And Justice for All

In memory of

A. Leon Higginbotham, Jr.,
Althea T. L. Simmons,
and Samuel C. Jackson

Contents

Illustrations

And Justice for All

Prologue

W HEN CONSERVATIVE COMMENTATORS criticized me for complaining when presidents and other officials refused to enforce civil rights laws, I recalled what my best friend, Minerva Hawkins, always said. "Remember, Mary Frances, when you're in the limelight you make a good target." Mrs. Hawkins, my high school teacher and mentor, offered this sage advice for whatever controversy erupted during my work as a member of the United States Civil Rights Commission. But her words apply equally to the commission itself. When effective, the commission has been a target for those who resist the need to purge our nation of its long denials of equal protection under the law.

I joined the United States Commission on Civil Rights in 1980, more than twenty years after its founding in 1957. The original members reached beyond the purposes set out by the commission's creators and chose to stay in the vanguard of the civil rights movement and protests. Both praised and attacked over the years, when reactionary politics held sway in the 1980s, the commission was stifled from fully carrying out its mandate. It had a resurgence of value, but sadly, during the George W. Bush administration its existence and utility remained compromised and questionable. Still, the commission's contribution to the struggle for civil rights and equal opportunity in our nation is incontrovertible.

The commission began in 1957, under President Dwight D. Eisenhower. He proposed a temporary commission on Civil Rights as a safety valve to relieve discontent and make it possible for him to avoid tough decisions about racial issues. Temporary commissions have a history of usefulness to a president who knows what he wants and appoints people who will deliver. In most cases, once such a commission has served its purpose, its reports are left to accumulate dust on library shelves. The 9/11 commission is an example of a temporary commission that received enormous praise, but many of its major recommendations are nevertheless gathering dust. Contrary to the usual pattern, the Civil Rights Commission became ongoing, and while its reports have met with mixed reactions, in the long run most of its recommendations have been implemented.[1]

From the beginning, Eisenhower's commission appointees explored the problems, investigated seriously, and made honest recommendations without great concern about how they would be received. The commission's work was so thorough—addressing such difficult problems and listening to people who were so grateful to be heard—and the civil rights movement was so powerful that soon it became unthinkable to end the commission. As Notre Dame president Father Theodore Hesburgh,[2] an initial commission appointee, explained in the 1960s, the commission was "becoming, more and more, a kind of national conscience in the matter of civil rights," helping Americans to move away from a horrible racial history.[3]

Successive commissioners challenged the nation first on race, then on national origin, sex, age, disability, and religious discrimination. It was not easy work. Commissioners were threatened physically in the early years and publicly harassed in the media and politics for most of the commission's history. But the commission became known for its integrity and its hallmark independence from political authority by doing its work without fear.

Presidents tried to use the commission—and some succeeded—and some escaped condemnation. Congress, presidents, activists, and scholars have acknowledged the role of the United States Commission on Civil Rights in helping to frame the nation's great civil rights laws. After conducting fact-finding investigations and studies, the commission recommended much of the language of the Civil Rights Act of 1964, the Voting Rights Act of 1965, the language minority protections of the Voting Rights Act passed in 1975, the Age Discrimination Act of 1978, and the Americans with Disabilities Act of 1990. The commission was also instrumental in monitoring government agencies to ensure enforcement of these laws once they were passed. Great progress toward equal opportunity resulted.

Eventually, the power of civil rights protest against racial inequality receded and positive change stalled. With progress toward equal opportunity and changing demographics, more complicated issues arose and the constituency in support of civil rights was fractured. In 2007 the Pew Foundation reported that by a ratio of two to one African Americans said the values of poor and middle-class blacks have grown dissimilar over the past decade while values of middle-class blacks and whites have grown alike. However, the foundation also reported that the children of middle-class blacks were more likely to skid back to the lowest socioeconomic status than to maintain middle-class status and that more than two-thirds of blacks believed race discrimination remained widespread, while whites disagreed, by majorities of two to one. Still, 53 percent of blacks believed that individuals are mainly responsible for their situation despite the discrimination, but they were increasingly less optimistic about making progress.

One result of the class divide was a dangerous complacency, based on the very visible success of a relatively few individuals. A sense of community responsibility was undermined. With Nancy Pelosi as the first female Speaker of the House, Hillary Clinton and Bill Richardson taken seriously as candidates for the presidency, Sarah Palin as the Republican vice presidential nominee, Barak Obama elected to the presidency, and Oprah Winfrey as the nation's super-influential media icon, it became easier to scoff at the need to fight race and sex discrimination. And yet discrimination, as the Pew reports suggested, persisted and became more complicated.

Incarceration rates as a result of the drug culture narcotized organizing efforts among the poor. Drug addicts are not able to organize a movement or a riot, and thus those who most needed to make demands succumbed to a kind of pacification. Quick crackdowns on any sign of protests, mayors and county executives dependent on state government, and gentrification all took a toll, eroding the prospects for social change. Most upwardly mobile African Americans became far removed from the people who suffered and from the reality of life in these neighborhoods.

Public discussion increasingly assigned the failings of poor blacks to personal responsibility and individual bad behavior alone. Discussion receded of the structural failings of society: bad public policy, economic neglect, and the failure of law enforcement to stop the drug trade.

Upwardly mobile African Americans expressed their outrage in quick bursts that soon passed—about discrimination in the criminal justice system in Jena, Louisiana, and nooses or about the removal of Don Imus, no matter how temporary, for making racist remarks about the Rutgers women's basketball team. A favorite reform activity for middle-class African Americans became engagement in electoral politics. They forgot that though elections and the right to vote are important, protest and pressuring elected officials are essential ingredients of politics.

The commission, since the end of the 1960s, has functioned in an environment where there was usually no national grassroots civil rights movement to push for critical change. Conflict over immigration policy led to large marches, and since the issues remained unresolved there was potential for sustained grassroots activism. Because of resistance to more equality under law, the gay and lesbian movement became sustained and vibrant and acheived some successes.

Evidence of a civil rights backlash on race could be seen in the 2007 Supreme Court's prohibition of voluntary desegregation efforts in Louisville, Kentucky, and Seattle, Washington; the successful passage of anti–affirmative action initiatives in California and Michigan; and the almost universal adoption of the label "preferences for the less qualified" to misrepresent affirmative action remedies.

Given the commission's proud history of major contributions to the civil rights struggle, it was sad that during the second term of President Bush the commission stopped supporting strong enforcement of long-standing civil rights laws. It also failed to use its own accumulated expertise, reports, and power to hold fact-finding hearings to analyze current problems and make recommendations. It may be that there was not enough public interest and little civil rights movement to urge action and to take the commission to task. Even with instances such as the 2006 New York police shooting of Sean Bell, an unarmed black man, the Washington civil rights lobby assumed that the commission would do nothing worthwhile, and hoped the commissioners would continue to be ignored.

The commission in the George W. Bush years suggested nothing to address the mismatch between the successful attacks on affirmative action in higher education and the need for more individuals from our country's increasingly diverse population to fill the ranks of employers and the military. Debate over the reauthorization of the grossly under-funded No Child Left Behind proceeded with no word from the commission on perfecting ways to achieve its goals of educating children without regard to race or national origin.

When the Bush administration's Justice Department corrupted its personnel practices and procedures, the commission made no comment, even though it had issued numerous reports since 1957 on effective management of the Justice Department and its Civil Rights Division. Faced with experiences that harked back to the heavy-handed disruption during the Reagan years, career lawyers fled the division because Bush appointees reassigned them from voting rights work and ignored their objections to the redistricting decisions that allocated congressional seats while discriminating against people of color. In addition, lawyers who applied for career positions were screened to determine their political affiliation and views. Further, the Justice Department process for hiring young lawyers as interns on temporary appointments to acquaint them with the Civil Rights Division, which had always been a responsibility of panels of career lawyers, was changed. The decisions would be made entirely by political appointees.[4]

The commission had nothing to say when the firing of United States attorneys in 2007 highlighted the Justice Department's continued emphasis on trying to find Democrats guilty of fraud on flimsy evidence, instead of ending discrimination and protecting voting rights of Native Americans, African Americans, Asian Americans, and Latinos. Meanwhile, the department shifted its agenda from combating racism to focusing on discrimination complaints from its supporters in the religious community who wanted federal taxpayer funds. Its interest in racial discrimination in voting extended only to a suit supporting whites who claimed that black political leaders in Noxubee County, Mississippi, were intimidating them at the polls.[5]

When Americans and the world complained about the treatment of African Americans in New Orleans and along the Gulf Coast in the aftermath of Katrina the commission was silent. With its subpoena powers, it could have cut through the White House's refusal to give documents to the Senate committee investigating the governmental response. The commission could have set off a fight that might have pried loose the truth. But no official body fully aired, much less laid to rest, the questions of whether race and class influenced actions that surrounded the response to the levee breaks and the rebuilding of the Gulf Coast.

Clearly, the need for bipartisan investigations using subpoena power "to put the facts on top of the table," as President Eisenhower suggested, remained. On-site investigations and hearings with sworn testimony including all who wish to testify can augment congressional oversight, which is sporadic, usually unsworn, and limited in scope. But there is a greater need to reclaim the moral authority and initiative that will make further progress possible. Much work to advance the quest for equal opportunity and social justice remains undone. Alongside the demand for more personal initiative and responsibility, continued discrimination persisted in voting rights, in police-community relations, in mortgages and automobile financing, in the search for quality education, and, most graphically, in government treatment of flooding victims in the aftermath of disasters such as hurricanes Katrina and Rita. An educational achievement gap and problems of crime and violence could be addressed constructively by a credible commission.

Public discussion included more talk of religion in government and less goodwill and commitment to social justice—widespread gay bashing and simultaneous raising of holy hands. All the while, no attention was given to single parents confounded by poverty and decay or to providing the tools to improve their families' lives. The civil rights movement and civil rights laws along with the work of the commission helped to move our nation closer to securing the constitutional promise of equal opportunity. But we have been consumed by denial and manipulated by distractions. No matter who is president, Obama's success could inspire a renewed determination to end denials of opportunity in our society. It could also result in self-satisfied stagnation. Rosa Parks and Coretta Scott King have gone to join Cesar Chavez, Fannie Lou Hamer, Medgar Evers, Martin Luther King, Jr., and my friend Minerva Hawkins, and still we are not saved. Yet, in the fullness of time, people of courage and imagination always emerge to advance the entire unfinished agenda of achieving liberty and justice for all. This is the story of the commission in the continuing struggle.

CHAPTER I

Responding to the "Negro" Protest

ROBERTA TUCKER slowly gathered herself to speak before the United States Commission on Civil Rights hearings in Tallahassee after the 2000 presidential election. It was her first appearance before any official inquiry, and it had not been easy to come forward. She faced a packed hearing room, the glare of a mass of television cameras, and a gaggle of print and radio media as she testified about how a white Florida Highway Patrol trooper stopped her on her way to vote. She was driving just south of Tallahassee on the only main road leading to her polling place in Woodville. The officer looked at the forty-nine-year-old woman's license and then let her drive on. She was puzzled because "nothing was checked, my lights, signals, or anything that they usually check." Angered by the memory, she spoke more rapidly. "I was intimidated by it and I was suspicious of it."[1]

John Nelson, fifty-two, another African American witness, at first was too nervous to speak. Then, finding his voice, he recalled the unmanned Florida Highway Patrol cars parked outside his polling place in Monticello, twenty-five miles east of Tallahassee. Nelson testified that he started to turn back and then forced himself to go forward. "I thought that was unusual. It makes you wonder, why is it there? What's wrong?" At his precinct the intimidation continued as, for the first time, instead of just asking for his voter registration card, the poll worker demanded two pieces of identification.[2]

Apostle Willie Whiting, unlike Tucker and Nelson, was eager to testify. The fifty-year-old African American pastor of the House of Prayer Church in Tallahassee relished describing his election-day experience before the commission. As he stood in the polling place with his family, a poll worker told him he was a convicted felon and could not vote. Whiting protested that he had never even been arrested, but to no avail. Asked by general counsel Edward Hailes how it felt, he answered in a booming voice, "It didn't feel good," having his family and "other people at the polling place" observing him. Whiting said he felt "sling-shotted back to slavery" by the shame it brought. One after another, African American, Latino, Haitian, older American, and other citizens who were disabled described a nightmare of official government-implemented disenfranchisement.[3]

The testimony in Florida resembled in some ways the commission's first hearing in Alabama, in December 1958. These were the early years of modern racial protest, when the term "race relations" began to take on new meaning. In Montgomery, blacks had refused to ride city buses for more than a year to end transportation segregation. In Birmingham, bombs were exploding, including one in the home of Alabama Christian Movement for Human Rights leader Rev. Fred Shuttlesworth and his family on Christmas morning. Meeting in the Fifth Circuit Courtroom in the Federal Building in Montgomery, the only venue in this cradle of the old Confederacy where blacks and whites could meet together, the commission heard testimony about the endemic violence and intimidation. Commissioners stayed at Maxwell Air Force Base because integrated hotels were legally impermissible.[4]

At the 1958 hearing, twenty-six African American witnesses, all of them educated, property-owning taxpayers who met the state's residence and legal requirements for voting, told the commission that they were denied the right to register to vote and faced implied and open threats. Risking their livelihood and their lives just by testifying, witnesses came forward to tell of their despair over their treatment and

Aaron Sellers, a Bullock County, Alabama, black farmer, tells the commissioners at Montgomery hearings in December 1958 how he and other blacks waited for nine hours in a separate room to register to vote and how he and the others were warned by a white man to "get the hell out of here" and left.

their burning desire to vote. Tuskegee resident Charles E. Miller, a Korean War veteran, told the commission, "I have dodged bombs and almost gotten killed, and then come back and been denied to vote—I don't like it. I want to vote and I want to take part in this type of government. I have taken part in it when I was in service. I think I should take part in it when I am a citizen."[5]

Aaron Sellers, owner of a 240-acre farm in Bullock County, told of waiting for nine hours, in a separate room, while whites were quickly registered. Intimidation capped off the boredom. As Sellers and five other "Negroes" waited in line, a white man asked what was their "trouble." When they answered, "We are waiting to register," the white man replied, "If I were you all—you are citizens already. If I were you I would go on back home." When he returned and realized they hadn't left, the white man yelled angrily, "Well, I thought I told you all to get the hell out of here." Although they had waited for hours, intimidated and frightened, they left.[6]

The five white and one African American men on the commission who listened to these courageous African Americans were just adjusting to their duties. In the wake of *Brown v. Board of Education*, the Montgomery bus boycott, continued black protest and white reaction, this new commission had been established by President Eisenhower and Congress as a response to the emerging civil rights crisis. By the end of the Eisenhower administration, these men would reach well beyond the president's political purposes, and the commission would play a major role in the struggle for civil rights.

John Hannah, the commission chairman, was a second choice after retired Supreme Court Justice Stanley Reed first accepted and then turned the president down. Reed said that it undermined the image of the Court for justices to take on other governmental roles after their tenure. Hannah, who had been Eisenhower's assistant secretary of defense, was president of Michigan State University. At Defense, one of his responsibilities was the completion of the integration of the armed forces and civilian personnel in the services.[7]

The son of an Iowa chicken farmer, Hannah earned undergraduate and graduate degrees in poultry husbandry at Michigan State and then made his way up the administrative ladder. He eventually married the daughter of the Michigan State president, and then succeeded his father-in-law as president of the university in 1941. As Michigan State president, he essentially transformed an agricultural college into a major Big Ten research university.[8]

The other commissioners appeared to fulfill Eisenhower's political needs. His staff understood that the president wanted a "Negro" on the commission and he wanted someone whom the Senate would easily confirm. E. Frederick Morrow, the first and only African American professional on the White House staff, recalled from his conversations with senior staffer Maxwell Rabb that a confirmable "Negro" requirement automatically disqualified any "social worker or member of NAACP, etc." from becoming a commissioner.[9]

White House staffers settled on sixty-two-year-old "sturdy, bulb-nosed" Ernest Wilkins, a Chicago lawyer and former president of the Cook County Bar Association, for the "Negro" slot. Wilkins, who was "accepted by the establishment black and white," had already been confirmed as an assistant secretary of labor for international affairs. In almost three years at Labor, he had quietly presided over the president's committee charged with preventing racial discrimination in government contracts, officially chaired by Vice President Richard Nixon. Wilkins apparently worked well with A. Philip Randolph, the organizer of the Brotherhood of Sleeping Car Porters, who led the 1940s March on Washington protests that were principally responsible for the creation of the contracts committee, and the only black vice president of the American Federation of Labor–Congress of Industrial Organizations union (AFL-CIO). Wilkins also received high marks for his representation of the United States in international labor organizations.[10]

Wilkins's publicly reported comments on racial matters as an assistant secretary of labor were benign and inoffensive to whites. When whites stoned Vivian Malone, a black woman, for trying to attend classes at the University of Alabama, Wilkins called the incident "deplorable." However, he suggested no remedy and tepidly said that it should be seen as affording some people the opportunity to gain "new insights into their own lives" from the problems "involved in change." He also told an Urban League dinner on February 15, 1956, that "the cloak of freedom is sitting much better on our collective shoulders these days—though not too well at that." He continued: "There needs to be a little tailoring done here and there—for instance, in Mississippi, South Carolina and Washington DC—I have no doubt that it will finally get done."[11]

Eisenhower also wanted "moderate" white Southerners on the commission. He appointed sixty-four-year-old Robert G. Storey, the dean of Southern Methodist University's Law School and a renowned Dallas attorney who had served as executive trial counsel for the United States at the Nuremberg trials of major war criminals after World War II. Storey had also served as president of the American Bar Association, as president of the Inter-American Bar Association, and as a member of President Truman's Hoover Commission on Organization of the Executive Branch of the U.S. Government.[12]

The president's other Southern "moderate" appointee, seventy-two-year-old Tampa lawyer Doyle E. Carlton, was the governor of Florida during the Roosevelt years. He had dealt successfully with the collapse of the state's land boom, a violent hurricane, the Mediterranean fruit fly infestation, and the nation's Depression. His only other foray into politics was an unsuccessful run in 1936 for a Democratic nomination for the U.S. Senate. Carlton, a friend and active supporter of then Florida Governor Leroy Collins and Senators Spessard Holland and George Smathers, was eminently confirmable.[13]

The commission was formed at a time when the Mason-Dixon Line demarcated race relations, a condition that had persisted since before the Civil War. But that North-South divide also determined seniority and power in the Senate. Eisenhower's nominees needed confirmation by the Judiciary Committee, chaired by Senator James Eastland (D-Miss.). To overcome this hurdle, the president also appointed former Virginia governor John S. Battle, a well-known and outspoken Southern segregationist, to the commission in November 1957. Senator Harry F. Byrd, Sr., of Virginia, Battle's political mentor, had denounced the idea of a commission as "a vehicle for witch-hunting at its worst, and dangerous beyond the comprehension of most living Americans." A staunch defender of the racial conventions of Southern society, Battle had made his views widely known through his speech at the 1952 Democratic convention defending Virginia for its refusal to accept a loyalty oath binding delegates to support the convention decisions. The tall, distinguished-looking Virginian pleaded that his state be allowed the "freedom of thought and freedom of action" that had been "enunciated by Thomas Jefferson—in whose County I happen to live—the great patron saint of this Party." At his confirmation hearing, Battle assured the committee that Eisenhower had chosen him because he believed "it might be helpful if there was some member of the commission who had . . . strong southern views."[14]

Charismatic and black-haired, with gentle features set off by a remarkable cleft chin, Father Theodore Hesburgh, the president of Notre Dame University, was Eisenhower's youngest commission selection. At forty years old, Hesburgh was head of the best-known Catholic

Governor-Elect and Attorney General John Patterson *(right)*
protests the delivery of Macon County voter list, seen on floor, to
the commission, during a December 8, 1958, hearing in
Montgomery, Alabama. At left is Commissioner John S. Battle.

institution of higher education in the country, a post he had assumed in
1952 at the age of thirty-five. With this bipartisan group of appointees,
Eisenhower expected easy confirmation and then moderate commission recommendations. Carlton, Battle, and Storey were Democrats, Hesburgh was an Independent, and Hannah and Wilkins were
Republicans.[15]

The commission had its first experience with the growing conflict
over race in the 1958 Alabama hearings. As the commission staff prepared for the hearings, Alabama voting officials defied subpoenas and
refused to make their records available for inspection. The registrars in
Macon County, source of most of the African American complaints,
refused to cooperate on orders from the state's attorney general, John
Patterson. In two other counties, Judge George Wallace, the future
governor, impounded all registration records and announced that he
would "jail any commission agent who attempts to get the records."[16]

When state and local officials testified, they were uniformly hostile. The commission's vice chair, Robert Storey, asked Grady Rogers, a member of the Macon County Board of Registrars, about the testimony that prospective voters were racially segregated. Rogers answered, "At times. But, I don't care to answer that question on advice of counsel." When Storey inquired, "Why do you refuse to answer it?" Rogers answered, "Because it might tend to incriminate me." When Storey repeated the line of questioning, Rogers consulted with Attorney General Patterson (soon to be governor) and replied that he was "a judicial officer under the State laws of Alabama" and his actions "cannot be inquired into by any body." Each subpoenaed Alabama state and local government official mouthed the same defense.[17]

Commissioner Ernest Wilkins asked Harrell Hammonds, judge of probate of Lowndes County, whether it was true that there were no "Negroes" registered in his county. He responded, "That's what they say." Wilkins continued, "In other words, out of a population of 17,000 or 18,000, 14,000 or 15,000 Negroes and 3,000 or 4,000 whites, you have approximately 2,200 or 2,300 whites registered and not a single Negro! Don't you think that is a rather unusual and peculiar situation?" Hammonds replied, "It might be unusual and peculiar in some places; yes." Wilkins and the other commissioners were quite startled at their first encounter with the raw racial exclusion that the Alabama officials regarded as commonplace and their defiance when questioned.

Dorothy Woodruff, one of three Lowndes County registrars, was asked whether white prospective voters were asked to demonstrate literacy. She answered, "After we meet, we discuss it and if their qualifications are up to par we send them their certificate. We have never had any that haven't been up to par."

Storey asked her, "Is that true as to both the blacks and the whites?" Woodruff responded, "We have no blacks."

Eventually even Commissioner Battle, the former Virginia governor, who supported segregation, was exasperated by the evasive, chilling responses provided by the state and local officials. The segregationist commissioner thundered, "I have come to the state of my ancestors. . . . My grandfather, Cullen A. Battle, was . . . the commanding officer of a brigade of Alabama troops which was honored by a resolution of the Confederate Congress. . . . My grandfather was subsequently denied his seat in Congress, to which the people of Alabama had elected him, because he had served the Confederate cause.

"So, I come to the people of Alabama as a friend. The President . . . was not in error when, in asking me to serve as a member of this commission, he said he wanted someone with strong Southern sentiments, which I have. . . . It is from this background ladies and gentlemen that I am constrained to say in all friendliness, that I fear the officials of Alabama have made an error in doing that which appears to be an attempt to cover up their action." He thought they should appear and defend their segregationist behavior.

At the request of the commission, the Justice Department obtained a court order for the information sought. However, the Alabama legislature instructed the counties to completely destroy all papers concerning rejected applications. Therefore the inquiry necessarily sputtered to an end.[18]

State officials in Louisiana, like those in Alabama, refused to cooperate when the commission scheduled more voting rights hearings, this time in Shreveport. Anticipating a court order, state officials went to court first to prevent the commission from holding the hearing by challenging the constitutionality of the commission provision in the Civil Rights Act of 1957. Federal district court judge Benjamin Dawkins issued an order that commission procedures were illegal because they provided no opportunity for witnesses to cross-examine their accusers. Dawkins announced that he doubted the constitutionality of his ruling, but the ploy forced an appeal that delayed the commission hearing until it had to be canceled.[19]

It was not until July 1960 that the Supreme Court, in *Hannah v. Larche*, overruled Judge Dawkins's Louisiana opinion. The Court decided that the commission had the right to hold hearings and to subpoena and question witnesses. Fact-finding bodies such as the commission did not have to function like adversaries in a courtroom proceeding, subjecting witnesses to cross-examination. At a later date the commission was free to hold another hearing.[20]

The commission that went to Alabama in 1958 and to Louisiana in 1959 had its origin during the Truman years. As World War II ended, American racism became a particular focus of Soviet propaganda and the contention for the hearts and minds of men and women in Africa, Asia, and Latin America. In 1948 President Harry Truman, already upset by the persistence of lynching, became outraged by reports of racist beatings of black veterans returning to the South from World War II. Truman, a Democrat, issued Executive Order 9808, establishing the President's Committee on Civil Rights on December 5, 1946, and announcing that this new committee would tell him what the federal government needed to do to ensure civil rights for all. Commissions and committees on racial understanding had already been established locally to address wartime tensions, including one appointed by the mayor of St. Louis in Truman's home state of Missouri and a statewide commission in Connecticut.[21]

Truman's committee lacked subpoena power because he did not believe he could persuade Congress to grant it, given that the most powerful committee chairs were segregationist Southern Democrats. However, Truman still did what he could to empower the committee. His order gave the committee access to all federal employees and directed every agency to cooperate, including J. Edgar Hoover's FBI, which resisted from the beginning.[22]

Before the end of his presidency, Truman had made the first public speech by a president committing the federal government to the enforcement of civil rights. Though he refused to order the end of discriminatory hiring in the transit system for Washington, D.C., he appointed William Hastie as the first African American to serve on a federal court of appeals, he appointed justices to the Supreme Court who struck down racial restrictive housing covenants, and he ordered an end to the exclusion of African Americans from white public university professional and graduate schools. In the *Brown v. Board of Education* case, Truman's Justice Department filed strong briefs supporting an end to school segregation.[23]

Truman also began implementing the recommendations of his Committee on Civil Rights. The committee specifically endorsed new legislation covering voting rights and criminal procedures, a federal anti-lynching law, and an end to race discrimination in the armed forces. The anti-lynching law, which the NAACP had advocated since its founding in 1909, never passed. However, Truman did act decisively on another of the committee's key recommendations, issuing an executive order to desegregate the armed forces. The Civil Rights Committee also recommended a new Civil Rights Division in the Justice Department to litigate cases and a congressionally enacted commission on Civil Rights with investigatory power, instead of a temporary committee. These suggestions had to wait for events on the ground before they were implemented.[24]

Worsening racial tensions and continuing international concern about racism during the cold war led the next president, Dwight Eisenhower, who had shown no particular interest in the race question, to move toward creating a commission. Clarence Mitchell, the lobbyist for the NAACP and a coalition of groups in the Leadership Conference on Civil Rights, pushed Congress and the administration very hard for a new civil rights bill. The Leadership Conference was established to lobby for federal legislation, in 1952, by A. Philip Randolph; Roy Wilkins, executive director of the NAACP (no relation to J. Ernest Wilkins); and Arnold Aronson, program director of the National Jewish Community Relations Advisory Council, a coalition of major Jewish organizations.[25]

Attorney General Herbert Brownell, a well-connected New York lawyer and a close ally and key supporter of Eisenhower in the 1952 campaign, decided that proposing a civil rights bill, which would include voting rights protection and the commission, would relieve the pressure for action on the part of the president. Brownell's legislative proposal was based on a memo prepared by Maceo Hubbard, the only African American attorney in the Civil Rights Section of the Justice Department, who had previously been chair of the Philadelphia legal committee of the NAACP and a staff member of the Fair Employment Practices Committee. Brownell took from the Truman Civil Rights Committee the proposal for a commission and the idea of a Civil Rights Division in the Justice Department as likely to "garner widespread congressional support." But he added the idea of congressional authority for the commission to subpoena persons and documents connected with a hearing. He hoped that, based on thorough fact-finding, its "products would unite responsible people . . . in a common effort to solve the problems."[26]

Eisenhower liked Brownell's proposal and placed it on the agenda for his cabinet to discuss. He saw the commission idea as a low-political-risk response to complaints about administration inaction on racial conflict in the South. Eisenhower said he wanted the commission to "put the facts on top of the table." Everyone in the cabinet meeting on December 5, 1955, took the proposal seriously and supported most of what Brownell suggested, but for differing reasons. Vice President Nixon also said it was an opportunity to "sucker" the Congress into legislating the commission, then proposed the vice president as its chairman. That way the Democrats could not nominate a Southerner as vice president in 1960, should the need arise to balance their ticket. They would want to avoid complaints about having a segregationist as chairman of the commission.[27]

Eisenhower ignored Nixon's suggestion, but he approved the bill, except for a provision allowing the Justice Department to bring lawsuits in non-criminal discrimination cases. Private parties would have to litigate their own complaints. The president admonished Brownell not to behave too much like a liberal in pushing the legislation. He told him not to "act like another Charles Sumner," the famous Massachusetts senator of the Civil War and Reconstruction era who was physically assaulted on the Senate floor in 1856 by Congressman Preston Brooks of South Carolina when he attacked Southerners for trying to implant slavery in Kansas. Eisenhower instructed Brownell to send the bill to the Congress as a measure urged by the Department of Justice, not as an administration proposal. Eisenhower wanted to move cautiously without having the bill identified as the president's. When Brownell testified, he told the House Judiciary Committee that the commission would collect data for a "useful analysis of the problem of racial conflict."[28]

Northern Democrats and Republicans in the House approved the civil rights bill, including voting rights and the commission, in 1956, but Southern senators threatened a filibuster in the Senate and it died in

WE HAVE IT UNDER CONSIDERATION

Delaying the civil rights bill in the Congress, 1957.

committee. Meanwhile, segregationist resistance continued to grow, creating more pressure for action. In 1956, when Autherine Lucy's attempt to break down segregation by attending the University of Alabama set off rioting, university officials suspended her, ostensibly for her own safety. Lucy was refused readmission by the university and state officials despite a federal judge's readmission order.

As matters worsened, Eisenhower resubmitted the civil rights bill to Congress in his second term. In May 1957, during the Prayer Pilgrimage for Freedom, standing before the Lincoln Memorial in Washington, Martin Luther King, Jr., still emerging as a national leader, pleaded, "Give us the Ballot, and we will no longer have to worry the Federal Government about our basic rights." The wrangling back and forth in Congress over the civil rights bill flowed from Eisenhower's refusal to advocate strong voting rights protection. Trying to influence the president, White House African American staffer E. Frederick Morrow asked baseball trailblazer Jackie Robinson and other prominent African Americans to urge Eisenhower to resist adding amendments that would weaken the bill. But Eisenhower ignored their pleas.[29]

Prayer Pilgrimage in front of Lincoln Memorial.
Martin Luther King, Jr., pleaded, "Give us the ballot." May 1957.

In an effort to defeat even the weakened bill, Senator Strom Thurmond of South Carolina filibustered, taking the floor for twenty-four hours and eighteen minutes. Although he had a secret daughter, Essie Mae, born of a relationship with Carrie Butler, a sixteen-year-old African American girl who worked in his family's home, Thurmond defended segregation and railed against "giving any federal agency carte blanche authority to probe and meddle in every phase of the relations between individuals." Nonetheless, then Senate Majority Leader Lyndon Baines Johnson, six years before he would assume the presidency, brokered the passage of the civil rights bill during the months leading up to the crisis in Little Rock. Eisenhower signed the Civil Rights Act of 1957, the first civil rights law since Reconstruction, on September 9, 1957.[30]

The act established the commission as an independent bipartisan agency with no enforcement power, but did give it the power to subpoena in connection with a hearing. Its charge was to

> investigate allegations concerning the denial of the right to vote based on color, race, religion, or national origin; collect information on legal developments constituting a denial of equal protection of the laws to any person; appraise the civil rights policies and laws of the federal government and report findings and recommendations to the President and Congress within the two years of the agency's existence.

The bill provided for six part-time members appointed by the president with the advice and consent of the Senate, paid only for the days they actually worked, and also for a full-time staff director and a small civil service staff.[31]

Under the legislation, the commission would conduct investigations, which would provide legitimacy for follow-up enforcement action by the Justice Department to end any discrimination identified. In supporting the legislation, despite the fact that it had established a commission without enforcement power, Martin Luther King, Jr., correctly predicted that its influence would depend largely upon protest and demands arising from "the sustained progress of a mass movement of Negroes."[32]

At the same time that the president was sending troops to Little Rock to implement a federal school desegregation order over the objections of Governor Orval Faubus, he began searching for commissioners.

Senator Thurmond filibustering to defeat congressional passage
of the Civil Rights Act of 1957, which created the
U.S. Commission on Civil Rights.

Eisenhower described dealing with the school crisis as standing between
"extreme firebrands and extreme diehards." The decision to use the
369th Airborne Division at Little Rock's Central High School was
motivated by Eisenhower's insistence on enforcement of his orders as
chief military commander, not by concerns over civil rights.[33]

In this atmosphere Eisenhower selected as commissioners "moderate voices" who would have a "very ameliorating effect on these aroused
feelings, prejudices, [and] passions." However, the chairman of the Senate Judiciary Committee, James Eastland, was in no hurry to have the
commission begin investigations and public hearings, such as the one in

Alabama, that might undermine embattled racial restrictions. He delayed the Senate confirmation hearings for almost two months after the president sent his nominations to Capitol Hill. The Judiciary Committee voted to recommend confirmation of the nominees in a voice vote on March 4, almost six months after the bill had passed. This left the commission only eighteen months to hold hearings, including the one in Alabama described earlier, and to produce a final report.[34]

From the start, Southern senators intimidated Eisenhower's staff director nominee, Gordon Tiffany, who had served as attorney general of New Hampshire under presidential assistant Sherman Adams when he was governor. After the president nominated Tiffany, Senator Richard Russell of Georgia insisted that the staff director's "views and activities will have more effect upon the work of the commission and its final recommendations than will any other individual including the Chairman of the commission." Eastland floated the claim that Tiffany showed an interest in Communist front organizations, although he said he did not believe "that Mr. Tiffany is a Communist." Senator Russell complained that Tiffany lacked the stature for such an important post. The Senate confirmed the commission membership in March 1958 and approved Tiffany as staff director two months later, on May 14. By this

Arkansas governor Orval Faubus with
National Guard at rally at state capitol.

time only fifteen months remained before the two-year commission's expiration in September 1959, under the terms of the Civil Rights Act of 1957.[35]

Having created the commission to show his concern for civil rights, Eisenhower lost interest in the issues and did little to fund the agency. After criticism on the House floor and in newspaper editorials for his inattention, the president stated on March 26 that he had "great hopes" for what the commission might do "watching and seeing what are the legal difficulties that may occur, as well as what can be done in what you might call the educational and even, indeed, the spiritual field." With that lukewarm endorsement, it took another three months, until June 25, before the congressional appropriation passed.[36]

The commission's chairman, John Hannah, complained to anyone who would listen that the congressional delays "stalemated" the commission. Once the appropriation was finally made, commission officials began hiring staff. The commissioners came to town once a month to meet and make plans. They agreed that each commissioner could appoint a lawyer as a personal legal assistant, who would also serve on the regular staff of the commission under the staff director. Commissioner Wilkins proved more assertive than his reputation for avoiding strong anti-racist stands while he was an assistant labor secretary had indicated. When he insisted on the appointment of some African American staffers for other posts in the agency, Battle, the former segregationist Virginia governor and supporter of Jim Crow, fought him every step of the way.[37]

Had they known more about him, the commissioners would not have been surprised at Wilkins's insistence on diverse staffing. Son of a Missouri preacher, light enough to have passed for white but enough of a race man to be a leader in his black fraternity, Kappa Alpha Psi, Wilkins had been particularly galled by the employment discrimination experiences of his son, Dr. J. Ernest Wilkins, Jr., born in 1923, who graduated at age seventeen with a degree in mathematics from the University of Chicago and received a graduate degree in the same field. Wilkins Jr. also earned a graduate degree in engineering from New York University. By the time the father was appointed to the commission, he had seen his son denied appointment at any research university because of his race. Wilkins did not have the opportunity to make an impact on the commission, beyond his influence on staffing decisions and participation in the Alabama hearing; he had battled high blood pressure for some time, and he became seriously ill and died from a heart attack in January 1959.[38]

Senator James Eastland, chairman of the Judiciary Committee,
resisted Majority Leader Texas Senator Lyndon Johnson's efforts
to pass the 1957 Civil Rights Act creating the commission and
still tried to derail civil rights measures pushed
by Johnson as President.

Upon Wilkins's death, George Johnson replaced him. Johnson, also
a black Republican, had been dean of the Howard University Law
School before joining the commission as director of planning and
research. After Johnson's confirmation, Eisenhower spoke to a conference of commission state advisory committees in June and swore him in
at that time.[39]

Among the first decisions the commission made was to appoint state
advisory committees (SACs) composed of local citizens. The citizens,
who would serve without pay, would act as the eyes and ears of the commission around the country. The Civil Rights Act suggested local advisory committees but did not detail any responsibilities. The commission
immediately appointed advisory committees in every state except Mississippi and South Carolina, two states where the staff found it difficult
to recruit residents who were willing to serve.

Once Tiffany officially came on board and hired staff, the commission set its priorities—voting, education, and public housing. The staff
began preliminary surveys and field investigations of complaints about
the right to vote that led to public hearings. By mid-August, Tiffany had

The swearing in of the first commissioners by President Eisenhower,
January 3, 1958.

hired sufficient staff to report to the commission that "the ground work is largely completed."[40]

From the beginning, the commission received numerous complaints about alleged civil rights violations, and the complaints increased as the commission's work became better publicized. Some came from prisoners who claimed bias in trials, and others concerned matters not within the commission's mandate, but a large number of the complaints came from ordinary Americans with seemingly valid grievances about interference with their right to vote. By August the commission had accumulated a sufficient number of voting rights complaints to authorize the hearing in Alabama. In education, the commission decided to focus on communities' desegregating under federal court orders. Commissioners planned a conference in Nashville, Tennessee, for exchanging views on common problems. They decided to begin with the upper South before tackling school desegregation issues in the Deep South.

However, in grappling with what they reported as "problems of schools in transition" over the next months, the commission expressed

Leola Bailey, Alda Boothe, Warren Brown, Rita Moseley, and
Barbara Spring, closed out of Prince Edward County, Virginia,
schools to preserve segregation.

alarm at Virginia's state policy of tuition grants for white students to
attend private schools. After providing either no education or poor-
quality education for the children of black taxpayers since emancipation,
Virginia's Prince Edward County closed the public schools to avoid
desegregation. The schools remained closed despite federal court
orders to reopen. The county then created a special foundation to establish schools and to raise funds for tuition grants for white children and
left black children who were seeking an equal opportunity for a quality
education with no schools at all.[41]

At that time, Warren Brown was about to enter first grade. His
mother, unable to afford to send him away to school, tried to teach him
at home for four years until she found a church that offered classes. Rita
Moseley was entering the sixth grade. Her mother sent her 120 miles
away, to Blacksburg, to live with an elderly woman and her mother, total
strangers, to attend school. The schools were closed in Prince Edward
County from 1959 to 1964. More than forty years later, as a form of
reparations, the State of Virginia passed a law in 2005 providing scholarship grants of $5,500 for any resident who was denied a proper educa-
tion when the schools closed.[42]

As the commission focused on the Alabama voting rights hearings, terrorism against African Americans seeking to register to vote throughout the South continued. By the end of 1958, Justice Department officials reported for the first four years of the Eisenhower administration six racially motivated voting-rights-related killings in the South, twenty-nine other shootings, forty-four beatings, five stabbings, forty-one bombings, and seven instances of arson of homes, churches, and schools. It was in this atmosphere of continuing violence and resistance that the commission convened the Alabama hearing to investigate complaints of voting rights violations.[43]

Feeling stymied and frustrated by the segregationist officials' resistance to the commission's investigations in Alabama and Louisiana, Hannah sought a supportive statement from the White House. After all, he thought, they were challenging Democratic Party officials, and a Republican administration would presumably have no need to protect Democrats. Eisenhower promised to help, but on his staff's advice that by doing so he would only roil public opinion and make matters worse, the president refused to take further action.[44]

With the Alabama hearing over and Shreveport adjourned, the commission staff prepared the final report, which was required by law before September 9, 1959. They needed commissioners' approval of the draft, which they had planned to discuss while in Louisiana for the hearing. After the adjournment in Shreveport, Hesburgh suggested they should escape the heat and humidity in Louisiana. He acquired the use of a private plane and flew the commissioners and staff to Notre Dame's Environmental Research Center in northern Wisconsin—also known as Land O' Lakes, after the nearby town of the same name. The center, some seven thousand acres of wilderness along the border of Wisconsin and Michigan's Upper Peninsula, served as the home of an undergraduate research program, year-round grant studies, and a getaway retreat for the university.[45]

After enjoying the cool weather, fishing, and relaxed discussions sitting in the moonlight, everyone agreed on almost every issue, although Battle said he might have to dissent in order to remain true to the segregationist perspective. The next morning, in the light of day, even though some of the commissioners may have been having second thoughts, everyone kept to the gentlemen's agreement.[46]

Commissioners reported to President Eisenhower that "in asking men of different backgrounds and different regions of the country to serve on the commission," he "could not have expected unanimity on some of the most difficult problems of civil rights." They decided, how-

John Hannah (on porch) and Father Hesburgh.
Commission meeting at Land O' Lakes Retreat, Wisconsin,
June 1959, while writing the report on the Montgomery hearing.

ever, to avoid issuing minority reports and to emphasize agreement, leaving dissent to be expressed in separate statements in the report or in footnotes. Battle, as he had told the group he would, submitted a lone general dissent. His short two-paragraph statement expressed his "highest regard" for each commissioner but disagreed with the "nature and tenor" of the report. He charged that instead of the impartiality that Congress had intended, the report presented an "argument in advocacy of preconceived ideas in race relations."[47]

A proposal made by both Johnson, the only African American, and Hesburgh in their individual statements was not preconceived but imaginative, however. They called for Congress to cut off federal funds for education and other services when the public's money was used to support discrimination. The two men insisted on the "prime importance" of such a policy even if some funding recipients were "inconvenienced temporarily." The seemingly radical funds-withholding idea gathered support only slowly. Such a policy suggestion was far ahead of the thinking of other commission members.[48]

The five members in the majority proposed that when the commission certified voting rights discrimination to the president, he should appoint temporary federal registrars to register the excluded voters. The commission pushed the federal registrars idea repeatedly over the next few years, but to no avail. The three Northerners wanted to recommend a constitutional amendment protecting the right to vote from abridgment for any reason except age, length of residence, or legal confinement at the time of registration or election. But all three Southerners disapproved.[49]

On housing, the commission recommended biracial local commissions on desegregation and asked the president to issue an executive order directing all federal agencies to work toward the goal of equal housing opportunity. They also asked that public housing authorities select target sites for change, with the goal of ending racially segregated projects.[50]

Storey, Battle, and Carlton objected that the report should not include any housing recommendations, since "no one pattern will serve the country as a whole." At a time when freedom of choice was used by Southerners to preserve segregation, they objected to the use of the term "freedom of choice" for minorities seeking housing. They asserted that the majority had "a fixed program of mixing the races anywhere and everywhere regardless of the wishes of either race." They predicted that such mixing of races would cause "dissension, strife, and even violence" in places where it might be least expected.[51]

In its first eighteen months, the commission had produced a report that reinforced knowledge about race relations with factual evidence and that made solid recommendations. The commissioners had identified facts and the problems, and most of the recommendations were agreed to by five of the six members. They had reached the general conclusion that "the fundamental interrelationships among the subjects of voting, education and housing make it impossible for the problem to be solved by the improvement of any one factor alone." Voting rights, equal educational opportunity, and housing opportunity should all be assured.[52]

Where they disagreed, in a North-South split, they did so without personal attacks. Predictably, they received favorable press coverage in the North and negative coverage in the South. The release of the report raised the question of whether this temporary panel had completed its work or should be extended. The continued conflict and racial tensions with no response from the administration save the creation of the commission and some tentative steps from the Justice Department meant that the administration could not afford to have the commission end.

President Eisenhower said repeatedly that he would support a two-year extension of the commission to continue its "useful" suggestions. However, he did nothing to push the issue. Congress failed to act until the eve of the deadline, forcing the agency to go through close-down procedures. Shortly before adjournment, a week after the issuance of the commission's final report, on September 15, 1959, Congress endorsed the two-year extension. The vote came from the same coalition of Republicans and Northern Democrats that had passed the civil rights bill in 1957.[53]

After the commission's reauthorization, Battle resigned, and upon Hannah's recommendation, Eisenhower appointed Duke University political scientist Robert Rankin to replace him. Rankin, a distinguished, widely published scholar, had been advising the staff. The Senate confirmed Rankin, although Southern senators thought him too moderate. The Southern senators continued to direct their ire toward Gordon Tiffany, the staff director, which undermined staff morale. Senator John McClellan of Arkansas, chairman of the Government Operations Committee, decided to investigate the commission's management. Such oversight can be very useful in uncovering problems and recommending solutions, but it also can serve as a political weapon to inhibit an agency's work when a congressional committee disagrees politically with the work being done. Such investigations can impede and embarrass staff by launching detailed management inquiries and implying to the press that something terribly wrong is afoot. The investigation that Senator McClellan spearheaded had that very effect.

McClellan ordered a time-consuming audit of the staff's day-to-day operations. He also harassed civil service staff members, who are usually not called before committees because they do not make policy decisions, and demanded that they criticize their boss in public committee hearings. Hannah protested the employees' treatment, but to no avail.

The Senate committee's consistent criticism of Tiffany and his staff achieved its purpose. Tiffany resigned voluntarily on December 2. Six months after his resignation the committee issued a report reiterating the charges of malfeasance and stating that Tiffany had left because of the investigation. Whatever Tiffany's administrative skills, the segregationists attacked him because they held him responsible for the commission's groundbreaking hearings and the recommendations in its first official report. The *Washington Post* defended Tiffany in an editorial, saying that he had suffered "a mean and pointless back-stabbing." The paper called McClellan's report "scandal-mongering." Moreover, the goal of demoralizing the agency was achieved as the staff, according to Berl Bernhard, the deputy staff director, felt that the McClellan investigation "cast aspersions on the entire Administration of the agency." Bernhard, a Yale Law graduate of the Class of 1954, who had been at the commission from the beginning, became acting staff director.[54]

In this early period, the commission, though focused on the South, also expressed interest in the civil rights problems experienced by African Americans in the North, as well as in discrimination against Native Americans, Asian Americans, and Mexican Americans. *Time* magazine complained that when the Montgomery hearings were announced, the commission "in a strained attempt to prove its fair-mindedness" said it was planning investigations in the North. In doing so, *Time* wrote, the commission "leaned so far backward to prove its fairness it almost lost its balance."[55]

The commissioners needed to pay attention to the North and to issues facing Mexican Americans and Asian Americans who had long experienced discrimination. As for African Americans, racial conflict over housing integration, sometimes leading to violent attacks from whites bent on maintaining neighborhood purity, was a prominent feature in the urban North of the post–World War II period. Police often did not defend blacks at all; if they tried to do so, they themselves came under attack from the rioters.[56]

In 1960 the commission held hearings in Los Angeles, San Francisco, and Detroit. In Los Angeles, the governor and the mayor testified, along with other officials and witnesses, about their attempts to solve problems facing Mexican Americans and African Americans.

Mexican Americans had formed the Community Service Organization (CSO), to monitor the discrimination they faced. The commission heard from Edward Roybal, the only Mexican American member of the Los Angeles city council and the first in one hundred years, and Philip Newman, who was counsel to the CSO. Roybal complained that with the recent elevation of Carlos M. Teran from the municipal court by Governor Pat Brown, there was no Mexican American on the superior court for the county of Los Angeles, despite the large Mexican American population. And Teran's appointment left "no Mexican on the municipal court," though both courts together had about a hundred judges. There were no Mexican American prosecutors, and out of seventy or eighty deputy district attorneys, only two were Mexican Americans. Among public defenders "there was, until recently, one Spanish-speaking attorney within the personnel of the public defender system. I believe as of now there are none." Also, "in the past 20 years there has not been one person of Mexican ancestry or descent serving on the grand juries of Los Angeles county."[57]

Few Mexican Americans served on juries because jurors were taken from the voting rolls, where discrimination limited Latinos. Roybal told the commission that in the last three elections, "anyone who spoke broken English was challenged by someone present at the polls, inside and outside, who asked them to recite the preamble to the Constitution, and, when they were unable to do so, they were challenged and they were refused the opportunity of casting their ballot." Anglos, in contrast, did not have to know the preamble to the Constitution, he said.

Roybal and Newman gave the commission eleven affidavits attesting to election abuse. Some victims who were mistreated were "gun shy," having in the past signed something unsuspectingly that "practicably signed their life earnings away," and would not sign the affidavits. The activists also had nine affidavits from an election board member who "may find that he is no longer a member of an election board next year." Roybal said everyone understood that the increasingly large Mexican American population was "a sleeping giant," politically.[58]

When Los Angeles Mexican Americans and African Americans charged discrimination in the administration of justice, the police chief, William Parker, countered their testimony. He told the commission that some problems arose partly from Latino class stratification and geographic dispersion: "The leadership moves out of the area when they become affluent and no longer identify themselves with the group." Further, "there is no desegregation or integration problem. . . . There may be an assimilation problem," occasioned by the "moving of people out of their culture to a strange culture." He said, "I think the adjustment will come, but I do think it will take time in that cultures are different." There is conflict, and "the poor hapless policeman who gets his orders from the State legislature as to what he should do is faced with this problem."[59]

Commissioner Johnson asked Parker what he meant by a conflict of cultures. The chief answered that part of the problem was that some Latinos came from "the wild tribes of the district of the inner mountains of Mexico." You could not "throw the genes out of the question when you discuss behavior patterns of people."[60]

As for African Americans, Parker emphasized that despite their poverty and high crime rate, Los Angeles had little racial tension. His comments came just four years before the Watts riot of 1965 and reports that race relations had been seething, largely unattended, for years.[61]

In San Francisco, Haruo Ishimaru of the Japanese American Citizens League warned the commission that housing discrimination against Japanese Americans could create foreign policy problems when it is "magnified by people in other countries." Erin Forrest, a member of the Modoc tribe and president of the Inter-Tribal Council of California, focused on unequal opportunity in public education for Native Americans and "the difficulty of explaining discrimination to children since their own language contained no such word."[62]

In Detroit in December 1960, after the presidential election, the commission listened to African American complaints of police abuse and to denials from the police commissioner, Herbert W. Hart. Commissioner Hesburgh suggested that fairness in the criminal justice system had to be ultimately worked out at the community level, but he hoped that "we have been able to contribute something just by listening to both sides."

When Africans Americans complained that police stopped them and frisked them on the street without evidence of wrongdoing and assaulted them without reason, Hart casually dismissed what he called their "uninformed misstatement." The audience balked at this, roaring disapproval until gaveled into silence. One witness suggested a community police review board, but Hart strongly resisted the idea. The commission report emphasized the conflict-ridden race relations and serious concerns about police abuse that were festering in the ghettos of Detroit.[63]

While the commission worked on the hearings and the 1961 report, the civil rights fight in the South moved in a new direction. On February 1, 1960, four African American freshmen from North Carolina A&T College in Greensboro sat down at a segregated lunch counter and refused to move, and thus began the sit-in era.

In the last few months of his term, Eisenhower faced a rapidly changing civil rights landscape. Countless young African Americans were caught up in a movement on college campuses across the South. White college students joined them, and the Student Nonviolent Coordinating Committee (SNCC) evolved. Southern police responded to sit-ins and civil rights marches with fire hoses, tear gas, beatings, and arrests. When white liberals, as well as blacks in Martin Luther King,

Jr.'s Southern Christian Leadership Conference (SCLC) and the Congress of Racial Equality (CORE), joined and supported the students' movement, the conscience of the nation was stirred. The federal government did not respond immediately. Unnerved, Eisenhower relied on the position that law enforcement responses to sit-ins, including any violent response, lay completely within the purview of each state.[64]

The commission and the Congress, like established civil rights leaders, were occupied with discussing a new civil rights bill, as promised at the end of the session in 1959. All were caught off balance by the changing course of civil rights protests on public accommodations. The new measure under consideration had many needed provisions, but nothing relevant to the demand for federal responsibility for protecting those who participated in sit-ins. The legislation that was passed included the commission's recommendation to criminalize interference with a court order for desegregation and also included federal penalties for those who crossed state lines to engage in bombing or burning of schools or churches.[65]

However, the commission's recommendations to strengthen voting rights enforcement went unheeded. The administration asked for the preservation of voting records for twenty-two months instead of five years (as the commission had asked) and proposed court-appointed referees instead of registrars for voting. Eisenhower issued a vague call for Congress to give consideration to both ideas. The Justice Department disliked the commission's proposal because it forced the president to take action. Civil rights groups and Northern civil rights advocates in Congress preferred the less cumbersome, speedier commission plan.

The idea of weak federal referees prevailed, with Eisenhower's attorney general, William Rogers, and Senate Majority Leader Lyndon Johnson cooperating on the final bill. Eisenhower tried to distract public attention from the bill by signing it at a ceremony on May 6, 1960, attended only by Rogers and the assistant attorney general for civil rights. As a bow to the commission and civil rights advocates, the White House responded to the continued racial conflict in the South by designating a sub-cabinet group on civil rights, with the commission participating ex officio because of its independence.

Despite the rash of civil rights violations and complaints that were within the jurisdiction of the Civil Rights Division of the Justice Department after it was established in 1957, the department brought few cases. For example, though charges of police brutality constituted 30 percent of the complaints from citizens, the department won only

Martin Luther King, Jr., Presidential Assistant E. Frederick Morrow,
President Dwight Eisenhower, and Brotherhood of Sleeping
Car Porters Union president A. Phillip Randolph discuss
implementing the Civil Rights Act of 1957.

four civil rights prosecutions between 1957 and 1960. None involved
abuse of African Americans.[66]

By 1961, the commission had settled into a well-established routine.
Meetings took place once a month, and the chair spoke for the commission to the press, although the press sought opinions from the other
commissioners and the staff as well. The commission made decisions
based on staff recommendations or individual commissioners' suggestions. The staff conducted the investigations and wrote the reports,
and the commissioners debated drafts over a one- or two-day period,
making revisions and striving to overcome the North-South divide,
although that goal was not always achieved.

During the Eisenhower years, mounting pressure from African
Americans and civil rights groups, as well as Northern white empathy,
and the enfranchisement of large numbers of blacks in Northern urban
areas increased pressure for legal reform. Eisenhower responded to

increasing public pressure and to the exigencies of maintaining moral leadership in the world with rhetorical commitments to racial equality and sporadic enforcement. Indeed, military power had been used to enforce a court order in Little Rock, though resistance to school desegregation elsewhere went unchallenged.[67]

The commission had pursued investigations without fear of political consequences. However, commissioners did not yet understand how they could influence congressional or public action without the support of the White House. They discussed John Hannah's complaint that during the last year of the Eisenhower administration, he did not have access to anyone on the White House staff who could follow up on the commission's inquiries or suggestions. He complained that in most instances, the commission "couldn't get beyond the front steps of the White House and its recommendations were ignored, its counsel was ignored, or not even sought."

Eisenhower's notion that the commission would be a temporary solution to his political problems was confounded by the growing civil rights protest movement. The commission had been extended, though plagued by resistance from the beginning. The commissioners, as historian Foster Rhea Dulles concluded, had determined that they would gather facts that would lay the foundation for civil rights legislation, stimulate action by Congress and the executive, and serve as the conscience of the nation by exposing failures to secure and protect civil rights.

Those opposed to racial change attacked the commission for being too radical, and the administration resisted cooperating as the commission exercised the independence that the president had unwittingly endorsed at its inception. The widely disseminated report of the commission set the stage for civil rights legislation. But as Martin Luther King, Jr., predicted when the Civil Rights Act of 1957 passed, the future would depend largely on the activities of the masses of African Americans mobilized to gain their rights.

CHAPTER 11

Among Friends

THEOTIS CRYMES had lost almost everything when he appealed to the Civil Rights Commission in 1961. He said he wanted to tell his story in the hope that "somewhere in America something can be done to help me and other victims of injustice." He stated:

> I am a veteran who served in the Armed Forces of the United States for six years. I have a wife and three small children. But after having been shot in the back by an officer, I have been paralyzed for life and am now confined to a wheelchair.
>
> On the night of March 19, 1960, I was driving home from Bessemer, Alabama to Montevallo, a distance of about 20 miles. I was driving about 60 miles an hour. A friend and neighbor, James Morrow, was with me. When we passed through Helena, Alabama, I noticed a car some distance behind us, but paid no attention. After driving about four miles further this car caught up with me and bumped into my car from behind, almost knocking my car off the highway. I pulled over and stopped. The other car stopped right behind me, a red light flashing on the top. It was not flashing when it was following me and when it hit me.
>
> I got out of the car and an officer came after me and would have struck me with his gun, but I threw up my hands to keep from being struck. I asked what this was all about and what I had done. He then asked if I had any whiskey in my car and I told him no. He made me put my hands up on his car, and he began to search me. And while I was standing with my hands up on his car, he shot me in the back, paralyzing me from the waist down.
>
> My friend, James Morrow, had gotten out of my car on the same side where we were standing. But a white man in plain clothes, who was with the officer, got out and pointed a car-

bine rifle at him and made him get back into the car. I had fallen on my back on the highway. I looked up at the officer and asked him why he shot me down like this. He only said "Shut up, Nigger."

The officer who shot Crymes was the police chief of Helena, Alabama.

After an FBI investigation, the Justice Department ordered prosecution, but the chief claimed that he had fired in self-defense when Crymes advanced on him with a knife, and he was acquitted. In May 1961 the commission wrote to the Veterans Administration, which had denied Crymes a veteran's pension. The VA then determined he had done nothing to cause harm to himself and awarded him a pension.[1]

During the Kennedy administration the Civil Rights Commission focused on the South, where the growing civil rights movement met massive resistance and many individuals like Crymes suffered life-threatening assaults. The commission's first series of hearings had persuaded its members that "the fundamental interrelationships among the subjects of voting, education and housing make it impossible for the problem to be solved by the improvement of any one factor alone." Consequently, the commissioners sought to establish a basis for a comprehensive civil rights law to end discrimination in government-funded programs and to protect citizens' right to vote. Commission members prepared a report based on what they had learned in hearings and investigations and on what they believed needed to be remedied.[2]

During the Kennedy administration, the commission also discovered the dangers of being seduced by a seemingly sympathetic president. During these years, the commissioners were as impressed by the Kennedy mystique as the public was. They welcomed the new administration, believing that the Massachusetts Democrat would strongly protect and defend African Americans who de-

Theotis Crymes. The commission helped Theotis Crymes keep his veteran's pension after he was wrongly accused of provoking a local police chief to shoot him in the back, resulting in paralysis.

manded first-class citizenship. But after the White House deliberately undermined a commission report demanding strong enforcement of desegregation in institutions receiving federal taxpayers' funds, they learned to guard their independence. In the process, the commissioners realized that they needed to push their own recommendations whether or not the White House agreed with them.[3]

The commission at first believed it had a "hotline" to the Kennedy White House through Harris Wofford. Once Hesburgh's assistant, Wofford had worked in the Kennedy-Johnson campaign and joined the new administration. Kennedy's campaign rhetoric criticized the go-slow civil rights policy of Eisenhower-Nixon and asserted that he would have forced non-discrimination in housing with the stroke of a pen. Wofford's appointment as special assistant to the president promised positive executive branch action on civil rights.[4]

As Camelot took shape, the commission sought the president's attention. But with cabinet appointments and other urgent priorities, the commission's requests for a staff director and a guarantee of cooperation from the Justice Department and other agencies in commission investigations were neglected. Impatient with the delay, Hannah and the other commissioners threatened resignations in a move to force the White House staff to act. More than anything, Hannah wanted the White House to seriously consider the commission's views.[5]

After the commissioners submitted their resignations, the White House scheduled a meeting for Hannah with the president. Chairman Hannah, the Michigan agricultural university president and a chicken farmer's son, confronted the scion of Boston Irish aristocracy directly. Hannah brought Hesburgh along to the meeting. Perhaps he hoped the presence of the Catholic priest, who was the president of Notre Dame and Wofford's former boss, might help to persuade the president to act. After the men engaged in small talk with the president, Hannah told Kennedy that if he were to continue as chairman he would need new appointees to enhance the likelihood of unanimity. He also asked the president to begin strong enforcement of anti-discrimination measures, including in the housing area, as he had promised during the campaign, and to consider withholding federal funds from segregated colleges and universities. He also insisted that Kennedy issue his promised executive order to ensure equal opportunity in housing funded or assisted by the federal government.[6]

Hannah also asked that a staffer with access to the president be designated and identified as a liaison with the commission. He told the president that "either the commission should have the opportunity to express its views based on the information that it had" or "it was a wasteful thing to have around."

Kennedy responded immediately to the easy part, appointing a liaison: "Well, I'm going to name Harris Wofford to do that. As a matter of fact, I'm going to do it today." Indeed, that day Wofford became special assistant for civil rights and head of the nonfunctioning sub-cabinet committee on civil rights that was established by Eisenhower. Although Kennedy took that easy step, he did not go on to issue the promised executive order. So much for forcing the president to act. According to internal White House staff records, Kennedy had no interest and saw no need to move on the executive order or any other civil rights policies at the time.[7]

Staffing and appointments gave the Democrats a chance to fill posts with individuals suggested by patrons and supporters. Berl Bernhard's background, including his Yale Law School pedigree, made it easy for Kennedy to accept him as the commission's choice for staff director. Kennedy then immediately nominated fifty-four-year-old Harvard Law School dean Erwin Griswold and Howard University Law School dean Spottswood Robinson to the commission. They would replace Governor Carlton and George Johnson, both of whom resigned in March. The president wanted to gain credit for making appointments to the commission, and Hannah used his patronage power to ease the way. He hired Johnson for Michigan State's programs in Nigeria, where he helped to found the University of Nigeria Law School. Kennedy's friend and chief counsel on Southern civil rights matters, Senator George Smathers of Florida, pushed Carlton into a "friendly resignation."[8]

The Griswold and Robinson appointments shored up Kennedy's support from civil rights advocates, especially African Americans. Thurgood Marshall's law firm, the NAACP Legal Defense and Educational Fund, had good professional relationships with both men. Griswold, "built like a granite block" and "just as inflexible in his conceptions of basic rectitude," was a Republican and a tax expert, and a supporter of civil liberties. He had also appeared as an expert witness in higher-education desegregation cases brought by the NAACP-LDF before the *Brown* case.[9]

The son of a Virginia lawyer, forty-five-year-old "tall, spare and mild-mannered" Spottswood Robinson loved fishing so much that he built his own boat in his basement. He had been one of the NAACP-

Howard Law School Dean Spottswood Robinson, one of the lawyers who argued *Brown v. Board of Education* along with Thurgood Marshall, was appointed to the commission by President Kennedy.

LDF lawyers who argued *Brown* and was an expert in property law and constitutional law. After attending Virginia Union University in Richmond, he received his law degree with honors from Howard University in 1939. He began his law career as a professor at Howard, specializing in property law, took a leave of absence in 1947, and returned as the school's dean in 1960. While on leave, he privately practiced law in Richmond and was a general counsel in the banking industry.

Jack Greenberg, who was also on the NAACP-LDF legal team that argued *Brown*, described Robinson as "one of just a very small handful of practicing lawyers who handled civil rights cases in the late '40's and early '50's in Virginia." He litigated civil rights cases involving interstate bus travel, public parks, and housing restrictive covenants.[10]

Both the NAACP's Roy Wilkins and Martin Luther King, Jr., lobbied hard for Kennedy to nominate Benjamin Mays, president of Morehouse College, as a commissioner, but Georgia's rabidly segregationist senators, Democrats Richard Russell and Herman Talmadge, objected. Wilkins and King complained to the president after the press reported that he had rejected Mays. On March 1, 1961, the NAACP head wrote that, of course, Dr. Mays "is biased (as the Senators assert) in favor of eliminating the unconstitutional, undemocratic and indecent prescription in effect against his own people." Wilkins continued: "If he were not, then the Civil Rights Commission post would be as well filled by any southern segregationists—and remain as empty, in terms of executing the task for which the body was created."

If Talmadge's and Russell's views prevailed, Wilkins asserted, no African American, except someone "parroting the views of their lily-white ventriloquists," would serve in any federal position. King, a Morehouse graduate, told the president in a telegram the same day that

Mays was one of the "truly great men of our generation." Of course, "he has not been an accommodating ultra conservative leader." He had always shown "unswerving devotion to the principles of American democracy." King wrote that all men of goodwill, and African American voters especially, would be "gravely disappointed" if these attacks defeated Mays's nomination. After telling them he shared "their high regard" for Mays, Kennedy let the idea die, believing that he could not obtain Mays's confirmation.[11]

As Kennedy chose what he regarded as confirmable nominees, White House staffers expressed some wariness about the commission's watchdog duties. They concluded, however, that though the commission's independence "might become a bit of a problem," it could be a "political asset." If the commission made "severe" recommendations, then Kennedy could appear moderate and "point to the commission and say we're really not as crazy as this wild bunch of people at the commission." The administration could in this way leave itself room to maneuver.[12]

President Kennedy in the Oval Office with the commission,
headed by John Hannah, November 21, 1961.

Even though Kennedy announced the nominations of Griswold and Bernhard in March, Senator James Eastland's Judiciary Committee ignored any party allegiance to the Democratic president and delayed their confirmation. Eastland was, as usual, against public investigations of race relations. After extended debate and objections from the Southerners about their liberalism, the Senate confirmed the nominations on July 27, 1961.[13]

Staff Director Bernhard eagerly nurtured contacts with Bobby Kennedy, the attorney general, and Harris Wofford, hoping they would respond positively to commission actions. Bobby Kennedy supported the selection of Bernhard as staff director but told him the administration wanted to avoid legislation that would only divide Democrats in Congress and anger Southern segregationists. Bernhard decided to stay "on the periphery" of administration policies and to participate in "some basic decisions" while reminding Justice officials and White House staff that his primary loyalty was to the independence of the commission. Despite his optimism about the civil rights commitment of the Kennedy administration, Bernhard found that balancing "independence and criticism" turned out "to be more difficult" than he had "anticipated."[14]

The commission continued working on a new final report to be issued before the agency's upcoming expiration date in September 1961. The report relied in part on information gathered in the reconvened Shreveport hearings permitted by the Supreme Court decision in *Hannah v. Larche*. In the hearings, in May 1961, the staff documented the White Citizens' Council sponsorship of the "segregation law package" designed to preserve "the existing social order," passed by the Louisiana legislature in 1960. It endorsed the purge of any blacks already on the rolls, set up a committee to reduce African American registrations, and issued a manual instructing local registrars how to maintain the "purity" of the ballots.[15]

The "package" required a registrant to be of good character. "Bad character" included misdemeanor violations, except for traffic and game law violations, common-law marriage, or having children out of wedlock. The Louisiana legislature redefined misdemeanors to outlaw participating in a sit-in. In addition, applicants had to sign an affidavit promising to abide by the state's laws, which of course included the segregation laws. Most of the registrars admitted to the commission that they used the procedures to prevent African Americans from voting.[16]

Joe Kirk, from Webster Parish in northwestern Louisiana, told the commission that when he went before the registrar in July 1960, the "first question she asked was did I have any illegitimate children. I said, Not as I knows of. If I has, I hasn't been accused of it." The registrar said, "You are a damned liar."

Vice Chairman Storey questioned: "Said what?"

Mr. Kirk: "You are a damned liar." I just smiled; I could still give the smile. Then she said, "I know you were going to tell a lie at the first place." Then she asked the question, "What were disfranchise mean?" I said "just like I am now, this is disfranchise from voting."

She said, "That doesn't suit me." I said, "Well, just like a bus company, any other company, has a franchise—is disfranchised, it can't operate." And she said, "Well, study your dictionary. That doesn't suit me."

Commissioner Rankin questioned Mrs. Clement, the Webster Parish registrar, about the testimony: "Another one said this: You asked him about 'how many illegitimate children do you have?' And he replied 'None.' And the answer to that was: 'That's a damn lie.'"

Mrs. Clement responded: "I don't remember that."

Commissioner Rankin: "That is the testimony."

Mrs. Clement: "But I could have said it. I could have said it to someone."[17]

The registrars understood that the legislative goal of "preservation of the social order" required purging any African American voters already on the rolls and blocking new registrations. The commission concluded that the entire process was discriminatory.

As the staff prepared their latest "final" report, including the Shreveport hearing, Hannah told them they had moved beyond all question of being a temporary commission. He believed their usefulness was clear. The civil rights protests made the problems they worked on a matter of greater urgency. In writing to Hannah, President Kennedy repeatedly expressed confidence in an extension, but he stopped short of recommending one. Hesburgh told Wofford that Hannah worried about "practical politics" interfering. Morale deteriorated and close-down activities began for the second time in two years. Several key workers resigned. Kennedy, not seeing the commission as particularly useful to his administration and not ranking an agency devoted to civil

Mrs. Lennie Linton, Claiborne Parish, Louisiana, registrar.

rights among his priorities, did nothing. Advocates in Congress had to take the lead.[18]

On September 9, 1961, during the reauthorization discussions, the commission issued its 1,400-page, five-volume report, which resoundingly underscored its usefulness in assessing civil rights. The commission observed that the "gap between the promise of liberty and its fulfillment is narrower today than it has ever been," but it remained "wide and deep, and the demand to close it more urgent than ever." Each volume reported on the progress to date and how to finish the work that remained undone.[19]

Most of the recommendations, which documented the need for legislation to end segregation by federal enforcement, were unanimous and were eventually endorsed by the administration. However, J. Edgar Hoover reacted furiously to the final volume, titled *Justice*. This was the first time any federal agency had had the courage to criticize the FBI— even indirectly. The report took a comprehensive look at racial tensions in police-community relations, and the FBI had essentially declined to give the commission information that it requested on how the bureau handled allegations of police brutality.[20]

The bureau had the responsibility of investigating, for possible prosecution, any official acting under [color of law] who committed abuse on the grounds of race. Some allegations involved whether the bureau "had only southern agents working with the southern police chiefs," which compounded the problem.[21] The commission's conclusion that the FBI "has little enthusiasm for its task of investigating complaints of police brutality" infuriated Hoover. But the commission reasoned that since an alleged police-brutality case required exploring whether state or local police had committed a federal crime, any investigation, no matter what the outcome, would create tensions between the FBI and the police. The FBI had to guard against downplaying complaints against police to preserve working relationships.

The bureau's policy of notifying heads of local police departments when the FBI investigated a law enforcement official could jeopardize any prosecution. The supervisors "might have an unduly protective attitude toward their officers" or "might share racial prejudices of their subordinates and their communities." African Americans, who suffered abuse and understood how the FBI worked with police in their communities, feared the FBI. These problems were compounded in instances when a U.S. attorney, most of whom came from the locale where they worked, would not prosecute a police-abuse case even with clear evidence. Further, even when the U.S. attorneys prosecuted, local juries usually refused to convict.

Hoover sent Hannah "a severe letter" disputing the findings. He wanted the commission to "furnish the identities of such individuals so that their complaints might receive immediate attention." The commission had no intention of subjecting complainants to possible harassment and agreed only to share allegations made by witnesses and to put the FBI's response, if any, on the record. Bernhard then graciously accepted Hoover's offer of an agent as liaison to the commission to prevent future misunderstandings.[22]

The liaison, who saw Bernhard every week and sometimes more, in unsolicited contacts, tried to undermine the credibility of Martin Luther King, Jr. He shared negative allegations about King's personal life with the staff director. The commissioners and Bernhard had generally warm relationships with civil rights organizations and leaders, who saw the commission as an ally. Because of this, Bernhard had come to know Martin Luther King and consequently rejected the unsolicited information.

We now know that the FBI wiretapped King and his associates and other civil rights leaders and spread information about King's personal life, including alleged sexual relations, to the White House and others in efforts to discredit the leader. Hoover was also, of course, eavesdropping on the Kennedy White House. We also know that King had Bayard Rustin resign in 1960 because of persistent criticism of Rustin's homosexuality and Communist ties and because of Congressman Adam Clayton Powell's threat to falsely accuse King and Rustin publicly of having an affair.

But the titillating information supplied by the FBI liaison to Bernhard was different. The FBI agent said that while Bernhard might regard King as a great American, the leader actually was "sexually perverted." The FBI, according to the spokesman, had full documentation that King not only had "sexual orgies" with more than one woman and "cavorted with people who were of doubtful loyalty to the United States," but was also "a switch hitter."

When Bernhard replied that he did not believe the stories, the liaison showed him a report that "purported to document what had been said." But it referred to an "informer of known reliability," without using names. Bernhard did not tell anyone at the time about the discussion or the report, but he knew "damn well" that some people in the administration, including President Kennedy, knew about both the surveillance and the reported findings.[23]

Despite Hoover's objections, all of the commission members agreed to the Justice recommendations in their report. In the areas where the commissioners disagreed, it was because everyone rhetorically supported protecting African Americans' rights, but the Southerners did not want to recommend any specific actions to advance this goal. On the recommendation to have the president—or Congress, if necessary— ensure that federal funds were not used to discriminate, Carlton objected that segregationists also paid taxes. He argued that cutting off funds for violating other citizens' rights should not be used as "a club" to force compliance.[24]

The commission's recommendation to strengthen the 1957 Civil Rights Act with a new law that would prohibit denial of the vote for any reason except length of residence, incarceration at the time of the election, or conviction of a felony also drew fire from the Southerners. They wanted state elections to remain totally under state control. Storey also insisted that "as the English language is still the official language of the United States, there is good justification for States requiring that voters have at least a rudimentary knowledge of this language."[25]

The recommendation to reduce federal assistance to schools that were not desegregated, or at least working toward that goal, drew a dissent from Duke political scientist Rankin. He saw the idea as "punitive," like Congressman Adam Clayton Powell's proposed amendment to cut off all federal funds. Rankin did not believe "schoolchildren should be made to suffer for the errors of their elders."[26]

Rankin and Storey disagreed with a requirement that banks and other federally supervised financial institutions end discrimination in mortgage loan operations. They believed that financial institutions had a right "to pursue their economic policies free from unwarranted federal control." Storey argued that these institutions are "primarily business institutions and not institutions for social reform." He continued, "they will pursue nondiscrimination when it is in their prudent financial interest." The issue is "freedom versus authority," required by democracy.[27]

The Congress and the administration used the commission's recommendations, but not until circumstances forced the crafting of new legislation. In the meantime, the commission noted that the Justice Department had become a bit more active in using existing law to enforce civil rights, in contrast to the practically bare record of Eisenhower's Justice Department. The Kennedy administration brought some voting rights cases, intervened in the New Orleans school desegregation suit, asked the federal district court for an injunction to protect freedom riders trying to desegregate buses, and sued in New Orleans and Montgomery to end segregation in airports built with federal funds.[28]

However, as continuing African American protests and voter registration drives were met with bombings, arson, and shootings, the Kennedy Justice Department did practically nothing to protect the citizens seeking their rights and those supporting them. Civil rights workers felt betrayed. Burke Marshall, assistant attorney general for civil rights, explained that, given states' rights, the department had limited powers and lacked clear authority and it was up to the protesters and workers to protect themselves.

The civil rights activists did not expect armed support from a national police force, but they believed that more aggressive Justice Department investigations and prosecutions would stop some of the violence. As the commission reported on this fault line in federalism—capitulation to local control of the police, thus allowing unpunished violence—in order to propose legislation, an inevitable conflict resulted. However, the commission hoped that Justice would work harder since it knew the commission would criticize the department's failings.[29]

The commission report strongly disagreed with the Kennedy administration's emphasis on voting rights almost to the total exclusion of any initiatives aimed at ending overall discrimination. Now King's message at the 1957 Prayer Pilgrimage for Freedom that with the vote protected "we will no longer have to worry the Federal Government about our basic rights," appeared naive. Without protection for the protesters, voting rights would never emerge, and it was clear that voting would not automatically end the problems in education, housing, administration of justice, and other areas. The commission continued to assert that "the need for broader action is underlined by the fact that problems of discrimination are often intimately related to other problems." For example, the report stated that the need for urban renewal may not seem to be a civil rights problem, "yet discrimination—in housing, in education, and in employment—contributes in major degree to the creation and preservation of slums."[30]

The commission repeatedly emphasized the need for the president to "utilize his leadership and influence and the prestige of his office in support of equal protection" of the laws. He should use all "means at his disposal," the report advised, and it urged "marshaling the Nation's vast reservoir of reason and good will in support of constitutional law not only as a civic duty but as essential to the attainment of the goal of equal opportunity for all."[31]

The commission released the report shortly after advocates pushed a bill for a two-year extension of its existence and an $800,000 appropriation to the Senate floor. Father Hesburgh's widely circulated additional statement expressed the view of commission supporters. He wrote that "as a kind of national conscience in the matter of civil rights . . . its effectiveness depends quite completely on whether it is heard, and whether the Nation and national leaders act accordingly."[32]

Hesburgh went on: "Lest I seem to be unduly harsh on the South, let me underline another story often repeated in these pages." Housing discrimination across the nation continues because of "the unspoken, but very effective conspiracies of builders, real estate brokers, and good neighbors who are downright arrogant in preserving the blessings of democracy for their own white selves alone."[33]

Hesburgh said he knew some might think him "intemperate," but "unless there is some fire, most governmental reports remain unread, even by those to whom they are addressed, in this case the President and the Congress." He indicated that he did not care about Kennedy's vow to put a man on the moon if at the same time we continued to "ignore the central moral problem of our times and appearing hypocrites to all the world."[34]

In this atmosphere, Attorney General Kennedy wrote Congress that if they would not enact permanent status, he thought four to six years "highly desirable." Scathing criticism from the Southern senators delayed a floor vote, but in the end a two-year extension passed, which President Kennedy signed into law on September 21, 1961.[35]

Tension between the commission and the administration grew as Southern whites responded with increasing violence to the voter registration drives that Kennedy had encouraged. Bernhard, Griswold, Hesburgh, and Hannah had unsatisfactory talks with Justice Department officials to try to resolve the working relationship. They continued urging action, to no avail.

The commission staff director tried to develop political networks with Congress and the White House without transgressing boundaries. Bernhard assigned William Taylor, from his public information office, to informally aid Wofford's sub-cabinet-level efforts on civil rights. The sub-cabinet group fell into disuse as the civil rights protests and the anti–civil rights violence grew in intensity. Everyone knew the Justice Department called the shots and saw Burke Marshall, the assistant attorney general for civil rights, as the one sub-cabinet-level official who really counted. Everyone also knew that Wofford, therefore, had little clout. He had been appointed, offhandedly, to the civil rights job, and Kennedy saw him as useful in keeping civil rights advocates under as much control as possible.

Taylor kept track of correspondence and prepared answers to routine inquiries. He continued to perform this function for Lee White, who assumed Wofford's duties when he left in 1962. White, an oil and gas lawyer on the staff of assistant to the president Theodore Sorensen, became assistant special counsel to the president. Assigned by Bernhard to help the White House staff, Taylor sometimes found himself in the odd position of drafting letters to Bernhard from White and then a response from Bernhard as well.[36]

Bernhard also carefully consulted with congressional staff and the administration before recommending names for the commission's state advisory committees. Upon becoming staff director, he found that the committees, set up near the end of the Eisenhower administration, were doing virtually nothing, that they were "cozy friends of some Republicans in Washington in the administration and that they just hadn't done any work." The commission agreed on the importance of creating new membership without "upheaval and public turmoil."

The commission reorganized committees instead of removing appointees and tried to maintain a balance between political parties, business and labor and religion, and civil rights and non–civil rights representation. The committees began to have some influence in their states. Some even criticized the commission for being too slow to act, just as the commission criticized the administration.

When the commission staff naively asked Vice President Johnson's office for some Texas names and then ended up not appointing them, it became temporarily a "hot political issue." However, the White House generally expressed interest only when they thought that a committee member was "personal anathema" or "had fought them vigorous in the campaign" or that the committee member would take positions solely in the hope of politically embarrassing the administration. Nonetheless, the administration usually believed that the commission's overall agenda, including committee appointments, supported its efforts.[37]

The Kennedy administration played a shameful shell game with the commission, using the commission for its own purposes, as White House staffers had suggested when selecting commissioners. Commission staffers complained that in Congress, when Justice wanted to promote legislation, they would rely on the findings and recommendations of the commission. However, when they wanted to show their reasonableness, they would cite some commission recommendation as extreme to show their comparative moderation.[38]

The president and Bobby Kennedy ridiculed the commission in private, irritated at its constant nagging. But the White House also manipulated the commission, drawing it into a clearly political enterprise when Martin Luther King, Jr., requested a presidential proclamation marking the hundredth anniversary of Lincoln's Emancipation Proclamation, which freed slaves in rebelling states in January 1863 and marked a turning point in the Civil War. King thought a presidential proclamation would give a lift to the non-violent direct-action movement. For fear of offending Southern Democrats in Congress, the White House staff and the president did not want to touch the idea. King discussed his proposal with an ad hoc working group comprising Louis Martin—*Chicago Defender* columnist, former editor in chief and president of the National Newspaper Publishers Association, and then deputy chairman of the Democratic National Committee—and White House staffers Arthur Schlesinger, Lee White, and Berl Bernhard. Ultimately, after Lee White advised him that politically, he had to issue something, the president issued a simple proclamation asserting that securing rights for blacks remained an "unfinished task of our democracy."[39]

Upon the recommendation of the working group, Kennedy decided to ask the commission to arrange a low-visibility White House social event that would not upset the white Southerners too much but would respond to the civil rights constituency. The commissioners reluctantly agreed after Bernhard presented the idea. They concluded that since the president had asked, and it concerned civil rights, they should not refuse. In an orchestrated, widely publicized "special meeting," the president also asked the commissioners to prepare a history of the hundred years of civil rights since emancipation. The cost, $62,000, was borne by the commission from its meager budget.[40]

To prepare this study, the commission hired John Hope Franklin, who was the best-known African American historian at the time, having been appointed chairman of the history department at Brooklyn College and thereby becoming the first black with such an appointment in a white institution of higher education. Franklin, with the assistance of historians Rayford Logan, Allan Nevins, and C. Vann Woodward, finished the work during the academic year of 1961–62 and presented it to Bernhard in June 1962.[41]

According to Franklin, the commission, "anticipating a story in a celebratory key," was disturbed at his "telling a darker history of civil rights that indicated how much remained to be done." After much unsatisfactory back and forth, Bernhard had the staff rewrite the document as a staff report. He directed them to work "like blazes" to complete the history for February 1963. The commission, totally seduced by Kennedy and his staff and wanting to curry favor, thus compromised its integrity. The result was a history emphasizing how blacks were "advancing toward a position of relative social and economic and political equality in the United States." Further, in contrast to the disturbing reality of race relations consistently reported on by the commission, the report declared falsely that "government at all levels as well as private associations and individuals are pressing determinedly and successfully towards the goal of equal opportunity for all."[42]

The commission sponsored commemoration ceremonies throughout the country with a theme of rededication to the advancement of civil rights. Before the reception and ceremony in Washington, Louis Martin, the African American deputy chairman of the Democratic National Committee, whose job it was to gain political advantage, saw to it that the guest list included every civil rights leader and black entertainer so that the Republicans, who usually staged a big Lincoln Day address, would have no one to invite to their events. Under the circumstances, Martin Luther King, Jr., remained unimpressed. Totally disgusted with Kennedy's unwillingness to propose civil rights legislation, or to even speak strongly about civil rights in his State of the Union message, King offered excuses and did not attend. John Hope Franklin, disrespected and "used by the United States Government," was in England as a visiting professor and did not bother to concoct excuses for not attending. Franklin thought the commission "did not do honor to itself or the country" by its "machinations," in which he had been an unwitting

John Hope Franklin.

participant. For his part, Bernhard, naively, thought the commission's unseemly service for Kennedy's political purposes might garner gratitude and more appreciation of the agency in the White House.[43]

However, the White House did not begin to address the commission's recommendations seriously until the "actions of Negroes," as Martin Luther King, Jr., predicted in 1957, forced its attention. The crisis in Mississippi over the admission of James Meredith, a black state resident, to the all-white state university "Ole Miss" in Oxford may have been a catalyst. This and other incidents of violent resistance to desegregation perhaps encouraged Kennedy to support the recommendations of the commission and civil rights leaders to issue the long-promised executive order outlawing federal support for discriminatory housing and to finally accept the need for federal civil rights legislation.[44]

While Kennedy reached these conclusions, the expiration date for the commission again approached, and the president this time seemed ambivalent about the future of the agency. If reauthorized, the commission wanted to play a role in implementing anti-discrimination policies through a proposed clearinghouse function to advise federal agencies, supply a mediation service, and administer a program to ensure equal protection in the distribution of federal benefits. The commissioners also made clear their opposition to another mere two-year extension because of the disruption of staff.

The president decided to propose a four-year extension instead of permanence to avoid a "pessimistic prediction that our problems will never be solved." He rejected the other ideas, but included the new clearinghouse function, even though the White House staff thought the commission could adequately advise on implementation of civil rights under its existing authority. The commissioners, on the other hand, wanted the statute to reflect some change in their role.[45]

The commissioners were more disappointed when the White House

Kennedy accepts the bland report that his staff had persuaded the commission to produce for the 100th Anniversary of the Emancipation Proclamation, February 12, 1963.

did nothing to push for the reauthorization as the time grew short. As in the past, staff started to exit, and planning became problematic. But Chairman Hannah, supported by the other commissioners—Hesburgh, Griswold, Robinson, Storey, and Rankin—refused to lobby to keep the commission alive. Despite their cooperation with the president on the emancipation commemoration events, the commission sensed that its tensions with Justice had "spilled over" into relations with the White House. Hannah concluded that "they had been kicked around badly by the administration; they had gotten no thanks from anybody."[46]

Wilkins, King, and other civil rights leaders, however, were appreciative of the commission's efforts and insisted that the commission must continue. In October 1963, after the March on Washington and the Birmingham protests, in which Eugene "Bull" Connor, the commissioner of public safety, blasted child protesters with fire hoses and unleashed police dogs, Congress enacted the commission extension with the addition of the clearinghouse function. So long as problems of discrimination remained, it had become the little agency that could not die.[47]

In a dispirited mood, the commission faced a frontal assault on its independence when the Kennedy administration, concerned about the reaction of Southern segregationists and Southern Democratic members of the House and Senate, manipulated the commissioners into delaying hearings in Mississippi. Intimidated, the commission was rendered useless at a critical time.

The commission was aware of the White Citizens' Council's growing violent response to black voter registration drives. Landmarks in the violence were the 1955 drive-by shooting death of the first African American in Humphreys County to register, Rev. George Lee, the leader of the registration drive in Belzoni, and the shooting of Gus Courts, another leader who, seriously wounded, left for Chicago. Also on August 18 of that year Emmett Till, age fourteen, was killed for allegedly wolf-whistling at a white woman.[48]

After the commission was established in 1957, the repression and violence continued without the commission's attending to the needs of the victims. There was the conviction and seven-year penalty for Clyde Kennard in 1958, for allegedly stealing twenty-five dollars' worth of chicken feed, when his only real crime was trying to gain admission to the all-white Mississippi Southern College. Between 1956 and the end of 1959, ten black men were killed by whites, but none of the murderers was convicted. NAACP field secretary Medgar Evers investigated, filed complaints, and asked for federal help, but to no avail. In Philadelphia, Mississippi, in October 1959 a black man and woman, Luther Jackson and Hattie Thomas, were sitting in a parked car when a police officer drove up, ordered them to get out, took Jackson around to the other side of the car, shot him twice, and then drove away. Jackson fell dead into the ditch alongside the car. The police officer, Lawrence Rainey, was acquitted by a local jury, and the Justice Department informed Medgar Evers that since murder was not a federal crime it could not prosecute. There was also the killing of Mack Parker, who, awaiting trial on charges of allegedly raping a white woman, was taken from jail by a lynch mob in April 1959 in Poplarville, Mississippi.[49]

These developments before the 1961 freedom rides and the new energy brought to the cause by college students who staged sit-ins and insisted on organizing voters in the 1960s, led the commission finally to plan hearings in Mississippi, which had originally been scheduled for 1959, after the tense Alabama voting hearings. Commissioners had kept abreast of the continued racial violence in the state, noting the weakness of the Eisenhower administration's response and the Kennedy administration's slowness in coming to grips with the problems. Meanwhile, civil rights advocates in Mississippi and national leaders had kept up the call for the commission to go to Mississippi.

Frustrated and irritated as the Kennedy administration tolerated the violence and resisted their efforts to address it, Commissioners Griswold, Hannah, and Hesburgh complained to the White House about the continued reports of arrests without cause, bombings, and assaults on civil rights activists with no convictions. Any local press that reported accurately on the violence was at risk. In January 1962, J. Oliver Emmerich, editor of the *Jackson State Times* and the *McComb Enterprise-Journal* was beaten by a white mob for opposing the White Citizens' Council's segregationist harassment and violence. In addition, the four whites and two blacks who had accepted appointments to the commission's state advisory committee received hate mail and telephone threats. A cross was burned at the home of a white member, the president of Mississippi Church Women United, Jane Schutt of Jackson, and the home of Dr. James Lucius Allen, a black Columbus pharmacist, was firebombed.[50]

The commission consistently wanted to go to Mississippi but also wished to avoid any actions that would worsen local problems or infuriate the Justice Department. The commission's most important power, to subpoena witnesses and information in connection with a hearing, required Justice Department enforcement when witnesses were uncooperative. Consequently, commissioners did not want to risk a public fight if the Justice Department refused to aid them. In reflecting on the commission's acquiescence to the administration years later, Bernhard concluded, "We were chicken."

After the violence attending the Meredith enrollment at the University of Mississippi, Attorney General Bobby Kennedy warned that if the commission went to Mississippi, it might interfere with obtaining convictions and registering voters and the gubernatorial race in 1961. The commission "was quite agreeable to holding off because they thought they were doing the right thing." However, as matters worsened, the commissioners asked Bernhard to tell the assistant attorney general for civil rights, Burke Marshall, that they wanted to go ahead with hearings, and Justice's opposition became even "harder." The commission wanted to listen to those who pleaded for their presence and provide more support for new legislation. A written explanation to Bobby Kennedy, designed to assure subpoena enforcement, received an unsupportive response. Hannah fired back, "We must state in all candor that this decision is difficult for us."[51]

Hannah asked to meet with the president, but Kenneth O'Donnell, special assistant to Kennedy, put him off. After "the Cuban situation" was resolved, the president planned to see Prime Minister Harold Macmillan of Britain in Nassau and then travel to Palm Beach for the Christmas holidays. Hannah replied, expressing the commission's "discontent" but under the circumstances, "there is no alternative but to accede to the Attorney's General's request" to continue holding off on hearings in Mississippi.[52]

The commission's continued delay despite the escalating violence became embarrassing. Its patience worn thin, the state advisory committee publicly criticized the commission for foot-dragging, and the coalition of civil rights groups in the Leadership Conference on Civil Rights charged the agency with compromising its independence by caving in to the Justice Department. The administration kept up its duplicitous dealings with the commission. At a press conference on March 21, 1963, in answer to a question as to whether the commission should submit to Justice's objections to a hearing, President Kennedy said, "No, that is a judgment the Civil Rights Commission should" make and pursue "any hearing they feel advances the cause or their responsibility which has been entrusted to them by law. Then they should go ahead with it."[53]

Behind the scenes, the Justice Department kept up its opposition. On March 26, 1963, Bobby Kennedy wrote to Hannah, reiterating his "reasons" for continuing to object to hearings. The commission decided someone had to "shake-up the administration." Since Justice did not want the commissioners to go to Mississippi and therefore could not be counted on to enforce subpoenas or provide marshals for protection, they could not go. Instead, Justice asked the commission staff to revise a preliminary report they had written and include recent civil rights incidents and a description of the federal funds received by the Mississippi state government.

Along with the conservative attitude toward civil rights enforcement in the administration, the commissioners found particularly distressing the Federal Aviation Authority's 1962 approval of the construction of a new airport with segregated restrooms and restaurant facilities in Rankin County, an airport serving Jackson, Mississippi. The staff had actually acquired copies of the approved plans.[54]

After the staff concluded the revision of its report, the commission unanimously voted to accept their draft as an interim report on civil rights in Mississippi in lieu of a hearing. However, despite the commission's independence, Hannah agreed with Bernhard that they "could not come out with a report and take the President by surprise when it was such a blast." The commission routinely released a draft of the pertinent portion of a report to officials in a covered agency for comment. Sometimes officials would respond by implementing recommendations before the report became public. However, this time the commissioners, naively, agreed that Hannah would give the entire report to the president and that if he did not release it in seventy-two hours the commission would make it public. This was an entirely new procedure.[55]

Bernhard called Burke Marshall, the assistant attorney general for civil rights, to give him a heads-up, and he also gave Presidential Assistant Lee White a copy of the report, telling him that Hannah believed they should talk openly with the White House about their work. Instead of respecting the commission's openness and addressing the problems, the administration decided on a strike against the agency's credibility.

Marshall wrote a scathing rebuttal of the commission's points, minimizing the severity of the problems in Mississippi and arguing that Justice routinely acted as aggressively as possible. Lee White used Marshall's memorandum to write the president a caustic criticism of the commission for even preparing the report, and declared it inaccurate and irresponsible. White insisted the administration bore no blame for inaction on civil rights. He suggested that the president should tell the commission to change the report and that he should consider not supporting reauthorization or even attacking the agency publicly.[56]

Bernhard, oblivious to the responses of Marshall and White to the report, joined White in meeting with the president on the subject. Kennedy raised a number of questions from the memorandum and implied that the commissioners had bad judgment. He asked whether the report would help or just be "disruptive." He wanted to know if they had "talked with Bobby or [deputy attorney general] Nicholas Katzenbach about it?" He also said he did not believe the information about the FAA and had talked to Najeeb Halaby, the head of the agency, who said the commission was wrong about the airport construction. Bernhard responded that the commission had the actual plans. Halaby said he had worked out a defensible way to use state funds to build the segregated restrooms and restaurant at the federal facility. Dissatisfied with the commission report, the president asked that Hannah come to see him.[57]

When Hannah and Bernhard met with Kennedy, he asked whether the commission had voted unanimously to approve the report and whether they planned to publish it. They replied in the affirmative. According to Arthur Schlesinger, Kennedy responded, "I still don't like it. If the Commissioners have made up their minds, I presume they will issue the report anyway. I think they are off the track on this one, but I wouldn't try to suppress it. That would be wrong—couldn't do it anyway. It is independent, has a right to be heard, but I do wish you could get them to reconsider." In both meetings, Bernhard recalled, the president appeared "totally cool." He "even joked" and "never raised his voice." He never hinted at what was to come.[58]

The commissioners soon discovered they had been too trusting. The president met with White House reporters and denounced as totally irresponsible the commission's recommendation that the president explore his authority to cut off federal funds to the state of Mississippi. He made it appear that the commission thought the president already had the authority to do so, putting the most "draconian" spin on the idea.[59]

The press, almost unanimously, dismissed the commissioners as misguided and accepted the White House spin. Kennedy said there would be no further extension of federal aid used to encourage or permit discrimination but he did not have the power to cut off aid in a general way, as if that was what the commission wanted. Even the usually sympathetic press questioned why the commission should "throw people already in poverty into anguish." As a result, some asked whether the president intended to cut off funds for the commission for making the proposal. He answered, "No, I don't," but then in a public letter to Hannah, Kennedy dismissed the report entirely.[60]

The commission staff felt deeply wounded by the episode. Civil rights groups, pleased but shocked that the commission could be so aggressive, rallied to its defense. Roy Wilkins wrote a supporting letter to the *New York Times*, which had editorialized against the commission's proposal. He later told Bernhard, "You know it's the first time in my life that I've been left in the dust." When he read about the report in the *Times*, he couldn't believe it. In writing the letter he hardly knew what to say because he "felt like I was an old conservative dog" since he had not had the temerity to propose cutting off federal funds at that point.[61]

Gloom settled in at the commission over the manipulation by the White House, but the commissioners felt no regret about their final decision. The report's recommendations had been approved unanimously, with even the Southern commissioners agreeing. They believed that the federal government should cut off funds in instances of publicly financed discrimination. They had urged the action before, and now they made no apologies.

They had learned not to be seduced by a "friendly" White House into abandoning control over the release of their own reports. The episode strengthened the commissioners' commitment to maintaining the commission's independence. Funding cutoffs became a central part of the Civil Rights Act of 1964, but in 1963 that glimpse into the future was not yet available to the embattled staff at the commission. Bernhard had done everything possible to ingratiate himself and the commission with the administration, including agreeing to the White House proposal for the Emancipation Proclamation commemoration events and lending Taylor to the White House staff, but there had been no reward.[62]

The Kennedy administration slowly stepped up its attention to civil rights matters, as the conflict in the South continued unabated. All over the South, police arrested citizens engaged in civil rights demonstrations and filled jails with protesters. At last Kennedy stepped forward. In June he sent in the National Guard to thwart Alabama governor George Wallace's schoolhouse-door stand to avoid desegregating the University of Alabama. After the confrontation with Wallace, Kennedy made a

Alabama governor George Wallace defies Deputy Attorney General Nicholas Katzenbach's attempt to implement desegregation of the University of Alabama, June 11, 1963.

nationally televised speech and expanded his February bill to an omnibus civil rights proposal. Kennedy described the cause as a "moral issue" of "whether all Americans are to be afforded equal rights and equal opportunities, whether we are going to treat our fellow Americans as we want to be treated." That same evening, as Medgar Evers arrived home and stepped out of his car into the driveway, he was shot and killed by White Citizens' Council member Byron De La Beckwith. Despite Beckwith's fingerprints on the rifle that shot Evers, he was acquitted. The Evers assassination underscored the need for strong action against racists. Then in August of 1963, the March on Washington pushed the need for civil rights reform further to the forefront of the nation's conscience.[63]

The omnibus bill covered much of what the commission had recommended, including a four-year extension of the commission, a sixth-grade literacy test for voting, authority for the attorney general to file suits to enforce school desegregation, and a provision cutting off funds for any discriminatory state or local programs. Another provision would end racial exclusion in restaurants and other public accommodations. Members of the commission and the staff director testified, offering strong support for the bill. With the federal fund cutoff now part of the Kennedy agenda, the press forgot its criticism of the commission for proposing it. The *New York Times* and other papers emphatically sup-

ported reauthorization of the agency. Nonetheless, the commission again required last-minute resuscitation. In the first week of October Congress added a one-year extension as a rider to another bill.[64]

In the commission's 1963 report, Hannah noted that "every step taken by Congress and the Executive department

Medgar Evers, NAACP field secretary, was killed by rifle fire from White Citizens Council member Byron De La Beckwith as Evers emerged from his car in his own driveway in 1963.

Byron De La Beckwith, arrested by FBI agents for Medgar Evers's murder. Survived two trials with the backing of the white establishment. He was finally convicted years later in 1994.

in the field of civil rights in the past four years originated with the recommendations of the commission or depended on the facts it gathered."[65] He was not exaggerating. In his February 1963 message to Congress, President Kennedy acknowledged that the commission's recommendations "have provided the basis for remedial action both by Congress and the Executive branch." The relationship had been consistently uneasy, but with the impetus of civil rights protests, it had been productive.[66]

On October 10, 1963, Chairman Hannah wrote to Kennedy that given the commission's extension, he wanted to discuss the future with the president. Several members wanted to resign. Bernhard planned to leave at the end of October, and many of "the ablest" members of the staff had already left. If Kennedy wanted new commissioners, Hannah would join Storey and Hesburgh in gladly resigning. Robinson had already left to accept the president's appointment to the District of Columbia federal court, but Hannah had not discussed with Rankin and Griswold their plans. Hannah asked for a phone call to talk with the president before the October 27 meeting of the commission.

Kennedy replied that he already had Storey's resignation. He had planned to leave after his wife died but agreed to stay on for a short time. The president hoped the commission would name a temporary staff director to replace Bernhard until the omnibus bill passed. The president also explained that he wanted the commission to make its plans first, and then he would discuss the future with Hannah.[67]

At their monthly meeting the commissioners approved a staff paper on future activities, including state and local reaction to racial unrest and finding ways to encourage greater protection for civil rights workers, since they expected and hoped the protests would continue. After the commission meeting, Hannah told the president that "about two-thirds of the staff have departed or are departing for greener pastures."

They had prepared a budget to submit with the understanding that the commission would continue indefinitely and instructed the staff to recruit replacements so that the work could continue.[68]

Bobby Kennedy, tired of the commission's criticism of the administration's conservative approach to civil rights enforcement, advised the president to ask for Hannah's resignation as chairman at a meeting the president had scheduled with Hannah for November 13, 1963. However, President Kennedy did not raise the subject. Instead, he and Hannah agreed that Hannah would persuade Hesburgh to stay at least until sometime in the spring. Hannah agreed to stay until then and assumed that Rankin and Griswold would also remain until the spring. Hannah encouraged the president to appoint replacements for Storey and Robinson and advised that one should be "a Negro" and, for balance, one other a "distinguished white person from the south." However, Hannah understood that Kennedy might have other qualifications in mind.[69]

Hannah told Kennedy that if the commission undertook to investigate allegations of fraud in voting, as proposed in the omnibus legislation, it would need more staff and perhaps an entire new section, but he

Puerto Ricans voting in New York City, 1959.

felt that bridge could be crossed when it was necessary. He liked the idea that the commission, in addition to continuing the handling of complaints and monitoring enforcement, would perform a field survey of some medium-sized communities throughout the county where there had been racial unrest and suggest solutions. They agreed that it would be useful for the commission to collect information on state and local anti-discrimination laws and on implementation of the laws by employers and unions.

Hannah suggested that they might examine whether federal programs had resulted in discrimination in rural areas. He also thought they might see what federal agencies had done to prevent or end discrimination at the Oak Ridge National Laboratory, established in eastern Tennessee in 1943, and at Cape Canaveral, established as a space launch center in Florida in 1962. But, he told the president, the commission would wait until after the civil rights legislation passed to pursue those goals.

Kennedy indicated an interest in a study of civil rights issues concerning Eskimos in Alaska, and Hannah agreed to look into what could be done at a reasonable cost. Kennedy also said he did not think the commission had done enough on problems facing Indians, Mexicans, Puerto Ricans, and possibly other minority groups. Hannah answered that they had done more than the president realized and he would send the president the relevant reports published by the commission. They agreed that the commission would continue its work with minimum visibility until after Congress had come to a final vote on the civil rights legislation.

Hannah, wounded by what the commission regarded as the Kennedy White House's abuse of their trust, ended by telling Kennedy that the commission wanted to cooperate with the administration, but the commissioners felt strongly that the Civil Rights Commission should be independent of other agencies of government and should always be in a position to exercise independent judgment. He knew the president agreed that this was a sound position.[70]

After the meeting, he wrote to Kennedy summarizing their discussion and including a list of studies during the last six years on issues facing groups other than African Americans, saying, "It may well be that we have not put as much emphasis here as we might have, but this results from the fact that . . . the overwhelming problem has to do with the discrimination and demands to which American Negroes are subjected. There are so many more Negroes, and the discrimination has been so much more intense that it represents the bulk of the problem."[71]

The White House and the commission had reached some agreement, but the large task of passing the civil rights bill with the commission recommendations and the four-year extension remained before them. Hannah's November 13 conversation with the president was the commission's last contact with Kennedy before his assassination on November 22, 1963.

CHAPTER III

"So Glad You Finally Made It"

I N EARLY 1965, Natchez black funeral home operator Archie Curtis and his ambulance driver went to answer what appeared to be a routine call for a heart attack victim. But when they arrived at the rural address they were accosted by armed and hooded white men, blindfolded, and driven "further into the country." One assailant ordered them to hurry out of the car before we "blow you to pieces." Another told Curtis to "drop them pants." As they "whipped him with a whip," he begged them to stop since he was recovering from a stroke. They asked him for his "damned NAACP card." While beating them, their assailants asked that the victims admit to NAACP membership and beat them some more and then let them go with an admonition that "you better not tell nobody" and drove away.[1]

Alfred Whitley, "a scared little man of middle age, undistinguished in every visible way," suffered an even more horrific experience. On February 6, as he drove home from his janitor's job at the Armstrong Tire and Rubber Company in Natchez, a car followed him onto the gravel road to his house, about ten miles outside of town. When he was about "a hundred yards from his house two cars were parked there and he couldn't get by." He blew his horn, but no one moved. Then the man in the car behind him and men from the cars in front emerged with their guns. When the eight men walked out his "car lights were shining" and he could see their hoods were down at first. Then seeing their faces were in the light they "covered themselves with one hand, and they had their guns pointed on me and in my car." He got out and they told him, "If you don't say nothing you won't get hurt." They took his glasses and tied his hands behind him, told him to close his eyes, and then said, "Put him in the Oldsmobile." They drove for about forty minutes and then stopped "out in the swamp somewhere." They "pulled" his "clothes off, tore them off, cut them loose, took them off. And they reeled out two bullwhips then and said 'You hear this?' "[2]

Alfred Whitley and his wife, Fannie Lee.

They "shoved" Whitley on his stomach and beat him "until they got tired of beating." He asked why and one answered, "Well, don't you know we know you're the leading nigger in Natchez, the NAACP and the Masonic Lodge! And you have a white leader, and you're going to tell me who he is." When Whitley denied the accusations and said he belonged to nothing except his church and had never tried to register to vote, they beat him again and kept questioning him. Then they forced him to drink a bottle of castor oil and one of the assailants "put a gun across his nose" and said, "Do you know what you are going to die of?" Then one assailant said, "Nigger Run." Whitley ran while they shone a flashlight on him. He fell on his stomach. They turned off the light, shot where they saw him last, emptied guns over his head while he lay there. Then they drove away. "With the looks of the blazes . . . the blazes was coming right straight over my head."

Whitley made his way nude to the road and caught a truck driven by a passing black motorist and called his wife, who took him to the hospital. He was treated at Jefferson Davis Hospital, where the physician found "numerous abrasions and contusions, swelling above both eyes and across both cheeks. He appears alert and well-oriented. He is weak, however, from having been forced to drink approximately 2 to 3 ounces of castor oil." The physician told him to call the sheriff, who came to the hospital to interview him. But no one was ever arrested.

Under questioning from the commission's general counsel, William Taylor, Whitley explained that he recognized the car in which he was driven as belonging to an employee at the tire factory where they both worked. The white employee had asked him "what I thought about the school and [I] told him the children ought to be educated, but also there ought to be jobs for them based on their learning, in Mississippi."

Commissioner Hesburgh asked Whitley: "Did you tell the sheriff everything you have told us?" When Whitley answered yes, Hesburgh said, "And after that you never saw him again." Whitley replied, "No sir." When Commissioner Freeman asked if he gave the sheriff the name of the man he recognized, Whitley answered, "Yes, ma'am," but reiterated under questioning that nothing was done about his complaint.

Vice Chair Eugene Patterson asked, "Do you think they really had you mixed up with somebody else, Mr. Whitley, or do you think they thought they knew who you were?"

Whitley responded, "Well evidently, they had to know who I was, because from the way they stated when they beat me up. They said 'We've been after you for five days' and 'You're the hardest one we ever tried to catch.' "

Patterson: "Do you think it might have resulted from what you said at the plant that day?"

Whitley: "That's the only thing I can think of."

In February 1965, when the commission at last went to Mississippi, it heard stirring testimony from these and other witnesses who had been waiting and anticipating the arrival of the commissioners. The commission was welcomed by Charles Evers, who had insisted on becoming the NAACP field secretary after his brother Medgar was shot and killed on the evening of June 11, 1963, just hours after President Kennedy's introduction of a civil rights bill that addressed the causes for which Medgar Evers fought and died. Charles Evers told the commissioners, "We had anticipated your coming over two years ago but we are so glad you finally made it."[3]

In the previous two years history had not waited for the commission's arrival in Mississippi, but the commission had kept its focus on resistance in the South. First, however, the commission had to deal with the new administration. Understanding the demands on President Lyndon Johnson, who assumed the presidency following Kennedy's assassination, Hannah sent Johnson his last correspondence with President Kennedy, saying the commission would simply sit tight with minimum visibility until he could focus on decisions about the appointments.

Members of the U.S. Commission on Civil Rights arrive at the Federal Building in Jackson, Mississippi, for the February 10, 1965 hearing. *left to right:* John A. Hannah, chairman; Robert S. Rankin; Father Theodore M. Hesburgh; Erwin N. Griswold; and Frankie Muse Freeman.

Hannah did not expect an immediate response. However, as the commission awaited the new president's decisions, the White House staff, as is customary at the beginning of an administration, requested resignations from all presidential appointees. And, disregarding the commission's independence, they included the commissioners in that request.

Since the commissioners had all told Kennedy individually that they wanted to leave, they took the opportunity to send resignation letters. When nothing further occurred before the commission's January 15 meeting, Hannah wrote the president reminding him of the resignations to take effect at his discretion. He urged Johnson to keep in mind as he considered appointments that the commission's work did not increase the popularity of its members in many quarters. However, even critics agreed that the commission had consistently contributed to the solution of difficult and complex problems. Hannah also wanted Johnson to know that with the uncertainty about the agency's future, some "able staff has been enticed away by other agencies of the government and by other employers."[4]

Hannah wrote again, seeking a meeting with Johnson when the commission would be in Washington for the February meeting. In the meantime, clashes occurred between Panamanian demonstrators and U.S. troops in January 1964, as protesters surrounded the Panama Canal Zone until Johnson eventually agreed to renegotiate the Panama Canal Treaty. Johnson wrote the commissioners that this crisis had absorbed a great deal of his attention, but he wanted them to stay and proceed in accordance with whatever they had discussed with Kennedy. He also hoped they agreed that "all of our efforts should be undertaken" to enact the civil rights bill.[5]

Commissioners worried over what role they would play when the civil rights bill that they had recommended eventually passed. Hannah reminded them that their recommendations, including the fund cutoff idea that had caused them so much grief, featured prominently in the legislation. He told them that they would have plenty to do. Civil rights issues, unfortunately, did not seem likely to disappear, and implementation would require a struggle. First, however, they needed two more commissioners to fill the vacancies.[6]

In pursuit of his civil rights agenda, Johnson settled on a number of unprecedented African American appointments, including Housing and Urban Development Secretary Robert Weaver, the first African American cabinet secretary, before he turned his attention to the commission. In February, the president made his first commission nomination, a Kennedy selection. He named Frankie Muse Freeman, who was the associate general counsel of the St. Louis Housing Authority. A forty-eight-year-old Howard University Law School graduate who had practiced privately and served as an assistant district attorney in St. Louis, Freeman would become the first woman appointed to the commission. She also served on the executive board of the local NAACP chapter and had already served on the commission's Missouri State Advisory Committee. The *St. Louis Post-Dispatch* applauded her selection as an excellent choice.[7]

In naming Freeman to the post, Johnson went against the recommendations of Roy Wilkins and Whitney Young, who, when asked, "had some man to recommend." In February 1964, when Johnson went to St. Louis to speak, he invited Freeman to meet with him. At the meeting, Freeman thanked the president, expressing her concern about fitting in with the academics on the commission. Johnson assured her that she could "handle deans."[8]

In the middle of the battle to gain passage of the civil rights bill,

National Urban League president Whitney Young, NAACP executive director
Roy Wilkins, Congress of Racial Equality president James Farmer,
and Student Nonviolent Coordinating Committee chairman John Lewis—
civil rights leaders who contended with the Johnson administration.

Johnson devoted personal time to obtaining the "right" person for the
job in order to gain the support of Southern senators for the pending
civil rights bill as well. Settling on Arkansas lawyer William Mitchell,
whom he had met at a social function, he talked to the state's two Democratic senators, John McClellan and William Fulbright, to ensure their
support for Mitchell's confirmation. Fulbright, apparently, agreed easily, but Johnson had to cajole McClellan, who said he had opposed the
commission from the beginning. Johnson told him he knew that but
wanted Mitchell because he needed a "Southerner who will stand up on
his hind legs, and say 'By God, wait just a minute,' " as the longtime
Speaker of the House of Representatives, Texas Democrat Sam Rayburn, would say.[9]

After neutralizing McClellan, Johnson invited Congressman Wilbur
Mills of Arkansas to sit with him while he phoned Mitchell. The
Arkansas lawyer did not seem very receptive, saying he would have to
talk to his partners before making a decision. Johnson told him, "Tell
your partners your President's got his tail in a crack."[10]

Johnson ticked off the impressive academic posts held by the four members still left on the commission—Hannah, president of Michigan State; Hesburgh of Notre Dame; Griswold, dean of Harvard Law School; and Rankin, professor of political science at Duke—and told Mitchell, "I want someone who won't be a damned idiot and want to eat a little Negro baby for breakfast."[11]

After Mitchell, who feared disadvantages to his law practice from serving on a civil rights commission, declined the president's offer, Johnson turned to Eugene Patterson, editor of the *Atlanta Journal-Constitution*, who had the support of the Georgia senators. Even though they did not like the commission, and had some concerns about his views, they decided not to oppose forty-one-year-old Patterson, a Georgia-born journalism graduate from the University of Georgia. During World War II, Patterson served in General George Patton's Third Army, and after a journalism career he became editor of the *Journal-Constitution* in 1960. Patterson courageously wrote to his fellow white Southerners during the conflict and violence of the civil rights movement, trying to influence them to change. His column about the Birmingham church bombing in which four little girls were killed in 1963 was so moving that Walter Cronkite had him read it on the *CBS Evening News*. "Only we can trace the truth, Southerner—you and I. We broke those children's bodies. We watched the stage set without staying it. We listened to the prologue unbestirred. . . . We—who go on electing politicians who heat the kettles of hate. . . . This is no time to load our anguish onto the murderous scapegoat who set the cap in dynamite of our own manufacture. . . . He thinks he has pleased us." Whitney Young told Johnson he had Patterson on his list as a "a good white Southerner." Johnson nominated Freeman and Patterson in March, but Senator Eastland dragged his feet, as usual, and delayed their confirmation hearings until the end of July 1964. The Senate finally confirmed Freeman in September and Patterson in October.[12]

In the meantime the debate over the Civil Rights Act of 1964, including the recommendations of the commission that had made it into the bill, proceeded in the House of Representatives. After House passage in February, the Southerners filibustered for eighty-eight days until May. During Johnson's strong push for the bill in the summer of 1964, whites and blacks joined in SNCC's Freedom Summer, a concentrated effort to register black voters in the South. On June 22, one black and two white civil rights workers, James Chaney, Michael Schwerner, and Andrew Goodman, went missing while traveling from Meridian to Philadelphia,

Andrew Goodman, James Chaney, and Michael Schwerner, three civil rights workers killed by Klansman Deputy Sheriff Cecil Price and sixteen co-conspirators near Philadelphia, Mississippi, in June 1964. Price and six others were convicted of federal civil rights charges in 1967 and received short sentences.

Mississippi, to investigate a church burning. Some weeks later, after the FBI paid an informer $30,000, officials found the bullet-riddled bodies of Chaney, Goodman, and Schwerner buried in an earthen dam. The national disgust and shock at the continuing violence in the South and the murder of the three civil rights workers fueled passage of the civil rights bill.[13]

On July 2, 1964, Johnson signed the Civil Rights Act of 1964, based on Kennedy's proposals that acknowledged the commission's recommendations as "the basis for remedial action." The act established an Equal Employment Opportunity Commission to handle employment discrimination claims and outlawed long-standing discrimination in public accommodations such as restaurants and hotels, which had been prohibited in the Civil Rights Act of 1875 until the act was found unconstitutional by the Supreme Court in 1883. Title VI of the 1964 act also prohibited the use of federal funds by institutions that discriminated on the basis of race, color, or national origin.[14]

The Congress also enacted the commission's recommendation for sixth-grade education as presumptive evidence of literacy. However, Congress rejected the commission's proposal for federal registrars and left punishment of voting rights abuses to the Justice Department and the courts. After the usual North-South disagreement, Congress renewed the commission for four years, the longest reauthorization to date. The legislation also gave the commission a requested clearinghouse function and the responsibility for investigating voting fraud and denials of the right to vote.[15]

The commission experienced a crisis of confidence after the election.

The Johnson administration began staffing the agencies created under the Civil Rights Act of 1964 while preparing proposals to send to the Congress for what became the Voting Rights Act of 1965. A period of reassessment began at the commission. The staff was at a loss as to what the commission's role should be in the changed environment. Commissioners and staff thought that the nonviolent protests and the violent response were spent. Figuring out how to obtain a positive response to the riots in the ghettos seemed impossible. The commissioners disagreed. Commissioner Eugene Patterson thought the agency should take on investigations of the violence in the North. Their best work always involved hearing from aggrieved people and officials out in the field. They would also need to determine how to address the social and economic problems of the black poor. The other commissioners were deeply interested but decided to have the staff recommend ways to change the course of their work.

After anguished reappraisals, the commission, at first, decided to use its accumulated knowledge to advise the new civil rights agencies on implementing the new civil rights act. The staff helped the Equal Employment Opportunity Commission and the Community Relations

Martin Luther King, Jr., and members of Congress as President Johnson signs the 1964 Civil Rights Act.

Service get under way, and gave technical assistance to civil rights agencies throughout the government through a new technical information clearinghouse center. The commission also advised the Justice Department and the Bureau of the Budget on the initial regulations for the fund cutoff provisions of Title VI. As Hannah had predicted, when the Civil Rights Act of 1964 was passed, the commission had more work than ever to do, but that work was not nearly as exciting as hearings and investigations in conflict-ridden areas.[16]

Based in part on the commission's contribution to the Civil Rights Act of 1964, especially the funds termination for which the commission had been "clobbered" and its work helping the agencies get started, the commission expanded its operations and requested a budget increase to hire new staff. Hannah also asked the president to appoint William L. Taylor, the general counsel and, like Bernhard, a member of the Yale Law Class of 1954, as staff director. Johnson agreed to Taylor's appointment, although Lee White noted that "his entire background is with the NAACP Legal Department, the Americans for Democratic Action and the Civil Rights Commission." Since the post required Senate confirmation, "there may well be some problem in naming him, although surely he merits consideration." After some objections from the Southern senators, Taylor was confirmed in August.

Hannah and Hesburgh wanted to resign, but not before completing the long-unfinished business of the hearing in Mississippi. At first Attorney General Nicholas Katzenbach seemed agreeable and promised that the FBI would provide any information the commission needed. After the Chaney, Schwerner, and Goodman murders, however, he asked the commission not to move forward with the Mississippi hearing.

When Katzenbach met with the commissioners to persuade them not to go, they reminded him that throughout the Kennedy administration they had accepted the suggestion to delay their hearings. They could not simply continue to wait. They had a responsibility to the activists who were risking their lives for change, including their own SAC members, to conduct their own investigation and to hear from people on the ground. After Katzenbach left, they discussed the perpetual topic of how going ahead would affect a cooperative relationship with Justice. After the staff pointed out that cooperation was always a sensitive issue, no matter what the commission did, the commissioners decided unanimously to hold the hearing, despite any resulting strain on their relationship with the Justice Department.[17]

In February 1965, when the commission arrived in Mississippi, Commissioner Freeman wanted to visit four black churches in Canton

Attorney General Nicholas Katzenbach, who tried to
persuade the commission not to go to Mississippi.

that had been burned after African Americans tried to register to vote.
The commission staff worried about safety, but reluctantly found a car
for the trip. When Commissioner Griswold learned of Freeman's proposed site visit, he and his wife and other staff decided to join her.
Deeply affected and moved by the site, the commissioners decided that
whenever the commission held a hearing thereafter, they would arrange
for a site visit if at all possible.[18]

The five days of hearings, broadcast live on television from the Veterans Administration Center in Jackson, led to unanimous recommendations that supported the enactment of the Voting Rights Act of 1965.
Before the commission hearing, WLBT, the Jackson television station,
had routinely censored broadcasts concerning civil rights. Station manager Fred Beard complained that the national networks were "overload-
ing the circuits with Negro propaganda." In 1955 the station cut off a
national program about the NAACP and put a sign on the air saying,
"Sorry Cable Trouble." The station weighed in with segregationist
appeals when James Meredith attempted to enter the University of Mississippi in 1962. Because of the station's overt bias and censorship, the
FCC gave WLBT a one-year probationary period for its license in

1964. Under this pressure the station taped the hearings and broadcast some as a documentary, but WJTV, with a ninety-mile signal, carried the hearings live. They could be seen in Philadelphia, Mississippi, where Chaney, Schwerner, and Goodman had been murdered the summer before, and in Belzoni, where voter registration leader Rev. George Lee was fired upon and killed in 1955.

Through the commission hearings, the people of Mississippi heard from some public officials who described a new moderation on race even as witnesses detailed one outrage after the other. In addition, Jackson's notoriously segregationist newspapers, reflecting the new moderate appearance, published columns on the hearings and an editorial including some details of the terrorism.[19]

The commission hearings afforded whites a view of the terror, violence, and discrimination perpetuated by whites against blacks in the state. African American witnesses for the first time appeared on television, seen by their white and black fellow citizens talking to a government agency, with the commissioners respectfully listening to what they said. The televised hearings, as Roy Reed of the *New York Times* concluded, were a "crack in the racial wall."[20]

The commissioners heard from thirty subpoenaed witnesses, public

VA Administration Medical Center in Jackson, Mississippi,
where the 1965 commission hearing was held.

officials, and citizens who claimed that their rights had been violated. After the publicity over the murders of civil rights workers and a continuing media focus on a state where violent attacks had become almost daily news, there was no need to have Justice enforce the subpoenas. Governor Paul Johnson and other officials welcomed the commission. Ignoring the state's record, Johnson assured the commissioners that Mississippi would continue to be the most law-abiding state in the nation.[21]

But Aaron Henry, the NAACP state chairman, was not impressed. He said the "statements we are hearing now coming from the official people of our state, to my mind it's because the state of Mississippi is right now in a show case. . . . I don't think that Governor Johnson could say anything differently if he wanted to. I am not at all convinced that this great change of heart he is now expressing is a genuine change. You wait until the commission goes back to Washington."

Charles Evers chimed in, "I agree."[22]

In addition to the testimony of Whitley, Curtis, and others, one witness told of returning home after trying to register and seeing five white men drive up to her house and leave a threatening placard that read: "Thousands of Klansmen watching . . . waiting!" Witnesses talked of routine hostile attitudes from officials. A circuit clerk who served as registrar gave testimony that showed he himself did not understand a section of the Mississippi Constitution that he had asked one of the African American witnesses to interpret in order to be allowed to vote.

Unita Zelma Blackwell, a housewife from Mayersville in Issaquena County, told the commission that she had joined the Council of Federated Organizations (COFO) and was trying to get people to "go down to the courthouse to register to vote." "They's afraid to . . . get thrown off the farms and everything else, but they're standing up and we're explaining everything."

She told the commission there were no blacks registered to vote in the county before the summer of 1964. She tried to register three times. When she went the first time, the registrar gave her a "slip of paper— because I had never saw one before—and I looked at it and took my time. And filled it out and she stood there hanging over the banister." Then the registrar gave her a section of the Mississippi Constitution on the power to tax corporations to interpret, which Ms. Blackwell read to the commission. The registrar told her that she had failed. The second time, Blackwell took affidavits showing she had more than the required sixth-grade education, but the registrar gave her another section of the

Mississippi Governor Paul Johnson, right, reads a statement before the U.S. Commission on Civil Rights hearing in Jackson, February 16, 1965. Listening (*from left*) are Erwin N. Griswold, John A. Hannah, chairman, and commission members Frankie Muse Freeman and Father Theodore M. Hesburgh.

Constitution to interpret, dealing with the judicial sale of land. Blackwell was failed again.

The third time Ms. Blackwell attempted to vote, the registrar was helpful. Blackwell took the test again and finished it, then noticed she had misspelled the word "length" and had not included the date. The registrar said, "Oh, that's all right," and she passed. Blackwell thought "the civil rights [commission] and Justice department, everybody running in," made a difference.[23]

Hesburgh asked Blackwell, "Do you anticipate having any difficulty because of coming here today and making this testimony?" She replied, "Well I don't know." Just a few days before her testimony, "we was coming out—we had been to Mr. Jackson's house, and was talking to him about coming to a parent's meeting, and some white guys came up in a truck and blocked us and got out and told us all kinds of nasty things: Get out of here and don't come back." The Sunday before, the same truck had come by, she testified. "They was down talking to people, and had a shot gun out and flashing it." They said, "I could have killed you

Unita Blackwell *(second from right)* in her ever-present boots, with unidentified fellow volunteers organizing voter registration around the time when she testified at the commission's February 1965 hearing in Jackson, Mississippi.

way back yonder in the woods," and other threats; "and you get to the place you know it's going to happen but you've just got to stand up and got to do something."[24]

Commissioner Frankie Freeman recalled that the commissioners were visibly "appalled" by the testimony of Carter, Whitley, Blackwell, and others who described their harassment and subjection to brutality, but she said she tried not to "get so caught up in despair that it would take over, because you couldn't be effective then." But try as she might, occasionally she would put her "hands together and just say 'Lord.' " Then she would wipe the tears away, sensing the camera coverage. She said she was strengthened by the belief that despite the "horror stories," "change was happening."[25]

The voices of moderation heard from some white leaders gave Freeman and the other commissioners reason to hope. E. J. Palmer of Natchez, president of the Mississippi Manufacturers Association, conceding the existence of the racist behavior that had been described, said change was coming. He believed, "Nothing can be gained by anyone by a continuation of what has happened in the past."

Leroy P. Percy of Greenville, a banker and cotton planter, a son of a senator, former president of the Delta Council and the Mississippi Economic Council, and a member of one of the Delta's oldest and most respected families, said they were tired of the dead hand of the past. "The people of Mississippi want a change and I believe they are going to get it."

Hannah, in closing the hearings, said that while the violence and denials of the right to vote had not ended, he hoped the leaders who had come forward "after a long silence will begin speaking clearly and forcefully for a progressive Mississippi." The commission had come to work on the conscience of Mississippi, and hopefully it had done so. Although the assassination of Malcolm X on February 21, 1965, captured press attention a day after the hearings, the proceedings helped to encourage change and provide impetus for the Voting Rights Act of 1965.

Soon the spotlight shifted to Alabama, where on March 7, 1965, Governor George Wallace sent state troopers who used tear gas, whips, and nightsticks to break up the march from Selma to Montgomery. On March 15, President Johnson called for a new voting rights act. On March 21, joined by prominent figures from all over the nation, a new march from Selma to Montgomery took place, protected by the National Guard under Johnson's orders and broadcast live on television. Four days later, the FBI had seventy agents in the area when a Klan sniper killed Detroit housewife Viola Liuzzo, who was murdered as she spent the day driving marchers from Montgomery back to Selma in her car. Johnson cited the violence to further encourage passage of the 1965 Voting Rights Act.[26]

The widely covered Mississippi hearings and the commission report released on May 18, 1965, helped the campaign for the act, which was before the Congress. The report traced the history of voting discrimination in Mississippi and pointed out that only 7 percent of the black population of voting age had registered to vote, the worst record of any Southern state. The Civil Rights Act of 1964, which required the litigation of every single complaint, could not solve this daunting systemic problem.[27]

The Congress added provisions, recommended by the commission, regarding sanctions, poll watchers, and poll taxes that ultimately made the final legislation even stronger than the original bill proposed by Johnson. The legislation prohibited the use of tests and devices at the polls to discriminate. Members of Congress effusively praised the commission's influence on the legislation. Senator Edward Kennedy wrote

State troopers, sent by Governor Wallace to break up the first March from Selma to Montgomery in 1965, beat the marchers.

Hannah, "You may be assured that your assistance in this matter was of real significance in our attempts to strengthen the bill." President Johnson signed the Voting Rights Act on August 6, 1965.[28]

The commission's work on the Voting Rights Act of 1965 reinforced the importance of its fact-finding investigations and hearings. When the constitutionality of the act was challenged in *South Carolina v. Katzenbach*, the Supreme Court's rejection of the challenge was based in part on data published by the commission.[29]

In August, President Johnson signed another progressive social policy bill that had been brewing since his June 4, 1965, Howard University commencement speech calling attention to the need to address poverty and inequality. In order to "Fulfill these Rights," Johnson called for affirmative action and social programs for the poor. On August 20, he signed bills implementing a War on Poverty, to be carried out by the Office of Economic Opportunity. Throughout 1965 Congress enacted an abundance of social legislation, establishing Medicare and urban renewal programs.

Even while Congress was passing the Voting Rights Act, public attention had already moved on. The Watts riot in Los Angeles in August 1965 exploded after a highway patrolman stopped an apparently intoxi-

Federal officials registering first-time black voters in Canton, Mississippi,
August 11, 1965.

cated black man for speeding and police tried to subdue the crowd that
gathered believing they witnessed police brutality. There had already
been a number of smaller riots in the summer of 1964 in Northern cities,
triggered by tensions in police-community relations, about which the
commission had repeatedly warned. The commission, although it had
done some work on inequities in the North and West and had pointed
early to tension-ridden police-community relations in Los Angeles and
Northern cities, had been focused largely on the South.[30]

Black leaders counseled patience, voting for officials who would
make needed changes, and time to work out the problems in Northern
urban areas. But this advice was largely, and increasingly, unheeded by
African Americans in the ghettos. Rioting in Los Angeles led to the
arrest of four thousand people, thirty-four deaths, and hundreds of
injuries, with property damage estimated at $35 million.[31]

During the riot, Congress, having just appropriated some $950 mil-
lion in August 1964 for President Johnson's War on Poverty, exploded
in recriminations. Congressman Adam Clayton Powell of New York
told his colleagues that civil rights legislation had absolutely no meaning to blacks in the North who were fed up with police abuse, de facto

President Johnson signing the Voting Rights Act on August 6, 1965.

segregation, unemployment and underemployment, inferior education, political tokenism, and Jim Crow justice. Powell correctly predicted that Los Angeles would be only the first of a long series of riots and episodes of lawlessness.[32]

After the Los Angeles riot, when a White House working group considered how to reorganize civil rights functions, the commission sought to play a central role. However, Vice President Humphrey persuaded Johnson that with the successful implementation of the Civil Rights Act of 1964 and the Voting Rights Act, they needed to work on enforcement by moving the Community Relations Service (CRS) from the Commerce Department to the Justice Department. That way, Justice could oversee conciliation, mediation, and litigation. Humphrey argued that the commission, as an independent advisory agency, should have only the clearinghouse or data collection responsibilities of CRS transferred to it.[33]

Then, shortly after the decision to reserve mediation and reconciliation functions for the Community Relations Service, Johnson found another major task for the commission. He asked the members to focus on a new survey of education throughout the country, examining racial isolation in the public schools. The president wrote to Hannah, saying for "our Negro children quality education is especially vital because it is the key to equality." Inferior education led to African Americans' being "seriously handicapped in taking advantage of opportunities afforded by new laws, new attitudes and an expanding economy."

Even though "substantial progress in ending formal segregation of schools" had occurred, "racial isolation in the schools persists—both in the North and the South—because of housing patterns, school districting, economic stratification and population movements." Since these problems fell within the study and investigation purview of the commission, he asked the commission to gather the facts and make them known "as quickly as possible."[34]

Instead of deciding to investigate the causes of the riots, the commissioners, impressed by the president's apparent interest, eagerly accepted the invitation to perform the more narrowly focused education study. This decision placed the commissioners squarely in the midst of increasing opposition to busing schoolchildren for purposes of desegregation and the reality of de facto segregation in Northern schools as a result of segregated housing patterns. Meanwhile, the McCone Commission, established by the governor of California, investigated the riot in Los Angeles. On December 22, 1965, the McCone Commission issued its report. The Civil Rights Commission's California State Advisory Committee, in response, made its own investigation and analysis of the McCone report and wanted the commission to come to Los Angeles. Chaired by James Pike, Episcopal bishop of San Francisco, the committee had begun work right after the riot but decided to wait for the McCone report before taking action. In early January, it sent the commission a blistering assessment of the McCone report. The commission's staff director, William Taylor, sent their analysis to the White House after the commission accepted it.

The state advisory committee expressed sore disappointment at the McCone Commission report, which "prescribes aspirin where surgery is required." At a cost of a quarter of a million dollars, with a staff of thirty and fifteen secretaries, the "superficial" report ignored public warnings from public officials well in advance of the riot. For example, a member of the California State Advisory Committee, Los Angeles municipal judge Loren Miller, publicly stated that "violence in Los Angeles is inevitable." He correctly predicted that nothing would be done beforehand but when it happened "a commission would be appointed." The United States Civil Rights Commission had itself predicted a crisis in police-community relations, in 1961, after hearings in Los Angeles. Since then the problem had only worsened.[35]

The California State Advisory Committee members pointed out the report's neglect of any findings at all concerning police practices while actually warning against criticizing the police department. The state advisory committee not only criticized the McCone report but also made a number of recommendations for ending discrimination in the administration of justice, and in housing, employment, and education. One member of the committee, Dr. Reynaldo Carreon, Jr., who served on the Los Angeles Police Commission, filed a dissenting statement, in which he praised Chief Parker as a "symbol of police honesty, discipline and integrity."[36]

The California State Advisory Committee recommended commission hearings on the whole array of issues, believing that the commission was best equipped, through use of the subpoena power, to do a thorough job. In the interim, the advisory committee wanted a federal official immediately appointed to coordinate programs, to participate in the implementation of the acceptable recommendations in the McCone report, and to set up a crash employment program. They also wanted Kennedy's housing discrimination order expanded. The commission demurred, refusing the state advisory committee's request to come to California. Its members did not believe the commission could withstand public scrutiny of a decision to perform what would amount to an inquiry into the McCone investigation. Besides, the president had asked the commission to conduct the study of racial isolation in the schools.[37]

The commission, therefore, ducked an opportunity to join the discussion over urban riots and to delineate a case for federal action, deciding instead to stick to monitoring the enforcement of the 1964 and 1965 acts and the study of racial isolation in urban education requested by Johnson. The commission's decision to focus on desegregation insulated the president from having to face an independent report on the riots, a report that he could not influence.

In addition to miring the commission in the swamp of de facto school desegregation, the White House worked at containing the commission in other ways. Three months after the passage of the Voting Rights Act of 1965, the commission issued a survey finding that the Justice Department was slow in appointing federal examiners in districts where needed, but administration officials quickly developed a strategy to reduce the public impact of the commission's criticism.

Lee White sent comments to the president at his ranch, telling him that "some of the report is mildly critical" of Katzenbach and the Justice Department. Katzenbach had already sent the commission a letter noting factual errors and improvements that the department had made since the staff investigators "were in the field." Katzenbach "was anxious that this information be available to those writing the initial story rather than waiting to catch up with it."

To undercut the force of the commission's report, the attorney general released his letter to the press before the agency issued the report. White and Katzenbach advised that the White House press office should tell the press that the attorney general had met with representatives of civil rights organizations just that week and updated them on their work and that "the reaction by all participants was favorable."[38]

After receiving Katzenbach's seven-page letter written for press purposes, Staff Director Taylor, ever mindful of the need to cooperate with Justice, explained that the agency meant no disrespect to the department. But animosities between Justice, which did not like being monitored, and the commission continued to fester.[39]

Progress continued in the voting rights implementation effort, however, as the commission and civil rights leaders prodded the administration. By the end of the year, nearly 250,000 African American voters had registered and blacks won seats in the Georgia legislature and on several Southern city councils.[40]

When the commission finished the law enforcement section of the report on the Jackson, Mississippi, hearing, in October 1965, Hannah asked Lee White for a meeting with Johnson before its release in November. They had last met with the president in February 1964. Hannah told the president that they, like most Americans, felt "inspired by your leadership in the field of civil rights and by your eloquent address at Howard University." They wanted to discuss their recommendations with him and have his guidance on what steps could be taken by the administration in response. Lee White declined Hannah's request. Citing the president's medical condition since his September 1965 heart attack, White explained that it was too early to know when the president could resume his schedule. It depended on his "convalescence program."[41]

Even with the riots and negative public reaction, the commission, as if oblivious, moved forward to finish work on the urban school racial isolation study. Hannah called it "the most important assignment this commission has ever undertaken." The commission gathered experts headed by Thomas Pettigrew, a social psychologist and race relations expert at Harvard, as the principal consultant and approved an advisory committee including some of the best-known educators and social scientists of the day, such as psychologist Kenneth Clark, whose work was cited by the Supreme Court as a basis for the decision prohibiting segregation in *Brown v. Board of Education*. They commissioned papers from experts and had local educators prepare studies of fifteen school systems throughout the nation. They also re-analyzed data in the Coleman Report, a huge survey of some six hundred thousand children mandated by the Civil Rights Act of 1964. The commission prepared the study at a time when the usual supporters of desegregation in the South had begun to criticize attempts to desegregate schools in the North.

In January 1967 the commission asked for a meeting to present the draft racial isolation report personally to the president. They had not met with Johnson since the beginning of his presidency, when he asked them to stay in office. Harry McPherson, a senior staff official whose portfolio included civil rights, recommended the meeting and tried to gain approval by noting that Hannah was a "close friend" of George Romney and therefore ignoring the commission might give Romney a campaign issue. Apparently Johnson did meet with the commission, but it was not put on his public schedule. He had asked the commission to conduct the racial isolation study because it served his political needs, allowing him to escape commission scrutiny concerning the riots. Further, it did not serve his current political purposes to associate himself with a report that attacked Northern school segregation and inequality.[42]

The commission report, *Racial Isolation in the Public Schools*, issued on February 20, 1967, was a comprehensive assessment that made specific suggestions to improve educational opportunity, including the need for new facilities. But it concluded that segregation presented a problem in itself. The report also called attention to the complicity of housing policy in the creation of the ghetto. It asked Congress to enact a law requiring the states to provide more racial balance in the schools in order to improve the quality of education of racial minority children. Freeman added a statement that as a nation, "we are now on a collision course which may produce within our borders two alienated and unequal nations confronting each other across a widening gulf created by a dual educational system based upon income and race." Hesburgh concurred with her views.

Commissioner Freeman recalls heated attacks on the commission for assuming that "a black child had to sit next to a white child to learn," ignoring the commission's greater school-quality recommendations. The *New York Times* predicted that the report would "stir wide interest" because it struck at "the center of the debate between those who would focus federal resources on improving the quality of ghetto schools" and those who wanted resources devoted to achieving integrated schools. However, members of Congress made it clear that they were not about to deal with the subject. The *Times* editorialized that, of course, "schools in which disadvantaged Negro children predominate operate under severe handicaps." But desegregation would require "massive reshuffling of pupils over great distances." In focusing on impractical integration the commission could encourage a "defeatist" attitude about improving ghetto schools.[43]

However, key civil rights leaders endorsed the commission's findings, and Frankie Freeman met with Roy Wilkins, Whitney Young, and Dorothy Height, president of the National Council of Negro Women, to discuss the report. From the administration, which had foreseen the findings, came efforts to distance Johnson from the report that he had requested, and the president's response was mostly silence.[44]

The press reaction to the racial isolation report confirmed the White House's view that it should say nothing. The Office of Education informed the White House on March 23, 1967, that of thirty-nine newspapers, including major publications, twenty had run critical editorials and nineteen had supported the report. The favorable editorials stressed the need for local action in accord with the recommendations. The critics thought the commission de-emphasized teaching individual children to learn wherever they attended school and emphasized integration too much.

Many of the editorials, both pro and con, made what Staff Director Taylor noted as factually inaccurate statements, "distortions of the commission's report, and misconceptions about what has or has not been proved to be sound educational policy." In addition, Taylor told White House staffer McPherson on April 12, 1967, that he thought the negative editorials from the usually supportive *New York Times* and *Washington Post* focused on the schools in New York and Washington and "decided that integration was an impossible goal and therefore were critical of the report."[45]

As the commission worked on the racial isolation study, urban racial disorders continued. In 1966 alone there were forty-three riots, all initially precipitated by some incident between African Americans and the police. Public officials and legal officers, ignoring the recommendations of many observers, including those of the commission, blamed everything except the social problems that lay at the root of the riots.[46]

While the experts were preparing the racial isolation report, the

"NOW HURRY UP, CHILD—YOU'LL BE LATE FOR SCHOOL."

Bill Mauldin segregation cartoon.
Original given by Mauldin to Commissioner Freeman.

commission decided to have a new series of hearings "to seek the facts concerning civil rights problems affecting Negro citizens and other minorities living in the inner city," wanting to reinforce its interest in civil rights in the North and not just the South. Chairman Hannah said the commission was interested in "problems that are representative of problems elsewhere." The commissioners wanted to determine how the multiplicity of federal programs such as urban renewal, education, and housing aid were helping the ghettoized poor. In legal terms they wanted to ascertain whether inner-city residents were accorded equal protection of the laws. The commission heard from federal and local housing and education officials, as well as individual complainants, and made site visits to augment the record.[47]

The commission held hearings in Cleveland in April 1966, in Rochester and Boston in the fall of 1966, and in the Bay Area in the spring of 1967. In November 1967, after the publication of *Racial Isolation*, the commission released *A Time to Listen . . . A Time to Act*, based on the hearings. In the report, Hannah stated they had sought to engender understanding in the atmosphere of Northern urban riots. They sought to give "possible answers to questions sometimes asked by white people about minority groups," such as "Why can't they, like early immigrant groups, simply better their condition and move out of slum areas through personal effort?"

The testimony from ghetto residents showed their despair at the lack of improvement in their circumstances. One poor Boston mother complained about rats in her apartment. She said that when her family had lived in a better neighborhood, "the street sweeper was there every morning with water and brushes" and trash was collected twice a week. In her current neighborhood, with mixed residential and business uses, "on Friday night . . . the store owners put out the trash and it's [not till] Tuesday when they pick it up it draws rats."[48]

In Cleveland, "although the greatest health problems were concentrated in the East Side Negro areas, the only public hospital was located on the west side." One mother complained that in order to get prenatal care she had to spend "an hour and a half to go there and an hour and a half to get back," plus the wait, which interfered with her work and child care responsibilities. Most of the women who gave birth at the public hospital came from the east side and most had no prenatal care.[49]

Many women in the Cleveland ghetto worked at domestic jobs. Attempts to better themselves by attending school often met with resistance. They told of missing classes because they had to stay late at night to keep a job. In trying to make it, many described the barrier of inadequate education in the schools they attended. They, like past generations, wanted to move up and out through education. A Cleveland woman described how her elementary school children were using the same textbooks she had used in school thirty years before. A Boston parent explained that his daughter made A's until she entered predominantly white Girls' Latin. "Now if a child is an A student in one school she should be an A student when she goes to another school" in the same school system. He decided the school quality was so poor that "nobody should think that an A student in a Roxbury or Dorchester school means anything."[50]

As for jobs and training, a young man who had dropped out of high school described how he held various restaurant jobs at low wages. He enrolled in a Labor Department Employment and Training stockroom training course. After he finished the course his employer, who needed a stockroom clerk, told him he did not have enough experience. The state employment service had no jobs available. He ended up working "a couple of jobs as a cook in a restaurant," the same type of job he had before he took the course.[51]

The commission concluded that many ghetto residents felt they lived in a "trap" from which they could not escape. The commissioners hoped the report would help those who were disgusted by the urban riots to understand that "violators of the law must be punished. But it would be a cruel paradox if after years of failing to reward patience or redress injustice, we were to use such violations by a few as an excuse for continued inaction on the problems which affect so many

Urban renewal, Cleveland, 1971.

and involve us all," mainly race and poverty and the absence of equal opportunity.[52]

The commissioners felt confident that the hearings had shown their determined emphasis on Northern problems. Staff Director Taylor welcomed a September 1966 editorial from Rochester's "conservative Gannett" paper applauding the "calm and businesslike" approach of the commission and the efficient staff work that "served Rochester—and the nation—well." Taylor sent the editorial to the commissioners and to Harry McPherson, who had inherited the White House staff liaison role from Lee White, telling him, "In the midst of the backlash, it is of some comfort to know that there are currents running the other way."[53]

While the commissioners worked on *Time to Act*, based on the hearings, they had to absorb the news that in July 1967, while the Detroit riot was under way, President Johnson appointed the eleven-member National Advisory Commission on Civil Disorders, chaired by Illinois governor Otto Kerner, to look into the riots that had begun in 1964 and to provide recommendations for the future.

The staff at the Civil Rights Commission felt marginalized by the temporary, though high-profile, Kerner Commission. After all, the Civil Rights Commission was already investigating underlying conditions in cities and had completed the racial isolation study, as the president requested. However, Johnson believed Hoover, who told him the

Illinois Governor Otto Kerner.

riots arose from Communist plots, and thought, mistakenly, that the Kerner Commission, as his creation, would confirm these "facts." He knew the Civil Rights Commission would likely continue on its well-established path of probing discrimination, and that once it began a study he could not tell the commissioners what to conclude.

The administration's manipulation with regard to the riots did not work. When the Kerner Commission made courageous findings that deviated little from the consistent advice offered by the Civil Rights Commission, Johnson ignored their report. As Commissioner Freeman, joined by Commissioner Hesburgh, had already noted, the Kerner Commission similarly concluded, We are "moving toward two societies, one black, one white." The commission forwarded a copy of the *Time to Act* report to the Kerner Commission in November 1967 when it was completed with the hope that it might prove useful.[54]

Other voices now weighed in on the public debate. In March 1965, Daniel Patrick Moynihan, assistant secretary of labor, issued the report *The Negro Family: The Case for National Action*. After Johnson's speech at Howard University, which built on Moynihan's work, the Northern urban poor, empowered by the War on Poverty, made more demands for change. With the August 1965 riots in Los Angeles, the White House Conference on Civil Rights in 1966, riots in several cities in 1966, and the Detroit and Newark riots in 1967, the commission continued to work, but largely without public notice. The commissioners felt buried in the details of Northern school desegregation with little public support, though their racial isolation report was a model study. They also needed to stay on the cutting edge of civil rights concerns.

As more and more deprived individuals found their voices, a host of demands emerged, including those from the National Welfare Rights Organization. The assertion of Black Power quickly led to demands from other minorities for Indian power and Latino or Chicano power. Johnson's accomplishments, including the civil rights bills, became overshadowed by the urban unrest and the Vietnam War quagmire. The commission struggled to remain relevant given the current crises.

After Johnson selected Harvard Law School dean Erwin Griswold, one of Kennedy's commissioner appointees, to become solicitor general in October 1967, Hesburgh and Hannah soldiered on. They had been there from the beginning and had first experienced White House disinterest in their work in the Eisenhower administration. Rankin, appointed in August 1960, had experienced the manipulation of the Kennedy years. Freeman and Patterson had been appointed in 1964, when the commission played a central role in the Southern crisis and now found it harder to feel a sense of accomplishment.

Believing that they had served long enough, Hannah and Hesburgh tried, unsuccessfully, to talk to the president about resigning. Hannah explained, "Ten years is a long time in the life of a man, and . . . we have served our stint." Congress extended the life of the commission for five years, although with an amendment, added by Senator Sam Ervin, to cap appropriations at $2.5 million without an increase. Senators McClellan and Thurmond persisted in their opposition to the commission's continuation.[55]

Martin Luther King's assassination in April 1968 further demoralized the staff and the commissioners, who were increasingly dispirited about the possibility of further progress on civil rights. Staff Director Taylor recalled that at a previously scheduled District of Columbia State Advisory Committee meeting the next morning, in the midst of their grief, no one knew what to say. Outside, smoke could be seen from the rioting that began with word of the news of King's assassination. Congress enacted the commission's long-standing recommendation for a national fair housing bill, though the result was weaker than what the commission proposed. This legislation made the purchase of housing on a non-discriminatory basis a matter of national policy but with little in the way of enforcement mechanisms. Responding to the racial disorders springing from Martin Luther King, Jr.'s assassination, Congress also enacted an anti-riot bill but ignored the Poor People's Campaign that King had envisioned, which died with no significant help for those in poverty.[56]

In this tumultuous period, the commission returned to some unfinished work on its Southern agenda. Beginning on April 27, 1968, it held hearings in Alabama for the first time since 1958, on the economic plight of African Americans in sixteen Black Belt counties, and issued the report *Cycle to Nowhere*. The televised hearings opened a window on Bellamy, Alabama, where the American Can Company operated a sawmill and ran a fully segregated company town. The town presented a horror of blacks occupying shacks and "a rickety all-black school owned by American Can down to its broken windows and outdoor privy." On the other hand, "all 45 white company houses have bathrooms and running water but only eight of the 123 black ones do." The other blacks shared outdoor privies and outdoor water spigots. The plant had separate black and white bathrooms and separate jobs. Only "one Negro works in the office and he is an office boy."

One black sawmill worker, Frank Fenderson, described reluctantly his four-year-long effort to pay for furniture he bought on credit at the company store in the town. He received no bills, but "every two weeks when his salary check arrives, deductions are already taken out of it." He produced his pay stub for two weeks ending April 12, 1968, showing that his gross earnings were $139.43 but "after deductions he received exactly five dollars." Embarrassed by the hearings, the company closed down the town and started a program of urban renewal called "Cycle to Somewhere."[57]

In June 1968 came the assassination of Bobby Kennedy. By that time staff morale had already reached a new low. In 1965 the commission had received praise and support from African Americans in the South and almost uniformly outside the region. However, by 1968 commissioners and staff believed that African Americans in the North and West saw the commission as irrelevant to their problems in the ghettos because of the commission's failure to address the riots directly and its inability to do anything about the education problems identified in the racial isolation study. Staff Director Taylor felt that Vietnam had spent the national conscience and civil rights progress was stalemated. He left the commission on September 7, 1968, and Eugene Patterson, who won the 1967 Pulitzer Prize for editorial writing, left on September 30, 1968, when he became managing editor of the *Washington Post*.[58]

The White House gave some thought to appointing a "Negro Republican" to the commission, but Johnson instead wanted a white appointee who was well thought of by civil rights leaders. He chose Maurice Mitchell, a white native New Yorker, who, though he never finished college, became prominent in several organizations. After building Muzak into a huge provider of background melodies, as head of Encyclopedia Britannica Films in the 1960s, he led the move to use film as a teaching device. He became chancellor of the University of Denver in 1967, where he gained publicity for expelling students who had occupied the administrative offices to protest the Vietnam War. An Independent, he had been recommended for either a United Nations post or the Commission on Civil Rights. The White House sent his nomination to the Senate in June 1968, which failed to act before the end of the session. Johnson gave Mitchell a temporary appointment in November and then resubmitted the nomination in January 1969 as he left office. Mitchell would need confirmation in the next Congress.[59]

While working to shift its focus to urban problems, the commission also sharpened its attention to Latino civil rights concerns. President

Kennedy had raised the subject with Hannah in their last meeting, and Hannah now wrote to Johnson, on October 3, 1968, encouraging him to consider a Mexican American to replace Patterson. He noted, "There never has been a representative of this important minority group on the commission." Further, the commission planned to hold hearings in San Antonio concerning the civil rights problems of Mexican Americans, and it would "contribute considerably to the success of the hearings and would be of great help to the commission if the Mexican American community was represented on the commission at the hearing."[60]

The commission had already discussed the subject of Latinos, and included supporting testimony at the hearings in Los Angeles and San Francisco, before scheduling hearings in San Antonio. On October 11, 1968, the president received a memo on the subject of a Hispanic commissioner from Mary Rather, an acquaintance and a member of the state advisory committee in Texas. She explained that when the commission held a hearing in California, "there were great protests from the Mexicans that there were all Negroes and whites on the commission but no Mexicans." Of course, "the commission began 8 or 10 years ago when the Negro question was the thing." The commission needed a Mexican American.[61]

Johnson nominated Hector Garcia from Corpus Christi, Texas, as the first Mexican American commissioner. Garcia was regarded by the Latino community as a national leader and was easily confirmed. A physician, a graduate of the University of Texas Medical School, and a World War II hero, Garcia was founder and chairman of the board of the American GI Forum of the United States for Americans of Latin American origin to help Mexican American veterans of World War II gain access to services of the Veterans Administration and admission to VA hospitals.

The GI Forum gained notice over the treatment of the burial of Felix Longoria, who was killed on patrol in the Philippines as he was pursuing Japanese soldiers. When his remains were identified and returned to his family four years later, a funeral director in Three Rivers, Texas, would not permit his funeral to be held in the chapel because he was Mexican American and it might anger whites. Garcia took the issue to the national press and public officials, prompting Lyndon Johnson, who was a senator at the time, to arrange for his burial in Arlington National Cemetery. The GI Forum became one of the largest civil rights organizations. Garcia, a Democrat, replaced Patterson.[62]

In December 1968, when the commission went to San Antonio,

President Johnson with his appointee Hector Garcia, the first Mexican American member of the Civil Rights Commission, 1968.

Garcia appeared at his first meeting. Over four days of hearings, the commission heard of law enforcement interference with rural migrant workers who attempted to organize a union, and it also followed up on the education quality and racial isolation study by investigating progress in teaching children English through the use of bilingual programs. The commissioners also heard testimony on economic development programs that created skilled and semi-skilled jobs for poor Mexican Americans. The media covered the proceedings exhaustively, and Mexican American organizations and individuals expressed gratitude for what they regarded as successful hearings.[63]

After Bill Taylor's resignation as staff director, African American White House staffer Clifford Alexander and Louis Martin, deputy chairman of the Democratic National Committee, agreed that Carl

Holman, the commission's deputy staff director, should be appointed as the first African American in the post. This entirely acceptable idea led unpredictably to conflict. Holman had the support of the civil rights community and he had the requisite experience. Also, "at this stage in the commission's history, it would be most appropriate to have a Negro appointed as Staff Director."[64]

The commission agreed. However, Holman had been offered a senior position at the National Urban Coalition, a partnership of business, government, and community leaders organized in response to the underlying problems that caused the riots. Preferring to join the coalition, Holman declined the commission's offer. Louis Martin suggested the appointment of another African American, Samuel Simmons, the field director. In the meantime the commissioners made a new recommendation, without notifying the White House. They named the general counsel, Howard Glickstein, to the position as acting staff director. Although the commission should have consulted with the White House about what was technically a presidential appointment, Harry McPherson decided the White House "should not attempt to interfere."[65]

Civil service staffers wrote to the president complaining that only three officially confirmed commissioners attended the meeting when they approved the appointment of Glickstein, and Freeman voted against him. Assistant to the president George Reedy summarized the facts for Johnson, telling him that "this means that two white, although liberal southerners [Patterson and Rankin] voted for a white man

against a Negro voting for a black man." Reedy found it a "touchy situation," but the commission had no more than four regularly scheduled meetings left during Johnson's presidency, and he thought it "better to do nothing." The president noted, however, "I agree with you."[66]

The Johnson years were a productive but continued learning experience for the commission. The commissioners had learned from the

Carl Holman, commission deputy staff director; later president, National Urban Coalition.

experience with Kennedy to go to Mississippi no matter what the Justice Department said. So long as the focus was on the South, Johnson's real commitment to ending segregation made the commission politically valuable to his administration.

The commission's reports and recommendations had helped gain the passage of new civil rights laws. In its most successful work, the commission had listened to complaints and investigated at the local level. It had helped the new civil rights agencies begin their work. During the riots, the commission had been led away from involvement by Johnson. But it was ready to monitor whether the government implemented the Kerner Commission recommendations for achieving racial justice. It was positioned to remain a contributor in the cause of civil rights.[67]

CHAPTER IV

"The Dinosaur Finally Opens One Eye"

IN A CROWDED HEARING ROOM at Kelly Air Force Base in San Antonio, Texas, in December 1968, Hector Garcia, the first Latino to be appointed to the commission, listened with his colleagues to the testimony of high school student Edgar Lozano. Over the din of a mass of demonstrators outside, Lozano spoke about the treatment of Latino students in his school. He recalled being beaten by his teachers, explaining that they "took a stick to me" for speaking Spanish from the earliest grades. "You know what your mother speaks is a dirty language," they said. It's "a filthy language, nothing but bad words and bad thoughts in that language." The beatings and the words of his teachers stuck in Lozano's mind.[1]

Growing complaints from Mexican Americans about police abuse and discrimination in education had brought the commission to Texas. Commission counsel David Rubin questioned local school administrators: "Would it be fair to say that you feel there are genetic factors involved which account for the differences in achievements of Hispanic students?" Principal W. Dain Higdon, from San Antonio's Hawthorne Junior High School, where 65 percent of the students were Mexican, answered, "When you [Rubin] were in my office, I made that statement to you and I will stick by it." Furthermore, he continued, for his faculty, the "first obligation was paperwork, then maintaining discipline and then to teach."[2]

Aurelio Mayor, who taught at San Felipe High School, explained why some Mexican students became "militant" and joined the Chicano movement. The young people resented being taught about Spanish heritage instead of Mexico's history and their native Indian origins. Senator Joe Bernal added that even little children understood that the word "Mexican" was used by Anglos as "a word of contempt."[3]

Migrant farmworkers talked about their low pay and terrible housing, and their support of Cesar Chavez's United Farm Workers of America union. Reynaldo de la Cruz, a father of six, said he had been arrested several times for union activities, yet he still joined the union because of "what every farm worker faces, that they have been cheated too long."

The famed Texas Rangers were deployed to disrupt union meetings and frighten farmworkers, according to Jose Martinez. "Many people hate them, many people are afraid, because the majority of the Mexicans are not armed. They [the Rangers] are armed. And when the Rangers are coming, then the people are afraid of being hit, or being pushed around. The minute you hear the Rangers are coming everybody hides. This is the feeling of the people in the Valley. They are afraid." He was not sure about the federal government but thought "if they are really our friends, then something would have been done."[4]

Texas Ranger captain Alfred Y. Allee, who had become well known

The Chavez family at the commission's San Antonio hearings.

for breaking up farmworkers' strikes, defended his men, saying: "Among the Mexican Americans they [we] have a good reputation. I worked around the Mexican people all my life."

Pete Tijerina, executive director of the Mexican American Legal Defense and Educational Fund (MALDEF), complained of federal neglect. The Justice Department, he charged, intervened on behalf of African Americans in the South but "not once, not once, has the Attorney General intervened in any Mexican American case."[5]

The commission's turn to Latino issues touched a chord. Press coverage of the hearing in San Antonio was greater and more positive than for any hearing in recent memory. The commissioners believed that "for the first time, barrio Mexican Americans went away feeling that the Government does care about them."

After the hearing, the commission sent the complaints of police abuse to the attorney general. Also, at the request of Father Theodore Hesburgh, the staff began analyzing the possibility that refusals to pay the farmworkers their wages constituted peonage. After they consulted with Justice, they concluded that technically it did not. It was only an effective form of harassment and intimidation.[6]

The San Antonio hearing marked the commission's emphasis on extending its reach into previously neglected communities. In the late

Texas Ranger captain Alfred Y. Allee *(left)* at the commission's
San Antonio hearings on complaints of discrimination
against Mexican Americans.

Protesters at the commission's San Antonio hearings, December 1968.

1960s, anti-racist and feminist activists, along with unions, turned their attention to the discriminatory treatment of other Latinos, Asian Americans, and Native Americans as well as to biases against women, and the commission shifted its agenda to respond to this wider perspective on discrimination.

When Nixon was elected president after the 1960 defeat by Kennedy and the hiatus in between, the commission had its first experience with political officials who staked no claim to responsibility for the civil rights changes that had transformed the South. Nixon as vice president had participated in discussions when Eisenhower proposed the commission and when the president handled civil rights conflicts, including the Little Rock crisis. But Nixon's suggestions had consisted mainly of plotting to manipulate Democrats for political advantage. In 1968 Nixon Republicans perceived bitter feelings about black ingratitude for new opportunities and saw urban nationalist movements and race riots as dominating the national consciousness. Long-standing racial conflict in Northern cities over attempts to integrate housing and police-community relations made white ethnics a particular target of the Republicans' electoral efforts. Nixon's Southern strategy deliberately dismissed a one-hundred-year history of black Republicans as part of the party's base and sought instead to garner the votes of disaffected

Dixiecrats and supporters of Alabama governor George Wallace for president in the North and South. In Nixon, the commission encountered for the first time a president who deliberately inflamed civil rights issues to gain political advantage.

Despite Nixon's political stance of distancing the Republican Party from its civil rights heritage, he wanted some of the black vote. He quietly supported major increases in the budgets of the civil rights agencies, including the commission. He also deferred to his minority business constituents by supporting increased government contracts for them, establishing the Office of Minority Business in the Commerce Department. Nixon also increased funding for black colleges and issued an executive order ending tax breaks for segregated private schools. Two African American staffers, Robert Brown and Stanley Scott, were among Nixon's appointees as special assistants.

Turning his attention to women voters who wanted equal rights, he signed Title IX of the Education Amendments of 1972, which outlawed sex discrimination in educational institutions, extended affirmative action requirements for government contractors to set goals to increase the number of employees from groups that had been historically underrepresented and to include women, and named Barbara Franklin as the first woman to hold the most senior staff title, assistant to the president.[7]

While downplaying the party's interest in blacks, Nixon, who was from California, paid attention to Latinos as a way of adding another bloc of voters to the Republican cause. He kept a campaign promise to name a number of Hispanics to political appointments. He also supported the creation of a federal bilingual education program along with agencies and committees whose sole function was to coordinate Latino programs.

Nixon's policies recalled his attempt to have Eisenhower insist on the vice president as the chair of the commission in the original 1957 legislation so that Democrats could not put a Southerner on the ticket as vice president in the 1960 election. To create order and counter the riots and militancy of black nationalist movements, Nixon proposed increases in funding for urban areas. But for electoral purposes he used African Americans as a polarizing weapon. He invoked fears of "forced busing" and refused to permit strong enforcement of the civil rights laws by the agencies whose funding he increased, an action that led inevitably to clashes with the commission. The commissioners wanted strong enforcement of the laws, committed appointees, and larger budgets, which conflicted with Nixon's race-based strategy aimed at wooing white voters in the South.[8]

Even before the inauguration, Chairman John Hannah, following protocol, informed Nixon that he would be resigning after the January 9 meeting. Hannah, who had known Nixon since the Eisenhower administration, told the president that Hesburgh was also resigning as vice chairman. Hannah asked for the nomination of replacements as soon as possible.[9]

After Nixon asked them to stay, Hannah wrote to Nixon asking that he meet with the commissioners when they came to town for their February meeting. Hannah used gamesmanship to force Nixon to pay attention to the commission. He told him, disingenuously, that "communications between the commission and the President, with whom they met several times, were excellent" during the Eisenhower administration. In contrast, he told Nixon, the commissioners had little contact with Johnson. They wanted the president's views on how he saw the commission's "role . . . in the months and years ahead."[10]

Hannah, attracting Nixon's attention by expressing his desire to leave, received a new appointment as administrator of the Agency for International Development and awaited Senate confirmation. He and Nixon agreed that, though it was not required, he should step down from the commission. He asked Nixon again to meet with the commission to boost "morale." He also urged Nixon to resubmit Hector Garcia's name to the Senate, because "having a Mexican American on the commission was very important."[11]

At first Nixon assigned Daniel Patrick Moynihan, assistant to the president and a former Kennedy and Johnson staffer, "coordinative responsibility" for the commission. Moynihan's briefing memorandum for the president praised the commission for doing "a credible job" and for surprising people by maintaining "a fairly vigorous role through three administrations." The commission, according to Moynihan, had adjusted its activities to address current problems as they arose, which kept it from being a one-year commission and reinforced the public perception that it was needed.

Moynihan pointed out "some concern in the Mexican American community" over whether the president would renominate Hector Garcia, who had not been confirmed by the Senate, "but I cannot say how serious it is." Garcia, nominated by Johnson, had been at the San Antonio hearing, was the first Mexican American selected for the commission, and was a leader in the Mexican American community. However, Nixon was more familiar with the Mexican American community in California and could probably name a political supporter from his home state.

Presidential assistant Daniel Patrick Moynihan
with President Nixon.

Nixon needed to keep in mind that the commission had no enforcement power and served symbolic political purposes on the cheap. Moynihan "knew of no one agency where you are likely to get more return for
less investment" in maintaining "relations with the Negro community,"
assuming that Nixon was concerned about relations with blacks.

It was clear that neither Moynihan nor any other staff who reviewed
the memo had any idea that the commission's independence and its
experiences with previous presidents meant that though Nixon might
make suggestions, the commission would not take kindly to any specific
direction to act. Moynihan advised Nixon to tell the commission to look
at "how far the federal government is complying with the letter and
spirit of civil rights legislation." The president also could direct the
commission to do a study of a "recent apparent rise in racial hostility
directed against other groups, including Jewish Americans and the
implications this has for racial and religious tensions in the nation."[12]

Hannah, who had had some experience with Nixon when he was vice
president, approached the commission's meeting with the president,
which took place on February 16, with due caution. However, he had
just agreed to accept a new appointment, and he treated the president,
with appropriate deference. Nixon was interested in how the commis-

sion's work could help his appeal to Latinos, whom he saw as a growing source of Republican votes. He asked for any data available to use in his upcoming White House conference on Mexican Americans. He also indicated interest in Puerto Ricans; Garcia and Hesburgh cited some information on Latinos, and Nixon asked that Moynihan gather a general review of the statistics they cited and other materials. Moynihan chimed in that Mexicans are a "conquered people," while Puerto Ricans are "immigrants, who are important only in New York and Chicago." Puerto Ricans had actually been protected as natural-born citizens of the United States since the Jones Act in 1917, whether they lived on the mainland or in Puerto Rico.

Hannah did not know that the president had already told the staff before the meeting that he would not nominate Garcia. He wanted, he told them, "our Mexican," instead of Garcia, who was not a political adherent, and he explained that they should strengthen the commission staff with "our people." He also did not tell the commissioners that Mitchell could stay. The president had decided that Mitchell was "so well respected within the business, academic and Negro militant community" that withdrawing him would create more problems than leaving him in place. Garcia, however, could easily be replaced.[13]

President Nixon and John Hannah discuss transition
at the commission, February 6, 1969.

Before the March commission meeting, Nixon accepted Hannah's resignation. When Hesburgh met with Nixon for what he thought would be a discussion of his departure, the president asked him if he wanted to run the poverty programs in the Office of Economic Opportunity, and if so, would he have to ask the pope for permission. Hesburgh answered that he was not interested in the OEO position, but he accepted the president's offer to stay on at least for a year as chair of the commission. The *New York Times* announcement of Hesburgh's designation as chairman called him "one of the most outspoken advocates of minority rights" on the commission.[14]

Despite the praise from the *Times* for Hesburgh's civil rights advocacy, Nixon thought Hesburgh's principles were closely aligned with his own. Nixon often recalled how steadfastly Hesburgh had resisted anti–Vietnam War protesters on his campus. On November 18, 1969, students gathered in the Main Building at Notre Dame to protest on-campus recruiting by the CIA and Dow Chemical. They were concerned about the use of napalm in Vietnam and CIA interventions in Chile. Police in riot gear came to the building, and five students were suspended and five expelled. Amid ongoing student activism, Father Hesburgh announced the "15 minute rule": disruptive students would be given fifteen minutes to disperse before being arrested. In the era of many protests and police and National Guard responses, Nixon praised Hesburgh for squelching the students at a time when opposition to his Vietnam policies dominated campuses.[15]

After Hesburgh accepted the commission chairmanship, he wrote to Nixon that he was "honored," but needed immediate action on the commission's priorities. His pleas to increase the budget were hardly necessary, since Nixon had decided that it was good politics to fund the commission so that it could reinforce his agenda of paying attention to Latinos and women. Hesburgh's requests for specific nominees to fill the vacancies on the commission went nowhere, however, because Nixon had already made his wishes clear to the staff. The president had no one in mind immediately for staff director, so he was willing to elevate Howard Glickstein, who had been serving for six months as acting staff director. Hesburgh's hopes to have a "close relationship" with the White House would be realized, but only to the extent that the White House tried to be more effective than previous administrations in manipulating the commission.

At the commission's March meeting, Hesburgh reported that the White House had decided to support raising the budget to $3.2 million.

However, despite his recommendation of John Gardner, a "good friend and superb candidate," for vice chairman, the president, on the advice of assistant to the president H. R. Haldeman and others, chose Stephen Horn, a Republican and former dean at American University who was at the Brookings Institution. Nixon had decided that instead of someone who would be an ally to Hesburgh on minority rights, he would appoint Horn, who had shown no particular interest in these issues. A native Californian, with an undergraduate degree and a Ph.D. in political science from Stanford, Horn had worked in the Senate for Republican whip Thomas Kuchel of California. In 1970 he became president of California State University Long Beach. He served on the commission from 1969 to 1982 and in 1992 was elected to Congress. As a commissioner, he was no conservative but generally sought to moderate the more liberal views of the commission on race matters.[16]

Following up on White House efforts to "direct" the commission, Moynihan suggested anti-Semitism as a topic of inquiry, since the "organized" Jewish community was "extremely concerned" about apparent increases in anti-Jewish sentiment. He also suggested something he had not discussed with the president: the "intimidation" of "moderate" civil rights leaders by militant groups. For the purpose of undermining radicals, the commission could find that "physical intimidation, including direct threats of murder have become all too common" and were infringing on the moderate leaders' civil rights.

Hesburgh ignored Moynihan to focus instead on his immediate concern about the president's plans for the reauthorization of the Voting Rights Act of 1965, scheduled to expire in the summer of 1970. Moynihan replied for Nixon that "the whole matter is under intensive review." They would get back to Hesburgh soon, and they would not let "this lapse." After deciding that it would not interfere with the strategy of using affirmative action and busing to increase racial polarization, the administration ended up agreeing with the commission and the Leadership Conference on Civil Rights coalition in supporting the reauthorization.[17]

Despite the San Antonio hearing and other initiatives, the commission moved too slowly for some "militant" Latinos. President Nixon, alert because of his effort to gain Hispanic support, noticed in his news summaries that commission staffer Nick Reyes had quit, saying the "Jewish-dominated commission is black-oriented to the almost total exclusion of the Chicano and the Indian." Nixon routinely scribbled instructions for the staff secretary, Ken Cole, to distribute to the staff.

This time he ordered, "Let's have a report on this. I believe it's probably true—the top man, as you recall, is a holdover."

White House staffer Martin Castillo, chairman of Nixon's Inter-Agency Committee on Mexican American Affairs, reported back that Reyes had resigned "in anticipation of termination." After talking to commission staffers, he thought the grounds were "just cause." However, it was true that the commission had five Jewish American executive staff members, including Staff Director Glickstein, two African Americans, including the director of field operations, Samuel Simmons, and general counsel John Powell, and no Mexican Americans. He found that staffing below that group reflected a similar pattern and that "the Mexican-American and the Indian are virtually unrepresented." He saw "similar imbalances" in budget allocations, outlays, and programs. He asked that the White House staff discuss this and similar concerns, then adopt a remedy. Neither he nor Nixon inquired about the absence of women on the executive staff.[18]

Consequently, the White House agreed to a commission request for a personnel slot to hire a political appointee, a Hispanic, as deputy staff director. The commission, wanting to reinforce its move into Hispanic issues and perceiving Nixon's interest, successfully argued that it expected to pay increased attention to Latino issues without neglecting its "traditional" concern with the problems of African Americans.[19]

On policy matters the commission made little headway with the White House. The president shifted duties to make African American staffer Bob Brown the coordinator of matters concerning minority groups, including the Equal Employment Opportunity Commission (EEOC) and the Civil Rights Commission.

When the commission sent its report, *For All the People, by All the People: Equal Opportunity in State and Local Government Employment*, to the White House, Brown's analysis, massaged by presidential counselor Leonard Garment and assistant to the president John Erlichman, rejected key recommendations.[20]

The commission report made several recommendations to empower the EEOC to address discrimination in state and local government employment. The president, on his staff's advice, did not respond to the commission, but the administration did support the proposal that Title VII, enforced by the EEOC, should cover state and local government and not just private employers. The administration announced this action in a bill submitted after the report was released, but it refused to endorse the commission's recommendation to give the EEOC the power to issue cease-and-desist authority. The 1972 amendments to the 1964 Civil Rights Act's EEOC provisions included the coverage that the commission wanted, but instead of cease-and-desist authority, the EEOC was authorized to seek relief through the federal courts, which took more time and resources. The commission also recommended legislation authorizing cutoffs of federal funds to punish employment discrimination.[21]

The commission quietly worked with Congress on the EEOC amendments, but Nixon's no-action policy of July 3, 1969, de-emphasizing fund cutoffs to segregated Southern school districts that openly opposed desegregation, caused a public conflict with the commission. Although fund termination operated mainly as a threat, the commissioners and civil rights advocates denounced the change as "a major retreat."

As segregation persisted, their opposition grew louder when, for the first time, the Justice Department went to court to ask for a delay in school desegregation. The request affected thirty Mississippi districts. In South Carolina and Alabama the government also took action to stay desegregation.

The policy precipitated a courtroom denunciation of the administration from the NAACP Legal Defense Fund, which handled most of the desegregation cases. There was also a protest from within the Justice Department itself, from its career lawyers. When Department of Health, Education, and Welfare Secretary Robert Finch issued statistics purporting to show that desegregation had already increased with fall's school opening, the commission found his figures "overly optimistic and misleading." In a public report on September 12, 1969, the commission noted that "more than a thousand of the completely desegregated" districts Finch included in his report had no African American students.[22]

Deafening silence met the commission's demand for corrective action at the White House. African American staffer Bob Brown thought that because of the "confused and volatile nature of this whole area" the president should not reply. Garment agreed, and the commission faced the same stonewalling treatment that it had experienced with the EEOC report and the Voting Rights Act reauthorization. Brown wrote Hesburgh that the report criticizing Finch's data "is presently being reviewed and its recommendations will be given careful consideration."[23]

Nixon then proceeded to name "his" Hispanic, Manuel Ruiz, to the

President Nixon appointed Republican Los Angeles lawyer Manuel Ruiz, instead of pushing for the confirmation of Latino nationalist activist hero Hector Garcia, who had been nominated by Johnson.

commissioner slot that Garcia had held instead of asking for Senate confirmation of the Texan. Just as he had designated Hesburgh as chair, thinking he would be somewhat conservative on civil rights, Nixon apparently thought he could rely on Ruiz to behave similarly. Ruiz was no radical. He was from a generation of Mexican Americans who emphasized their American citizenship and urged gradual reform of discriminatory practices. They desired recognition as ethnic whites, not as racial others. This ethos of hyphenated Americanism meant that Ruiz did not like the word "Chicano," which, he explained, was not in any dictionary. He preferred to use the terms "Spanish-speaking element" or "Spanish-speaking persons." Ruiz's argument influenced the commission to use the label "Spanish-speaking persons" during his tenure, which ended in 1980.

Ruiz also sharply distinguished between legal immigrants and undocumented ones, just as Cesar Chavez and the farmworkers union did. Chavez's concern at the time was based on the reality that illegal immigration was driving down living wages—a key demand of the farmworkers' struggle.[24]

Ruiz was the first Mexican American to receive a law degree from the University of Southern California, in 1930, having gone there from his parents' home in the Belvedere Gardens section of the East Los Angeles barrio. In high school he was valedictorian, a track star, a member of the school orchestra, and captain of the debating team. He was one generation removed from his parents' origins in Mazatlán. As a teenager, he worked in the fields picking apricots and baling hay.

Ruiz had a private law practice specializing in international business law in Mexico and other Latin American countries. He remained deeply involved in ethnic, civic, political, and labor Latino activities in Los

Angeles, where he was one of the most important community leaders. While serving on the commission he generally supported measures to end discrimination.[25]

Though the commission was in conflict with Nixon over school desegregation, it and other civil rights advocates strongly supported his approval of the Philadelphia Plan, requiring an increase of black membership in the skilled trades to 20 percent within five years. Nixon allowed his secretary of labor, George Shultz, and his African American assistant secretary of labor, Arthur Fletcher, to announce the plan in June 1969.

Fletcher was a football star while studying under the GI Bill at Washburn University in Topeka, Kansas. After working in Republican politics and running a Kansas state transportation program that awarded contracts, Fletcher became firmly convinced that contract awards were one way to develop black entrepreneurs. He organized a community self-help program in East Pasco, Washington, which caught the attention of President Nixon, who appointed him as an assistant secretary of labor.[26]

The construction unions persuaded AFL-CIO president George Meany to urge congressional attempts to sink the Philadelphia Plan legislatively. They did not want to have white union members lose job opportunities to blacks. Opposition quickly grew against the implementation of the policy in Philadelphia and nationwide. The commission issued a strong supportive statement and then arranged for House Minority Leader Gerald Ford to use it on the floor. The administration, after first embracing the plan and Fletcher, moved Secretary of Labor Shultz to the post of director of the Office of Management and Budget and abandoned the initiative in order to pursue skilled trade unionists' votes in the 1972 election. After the election, Peter Brennan, a firm opponent of the plan who had garnered labor votes for Nixon, was appointed secretary of labor.[27]

At its January 1970 meeting, the commission discussed a request from Congressional Black Caucus founders Augustus Hawkins (D-Calif.) and John Conyers (D-Mich.) that the commission conduct an investigation into the deaths of Black Panthers Fred Hampton and Mark Clark the previous December 4 in Chicago. The Black Panther activists had been killed by the police in a raid on Hampton's apartment. The police were aided by a floor plan and information on when Hampton and Clark would be the most vulnerable, provided by an FBI informant. A federal grand jury in Chicago concluded that although the

California congressman Augustus Hawkins; his wife, Elsie; and
the author. Hawkins wanted a commission investigation
of police involvement in the deaths of Fred Hampton
and Mark Clark, two Black Panthers.

police fired eighty-three shots into the apartment, only one shot was
directed at the police. The grand jury also determined that Hampton
was shot to death while lying, unresisting, in bed with his pregnant girl-
friend. No indictments were issued, and the informant received
$100,000 from the FBI for his work.[28]

William Timmons, deputy assistant to the president, told the commission and the congressmen that "all aspects of this entire matter are
being fully considered and examined by appropriate individuals within
the Executive Branch." The commission, after much discussion, could
only agree to monitor and consider the issues in a study of crime, police,
and the minority community that was already under way. Thirteen years
after the murders, in 1982, Hampton and Clark's families accepted a
$1.85 million settlement after a long civil rights damages trial.[29]

The commission became increasingly anxious over the situation in
St. Louis, where longtime Congress of Racial Equality (CORE) leader
Percy Green and other civil rights activists had organized protests against
McDonnell Douglas Corporation, one of the country's largest defense
contractors. Green had worked for the company as a mechanic and lab-

Michigan congressman John Conyers
joined Hawkins in calling for a
commission investigation.

oratory technician from 1956 to
1964, until he was laid off in a general
reduction in force. Green believed
the layoff was racially motivated, and
he and other members of CORE
protested by illegally stalling their
cars on the main roads leading to the
plant during shift changes. Green was
arrested one day as he blocked the
street in his car and refused to move.
He pleaded guilty to obstructing traffic and paid a fine. Protesters also
staged a lock-in, padlocking the doors of one of the company's facilities,
but there was no evidence that Green participated.[30]

Green filed an EEOC complaint and sued for race discrimination.
The federal district court in the Eastern District of Missouri decided
against him, but the court of appeals and the United States Supreme
Court ordered a new trial, requiring the company to prove that it fired
him for non-racial reasons. The district court, after a full trial, decided
that he was not rehired because of his participation in unlawful demonstrations and not because of his race and that since his layoff in 1964 the
firm had substantially increased the number of blacks hired.

During this dispute, in January 1970, the commissioners went to St.
Louis for a hearing focused on the racial implications of suburban
development on ensuring opportunities for minority housing and
employment. The commission worried that jobs were moving beyond
the reach of African American workers in the city, who could not afford
to live in these newly created suburbs and had limited access to transportation to jobs. Commission members also wanted to review employment practices at large companies, including the McDonnell Douglas
Corporation, the largest employer in the St. Louis area, with about
thirty thousand employees.

Rev. Paul Smith, a black minister who worked as a regional contract
specialist for the Department of Defense, gave the commission information that buttressed Percy Green's claims and the commission's concern. Smith told the commission that McDonnell Douglas had failed
to develop a viable affirmative action plan. Therefore, he insisted, the

Percy Green, St. Louis local protest leader, at the time of the commission's hearings in St. Louis, January 1970.

Department of Defense had wrongfully awarded the company a multi-billion-dollar F-15 aircraft contract. The commission discovered that even though the company, as a government contractor, needed to show a plan for hiring and promoting African Americans, its plan was totally inadequate. Moreover, in a clear reflection of the need for such a plan, McDonnell Douglas maintained a workforce of more than 40,000 managers and officials, and only 40 were black. Among skilled craftsmen and semi-skilled operatives, the same disparity existed. Most African American employees held unskilled jobs, and none were in semi-skilled employment. Indeed, of the 1,101 assistant foreman positions, only one was held by an African American.[31]

The commission weighed in on the issue, asking Defense Secretary Melvin Laird to correct the error of awarding a contract for making military aircraft without assuring compliance. The commissioners alerted McDonnell Douglas of their finding that a management official had dismissed the compliance requirement, in the midst of the Vietnam War, saying, "We have our hands full trying to run our plant and build airplanes."

The Defense Department's secretary of the U.S. Air Force, Robert Seamans, Jr., met with company officials to resolve the problem. After a four-hour meeting, he emerged with a letter indicating their "commitment" to meet the EEOC requirements and a warning that if they did not, "failure to achieve this result promptly will require that we initiate action to terminate the F-15 contract." Defense Department officials would remain at the plant to work out the details of compliance.

On February 4, a *St. Louis Globe-Democrat* editorial defended the company, connecting the commission's intervention with the Green case. The commission met on February 5, and Commissioner Freeman, given that she was from St. Louis, wrote a reply, which the paper published on February 6. She stated that McDonnell Douglas's record was less than stellar, and she produced data from the Defense Department's contracting compliance officer on the inadequacies of the latest proposed plan.[32]

On February 10, 1970, the Pentagon announced that after negotiations, a new plan, including goals for hiring African Americans, had been agreed to with McDonnell Douglas. The plan also included training programs and a commitment to seek open housing for minorities working in the St. Louis area. Ironically, the progress in including African American employees under the plan helped the company to win its case against Green four years later.[33]

Retaliation against Freeman for the stance she took in her letter to the editor came swiftly. The board of the St. Louis Housing Authority, her employer for fourteen years, fired her; she was directed to leave by close of business on the same day the letter was published. The commission wrote to HUD Secretary George Romney asking for an investigation, but after repeated tries, nothing was done. Freeman refused to file a complaint. She decided that "even if they offered me the job again, I did not want to go back there." An attorney, she built a successful private practice and continued to serve on the commission until the Carter administration.[34]

After the McDonnell Douglas conflict in 1970, interactions between the commission and the White House became increasingly tense. The commission issued a report on discrimination in determining where to locate federal office buildings and other facilities shortly before Nixon issued a weak executive order on the same subject. When White House staff complained, the commission replied that the White House had "missed an opportunity to get the commission's input in this order, and if he had gotten input he could still have taken his choice as to whether or not to use it." The commission would inform the White House of future projects and "offer our help on any other White House pronouncements that might be issued concerning areas in which we are working."

White House staffers met with Staff Director Glickstein to "assure closer coordination in the future with the commission and to better use its resources." However, John Erlichman, an assistant to the president, considered taking reprisals against the agency by reducing its budget in the president's next request to Congress.[35]

Hesburgh tried to ease tensions by finding a way to compliment Nixon. His opportunity arose in May 1970 when the president requested $1.5 billion from Congress for emergency school assistance for desegregating schools. Hesburgh issued a statement saying that "the President's message represents a most positive statement. The goals he has stated deserve the support of all Americans." However, Hesburgh did not go overboard. He warned that the commission might have specific ideas for strengthening the proposed legislation, which seemed to limit busing and lacked incentives for districts to develop full desegregation plans. His caution was justified. The program became nothing more than a discretionary fund for local districts that often did nothing to desegregate schools.[36]

Fed up with the slow pace of school desegregation, during the last day of a three-day commission hearing on minority job and housing opportunities in Baltimore County in August 1970, Hesburgh complained bitterly, "This commission has had it up to here with counties and communities that have to be dragged kicking and screaming into the US Constitution." He went on, "All we get in these hearings is that people aren't serious about equality of opportunity, and the Government isn't serious about equality of opportunity." Witnesses during the hearings made Vice President Agnew, the former governor of Maryland, peripherally to blame, but the White House regarded Hesburgh's closing statement as another attack on the president.[37]

The commission had learned from its experience with Kennedy about the potential problems associated with sending advance copies of reports to the White House. However, throughout the year, the commission sent advance notice of the publication of reports, in an effort to avoid escalating tensions. White House staff members responded quickly when they saw that a highly critical 1,400-page report on federal civil rights enforcement would be released in September 1970. The commission, following its usual procedures, also sent specific findings and recommendations to the covered agencies for responses before publication.

After reading the report, presidential counselor Garment advised Erlichman that the report "had some good, but mostly bad, to say about the overall civil rights effort." It highlighted the lack of staff, lack of commitment, and lack of sufficient authority for the official in charge of civil rights to ensure that civil rights remained a priority. Garment noted that "some agencies have failed to recognize that they have any civil rights responsibility." Others knew but failed to take any action. The agencies had dealt inadequately with civil rights problems of Indians, Spanish-surnamed people, and women, and they had not collected or maintained data to determine compliance and impact. "Many have been passive waiting for complaints and not initiating compliance, they don't use available sanctions—fund termination and debarment [exclusion from future contracts] are so rare as to underline the credibility of the effort."[38]

Garment suggested that in order to preempt press coverage the White House should not "fuss" about the report. The administration could announce a newly created Domestic Council to review it and make recommendations. Then they could have the council recommend a permanent White House Subcommittee on Civil Rights. The White House action would drown out attention to the commission's report. If the White House wanted to do as Garment suggested, he could persuade Hesburgh to "announce this response concurrently with the issuance of the commission report."[39]

In October, the White House still was not ready to move. Hesburgh wrote Garment on October 1, saying, "As you know I have been perfectly open to your suggestion of doing whatever would be best regarding this report in obtaining the improvement to which it addresses itself." However, he indicated that when he saw the almost three-inch-thick report all printed and ready to go, he knew he would have trouble keeping it "under wraps" until October 12, the commission release date. To delay until November 9 "would be like keeping an elephant in a phone booth."

Hesburgh told Garment that waiting would hurt the administration because it would lead to "allegations of suppression," which would be "entirely counterproductive." He promised that in releasing the report, he would emphasize that the problems discussed had existed throughout four administrations and that the creation of the White House Office of Management and Budget promised to help. His reaction to hiding "this big fat report" was underscored by conversations with his fellow commissioners. He was sure Garment would agree that they should deal with the report "without guile, without political intent, and without creating unnecessary difficulties for anyone."[40]

Senior White House officials took a more caustic view of how to deal with the commission when Hesburgh refused to cooperate in their duplicity. Garment's suggestion that they nonetheless announce a new subcommittee of the Domestic Council and that he would influence Hesburgh to comment approvingly on it did not impress Erlichman.[41]

Erlichman responded by deciding that "lacking quid for our quo," they would not announce a new committee. Instead, he told OMB

director George Shultz, former secretary of labor, to have his staff prepare a confidential report on the commission's report for Shultz and
Erlichman that might become a public statement.

Their public reactions would be guided by "where they wanted to be
in election year 1972 on these issues." They should show progress for
minorities while doing nothing to lose supporters, or "keep from
achieving additional supporters of rt-of-ctr or in Blue Collar, won't get
black support no matter what nor will libs [liberals] support" Nixon.
They should be interested only in determining when to use "escalated
rhetoric" to appeal to their supporters and where to talk about African
Americans for purposes of the campaign.[42]

The OMB report concocted by Shultz and his staff to use as a
response lambasted the commission for not understanding that in "most
programs, civil rights considerations must be balanced against other
needs which are equally—or more—pressing." The commission's
emphasis on funding was misguided because, as the commission itself
usually emphasized, there was a need for "moral leadership of the nation
and changing attitudes of the public, as well as the furnishing of additional resources."[43]

Consistent with President Nixon's political emphasis on Hispanics,
the report applauded the commission's desire for increased attention to
Indians and Spanish-surnamed people. However, it criticized the commission for suggesting that "women should be treated as a minority"
and denounced its support of affirmative action to include more women
and minorities in the quest for well-paying jobs and educational opportunities. Garment sent some of the comments to Glickstein, but the
commission ignored the attempt to make it conform to the administration's line.[44]

On October 9, 1970, Hesburgh briefed thirty-five reporters, with
the understanding that the report should not be commented on until its
release date of October 12. He told them that the major conclusion was
that civil rights laws provided ample penalties for discrimination but
enforcement needed improvement. The report did not refer to the present administration alone, because the problems "have their roots in the
past." Hesburgh emphasized that "the report is a criticism of the civil
rights enforcement structure as it has taken shape in all of the Administrations in recent years." Nixon should exercise "courageous moral
leadership" on the issue of racial justice. Hesburgh took Garment's idea
a step further by indicating it would be a good idea to establish in the
White House a subcommittee of the cabinet-level Domestic Council to
oversee the enforcement of civil rights laws.

The media reacted just as White House staff had feared, emphasizing the commission's criticism of a "lack of Presidential leadership" for the failures in enforcement. Correspondent Daniel Schorr of CBS noted that the White House had failed to delay the report until after the congressional elections. The independent commission did not see itself as a partisan political body and had consistently issued reports, including the staff report on Mississippi that President Kennedy rejected, without being influenced by political considerations.[45]

President Nixon's reaction to the news summary was a simple instruction: "I think it's time to get a hold of the staff of this." His staffers immediately prepared a memo describing the appointment process for the staff director and a list of the commissioners and staff.[46]

Completely unaware of Nixon's plans, the commissioners were elated at the publicity. The press office reported more coverage than on any other report done recently. Newspapers followed up with editorials nationwide. The *Harvard Law Review* asked for a copy for a series of articles for the spring edition. Hesburgh appeared on television's *Dick Cavett Show* and on *Issues and Answers* to discuss the report.

In view of the enormous publicity about the commission report, the response that the OMB had prepared seemed too defensive. Instead, the Office of Management and Budget announced that budget examiners would begin to take civil rights considerations into account when evaluating agency requests. Also, OMB announced that the Department of Housing and Urban Development (HUD) had started a process of collecting racial and ethnic data. The commission announced that it would wait six months for a follow-up on the report and then hold a press conference regularly every two months with a chart showing progress in enforcement in agencies across the government.[47]

In December, White House concern over the commission's criticism of the administration and its steadfast independence continued unabated. Hesburgh repeatedly told Garment that they tried to balance commission "criticism" of the president with praise for specific presidential initiatives. For example, the commission announced support of the Family Assistance Plan, Nixon's welfare reform proposal, and sent Hesburgh's statement on the subject to every member of Congress. Hesburgh also gave Garment his article on civil rights policy, which he submitted to *Life*, but the magazine declined to run it. Garment passed the article, which asserted that the president "should not be made the scapegoat for every unsolved national problem," along to senior staff and the president.

Garment also shared with senior White House staff Hesburgh's letter in which he explained that as an independent bipartisan agency, the commission had to "speak frankly" to the president. The resident White House staff had to see that many people believed the administration "is not interested in civil rights, has written off the blacks and the Mexicans (not to mention the Indians) and really will not do anything to signal a deep interest in civil rights." He suggested that the president should make a statement that equal opportunity in education, housing, and employment are primary goals for the nation.[48]

Nixon ignored Hesburgh's pleas, but he and the staff still responded cordially, as if nothing was amiss, to routine letters from the commission. However, in March, Erlichman attacked Garment for circulating a memo to staff that appeared to agree with the commission that exclusionary zoning, which had the effect, if not the intent, of discriminating against minorities, violated Title VI and required the termination of federal financial assistance. Garment replied that he did not intend to "virtually repudiate" the president's position on "forced integration," though the commission's report did and the "law seems in fact to be moving in that direction."[49]

In order to undermine the commission's follow-up reports on enforcement, the White House Office of Management and Budget "intercepted copies of the proposed agency responses, analyzed them in OMB and with Len Garment, and in some instances made decisions that resulted in a more positive agency response." They then had the agencies send the revised copies to the commission. They also prepared doctored responses for inquiries about enforcement from the Congressional Black Caucus and prepared responses for use by the administration.[50]

At the commission meeting in April 1971 while the administration worked on responses, the staff denied a press report that they had agreed to let the White House staff review the agency submissions before sending them to the commission. They insisted that the agency reports were so bad it would be "difficult for the answers to be fudged." Although Hesburgh said he was impressed that at least the White House was paying attention, Mark Alger at the White House Office of Management and Budget had already told senior White House staffers that despite being "dressed up" the agency reports were still "pretty bad" because "not much was being done."[51]

Frustrated with the failure of efforts to undermine the commission's work, Haldeman assigned the task of dealing with the commission's criticisms to political operatives on the White House staff. Dwight Chapin, a deputy assistant to the president, told special counsel Charles Colson on May 26, 1971, to work with Garment "and start determining early as to what the commission is going to be releasing and getting ourselves positioned."

Staffer John Campbell notified all of the senior staff when an advance copy of a report on a government program to increase home ownership for low-income minority families arrived at the White House on June 9, 1971. The commission had followed this issue in hearings in St. Louis and in Baltimore. The staffers seethed at the commission's finding that while HUD successfully increased the "volume of minority participation," it was "responsible for perpetuating segregation." Departmental officials promoted the placement of whites in suburban areas and minorities in "ghetto areas" or "changing neighborhoods" in the central city.[52]

Over the month of June, the White House's irritation with the commission increased in the conflict over the commission's issuance of subpoenas in May 1971 to various administration assistant secretaries to appear at hearings. The White House staff ultimately decided not to have a public confrontation only when John Hannah, now their Agency for International Development administrator, assured them that the policy of issuing subpoenas to everyone, whatever their status, was initiated when he was chairman. It required subpoenas to compel an appearance to testify for all witnesses, except cabinet officers. The staff notified everyone who was invited to testify of the policy, including the "willing" and the "hostile," "so that the person affected will not feel distraught." The policy was necessary to obtain information that the commission needed to monitor enforcement and make recommendations.

Hesburgh also upset White House staffers when he wrote Nixon expressing the commission's pleasure that his proposed budget included a large increase for the Equal Employment Opportunity Commission. The commission had cautioned in the enforcement report that the EEOC would remain an "enfeebled" agency so long as it remained underfunded. However, Hesburgh had just learned that the House of Representatives Appropriations Committee was disinclined to agree to Nixon's request. Trying to reinforce the EEOC, he wanted Nixon to pressure the committee to fully fund the request of $26 million. However, the administration had other plans. They pressured the committee for only a small increase over the previous year. To seal the deal, the White House had the EEOC chairman, William Brown III, withdraw his request for a presidential letter asking the committee for the higher

John Buggs, the commission's first
African American staff director,
was appointed in 1971.

amount. This way the administration could claim credit for requesting a large increase but use the
dollars in question for some other
priority.[53]

Before the next commission enforcement report in July 1971,
Glickstein resigned as staff director
and joined Father Hesburgh at
Notre Dame, where he became
director of the university's Center
for Civil and Human Rights. After
Glickstein resigned, upon the com-
mission's recommendation, the president named John Buggs as the first
African American staff director. Buggs had joined the commission from
the National Urban Coalition as deputy staff director in February 1971.
At the coalition he had been vice president for field operations. He was
not a lawyer; rather, he held a master's degree in sociology from Fisk
University.[54]

Buggs's preparations for the commission's next reauthorization
deadline of January 31, 1973, were complicated by the tense relations
with the White House and the release of the follow-up enforcement
reports. The commissioners suggested a three-year extension and other
changes that they thought the agency needed. The commission proposed a requirement that agencies respond to commission recommendations and furnish requested information, protection of witnesses at
state advisory committee open meetings, a removal of the cap on commission appropriations, and the right to file amicus curiae (friend of the
court) briefs.

Father Hesburgh proposed an entirely new direction to his colleagues. He wanted the commission's role expanded to human rights
instead of just civil rights issues. Experience had taught the commission
that a broad social justice agenda, including issues of poverty and deprivation, without being bound by considerations of only race or national
origin, made the most sense. The commissioners decided that the idea
would have a better chance of adoption if, instead of making it a commission proposal, Hesburgh wrote to the president to suggest that he

initiate the idea on his own and propose it to the Congress. In the meantime, the commission would "work into all its reports and statements as they evolve in the months ahead the human rights aspect, as appropriate."[55]

As reauthorization was under discussion, the commission's May 1971 six-month update on the federal agencies' civil rights enforcement noted some improvement since the 1970 report. As Hesburgh put it, "The dinosaur finally opened one eye."[56]

The White House was somewhat pleased at the six-month report, but the November 17, 1971, one-year evaluation severely disappointed the staff. The commission issued performance ratings on the government's effort, and not one agency was rated as adequately enforcing civil rights laws. Director Shultz at the White House Office of Management and Budget, which was not an enforcement agency, received a rating of adequate, the highest rating, for his establishment of a civil rights office to review budget requests.

The commission called attention to the lapses in administration enforcement of civil rights policies. In one example, the Internal Revenue Service continued to give tax exemptions to all-white private academies created in the South to avoid desegregation, despite court decisions and a July 10, 1970, announcement by the Justice Department that racially discriminatory schools would no longer receive tax exemptions.

While enforcement had gradually improved, the commission concluded, "It is no consolation to the black farmer who continues to receive assistance from the extension service on a racially separate and unequal basis that the Department of Agriculture is making progress." Likewise, "it is no source of satisfaction to the Mexican-American or Puerto Rican job seeker turned down by a Government contractor that the Office of Federal Contract Compliance is gradually improving." Hesburgh added, "No one can get greatly excited about progress that is made after he is dead."

The commission highlighted the civil rights responsibilities of often overlooked agencies, such as the Federal Reserve Board. Those government entities, like others, needed to ensure non-discrimination in the use of any federal dollars they controlled. The Federal Reserve Board resisted even an acknowledgment of any civil rights responsibilities. And while the Office of Management and Budget, which had been found "adequate," had begun to collect data on funds used for enforcement, that oversight agency had developed no method for measuring the performance of the agencies it monitored.[57]

On the commission's reauthorization, the White House staff decided that politically they could not let the agency expire. They supported removing the $2.5 million cap on the budget but opposed the right to file "friend of the court" briefs, which White House counsel John Dean advised "would raise too great a potential for conflict with the Justice Department." The commission thought it would be helpful to advise the courts directly of its views based on hearings and investigations concerning the matters under consideration, but Dean rejected that argument. The commission's role was to find facts, not to support changes in court.

The White House decided against Hesburgh's human rights commission idea. Garment's reaction prevailed; in his view, looking into "nutrition, welfare, compensatory education and dozens of such issues" would require a large budget and staff, and there were already other advisory bodies monitoring these areas. There was plenty to do on civil rights without the commission's assuming "amorphous new powers."

Garment and Dean wanted the White House to support the addition of sex discrimination to the commission's responsibilities. In addition to the administration's interest in expanding attention to Latinos and Asian Americans as a means of expanding its political base, Nixon agreed with the suggestion of Moynihan and others that the president take political advantage of the burgeoning women's movement. Nixon's Presidential Task Force on Women's Rights and Responsibilities, established in 1969, resulted from this idea, and pressure by Republican women kept it afloat. The task force issued a report that recommended adding sex discrimination to the commission's jurisdiction, and also recommended administration support for the Equal Rights Amendment.

The idea of adding sex discrimination to the commission's jurisdiction elicited spirited objections from some White House staff. Speechwriter and political advisor Patrick Buchanan objected that the commission was "a thorn in the side" of the president. Giving it additional authority meant empowering "a little clique of individuals, whose stock in trade is moralistic preachments to the President for the benefit of the national press." Buchanan could see no benefit for the Nixon administration or the Republican Party in "expanding the powers of the Reverend Hesburgh."[58]

Frank Carlucci, associate director of the Office of Management and Budget, summarized OMB reactions on January 8, 1972. OMB made no recommendation, however, since it was a "political" decision. Carlucci thought it was probably "inevitable and not worth the flack to oppose it," but Shultz and OMB deputy director Caspar Weinberger "lean[ed] toward not including women." Carlucci pointed out that Hesburgh was seeing Shultz on January 17 "and they needed to tell him something." After Carlucci typed the memo, he later added that Shultz had reconsidered and would support it, while Weinberger was "strongly opposed."

Carlucci argued that giving this role to the commission could "dampen" some of the more "irresponsible" legislative and constitutional proposals on this issue. But to the extent that the commission's statements have been "inflammatory," adding gender would increase the problem. "Sex discrimination is less aggravated than other forms of discrimination. There's too much to do on race and this will add pressure for increasing the commission's budget." With Buchanan and Weinberger opposed, women's advisor Barbara Franklin vacillating— she thought women were important but there was "political risk" for the president no matter what he decided, because it was a "tough call"—and Garment, Shultz, Dean, and Clark MacGregor in favor, Nixon decided to support the inclusion of sex discrimination.[59]

Nixon mentioned the extension of the commission in his State of the Union message. And when the bill was introduced extending the commission for five years, until June 30, 1978, Commissioner Freeman testified in support before the Congress. It became clear that the commission would have sex discrimination added to its jurisdiction, even if it was not supported by the president. As a result of requests from women's rights leaders, numerous bills had already been introduced in the Congress for that purpose.

The commissioners were already at work on women's issues. They reviewed the report, in February, of a task force that the staff director had organized on sex discrimination programs, which Carol Bonosaro chaired. The purpose was to start a program approaching sex as a cross-cutting issue with a diverse staff. Several speakers were invited to talk to the staff in preparation, including Gloria Steinem, who came with Margaret Sloan, the first chairwoman of the National Black Feminist Organization. Sloan, a longtime civil rights activist, traveled extensively with Steinem, giving talks on feminism. Some of the staff opposed inviting her because they decided she might be a lesbian. In addition to possible homophobia, their strained reasoning included a worry about criticism of her participation because the commission had only a very narrow claim to jurisdiction over sexual orientation discrimination.[60]

In New York, in February 1972, the commission tried to show its interest in the denial of equal opportunity to Puerto Ricans by holding hearings. State advisory committees in Massachusetts, Connecticut, New Jersey, and New York had held fact-finding meetings on the subject, and the commission planned four days in New York devoted to education, public housing, employment opportunity, and the administration of justice. Puerto Rican dissidents interrupted the hearings, calling them farcical since "Commissions never accomplish anything." Others shouted, "We want Puerto Ricans to speak for us, not blacks, whites, or anyone else." At one point they took over the microphones. For the first time at a commission hearing marshals could not restore order and the commissioners left the stage. National television news covered the proceedings.

Most of the protesters wanted to discuss Puerto Rican independence, which was not on the agenda, and saw an opportunity to have their views televised. Some threatened witnesses and made bomb threats if the hearings proceeded. The commission decided to conclude the hearing after two days of disruptions. They asked Puerto Rican author Piri Thomas, who had already been hired to cover the hearings for publication in the commission newsletter, the *Civil Rights Digest*, to prepare an account of what had been heard before and between the disruptions.[61]

The Nixon White House, in pursuit of his Southern strategy of appealing to white voters through race-baiting, kept civil rights at arm's

Puerto Rican Socialist Party members displayed signs and shouted during hearings before the commission in New York City, February 1972.

length in an election year. When Congress enacted the legislation giving the EEOC jurisdiction over state and local government employment, as the commission had recommended, the White House staff debated how much publicity to give it. Political counselor Charles Colson won the debate: no publicity and "absolutely no signing statement" when Nixon signed the bill on March 24, 1972.

In April 1972 Hesburgh further irritated the political operatives at the White House when ABC and NBC television reported that he said George Wallace "heated up the phony issue of busing and everyone jumped aboard including Richard Nixon." Hesburgh went on: "We live in an age of midgets; I feel like vomiting when I hear them, all of them." Hesburgh, when asked, said he did not intend to resign; he would "get a headline" and then Nixon would appoint "a rabbit." Nixon wrote in the news summary that we "need for some responsible opponent of busing to speak out." Staffer Bruce Kehrl wrote to political counselor Colson, "Busing spokesman get on it."[62]

White House patience with Hesburgh and the commission was wearing thin as 1972 headed toward the primary and general election season. The commissioners agreed at their May 8, 1972, meeting that, if invited, Hesburgh would appear before the platform committees of both parties, or either party, and give exactly the same testimony with the same recommendations.

To the chagrin of the White House, on the May 17 anniversary of *Brown v. Board of Education*, the commission issued a report titled *Your Child and Busing*, which stated that busing did not hurt the quality of education for anyone and that "neighborhood schools mean segregated schools." Upon the release of the report, Commissioner Freeman said that "less than 4 percent of all public school children are being bused for desegregation. However, 43.5 percent of the pupils enrolled in school are being bused for other reasons."

The commission and the Nixon White House remained at odds during the last months of the president's first term. The commission had concluded that no matter what it did, Nixon would refuse to insist on strong civil rights enforcement, but it was determined to keep reporting on his performance, no matter the consequences. When Nixon crushed McGovern in winning reelection the commission hoped he would abandon his race-polarizing policies, instead of becoming more emboldened by the victory.

CHAPTER V

Killing the Messenger

RIGHT AFTER HIS REELECTION, Nixon did to the commission's chairman what Father Hesburgh had done to student anti–Vietnam War protesters who refused to be obedient. He silenced him by taking away his podium. Nixon fired Hesburgh because his eloquent criticisms, requests, and preachments had created considerable animosity in a White House staff that had no interest in actually enforcing civil rights laws.

Among Hesburgh's accumulated sins was his testimony at the July 1972 Democratic Party platform hearings. Even though the Republicans would not have him testify, Erlichman told Garment, he was "fascinated" to see Hesburgh's presentation, since he "wasn't aware that he had a partisan stripe." Anticipating that their "dirty tricks" would help defeat George McGovern, Erlichman indicated that Hesburgh would be asked to resign right after Nixon's reelection. Erlichman acknowledged, "I realize that we have no actual leverage," but Hesburgh would probably do the "honorable" thing and resign if asked.[1]

In the months leading up to the 1972 election, the commissioners had no idea that the termination of their leader was imminent. Continuing their work, they planned a conference on new Asian immigrants. Also, contemplating the first addition to their jurisdiction since the commission's founding in 1957, they designated an advisory committee to address their new mandate on sex discrimination.[2]

The commission reauthorization legislation in August 1972 stirred no congressional debate and no warning signals. However, unknown to the commissioners, over at the White House, Erlichman was looking for "any pretext" to have Nixon veto the commission extension bill. Staff secretary Ken Cole discouraged him, pointing out that Nixon was on record as supporting the extension, with the addition of sex discrimination. Besides, the agency's continuance was so widely assumed that the bill passed without objection even from the Southern Democrats who had always complained before. When the bill passed, news reports gave Nixon credit for urging its passage.[3]

After McGovern lost every state, including his own, in the November election, Nixon's staff moved quickly to reinforce the strategy of solidifying Southern white support for the Republican Party by de-emphasizing civil rights. Hesburgh made himself an easy target by announcing before the election that he was so disappointed with Nixon that he probably would not remain at the commission should the president win reelection. Erlichman now sought to hold Hesburgh to his "promise" as a matter of "both form and substance." However, "form and substance" meant something else to Hesburgh, as White House personnel director Fred Malek discovered when he demanded letters of resignation from commissioners. It might be good form for a political appointee to offer his resignation at the end of a term, but the pressure to leave threatened the commission's independence. Hesburgh had long ago wearied of serving on the commission and had offered to resign more than once, but he objected to Malek's imperious demands. Hesburgh responded that legally the White House could designate another chair, but it could not force him or anyone else off the commission.[4]

After Hesburgh made his points, he resigned as chair and from the commission altogether. The reporters pressed the White House for a response for weeks. Just before Christmas, Nixon sent Hesburgh a letter of acceptance, but Hesburgh, who did not recognize the president's authority on this issue, had stopped participating on November 16 when he resigned.

Nixon and Erlichman resented the commission's frank evaluations of the administration's civil rights record, but Hesburgh was only meeting the responsibilities of his chairmanship. The White House sought to fire Hesburgh for doing his job. In issuing a statement complaining about Nixon's interference with the commission's independence, Commissioner Mitchell noted: "The President never consulted or saw the commission in the four years he has been in office." Instead, Garment behaved like White House staffers before him, attempting to manipulate the commission through bureaucratic machinations.[5]

Hesburgh's tenure as chairman marked a critical shift of the government on civil rights issues, just at a time when the white majority was beginning to accept change. Hesburgh showed great courage by insisting on the commission's independence, refusing to comply with orders from the Nixon White House and demanding enforcement of the civil rights laws. The commission, under Hannah and then Hesburgh, had established its role in listening to complaints and attempting to preserve individual rights.

Independence, Hesburgh wrote in 1972, is a "vital commission attribute." He continued: "We do not criticize because it is easy or pleasant, or because six Commissioners are naturally cantankerous. We criticize because Americans continue to be victimized by discrimination and the Federal government is doing too little about it."[6]

From his Notre Dame office Hesburgh was asked by the press about the prospects for his replacement, and he responded that no one in the administration except Garment understood that they "can't fault the commission for doing its job." It is the "conscience of the Government." Other presidents had disagreed with the commission without "getting rid of Commissioners." He hoped the White House would "get the best people it can find regardless of political parties to work on these problems." The work required White House understanding that "the day the commission doesn't say anything unpleasant to the Congress or the President, it ought to go out of business."[7]

Although the White House press office and the congressional liaison staff complained that the media were relentless in asking about a nominee, Nixon refused to designate a new commission chairman. He left Vice Chairman Horn to preside for more than a year after Hesburgh's resignation. During this period, officials charged with enforcing the nation's civil rights laws were given larger budgets, but without commission prodding or White House guidance, enforcement waned. The media reported on the backlog and slow movement on complaints at the Equal Employment Opportunity Commission. The Office for Civil Rights in the Department of Health, Education, and Welfare scarcely moved to ensure that recipients of government contracts complied with anti-discrimination mandates and outreach to women and minorities.[8]

Civil rights advocates and commission studies had persuaded Congress to enact the increased budgets that the administration had requested for the agencies. Lack of leadership in utilizing the funds by the White House angered the civil rights coalition. The Women's Equity Action League, the NAACP Legal Defense and Educational Fund, and the National Women's Law Center sued several federal agencies to force action on their responsibilities. Most of the major civil rights and women's rights gains of this period were the result of action by these private nonprofit organizations, not the result of federal initiative. The litigation seemed endless and the administration continued to drag its feet. With Vice Chair Horn presiding, the commission limped along, following the agenda set under Hesburgh's leadership while awaiting new appointments.

The White House, distracted by the Watergate hearings and knowing that whatever the outcome they need not worry about reelection, responded listlessly to the criticisms in the commission's 1973 enforcement report, which "reinforced the findings of the three preceding reports that the Government's civil rights program is not adequate or even close to it." The report again blamed Nixon's leadership for the continuing neglect. The commission found "inertia" accompanied by "delay" in the inaction of the federal agencies. With Watergate and no reelection campaign in mind, the administration did not mount an extensive public relations defense, as in previous years.[9]

Nixon continued to ignore the commission as the months went by. Watergate became well-nigh all-consuming, but the administration faced other domestic crises as well. Nixon had followed up on Lyndon Johnson's pronouncements in favor of a change in Indian policy by issuing a message to Congress in July 1970 urging a policy of Indian self-determination. Congress responded by enacting legislation reinforcing partial sovereignty for Indian tribes. With the supervision of the Bureau of Indian Affairs, American Indians would have control over their own reservations, to the exclusion of state law. Increasingly restless, they created the American Indian Movement, which in November 1972 brought a caravan of Native Nation representatives to Washington, where they occupied the Bureau of Indian Affairs headquarters and demanded attention to their claims for land, enforcement of treaties, and equal justice.

Amid the protests, Secretary of the Interior Walter Hickel, whose duties included the Bureau of Indian Affairs, sought to quell tensions through the use of the commission. He suggested, unsuccessfully, that Nixon should appoint Ernest Levato, secretary of the All Indian Pueblo Council, to the commission to "demonstrate your commitment to the advancement of American Indians."[10]

The commission had already begun attending to Indian issues during Hesburgh's chairmanship, but the sit-in led the commissioners to plan hearings in Phoenix and Albuquerque. The Albuquerque hearing began a few days after the Indians ended their sit-in at the Bureau of Indian Affairs office in Washington. Several Native American witnesses criticized the commission for focusing on blacks and Hispanics and paying too little attention to Native Americans. Hubert Velarde, an Apache, told the commission that if Native Americans had been afforded an opportunity to testify and "air our grievances" before, perhaps "the unfortunate events which took place in Washington earlier this month involving some of our Indian brothers could have been avoided." He did not understand why they, "the legitimate Americans," had to stage sit-ins and protests before they could be heard.

After witnesses from different tribes in the Southwest testified on the dismal state of Indian health, education, and housing, the commission documented the deteriorating conditions under which the eight hundred thousand Indians in the region lived, including an "unemployment rate eight to thirteen times greater than the overall rates for New Mexico and Arizona, an average educational level far below that of the general population, a relatively high infant mortality rate, and a short life expectancy."[11]

The state of American Indians became a continuing commission concern. In March 1973 the commissioners discussed the Wounded Knee conflict. In February of that year about two hundred Sioux, led by members of the American Indian Movement, seized the tiny village of Wounded Knee, near the Pine Ridge Indian Reservation in South Dakota, where the last great massacre of Native Americans by the U.S. Cavalry occurred in 1890. Among their demands was a review of more than three hundred treaties between the Native Americans and the federal government that the American Indian Movement alleged had been broken. Wounded Knee was occupied for seventy days before the Indians surrendered. The leaders were subsequently brought to trial, but the case was dismissed on grounds of misconduct by the prosecution.

Joe Muskrat, from the commission's Denver office, had been sent to Wounded Knee and the Pine Ridge Reservation as an observer. The same problems existed there that the commission documented in its report on Indians in the Southwest. South Dakota's Native Americans also suffered from internal tribal disputes. Joe Muskrat thought that the American Indian Movement had used all of this to its advantage, and that federal officials were negotiating fairly. The commission wrote to the attorney general asking that the utmost care be taken in the situation. After the protest was settled, commission staff investigated the complaint of the movement that tribal council elections were unfair and agreed with them in some particulars, recommending action by the federal government to monitor the elections.[12]

Although worried about the logistical problems and the costs, the commission scheduled two more hearings concerning Native Americans. In October 1973 commissioners went to Window Rock, Arizona, the headquarters of the Navajo Nation, where they focused on whether the government's affirmation of Indian self-determination had changed the Indians' circumstances for the better. Tribal chairman Peter MacDonald was asked by the commissioners if he had "seen any change in the relationship between the tribe and the Bureau of Indian Affairs or the Indian Health Service since the philosophy was established three years ago." Cynical about the government's changed rhetoric, he answered, "Yes, I have seen a change of three Commissioners of Indian Affairs," eliciting laughter from the audience.[13]

The September hearing had to be delayed because of disputes over strategy between younger, more militant Indians and the older, established tribal leadership. The younger leadership there and in other places and on other reservations supported the American Indian Movement, believing the established leaders had been co-opted by the Bureau of Indian Affairs, which they blamed for many of their problems.

Emblematic of the failure of self-determination, the commission found that the tribal council approved an Office of Navajo Labor Relations in 1972 to press the firms that operated on Indian land to hire and train Indian workers. The Bureau of Indian Affairs withheld approval of the office until the announcement of the commission hearing, although the office was actually staffed and attempting to function.[14]

Despite massive Indian unemployment, officials of the Bureau of Indian Affairs told the commission that they did not bother to enforce the federal non-discrimination law in their contracts for the operation of bureau programs. Although Indians had an "absolute preference" for jobs on or near the reservation, Thomas Brandt, the local bureau contracting officer, said his agency did not enforce the preference in hiring contractors because we "lack the staff and we lack the time." Instead they used "local preference," which meant anyone in the locality could be hired. In almost 90 percent Native American areas, instead of holding an expected 60 or 70 percent of the jobs on or near the reservations contracted by the federal government, the Native Americans were only 22 percent of those employed.[15]

Thomas Brose, head of the Office of Navajo Labor Relations, said the tribal council required contractors to at least hire Navajo trainees, but contractors already operating on the reservation refused to do so. In discussing the companies holding leases, he pointed out, "You're talking about the Fortune 500. If the Navajos sue them they will fight all the way. It will cost $2,000,000 a suit and we don't have that kind of money."[16]

The commission recommended that the EEOC establish an office at the reservation to handle employment discrimination complaints. They also asked the Bureau of Indian Affairs to enforce the Indian preference for jobs on the reservation and that Congress give the Bureau additional appropriations for that purpose. The commission also wanted development aid, including small business development loans, made available for the Navajos.[17]

Tensions in Indian country grew worse when, in April 1975, the bodies of two men, Herman Dodge Benally, thirty-four, and John Earl Harvey, thirty-nine, were found near Farmington, New Mexico, in Chokecherry Canyon, partially burned and bludgeoned. One week later, a third body was discovered, that of fifty-two-year-old David Ignacio. All three men were Navajo. On May 1, 1974, three Farmington High School students were charged with the murders.

These crimes provoked an angry Native American community to begin protest marches through downtown Farmington, denouncing the pervasive racism and bigotry of the community. The white youths were adjudged guilty of torture murder but sentenced only to the state school for boys until the age of eighteen. As tensions mounted, much of the white community in Farmington was unsympathetic to the Indians' distress. In the midst of this crisis, in August 1974 the commission's New Mexico State Advisory Committee (SAC) went to Farmington to hold three days of public hearings.[18]

The SAC heard whites complain repeatedly about benefits given to the Navajos, including free health care tax exemptions and public assistance. One store clerk told the SAC that "their money spends like anybody else's. I should say our money. We have to keep them. . . . It is our money they are spending." Navajo leaders resented such remarks. One tribal leader, John Redhouse, retorted: "They are just returning some of the money we gave to them to support the tax base. . . . The resources that are being exploited on the reservation are . . . the property of the Navajo people. The income that is derived from the exploitation of these resources should be spent to provide adequate resources to the Navajo people." The committee noted that Navajo oil, gas, and mineral resources made San Juan County the second-richest county in New Mexico.[19]

Redhouse focused on the murders, saying they were part of "a whole racist picture. For years it has been almost a sport, a sort of sick perverted tradition among Anglo youth of Farmington High School to go into the Indian section of town and physically assault and rob elderly and sometimes intoxicated Navajo men and women of whatever possessions they had for no apparent reason other than they are Indians." Indian requests to the local government to limit liquor licenses (alcohol could not be purchased on the reservation) were opposed by whites.

The SAC recommended that the local government establish a human relations commission and an office to receive complaints of abuse and discrimination. It also recommended the recruitment of Native Americans for the local police force and the hiring of translators for the courts, since many Navajos were functionally illiterate in English. The SAC also wanted the federal government to provide more public health money for health care in general, and alcohol treatment in particular.[20]

Thirty years later, in 2004, the SAC revisited Farmington and found improvements, and two years after that, in 2006, calm seemed to prevail. There was a citizen police advisory committee and a Navajo behavioral health center, and 12 Navajos on the local police force of 124 officers. However, protests and marches erupted again after the bludgeoning death of a Navajo woman by two white men, the beating of a Navajo man by three white men who shouted racial slurs at him, and the killing of an unarmed Navajo man by a white police officer, who claimed the deceased was moving aggressively toward him and grabbing his baton. Again Native Americans demanded federal intervention.[21]

In addition to Native American concerns, the commission, under the new sex discrimination jurisdiction, named Carol Bonosaro as director of women's programs, and discussed what position to take on the Equal Rights Amendment. Bonosaro gave the commission a compilation of information on sex discrimination throughout federal law and policy. Reflecting the recurring debate within the commission on whether to address issues beyond race and national origin first, Vice Chair Horn wondered if "government enforcing agencies might emphasize sex discrimination to the exclusion of proper consideration of racial discrimination." Commissioner Mitchell said at his campus, the University of Denver, in trying to develop an affirmative action plan "the black and Chicano communities have reacted vigorously against the women's rights proponents." They argued that white women already had advantages. After the debate, the commission decided to send letters to the states encouraging ratification of the ERA.[22]

The commission reviewed the regulations issued by the Department of Health, Education, and Welfare to implement Title IX of the Education Amendments of 1972, which prohibited educational institutions that received federal funds from discriminating on the basis of sex. Bonosaro advised that the section on affirmative action was "so vague

Commission chairman Arthur Flemming, who surprised Nixon with his aggressive leadership on school desegregation, at a White House Conference on Aging, March 23, 1972.

and general as to be almost worthless." The commission made suggestions to strengthen the regulations, which lay dormant until signed by President Gerald Ford on May 27, 1975.[23]

In December 1973, Nixon finally nominated Arthur Flemming, with whom he had worked during the Eisenhower administration, and whom he had named commissioner on aging, as the new commission chairman. Awash in Watergate, the president needed an appointee who could sail through confirmation. Flemming had been a presidential appointee in every administration since his service on Franklin Roosevelt's Civil Service Commission. He had been a cabinet secretary and received the Presidential Medal of Freedom in 1957. He had also recently been cleared and confirmed to the Commission on Aging post by the Senate. He was confirmed on March 24, 1974, and continued as the commissioner on aging while serving on the Civil Rights Commission.[24]

After Nixon resigned, on August 8, 1974, Gerald Ford, a moderate Republican from Michigan and House minority leader since 1965 (who was named vice president by the Congress upon Spiro Agnew's resignation as vice president because of tax evasion dating from his time in Maryland), became president. Ford had supported civil rights legislation and had warm relations with the NAACP's Roy Wilkins, chair of the civil rights coalition. However, the new president inherited Nixon's Southern strategy and the Republican Party's practice of appealing to conservative reaction to civil rights progress. Nixon had made what he believed to be conservative Supreme Court nominations of William Rehnquist, Harry Blackmun, and Chief Justice Warren Burger, and, in his 1972 reelection campaign, supported a constitutional amendment to outlaw busing even as the public controversy and debate in Congress were under way.

Ford deserves credit for managing the end of the Vietnam War and the handling of refugees, for achieving the 1973 Helsinki Accords, in which the Soviets agreed to respect personal liberty and human rights, and for careful fiscal policies that reduced inflation and improved the economy. But on civil rights, the commission and civil rights groups, like the country, confronted a holding-action presidency. As one White House staffer put it, the president did not see his role as initiating government action or even reacting to anything, unless absolutely necessary. Ford, preparing to run for president, saw any civil rights quarrels with the former president as Nixon's legacy and not his to defend.

Still, Ford continued Nixon's policy of supporting funding for black colleges, more contracts for minority businesses, and increased budgets for civil rights enforcement agencies, though with little enforcement of penalties for noncompliance. He kept the Hispanic outreach programs Nixon had established and appointed John Calhoun, an African American, to handle outreach to minority communities.

He named African American Daniel "Chappie" James as the first black four-star general, and appointed the second African American cabinet officer in the nation's history, William Coleman, as secretary of transportation. He also appointed female senior staffers, including Anne Armstrong as assistant to the president.[25]

Eleven days after Nixon's resignation on August 8, 1974, Flemming began efforts to obtain a meeting of the commission with President Ford. He first sent a personal note from "Arthur" to Ford, congratulating him on his "superb" address and message to the joint session of Congress. "Like the late President Eisenhower," Ford had demonstrated by "deeds" that his "spiritual roots run deep." If Eisenhower were alive, "he would feel that the nation was in good hands."

Flemming followed up with a letter on behalf of the commission formally explaining the commission's functions and asking for a meeting. Bill Casselman told Bob Hartmann that since the president had meetings scheduled with minority groups, it "might be useful" to meet with the commission. He misinformed him that President Kennedy, "who created the commission," met with it two or three times and Nixon and Johnson once. Given Flemming's long experience, he could talk to the president about government organization.

On September 19 Casselman tried again, describing Flemming as a "storehouse of knowledge on government organization." Also, he added, former governor William Scranton of Pennsylvania, a moderate Republican and member of Ford's transition team, was a Flemming protégé during the early Eisenhower years. Hartmann responded that the president had seen the request and would meet with Flemming later. Finally, on October 7, 1974, the appointments secretary wrote Flemming on behalf of the president that "his heavy schedule" had intervened. They would get back to him. They saw no reason to take time for a meeting with Flemming.[26]

When electoral politics entered the picture, however, the White House staff expressed a sudden interest in the commission. Before the upcoming 1974 congressional elections, William Walker wrote the president and Donald Rumsfeld, Ford's chief of staff, that Congressman William Hudnut of Indianapolis wanted the nomination of Rabbi Murray Saltzman, of the Indianapolis Hebrew Congregation, to fill a vacancy for a Democrat, or an Independent, on the commission. Hudnut needed the appointment because "he had been re-districted into an area with a high Jewish concentration, and Saltzman's appointment would serve to neutralize this constituency in Hudnut's favor."

Saltzman was an activist leader of the Indianapolis Hebrew Congregation. He co-hosted an interfaith local WRTV–Channel 6 program that aired from 1967 to 1972 with Hudnut, then pastor of Second Presbyterian Church. They had made public their shared concerns for the well-being of Indianapolis and for human rights during the period of the civil rights movement. Civic leaders at the time referred to the weekly television programs as "an illustration of civility through dialogue."

Hudnut did not expect the White House to announce Saltzman's appointment before the next week's election, but if he could tell Saltzman of his nomination that would be enough to help in the election. The entire staff had decided "it would be advantageous to appoint a woman," but Anne Armstrong deferred and agreed that "Hudnut deserves our strong help." The senior staff all concurred. Mary Louise Smith, the first and only woman to chair the Republican National Committee, also agreed. When asked, Flemming said he thought it would be useful to appoint someone of the Jewish faith since the commission dealt with religious discrimination. Gerald Ford nominated Saltzman as "an excellent appointment on the religious grounds." After his confirmation Saltzman began serving, officially, in January 1975. Despite the White House machinations, Hudnut was not reelected to Congress, but he subsequently served as mayor of Indianapolis.[27]

None of this, of course, signaled any interest in civil rights on the part of the White House. In addition to the litigation brought by civil rights groups to force the administration to enforce contract compliance to give more job opportunities to women and minorities, the NAACP-LDF's cases addressing segregation in public education dominated the civil rights agenda. One suit against the Department of

Health, Education, and Welfare sought to gain greater resources for the black public colleges and universities in the South that had been established under state law to avoid desegregation, and to desegregate the black and white institutions. It dragged on for years with resistance from politicians and from locals who worried whether black students, faculty, and administrators would be negatively affected.[28]

Busing of schoolchildren to achieve desegregation, required because neighborhoods were segregated, continued to attract a great deal of the commission's attention. The commission asked the president to issue a presidential order on school desegregation prior to his State of the Union message. Given the assignment, Stan Scott discussed it with Chief of Staff Rumsfeld, Dick Cheney, assistant to the president, and William Baroody, assistant to the president for public liaison, but Ford wanted advice on how to proceed to come from Edward Levi, president of the University of Chicago, his nominee to become attorney general. Ford selected Levi, who had worked in the Justice Department and been a staffer on the House Judiciary Committee in the 1940s, in January 1975, upon Rumsfeld's recommendation. In the end, the president decided to adhere to Nixon's policies and declined to issue the order.[29]

The issue of Northern school desegregation went largely unattended in the White House, amid growing discord at the time of Nixon's resignation. The commission hoped a presidential order would help alleviate accelerating tensions.

In early 1972 the NAACP aided Boston African American parents who had sued the segregated school system. Boston school committee chair Louise Day Hicks ridiculed the parents' complaints about the racism and segregation in the schools, even as conflict worsened in the city. When federal district court judge Arthur Garrity issued his order, in June 1974, he required the busing of some African American children to South Boston High School and some white children to Roxbury. The school committee ignored Garrity. Hicks led an anti-busing group known as Restore Our Alienated Rights (ROAR). The state tried to implement desegregation, but to no avail.

On September 12, 1974, nine African American children were injured when mobs attacked eighteen buses in South Boston. Throughout the year protesters yelled "monkeys" and other epithets at bused-in black children, and white children stayed away from school. On October 7 came the beating of a Haitian man pulled from his car by a South Boston mob. On December 11, 1974, after the non-fatal stabbing of a white student at South Boston High School, white students held black

Protesters against the busing of black children in Boston, 1974.

students prisoner and would not let them go home. The students ignored Louise Day Hicks when she asked them to relent. After the students smashed police cars, the officers devised a ruse to rescue the black students, bringing the buses to the front door of the school building while ushering the African American students out through the back doors.

The only African American in the Ford cabinet, Transportation Secretary William Coleman, a corporate lawyer from Philadelphia who had been a member of the NAACP Legal Defense and Educational Fund board, pressed the president for action, even though it was not his portfolio. Ford put troops on alert but then announced publicly that he respectfully disagreed with Garrity's order.

The commission staff produced a report taking Ford to task and accusing him of having "contributed to the problem." The commission described Boston as a place where blacks were poorly organized but whites were "well organized towards destructive or anti-social ends." The busing controversy "exploded the thin veneer of civilization" prominently claimed for this "liberal" city. The commission thought the situation required strong support for Garrity's decision to "strengthen the vacillating" public officials, and a stronger federal presence. On December 27, 1974, Garrity cited three members of the school committee for contempt for not complying with his order.[30]

On January 6, 1975, the commission sent a letter to Ford, Attorney General Levi, and Secretary of Health, Education, and Welfare Caspar Weinberger, appealing for greater involvement in the Boston case. Ford did not respond. Later in January the Boston school committee submitted a desegregation plan. When school opened in the fall, the committee implemented the plan, including expanded busing. Many white parents kept their children out of school.

Meanwhile, after his swearing in on February 7, 1975, Ford told Levi to look for a case to promote a wide scope of remedies but to exclude busing. The administration had not found a case before the end of Ford's term. Ford and the Congress continued to ignore the commission's advice. The president consistently supported the anti-busing position adopted by Nixon, which was signed into a law in 1975 and prohibited the Department of Health, Education, and Welfare from requiring school systems to transport children beyond their neighborhood schools for purposes of racial balance.[31]

The Massachusetts State Advisory Committee asked the commission to investigate the situation in Boston. The commission agreed, and its inquiry culminated in a weeklong series of public hearings in the summer of 1975. The commission's efforts in Boston demonstrated its commitment to resolving an urgent and controversial issue.[32]

Chairman Flemming insisted that Northern desegregation remain a strong focus of the commission's efforts despite its dim prospects. The staff grumbled that the commission had spent about half of its resources in producing thirteen reports on school desegregation. Staff Director John Buggs and some staff thought the commissioners should not expend resources on an issue that generated strong white opposition. In addition, African Americans were increasingly impatient with bearing the burden of busing, attacks on their children, and unrelenting hostility. Flemming thought it a matter of principle to support desegregation and to support Judge Garrity as a good example of a judge's lonely efforts to enforce the law, whether he prevailed or not.[33]

Meanwhile, the commission continued to produce the routine reports monitoring the federal government that had become part of its agenda. Beginning in November 1974, and extending over the next seven months, the commission issued six volumes of its civil rights enforcement study, the fourth follow-up study to the September 1970 analysis of federal civil rights enforcement efforts. The volumes evaluated the regulatory agencies, programs in housing, education, employment, and policymaking. The report covered not just the cabinet departments and the EEOC but also the Office of Management and Budget, the Office of Revenue Sharing of the Treasury Department, and the Federal Deposit Insurance Corporation. Two volumes of *The Federal Civil Rights Enforcement Effort 1974* went to the White House on November 15, 1974, covering the activities of the regulatory agencies: the Federal Communications Commission, the Interstate Commerce Commission, the Civil Aeronautics Board, the Federal Power Commission, and the Securities and Exchange Commission.

The comprehensive study, like the other enforcement reports, described "the structure, mechanisms, and procedures" used by federal agencies in "their efforts to end discrimination" not just against minorities but also now against "female citizens." In conformity with its new mandate, the commission now included an analysis of sex discrimination. The commission found that, except for the Federal Communications Commission, "none of the [regulatory] agencies have acknowledged responsibility for dealing with one of the most important components of their responsibilities, eliminating employment discrimination in the industries they regulate."

The commission found "neither legally nor morally justifiable" the apparent assumption at the regulatory agencies, except at the FCC, that they stood "above the national commitment to equal employment opportunity." The FCC had rules prohibiting its licensees from discriminating in their employment practices, but the agency neglected enforcement within.[34]

To combat housing discrimination, the commission reiterated its view that the Department of Housing and Urban Development (HUD) needed real enforcement authority. Therefore, the commission recommended that the Civil Rights Act of 1968, mandating fair housing and passed after the assassination of Martin Luther King, Jr., should be amended to authorize HUD to issue cease-and-desist orders against Realtors who discriminated when offering HUD mortgages to home buyers. The commission pointed out that since the 1974 amendment to the 1968 act prohibiting sex discrimination in housing, nothing substantial had been done on the subject. They asked Ford to order the implementation of the recommendations.[35]

Even an innocuous response to the commission's recommendations emerged only slowly from the White House, after proposed responses went through several changes. A staffer at one point noted that since "Ford probably knows Arthur Flemming," they might "wish to make the letter or greeting less formal." The response from President Ford in a letter signed "Jerry Ford," thanked the commission for raising "important questions about which I have requested the views of appropriate officials within the Executive branch and the regulatory agencies." He blandly assured Flemming that the recommendations would be "fully and fairly considered."[36]

Ken Cole, who had moved from his post as staff secretary under Nixon to assistant to the president for domestic affairs under President Ford, asked the agencies to send him their comments on the reports for review. By March 12, when most of the responses arrived, James Cannon, who had become staff secretary, noted that the agencies, in general, had already sent comments to the commission.

Most agencies expressed appreciation for the evaluation and claimed to be working on the issues. The regulatory agencies showed the most reluctance, explaining, as the Securities and Exchange Commission did, that they had always believed it "doubtful" whether Congress intended that they issue regulations concerning employment discrimination "where a nexus has not been shown to exist between alleged discrimination and matters that are within the objectives of the securities laws." However, since being informed by the commission of their legal responsibility to not use federal funds to support discrimination, they produced regulations consistent with their mission.[37]

The commission's annual enforcement report on January 22, 1975, focused on the recalcitrants. It cited the failure of the Department of Health, Education, and Welfare, the Internal Revenue Service, and the Veterans Administration to enforce equal educational opportunity through use of the fund termination authority in Title VI of the Civil Rights Act of 1964. The Internal Revenue Service had not fully used its powers to deny tax exemptions to segregated nonprofit private academies established in the South to avoid public school desegregation. The Veterans Administration had not attacked discrimination in vocational schools that received federal aid through Veterans' benefits. The Department of Health, Education, and Welfare still relied primarily on voluntary compliance. Although the Ford administration received the report in advance, the staff decided it required no politically calibrated response because it covered Nixon's presidency and not theirs.[38]

The commission also issued *The Voting Rights Act: Ten Years After,* a report that recommended the act's extension upon expiration in August 1975. The commission conducted investigations in thirty-four jurisdictions in ten different states—in the South and in California, Arizona, and New York—in order to produce the report. According to the commission, the act "has contributed substantially to the marked increase in all forms of minority political participation in the last ten years." However, the report documents that "discrimination still exists in the political process."[39]

In February 1975 the commission issued a report declaring the existence of "widespread discrimination" in the use of general revenue sharing funds and asked Congress to increase the enforcement budget to hire more monitors for the program, which, ironically, had been initiated as a way of dealing with urban riots, discontent, and as a replacement to Johnson's War on Poverty. The Nixon-generated program, providing federal money under the State and Local Fiscal Assistance Act of 1972, distributed $30.2 billion over five years to 39,000 states and localities with few strings attached. Although the Revenue Sharing Act prohibited discrimination and had been touted as a support to struggling communities, the commission had collected evidence of widespread violations in employment practices and distribution of benefits by state and local governments. The commission, along with civil rights groups, had worried about fairness when Nixon first proposed the program in the wake of race riots and the end of the War on Poverty.[40]

Ford eventually met with the commission in March 1975 after his staffers agreed that it might be useful, or at least not counterproductive. Stan Scott, an African American special assistant to the president, recommended the meeting because he saw "no liability," even though the commission had "leveled criticism at the administration on such controversial issues as Boston busing." He pointed out, "It is also the fact that the President has taken the initiative in such areas as voter rights, [ending] trade with white Rhodesians in the struggle for democracy in Zimbabwe, and meetings with a wide cross-section of civil rights and social advocates."

Jack Calkins, executive assistant to Robert Hartmann, who had been a principal Ford staffer on the Hill and served as counselor to the president, thought a meeting would offer an opportunity to discuss "extending enforcement nation-wide of the pre-clearance requirement in the Voting Rights Act." This was the provision in the 1965 act requiring states that had discriminated against black voters to clear with the Justice Department, or a federal court, any changes made in their voting laws in advance of their implementation.

Ford's press secretary, Ron Nessen, thought Ford was expected to meet with the commission "at some point." Hartmann disagreed but lost the argument. He thought the president should pass: "I see no burning reason at this time; maybe he'd have an hour to himself if we quit ceremonial meetings like this."

The staff scheduled a twenty-minute meeting with Chief of Staff Rumsfeld, staffers Dr. James Connor, James Cannon, and Stan Scott, accompanying the president. Staff Director Buggs and Commissioners Freeman, Horn, Ruiz, Rankin, and Saltzman joined Flemming. In addition to a photo op for the White House press corps, the White House photographer took photos for "distribution to minority media."[41]

Augmenting the White House staff records of the meeting were Manuel Ruiz's more detailed handwritten notes, which he left in the conference room by mistake and which ended up in the White house file. Ruiz commented that after Flemming gave an overview about the commission, Ford expressed pleasure at the work on ethnic and religious discrimination and "enforcement of civil rights legislation was noted." After that, Ruiz wrote, "I'm in the forest and have deep feelings in this area involving my own experiences as a Mexican-American. I was the first Mex-American to graduate. I'm considered the Dean." The president recommended a five-year extension of the Voting Rights Act and remarked that "something ought to be done for the Spanish speaking." Ford also mentioned members of Congress "who are influential."[42]

The commission issued the voting rights report in January, recommending the language minority protections that were included in the new legislation. Father Hesburgh testified in favor of the extension of the act in the Senate on March 5, and Chairman Flemming testified in the Senate in favor of the extension and the language minority provision on April 9. The commission disagreed with Clarence Mitchell, the NAACP Washington bureau director and legislative director of the Leadership Conference on Civil Rights coalition, who wanted to have the act extended without delay and to include the language provision and a national ban on literacy tests in a separate bill. Mitchell worried that the Voting Rights Act might expire if a fight developed over the amendments.[43]

Contrary to Mitchell's fears, when the civil rights coalition decided to support the language provisions, the voting rights extension passed and President Ford, like Nixon, signed it. The new minority language provision required language assistance for American Indians, Alaskan Natives, Asian Americans, and the Spanish-speaking without sufficient

English language proficiency, in areas where they resided in large numbers.[44]

In February 1975 the commission returned to a review of research on desegregation. It had spent about $157,000 on a RAND Corporation study and in several briefings on the work had found it wanting. The researchers proceeded from an anti-desegregation stance and used a methodology that did not sufficiently take into account the impact of segregation on minorities. The commission decided to withhold approval but to release the design of the study publicly and to have the staff use it for preparing their own projects on the subject.[45]

At the April meeting the commission issued its reproductive choice report, *Constitutional Aspects of the Right to Limit Childbearing*. After the Supreme Court decided *Roe v. Wade* on January 22, 1973, the women's program had recommended to the staff director a commission report on the right to choose abortion. The report, opposing a constitutional amendment to cut off abortion rights or legislation restricting abortion rights, warned that such proposals would violate the First Amendment by forcing a person who did not believe life began at conception to accept that view. The commission also noted that abortion went generally unpunished at the time the Constitution and the Bill of Rights were written. Also, the report denounced congressional legislation that forbade the federally funded Legal Services Corporation, which provided lawyers for the poor, to represent poor women seeking to litigate the right to an abortion, and it also denounced other similarly punitive measures.

Abortion rights opponents, including Cardinal Cooke of New York, denounced the commission report. He wondered about the "role of the commission" and about the "legal mandate under which it was established." He thought this study, violating "the rights of the most powerless among us—the unborn child," was not expected from a civil rights commission. Anti-abortion advocates sent jars containing what they described as dead fetuses to the commission in protest. In the 1980s, Congress prohibited the commission from ever producing another report on abortion.[46]

The commission expanded its traditional concern about economic opportunity in the Nixon and Ford years to include women. In addition to approving a study of poor women and their children in poverty, the commission monitored opportunities for minorities and women to become entrepreneurs through participation in government contracting. The government's efforts in this area began when, as part of his anti-riot policy, Lyndon Johnson issued Executive Order 11458, to assist minority businesses by providing loans, technical assistance, and government-contracting opportunities. The 8(a) disadvantaged businesses subcontracting program, and the Buy Indian Act, emerged from the policy and gained the support of Presidents Nixon and Ford. They knew that many minority Republicans were entrepreneurs who, like Arthur Fletcher, supported the party primarily because of its support of contracting opportunities.

In 1971 newly elected black congressman Parren Mitchell from Baltimore, along with other members of the Congressional Black Caucus, with the help of leading congressional Democrats, had begun to explore discrimination in extending contracting opportunities. Mitchell and his colleagues created an ad hoc oversight committee, which found that discrimination was a barrier to the participation of minorities in contracts. In 1972 the House Subcommittee on Minority and Small Business Enterprise, concluded that minority businesses faced barriers as a result of lingering discrimination. In 1973 the commission, attuned to the issue by the congressional discussions, decided to undertake a systematic study. No contracting program existed for non-minority women, but the commission included women in its study, after a recommendation from staff that sex discrimination needed attention.[47]

The commission's 1975 report *Minorities and Women as Government Contractors* found that these groups faced "problems of staggering proportions" in obtaining information about 120 billion federal, state, and local contracts in time to bid and in accessing working capital for effective marketing and bidding. Minority and women entrepreneurs faced "a great deal of [official] skepticism" about their ability to perform, even though contracting officials brought "no specific cases of inadequate performance by minority firms" to the attention of the commission's staff.

The commission recommended set-asides to achieve a goal of increasing the annual dollar value of contracting to minority males, females, and non-minority females to an amount at least equal to their representation in American business over the next five years. In the last days of the Ford presidency, the House Committee on Minority and Small Business Enterprise embraced the findings and concluded that though the system seemed racially neutral, it perpetuated past inequities.[48]

In 1975 the commission also released a report documenting the slow progress in extending job opportunities to women and minorities. The commission found that the EEOC still had major problems, including insufficient funds to pay state and local agencies to whom the EEOC could defer cases to ease its own backlog. The EEOC routinely failed to tell complainants whose cases were not resolved in 180 days that they had a private right to sue. The commission recommended that the EEOC concentrate efforts on one large industry as an example to others and that it also require federal agencies to have affirmative action plans with targets for women and minorities.[49]

The commission also continued work on its agenda concerning Hispanics and Asian Americans. After the 1974 Supreme Court *Lau v. Nichols* decision ordered school districts to provide special language programs for children who spoke little or no English, a huge debate ensued over the best way to do this. Some advocates insisted that teaching children in English and then providing extra language training was the proper approach. The commission adopted the view of others who wanted some language instruction to begin even before the children learned English. Commissioners decided that "without a doubt, it is easier for children to learn in a language they already understand."

The commission had heard too much testimony about children dropping out of school because they did not understand the English language instruction. It emphasized that bilingual education should lead to having the student eventually learn English so that he or she no longer needed instruction in the native language, but it also stressed that this would take time.

Although Asian Americans favored varied approaches to English language assistance, most advocates for Hispanic civil rights supported the commission's approach, and Hispanics constituted the largest group of non–English speakers in the schools. Therefore, bilingual education soon became a hot political issue. The approach required an enormous number of bilingual teachers and, with more diverse immigration, many different languages. Opponents also raised questions about whether the children ever learned English. Some worried that Spanish might become an accepted language, which might reinforce separatist tendencies. Some Latinos began to object to the use of bilingual education as delaying the learning of English, an objection that only emboldened the opposition.[50]

The commission soon moved into an entirely different area that expanded its jurisdiction again. When Flemming first became chairman, he had announced his belief in the importance of ending age discrimination, based on his experiences with the White House Conference on Aging and as commissioner on aging. Johnson had signed the first age discrimination act, limited to employment of people over forty, into law in 1967. In 1975 Flemming compared age discrimination to racism and sexism, thus spurring a flurry of demands for action from constituents to their congressional representatives. As a result, in November 1975 Congress mandated a commission study of age discrimination in federally assisted programs. The initiative resulted in the Age Discrimination Act (ADA) of 1975. The ADA states that "no person in the United States shall, on the basis of age, be excluded from participation in, be denied the benefits of, or be subjected to discrimination under, any program or activity receiving Federal financial assistance." The act called for the commission to report on the extent of age discrimination in federally funded programs.[51]

The commission had little contact with the Ford White House after the March 1975 meeting with the president. The administration responded with a polite acknowledgment of the commission's enforcement report in November 1975. This report, like others, decried the expenditure of federal funds by agencies without ensuring civil rights compliance. Unlike previous administrations, the Ford White House did not regard criticism of its inaction from the commission as meriting damage control.

Ford was essentially a placeholder in domestic affairs, offering the same policies as Nixon until he could gain election in his own right. White House files show that the only civil rights issue that captured presidential attention in the Ford administration was Boston school busing, with its implications for his political prospects.

Given Nixon's troubles and the need to name an easily confirmable appointee, the commission ended up with Flemming as chair, who was not the "rabbit" Hesburgh feared. The commission still pursued an agenda that pushed for more progress to fulfill the promise of equality of opportunity. It had reasserted its independence and successfully disengaged from the idea that it needed a president's attention to have influence. The commission's enforcement reports kept up the pressure for resources and improvements in enforcement in federal agencies. The commission made major contributions to the initiatives to end age and sex discrimination. It had successfully undertaken projects assessing the circumstances of women, Latinos, Native Americans, and Asian Americans, and it had helped to lay the groundwork for improving government contracting and the fair housing laws. However, on issues of race and national origin, the commission had become mired in Northern school desegregation fights, and its position supporting bilingual education had become politically charged and hotly contested.

CHAPTER VI

Fulfilling the Spirit of the Law

D R. ETHEL ALLEN, who had been the first black city council member of Philadelphia, told a packed commission on Civil Rights hearing in her city on April 16, 1979, that more than a million dollars in damage awards had been paid out by the City of Philadelphia in the last two and a half years. However, "there's still the statement that there does not exist any police brutality."

Dr. Allen, who described herself as a "B.F.R., a black, female Republican, an entity as rare as a black elephant and just as smart," said, "Speaking as a member of a minority race we are just about tired of it." She continued, "It's bad enough to have to exist in a situation where the environment and the economic situation is detrimental to your well-being, but to have the additional mental harassment of knowing that your blackness or your brownness or your language barrier becomes an additional threat in the right circumstances" simply showed the "dereliction of duty" by the head of the police department.[1]

The commission's Philadelphia hearing was designed to examine police–community relations and to make suggestions for improvement. Allen recalled that at the time of the 1978 confrontation between MOVE, a predominantly black anti-authoritarian, dreadlocked, back-to-nature, anti-technology group, and then mayor and ex–police chief Frank Rizzo, she and other concerned citizens had met with Attorney General Griffin Bell and tried to make him understand "the pattern of abuse in the city." Later, in May 1985, a second confrontation with MOVE led the police, using a state helicopter, to drop a bomb made from federally supplied military explosives on MOVE's row-house headquarters. Thousands of rounds of ammunition and the fire that resulted from the bomb left eleven MOVE members, and some of their children, dead. Some sixty-one West Philadelphia homes were burned to the ground, and 250 people in the working-class black neighborhood were left homeless. The roots of that later tragedy, as Allen described it, lay in the 1978 confrontation.

Dr. Ethel Allen, who testified on police–community relations at the commission's 1979 Philadelphia hearing.

In 1978 Philadelphia police tried to forcibly remove members of MOVE from a house in the Powelton Village neighborhood of West Philadelphia. MOVE members had built a fence around their house and started a car-wash business out front. They began repeatedly yelling anti-government and anti-authority statements using a loud bullhorn. Neighbors complained about the disorder, chaos, and lack of sanitation at the site. When MOVE denied entry to inspectors and police and marched along the fence carrying rifles, Mayor Frank Rizzo blockaded the neighborhood to starve them out, requiring neighborhood residents to show identification to enter their own houses.

When the blockade failed, the police attempted to clear the house using fire hoses, on August 8, 1978, and a shoot-out ensued. It was never determined who began shooting, but a police officer was killed. Nine MOVE members were sentenced to prison for murder, though none of those taken into custody had weapons. Rizzo had the house demolished for health code violations, which removed any possibility of recovering evidence related to the siege. As a result, even some city residents who found MOVE disruptive felt that police had been too aggressive. The 1985 confrontation began with MOVE's protests over the convictions of its members.

At the commission's 1979 hearings, the city council president, George Schwartz, disagreed with Allen's criticism of the police. He defended officers who worked hard in some "pretty vicious neighborhoods and around the clock." Also, when he went to forums in his council district, most of the attendees were black "and they want more police enforcement, rather than less," he said. Horn, the commission's vice chair, admonished him: "More enforcement is not synonymous with condoning abuse of power." The commission was in Philadelphia precisely to make this distinction.[2]

The police commissioner, Joseph O'Neill, told the commission that even having a hearing about alleged police misconduct was detrimental to police morale. Conducting investigations and releasing findings

"Eddie Africa" uses a public address system to talk to people outside MOVE
headquarters, March 3, 1978.

would turn the police into "a bunch of pansies running around out
there." They should "just imagine the effect that would have on people
in the Community."[3]

When Horn suggested that the police might survey citizens to determine their satisfaction or dissatisfaction with the police, O'Neill scoffed
and elicited laughter from the audience when he said surveys are used
when people "are paying for those services," unlike "the customers we
generally have." When Horn said that people who complain about the
police are taxpayers, O'Neill responded that "a good many of them
aren't," but he backed off when Horn asked how he knew. Apparently he
assumed that everyone who complained about the police was a criminal
and paid no taxes. O'Neill also resisted when the commissioners tried to
persuade him to describe when it was proper to use deadly force.[4]

Then Mayor Frank Rizzo testified that "a pattern of police abuse
does not exist in Philadelphia." It was "media generated" by the
Philadelphia Inquirer. After all, Rizzo noted, only one officer had been
convicted of misconduct in court. He felt the *Inquirer* generated the stories "to sell papers, absolutely. The bleeding hearts have control of the
press."[5]

Rizzo dismissed the critics, calling attention to black-on-black

crime. Then he sneered at the commission for not including police officers as commissioners. The audience applauded when he asked bitterly
if the commission would accept him, as he would be unemployed in a
few months.[6]

The commission had come to Philadelphia for two days of hearings
to inquire into allegations of police misconduct and abuse toward citizens. In 1969 the commission's Pennsylvania State Advisory Committee
had begun investigating charges that the police denied equal protection
of the law to minority citizens and that the city government had no
process for redress. During the latter part of 1970, community tensions
escalated, and a major racial crisis threatened Philadelphia as a result of
the shooting of three police officers and the subsequent police raid on
Black Panther headquarters. In 1972 the commission's state advisory
committee held public hearings on police-community relations. By the
time the report was published, in June 1972, Frank Rizzo, who had been
police commissioner at the time of the hearing, had been elected mayor.

The SAC found that the use of excessive force was a recurring complaint. While some Puerto Ricans and poor whites were abused, blacks
were a particular target. The police department was indifferent to complaints and felt that it was accountable only to itself. The SAC recommended a citizens' complaint system, but in 1978 the system had still
not been enacted by the council, despite support from more than forty-
four representative and respective civic groups. These groups asked the
commission on April 1, 1978, to conduct an investigation. Nothing had
improved, conditions had worsened, and the mayor stated publicly that
"he would stand behind every policeman right or wrong, and when
wrong, trying to do what is right."[7]

The commission added the testimony from Philadelphia to testimony it received in hearings in Washington, D.C., and Houston and
prepared a report urging constraints on the use of deadly force and
more-forceful federal government prosecution of police abuse as a civil
rights violation. The report also recommended improvements in the
training of officers and the establishment of citizen review boards to
receive and settle complaints. The commission had found the Carter
Justice Department agreeable in conducting the hearings.[8]

The election of President Jimmy Carter marked the beginning of a
period of anticipated cooperation between the commission and the
White House. The commission was pleased that the administration
moved with new energy on ending discrimination even though Carter
rode post-Watergate sentiment into office in 1977 without any specific

civil rights promises to keep. African Americans supported Carter's election during a campaign in which his only comment that bothered them was when he said he opposed government efforts "to inject black families into white neighborhoods just to create some sort of integration." Carter went on to endorse the "ethnic purity" of neighborhoods, oblivious to long-standing racial conflicts, including violent attacks on blacks as Northern whites tried to keep their neighborhoods segregated. He apologized for the remark a few days later.[9]

When I became the highest-ranking education official in his administration, my work with civil rights appointees had to take into account that Carter, like Nixon and Ford, had deliberately shown little interest in civil rights and opposed school busing for desegregation during his campaign. As a historian and a lawyer educated at Howard University and the University of Michigan, I joined the Carter administration as assistant secretary for education in 1977, when education was still ensconced in the Department of Health, Education and Welfare. I was chancellor of the University of Colorado at Boulder, the first woman to serve as head of a major research university.

Inexperienced in Washington politics and lacking charisma, Carter seemed, to the press, disengaged and stubborn, sticking to his fundamentalist Christian values, which were unusual in Washington at the time. But the Georgia governor had established a record as a reconstructed Southerner who supported racial justice, and as president he appointed experienced political activists who pushed a civil rights agenda.

Using the issues highlighted by the commission in its Philadelphia hearing, Carter's Justice Department sued the city, alleging a pattern and practice of police abuse on racially discriminatory grounds. Not surprisingly, since police officers are usually acquitted by juries no matter what the evidence, the federal government lost at every stage. The courts rejected the complaint on the grounds that the attorney general had no authority to sue on behalf of third parties. The city government's victory meant that individuals had to sue on their own and the problem remained unresolved. Indeed, police-community relations remain a critical problem today in Philadelphia and elsewhere.[10]

During the Carter years, Chairman Flemming, whom I already knew from consulting with the commission on the abortion rights report, attended meetings of an interagency committee that I chaired, in his role as commissioner of aging. During Carter's presidency, the commission remained an outspoken critic of governmental, economic, and social forces threatening civil rights even though it had been in conflict with every previous presidential administration. The commission had, however, maintained its credibility and its independence. The Carter administration's relations with the Civil Rights Commission were often amicable—the result of the appointments he wisely made to key posts. The relative serenity led the *Washington Post* to suggest that the commission was a sleepy little agency that might well be abolished.

For more than half of his administration, Carter appeared successful primarily because he brought a renewal of respect and integrity to the Oval Office. In the post-Watergate years, the public had no specific policy concerns beyond ethical behavior, according to Stuart Eizenstat, Carter's domestic policy chief and issues coordinator during the campaign. Eizenstat was committed to fulfilling the president's campaign promises: zero-based budgeting, governmental reorganization, and reform of the civil service system. After an angry mob of young Islamic revolutionaries overran the U.S. embassy in Tehran, taking more than sixty Americans hostage on November 4, 1979, Carter spent much of his time focused on their fate, reported on nightly by Ted Koppel. The hostages were not released until minutes after Ronald Reagan took his oath of office.

By Carter's inauguration in January 1977, the Leadership Conference on Civil Rights coalition had expanded to include Latino and Asian American organizations along with the African American, women, and labor representatives, reflecting the growth of the movement for rights. The civil rights groups could point to numerous accomplishments. Through legislation, litigation, and grassroots organizing, they had established a legal framework for prohibiting discrimination on the basis of race, sex, religion, disability, national origin, and age in almost all realms of public life.

Consequently, women could not legally be denied a job or a promotion on the basis of their sex. Asian American and Latino citizens who had difficulty reading English could ask for ballots in their native language so they could vote. Disabled children had a right to education that would meet their needs. Civil rights advocates and the commission believed that the new administration would enforce federal civil rights laws, affirming its work.[11]

Carter entered office with a strong minority political base and at a time when the seeds of the civil rights movement had taken root, and his political appointments reflected increased diversity. He appointed the first black woman cabinet officer, Secretary of Housing and Urban

Development Patricia Roberts Harris, who later served as secretary of the Department of Health and Human Services; he also appointed as ambassador to the United Nations Andrew Young, a former member of Congress from Atlanta and before that a civil rights leader who served with Martin Luther King, Jr.

The Carter administration had at least one black, one Latino, one Asian American, and one white female assistant secretary in every agency and on the White House staff. Longtime African American newspaper columnist and publisher Louis Martin, who had been deputy chairman of the Democratic National Committee and presidential advisor in the Kennedy and Johnson years, returned to give political advice as an assistant to the president. Carter also appointed Hawaii congresswoman Patsy Takemoto Mink as the first female Asian assistant secretary of state.

The commission at the time decided to begin monitoring the political staffing patterns of the White House and the agencies to see how diverse they were. By January 14, 1978, the White House reported 22 minority policy professionals among a total of 186 employees. There were 18 black, 2 "oriental," and 2 "Spanish-surnamed" employees. By February 1980, the commission reported steady gains throughout the administration except among ambassadors, and in the Agriculture Department.[12]

Despite the unprecedented diversity of Carter's appointments, his administration endured criticism as African American unemployment reached astronomical highs, rising to 50 percent among black youth. I recall how I, as Carter's assistant secretary for education, and other political appointees daily tried to figure out ways we could help to reduce the unemployment numbers, even though Congress seemed more concerned about high taxes and waste in federal programs. The fiscally conservative Carter was ambivalent about funding new programs, but the urban employment and social services programs that he did promote to assist African Americans were viewed by his congressional opponents as more wasteful spending by the federal government.

As recently as its February 1977 report, *Last Hired, First Fired*, the commission explained that the 1974–75 recession had wiped out gains that minorities had made in employment. The commission predicted that the prospects for high unemployment and future recessions remained strong and pointed out that "a particularly serious unemployment problem continues to plague black youth." The commissioners feared that under the current economic conditions, without targeted jobs and training programs, the gains made during the 1960s "may soon be virtually extinguished."[13]

The commission asked that employers use alternatives other than seniority lists, to avoid laying off newly hired workers, suggesting options like reduction of hours or cuts in costs and other wages to give some protection for those who had found work only when laws prohibiting race and sex discrimination were enforced. The seniority proposal went nowhere. Labor unions, for whom seniority was a fundamental principle, insisted that the federal government should not interfere in a matter of collective bargaining. The commission continued to track black unemployment and produced a report in 1980 reiterating its recommendations for training and education and for ending stereotypes and asking for particular attention to the problem of black youth unemployment, as it soared during the Carter years.[14]

Although the unions opposed the commission's recommendations on seniority rules, members did not mount opposition to its support of minority contractors. As a result of congressional hearings and the commission's work, Congress passed a minority set-aside provision as an amendment to the Public Works Employment Act in May 1977. The amendment, offered by African American congressman Parren Mitchell (D-Md.), outlined a process earmarking 10 percent of the $4 billion appropriation for contracts with qualified minority business enterprises. Mitchell emphasized continuity with the Small Business Administration's Section 8(a) Program to help economically or culturally disadvantaged groups, a program that had been established by President Johnson in a 1968 executive order responding to the riots after Martin Luther King, Jr.'s assassination.

Despite the opposition of Eizenstat, Carter's domestic policy advisor, the president, like Nixon and Ford before him, supported the program because it was more palatable to conservatives than were goals and timetables for including minorities in employment and education. Carter supported Mitchell's bill not necessarily as a matter of racial justice but as a political calculation. African American critics had blamed his administration for dragging its feet on affirmative action and failure to address increasing unemployment.[15]

The commission spent months trying to find out who in the very disorganized Carter White House could arrange a meeting for its members to get acquainted with the president. The commission wrote to ask the president to appoint a staffer with direct access to him as their liaison, as previous presidents had done. Carter, however, ignored the request.[16]

The commission did not yet grasp that Carter and the White House staff were focused on his plans to reorganize various government functions as the solution to any problems, including civil rights enforcement. Moreover, Carter's people believed that their diverse, carefully selected appointees gave them political cover with constituencies who had an interest in civil rights. OMB had even enlisted former commission Staff Director Howard Glickstein to direct the civil rights portion of their reorganization plans. Because of the White House's self-confidence, the commission elicited little White House concern.[17]

The commission succeeded in obtaining a meeting with Carter only after Flemming wrote him that the annual enforcement report would be useful in Glickstein's reorganization project. Martha "Bunny" Mitchell, an African American special assistant to the president for minority issues and liaison with civil rights groups, had the responsibility for briefing the staff on the commission and preparing the president for a possible meeting. Carter was perhaps less sexist than black male civil rights leaders, who spread the word that Mitchell would have no clout at all because as a woman she could be presumed to have no power with the president. The black male civil rights leaders' complaints led in part to the White House's bringing in Louis Martin, an old warhorse dating from the Kennedy years, to advise on black affairs.

Mitchell seemed as competent and connected as special assistants for civil rights in other administrations had been. Her briefing memo for the White House staff covered all the bases. She recommended that if the press asked about the enforcement report, the White House press office should commend the commission, point out that it covered the activities of the previous administration, and emphasize Glickstein's reorganization study as the place where their recommendations would receive "full consideration."

She told the president that Glickstein believed a meeting with the commission would be timely, in view of the report and the civil rights reorganization study. When Tom Kraft, an assistant to the president, sent her memo to senior staffers for their recommendations, the mixed understandings of the role of the commission became evident.

OMB director Bert Lance, reflecting Glickstein's advice and knowledge of the commission, thought the meeting should occur and offered his staff to help with briefing papers. Eizenstat and his staffer Annie Gutierrez supported the position of OMB, which had the lead on reorganization, but they did not understand why the president should bother with the commission, since it had no enforcement authority.

Associate counsel Margaret McKenna had no objections to the meeting, but she told the other staffers to keep in mind that "the Civil Rights Commission represents only one of many viewpoints." Whatever the commission recommended did not necessarily reflect a "consensus within the civil rights community." The narrow perspective of the Carter administration did not contemplate the institutional role of the commission as a promoter of civil rights without regard to changes in administration. Given this reality, the commission could expect to be treated like just another advocacy group and not as an independent monitor of Carter administration performance and the governmental conscience on civil rights. The agency was seen as not even worth attempting to manipulate.

Reflecting the disinterest, the commission was given fifteen minutes in the cabinet room on July 8, 1977. Margaret McKenna and three black appointees—Robert Malson, assistant to Eizenstat; James Dyke, Vice President Mondale's issues development staffer; and Mitchell—along with Glickstein, from the reorganization project, joined the president in the meeting with the five commissioners and Deputy Staff Director Louis Nunez since Staff Director Buggs was ill. Given the political emphasis on women since the Nixon administration, it was curious that no one who dealt with women's issues was invited to the meeting.

The commissioners prepared extensively for a detailed presentation, thinking that, as an engineer, Carter would delve deeply into matters. They did not understand that his engineering bent had been exhausted with the decision to focus on structures, procedures, and reorganization. As was his style in the first few months in office, Carter listened, took notes, and said nothing to signal his intentions as the commission discussed the report and the authorization of the commission that would be ending in September of that year. When the commissioners raised concerns over congressional proposals to completely outlaw the enforcement of school busing for desegregation, Carter was wary. He had spoken against busing for desegregation and had made a campaign gaffe by saying it threatened neighborhoods' "ethnic purity." The commissioners and Nunez concluded that the president was "cold and unresponsive," and they left believing, correctly, that the issues they raised would most likely not receive attention at the White House.[18]

Chairman Flemming kept in touch with White House staffer Mitchell, sounding her out on the president's reactions to the commission's recommendations. He was impressed that she could arrange meetings with the president and seemed to understand the issues.[19]

The commission was able to support the administration's policy agenda in some areas. The commission joined the president's opposition to congressional efforts to give federal dollars to private religious schools by providing tuition tax credits to parents who paid private school tuition. The commission opposed the proposal as a violation of separation between church and state and also as a threat to the funding for equal educational opportunity in the public schools.[20]

When Carter came to office the Internal Revenue Service, despite Nixon's executive order, continued tax exemptions to white private academies established to avoid desegregation. The commission announced in May 1978 that at least seven segregated schools in Mississippi still had tax-exempt status. In August the Carter administration addressed the problem by issuing standards to establish eligibility for an exemption. To qualify, a school had to have at least 20 percent of the minority school population in the community in attendance or meet other criteria of non-discrimination, with rare exceptions. The commission gave strong support to the administration rule, which was criticized by opponents as creating a "quota" and subjected to continual attack in the Congress.[21]

Chairman Flemming tried unsuccessfully to enlist the president in the increasingly hopeless cause of Northern school desegregation. Flemming sent Carter the commission's *Fulfilling the Letter and Spirit of the Law* report, published in August 1976, and told him, "If we lose the fight for school desegregation all civil rights gains of the past two decades would be in jeopardy." Flemming asked Carter to show leadership by convening one hundred to two hundred American leaders in every field of endeavor as a national citizens' committee for the desegregation of the nation's schools. Flemming suggested that Carter tell the group's members that he would give the keynote address if they held a national conference as their first project.[22]

Flemming was fighting a losing battle. Carter replied on February 16, 1977, thanking him for the report but declining the summit suggestion. The president indicated that the request for a conference had "been considered with care." His administration was "now learning what our needs are and what we can do within existing law." The president indicated he believed "it too early to call a conference, which would probably duplicate your own recommendations."[23]

Continuing to press the commission's interest, Flemming also failed when he asked the president to oppose legislation, proposed by Senators Thomas Eagleton (D-Mo.) and Joe Biden (D-Del.), that prohibited busing for school desegregation, reflecting conflict in Kansas City, Missouri, and Wilmington, Delaware, over its use. Domestic policy advisor Eizenstat responded for the president that the commission's views would be given serious consideration, but Carter rejected Flemming's request. Eagleton-Biden became law, with the Carter Justice Department defending its constitutionality.[24]

The commission's strong criticisms of racial segregation in higher education were just as much in conflict with the Carter administration as its position on K–12 school desegregation was. However, the commission was almost alone in its insistence on Northern school desegregation, as civil rights groups no longer made it a priority when blacks became impatient with having to bear the burden of busing out of their neighborhoods and the hostility their children met at the desegregated schools. But on the issue of desegregation of predominantly white institutions of higher education and admissions policies that took race into account the commission was aligned with the views of the advocacy groups.

Tensions similar to those that characterized the relationship between the commission and Nixon surfaced in the months before the administration finally decided to support affirmative action in higher education in *University of California Regents v. Bakke*, decided by the U.S. Supreme Court in 1978. The commission and civil rights advocates criticized Carter for vacillating, at first, despite pressure from his African American constituency. In *Bakke* a white student claimed that he was denied admission to the University of California at Davis Medical School when some less-qualified students—as measured by standardized test scores— who were black were admitted, on account of their race.[25]

Before the *Bakke* decision, the commission endorsed voluntary affirmative action programs in professional schools, including the use of goals or targets and timetables. Just as the case was about to be argued, the commission stated that a decision by the Supreme Court "implying that in 1977 this nation has reached a state of progress sufficient to justify the abandonment of any significant component of affirmative action programs would have disastrous consequences." The commission warned that "abandonment of affirmative action programs, of which numerical goals are an integral part, would shut out many thousands of minority students and minority and women workers from opportunities that have only recently become available to them."[26]

After the Supreme Court announced the *Bakke* decision on June 26, 1978, affirming that, in the interest of diversity, race could be a plus factor, taken into account along with other variables, such as grades and test scores, for example, in higher education admission decisions, the commission, in a special meeting, praised the Court. The decision was criticized by University of Chicago law professor Antonin Scalia, who argued that Supreme Court justice Lewis Powell was wrong to endorse any form of affirmative action. Scalia, who would later join the Supreme Court, opposed any restorative justice based on racial indebtedness.

Supporters of affirmative action noted that the Court in *Bakke* retreated from earlier doctrine that made remedying the harm done to minorities a priority in assessing governmental actions. But the commissioners, content that the Court had left untouched the ability for courts and administrative agencies to order "preferential classifications" after proof of discrimination, unanimously concluded that they "were heartened by the action of a majority of the court because the Court expressed its unequivocal support for the consideration of race and ethnicity in admissions programs."[27]

White House staffers Eizenstat and his deputy, Bert Carp, resisted efforts to solicit a statement from the president expressing support for the very limited Court decision. Showing his reluctance, Carter waited several days to issue a memorandum to heads of executive departments and agencies that "the recent decision by the Supreme Court in *Bakke* enables us to continue these efforts [affirmative action] without interruptions." He wanted "to make certain that, in the aftermath of *Bakke*, you continue to develop, implement and enforce vigorously affirmative action programs." In January 1979 the commission approved a report, "What Happens After *Bakke*," to encourage the voluntary use of affirmative action, now defined as using diversity as one factor.[28]

The commission's recommendations on other unresolved issues met with mixed results at the White House. When the commissioners issued a report titled *Window Dressing on the Set*, asking for broad changes to achieve diversity in the broadcasting industry, they were criticized as interfering with the broadcasters' freedom of expression and were ignored. The report was a culmination of years of concern regarding influence of the broadcasting media on attitudes about the need for greater opportunity for victims of historic discrimination. The Kerner Commission, in its report following the 1960s riots, recommended attention to this issue, saying, "There must be greater use of the Negro in journalism, since the Negro journalist provides a most effective link with the ghetto."

At the urging of the commission and civil rights and religious

Following President Carter's July 8, 1977, meeting with the
Civil Rights Commission, commissioners left sensing
that Carter was "unresponsive."

groups, the Federal Communications Commission finally issued a non-discrimination requirement for broadcast licensees in 1969. It prohibited employment discrimination based on race, color, religion, and national origin.[29]

Shortly thereafter, under continued pressure, the FCC amended the rule to require affirmative action based on race in license renewal applications. After heated criticism from both the Civil Rights Coalition and the commission, in May 1971 the FCC added affirmative action for women. In 1975 the FCC, after defending several lawsuits, issued proposed new rules, saying that "equal employment programs must be active and affirmative and not merely passive or nondiscriminatory." But the agency exempted a majority of the licensees from the new rules. Benjamin Hooks, later executive director of the NAACP, then a Republican Nixon appointee, former Memphis, Tennessee, judge, and the first black FCC commissioner, dissented. Hooks objected that "all licensees are public trustees and all have an equal mandate to serve the same public interest."[30]

With this background, in August 1977 the commission, concerned about the slow progress in achieving diversity, especially in decision-making roles, issued the *Window Dressing* report asking the media and the FCC to make improvements at the networks and broadcast stations a priority. The commission hoped that changes in employment would lead to the end of sex and race stereotyping in the media and more diverse and inclusive programming.

Although the report had been carefully researched and written with investigations and surveys of stations and programming, the commission was criticized by the FCC and the media for having the temerity to move into this area.[31] The commission acknowledged that some progress had occurred, but it wanted more aggressive efforts to find, recruit, and train minorities and women.[32] The commission believed that television and the mass media confer status on individuals and groups and issues selected for placement, indicating who and what is important. If a people are rendered invisible by the mass media, they remain unworthy of public attention and concern. The report emphasized that "minorities and women should participate fully in bringing about change," and "the Federal Government should ensure that it is done."[33]

Louis Martin, responding to the interest of the president's African American constituency, convened heads of agencies across the government, including Labor and Education, to consider the lack of diversity in the media. They each assigned a staff person to what he called a media task force to consider how to encourage the industry to implement the commission's recommendations and also the suggestions in a report the commission had done on the motion picture industry. However, the administration decided against discussing the subject with industry representatives, and despite Martin's interest nothing transpired and the issue was buried.[34]

Tom Shales, a media critic at the *Washington Post*, unlike his paper's editorial that accused the commission of meddling with freedom of expression under the First Amendment, did not find the work offensive. He said the report "has its muddled moments and relied on statistics not always crispy fresh," but it made the point crystal clear that "women and minority-group members may be getting hired, but they have a devil of a time gaining access to those rooms at the top of the white male country club that runs television."[35]

Despite the FCC's criticisms of the commission, the stations, the networks, and the FCC itself paid increasing attention to the issue. They were pressed by civil rights advocacy groups and also changing audience demographics. With the passage of time the FCC began not only to emphasize diversity in employment and among on-air guests but also to reach beyond what the commission suggested and to influence programming content—though not for reasons of racial and gender diversity. The FCC began to focus on content in the 1990s in order to exclude what it regarded as sexually offensive programming from the airwaves.

In another initiative that started out with promise and then sputtered, the commission turned to issues of sexual orientation in response to the activism of an organized gay and lesbian movement. As early as April 28, 1977, White House staffer Marilyn Haft reminded presidential assistant Midge Costanza that representatives of the National Gay Task Force were meeting with the Justice Department that day. Haft had also obtained the commission's agreement to meet with the task force in May.[36]

The commission debated whether it had the authority to study discrimination based on sexual orientation. Members did not reach a decision until the August 15, 1977, meeting, when they passed a narrowly defined policy statement. The commission announced that it could consider gender discrimination only under sex and that under the language in the law authorizing the commission, it could not consider discrimination based on sexual orientation in education, housing, employment, or health, for example. However, the members agreed that the commission's jurisdiction under administration of justice was "considerably broader." The commission could consider disparate treatment of any class of persons by law enforcement, corrections, probation and parole, and the courts. However, commissioners decided against any such studies in the 1978 and 1979 fiscal years.

At the October 1977 meeting, the commission heard from Dr. Bruce Voeller and Ms. Jean O'Leary, executive directors of the National Gay Task Force. They were invited to brief the commissioners on sexual-orientation discrimination, primarily in the administration of justice. The pair asked the commission to "perhaps conduct a separate study of police brutality issues within the gay community, devote an issue of the commission's *Civil Rights Digest* to these issues, and include gay rights leaders among respondents for the commission's survey on future civil rights issues." Midge Costanza and Marilyn Haft from the White House staff attended and were introduced during the briefing. Unable to reach a consensus about whether to redirect resources after this initial step, the commission "took the matter under advisement."[37]

The commission successfully pursued its focus on age discrimination. In January 1977, its study of age discrimination in federally funded programs, authorized by the Age Discrimination Act (ADA) of 1975 in January 1977, was completed. The study analyzed a variety of institutions, ranging from community health centers to universities. Defining age discrimination as "any act or failure to act, or any law or policy that adversely affects an individual on the basis of age," the study forcefully discounted a number of usual justifications for age discrimination. Although some commentators criticized the report for its statistical methodology, Congress adopted the commission's 1977 recommendations in the 1978 amendments to the act.[38]

On fair housing, the commission continued to push its repeated recommendations in the enforcement reports that HUD needed enhanced authority to conciliate and receive complaints, and to have the Justice Department sue when a pattern and practice existed. Commission efforts to see legislation enacted were thwarted by disagreement in the Carter administration over how the legislation would be implemented and by conservatives, who opposed the whole idea of effective enforcement. As the 1980 election approached, Senators Orrin Hatch and Strom Thurmond, hoping that Carter would not be reelected, filibustered the bill, and Congress did not pass a stronger fair housing bill until 1988.[39]

The commission extended its work on women's issues, begun in the Nixon years. With continued debate over ending sex discrimination in education, and particularly the effect on expenditures in athletic programs, the commission instituted a study. The commission report, *More Hurdles to Clear*, issued in July 1980, reviewed the history of women and girls in sports, assessed their current status, and summarized the most recent policy interpretations of Title IX. It described the progress attributed to Title IX and the continued disparities in resources available to women and girls in federally funded educational institutions.[40]

Since the passage of Title IX in 1972, the commission had repeatedly criticized the Office for Civil Rights (OCR) in the Department of Health, Education, and Welfare for delays in enforcement. David Tatel, Carter's director of OCR, publicly recognized this history and promised improvements. The commission found some improvement but recognized that major problems persisted. The review of athletic programs started six weeks after it had been scheduled for completion. Information on the percentage of students who applied for scholarships and who received them, expenditures by program and services, and information on which programs students were enrolled in, all went uncompiled.

Staff training and investigations into employment cases had barely begun. Tatel promised to improve compliance.[41]

The commission cooperated with the White House on some women's issues. In support of the administration's position, the commissioners also decided to support an extension of the time for the ratification of the Equal Rights Amendment (ERA) to the Constitution, outlawing discrimination based on sex, which had been passed by the Congress and sent to the states. Congress granted the extension, but the ERA failed.[42]

Carol Bonosaro, director of the commission's women's rights program unit, went to a series of White House meetings on the subject of violence in the family, organized by Jan Peterson in the president's Office of Public Liaison in the summer and fall of 1977. Bonosaro described the commission's planned project on domestic violence, which began in 1978. The commission held a consultation in Washington and two hearings, one in Harrisburg and the other in Phoenix, on the subject. At the Washington proceeding, advocates from around the nation organized the National Coalition Against Domestic Violence. The White House established the Interdepartmental Committee on Domestic Violence, chaired by HEW Secretary Joseph Califano, in April 1979, to "co-ordinate a review of federal programs which currently provide or could provide assistance to victims of domestic violence." The work was actually done by the Interdepartmental Task Force on Women, chaired by Sarah Weddington, an assistant to the president. The commission issued a report from its domestic violence hearings held in Harrisburg, Pennsylvania, and in Phoenix, in 1980, with recommendations to help police departments handle the issue of spouse battering.[43]

Weddington's office worked aggressively on a range of women's concerns. She asked Chairman Flemming on August 10, 1979, for help with Secretary of Labor Ray Marshall. She had written Marshall, citing the commission's work in the 1976 report *Challenge Ahead* and elsewhere showing that upper age limits in apprenticeship programs restrict women's ability to enter these "lucrative jobs," since many women entered the workforce after their children were old enough to enter school. She asked Marshall to "move forward in this area, perhaps by abolishing age limits in registered apprenticeship programs under his National Apprenticeship Act authority or by issuing a proposed regulation to abolish the age limits in apprenticeship for public comment." She thought "it might be useful" if Flemming also wrote to Marshall.

Flemming wrote to the secretary, urging him to act, and sent Wedding-ton a copy of the letter. However, Marshall did not outlaw age limits, and upper age limits remained a barrier to women's participation.[44]

The commission also weighed in on the immigration policy debate that ensued from the recommendations of a congressionally created Select Commission on Immigration and Refugee Policy, led by former commission chairman Hesburgh. The select commission had endorsed identification cards and employer sanctions to reduce illegal immigra-tion. In September 1980, the commission released its own immigration report, *The Tarnished Golden Door*, which reiterated its opposition to employer sanctions and ID cards, which could cause employers to "dis-criminate against easily identifiable minority groups whose members, although legally in the United States, might be mistaken for undocu-mented aliens." Commissioner Freeman dissented, explaining that the government should make it "more difficult for persons entering illegally to secure employment." She wanted an ID system that would avoid dis-crimination against those who were already in the country legally. Vice Chair Horn said he supported an employer sanctions law if there could be a "secure and counterfeit-proof social security card" for employers to use in determining legality.[45]

The commission had kept poverty and discrimination among Puerto Ricans on the mainland on its agenda since the disrupted hearings in New York City in 1972. Nixon had appointed a number of Puerto Ricans to political office, including the commission's deputy staff direc-tor, Louis Nunez, but little change had occurred. In May 1978, Chair-man Flemming updated the president on the commission's work and the need for action. In a widely covered 1976 follow-up report, *Puerto Ricans in the Continental United States: An Uncertain Future*, the commission had described dire problems among the 1.7 million Puerto Ricans in the United States. Poverty among Puerto Ricans was "more severe than that of virtually any other ethnic group," and Puerto Ricans were often "last in line" for the opportunities and protections made possible under the laws passed since the civil rights movement. Despite all this, three-fourths of the families on the mainland were "self-sufficient and receive not one cent of welfare or other federal aid." The report asked for White House attention in making sure Puerto Ricans received the same opportunities and protection of the laws that others received.[46]

Chairman Flemming told the president that in September 1977 the commission had invited a group of forty Puerto Rican leaders to discuss the best methods of implementing the recommendations. The meeting led to the formation of the National Puerto Rican Coalition, devoted to community-based solutions. Flemming had alerted the White House about the conference, and the Puerto Rican leaders had followed up by pressing the administration to support their initiatives. However, Flemming complained, "Government at all levels had failed to adequately address the special needs of the Puerto Rican community." He asked the White House to set up a cabinet-level committee to begin addressing the issues and suggested that the commission, "because of its mandate to monitor and evaluate Federal laws and policies," act as an "observer."

The media coverage stimulated White House concern. Staffer Bob Malson wrote the domestic policy chief, Eizenstat, on May 24, 1978, explaining the commission's report and its suggestion of an interagency coordinating committee review of the impact of federal programs on the Puerto Rican community. Consequently, Eizenstat asked cabinet secretaries to review the impact of federal programs on the Puerto Rican community. Political appointees in the agencies began to pay greater attention to this constituency. In the summer of 1979 the White House established an Office of Hispanic Affairs, headed by Esteban Torres, an international director for the United Auto Workers before Carter appointed him U.S. ambassador and permanent representative to UNESCO in Paris. Although Torres was a Mexican American who resided in California, where the ferment around Cesar Chavez's United Farm Workers mobilization had heightened political consciousness, he monitored the response of federal agencies to requests from Puerto Ricans.[47]

White House obliviousness about the commission's institutional role led to political conflict over the president's reorganization plans, which could have easily been avoided. Former Staff Director Howard Glickstein, given responsibility for the civil rights reorganization study, effectively used the commission's work in reorganizing the enforcement agencies but made a misstep in proposing changes at the commission. Glickstein was unable to save the administration from the fight. The president's reorganization was designed in part to produce cost savings through budget cuts, and there was little in the commission's small budget to reduce. Glickstein recommended that the commission consolidate the state advisory committees into regional committees, but the commission needed the information received from the SACs. And politically, since SAC members were influential citizens in their states, there was no way Congress would permit their own state members to be cut. Besides, the savings were negligible. The committee members, as unpaid advisors, received reimbursement only for travel and expenses for meetings.

The announcement of the downsizing on August 20, 1977, and commission preparations to consider consolidation led to relentless criticism from the SACs. Some SAC chairs resigned. The Washington state chairman, Carl Maxey, who had served since 1963, wrote President Carter on September 6, 1977, "It is with chagrin and shame that I suggest to you that your administration has given strong evidence of insincerity and neglect to the problems of the old, the poor and the minorities." He thought that "having one President promise that he was not a crook was enough, but to have him followed by a President claiming to be a friend" who turned out "faithless" was too much.[48]

The chairs of the District of Columbia, Delaware, Maryland, Pennsylvania, Virginia, and West Virginia SACs told the president they were "appalled" to learn of the regional consolidation plan. The chairs of the Missouri, Iowa, Kansas, and Nebraska committees wrote the president that the plan "offered no foreseeable new benefits, would probably cost more than the current system, and would weaken committee contacts with decision makers at the State and Local level." They wanted to meet with Carter.[49]

The OMB director, Jim McIntyre, met with members of the SACs and simply reiterated his decision. He explained that the regional committee structure "will put the commission in an even better position to perform its vital role in ending all forms of discrimination."[50]

The commission began implementing the decision by holding a conference of SACs and, at about the same time, issuing a compilation of 1977 advisory committee reports, which were sent to the president and the White House staff. Chairman Flemming's letter to the president emphasized that the reports, covering the major problems of two decades, "provide an overview of national civil rights progress, both achievements and failures" from the state perspective. They also reinforced the belief that "completion of the unfinished civil rights business will require renewed dedication to the principles of equal justice for all."[51]

White House staffers defensively replied to complaints, insisting that the change will "strengthen the commission's national progress." Congressional liaison Frank Moore took a similar line, telling members of Congress that their "comments are under consideration." As the commission expected, Congress ignored the administration's recommendation to consolidate the SACs. Instead, the Congress enacted a mandatory provision requiring instead of recommending an advisory committee in each state and the District of Columbia in the commission's 1978 reauthorization.[52]

The commission reauthorization stimulated a number of proposals for additional responsibilities. A suggestion made by senior commission staffer Eileen Seidman to consider converting the commission into a human rights commission went nowhere. She hoped to resurrect Hesburgh's proposal, believing that Carter's "expressed concern for international human rights" would be facilitated by a "U.S. Commission on Human Rights whose mission would include liaison with similar organizations in other countries as well as the important 'conscience' role we play."[53]

Seidman sent materials to Annie Gutierrez on the White House staff after talking to her about the idea, but the White House was not even persuaded that the commission should be reauthorized in any form. Annie Gutierrez told her boss, Carter's domestic policy advisor, Eizenstat, that on reauthorization "there are many who feel that the commission on Civil Rights should be abolished, since its major effort has been writing reports." It has no enforcement powers "and has been regarded by some as a fairly weak element in the civil rights field." She concluded, however, that it would not be "politically feasible to try to abolish the Civil Rights Commission at this time." Instead, she thought the commission ought to have only a one-year extension, to avoid forgoing the possibility of future abolition or change.[54]

Luckily, the administration was saved from this narrow shortsightedness since others disagreed. In December 1977 presidential assistant Midge Costanza told senior staffers that Glickstein's reorganization project was "unlikely" to recommend the abolition of the commission. The administration cleared the five-year reauthorization bill, sending it to the Congress.[55]

No matter what the White House staff thought, Senate judiciary chairman Birch Bayh (D-Ind.) kept in close touch with Chairman Flemming and the work of the commission, and he had no doubts about the necessity for at least a five-year reauthorization. Bayh called the commission a "unique" agency that "deals with areas of our national life that some would prefer to gloss-over." Bayh also agreed with the commission to add disability rights to the agency's jurisdiction.

Assistant attorney general for civil rights Drew Days gave the administration's testimony before Congress on the commission's reauthorization. He credited the commission for help on the enactment of all of the major civil rights legislation of the 1960s and the Equal Credit Opportunity Act, the Civil Rights Attorney's Fees Awards Act, and the non-discrimination provisions of the Revenue Sharing Act and the Voting Rights Act extensions in 1970 and 1975.

He also pointed to the *Minorities and Women as Government Contractors* report, which had been used to defend lawsuits seeking to enjoin implementation of minority contract programs, and noted that the reports on Native Americans had been used by the Indian rights office. The task force in the Justice Department, charged with developing a plan for eliminating sex discrimination in the public sector, utilized the commission's report *Sex Bias in the U.S. Code.*

Days noted that the recommendations made in the commission enforcement reports are "carefully considered," although "no agency delights in criticism directed toward its administration." The commission's studies on Hispanics "were being used by his task force on making the federal government effective in this area." Finally, adding age and disability meant even more need for the commission's work. There is no other agency that "brings this material together, analyzes it with impartial scrutiny, issues recommendations designed to improve effectiveness and coordination, then publishes this material in a form accessible to the general public."[56]

The price of achieving reauthorization, however, was accepting Congressman David Treen's (R-La.) floor amendment to prohibit the commission from studying federal and state laws and policies concerning abortion. Anti-abortion advocates were still upset about the commission's 1975 report that supported abortion rights. The bill with the amendment passed both houses by voice vote. Congressman Treen noted that the 1957 statute creating the commission prohibited it from investigating membership practices of sororities and fraternities, private clubs, or religious organizations. Therefore, they could exclude abortion issues without interfering with the commission's independence. Ironically, Sarah Weddington, who had argued *Roe v. Wade*, as an assistant to the president handled the White House staff work on the amendment to exclude abortion studies.[57]

Domestic policy advisor Eizenstat told the president that Weddington and others on the White House staff agreed with the commission and the Senate conferees that the amendment is bad "on the merits." However, he should sign the bill with the amendment because *Roe v. Wade* still protected abortion rights, and the bill extended the commission for five years and authorized the appropriation requested by the

president. Carter, who did not believe in abortion anyway, took Eizenstat's advice that he should avoid conflict by not issuing a signing statement since "a number of groups have requested that you issue a
statement indicating your opposition to the abortion amendment."[58]

After the reauthorization, the commission pleased congressional
advocates, who wanted to counteract the commissioners' support for
affirmative action, by focusing on problems of religious minorities,
white ethnics, and the success of Asian Americans and holding three
consultations in which unsworn expert opinion was heard unlike a hearing. They included "Religious Discrimination: A Neglected Issue" in
April, "Civil Rights Issues of Asian and Pacific Americans: Myths and
Realities" in May, and "Civil Rights Issues of Euro-Ethnic Americans in
the United States: Opportunities and Challenges" in December. In the
Euro-ethnic proceeding, the commission heard from witnesses who testified on an array of issues, including housing and social services.[59]

Despite the commission's conflict with the reorganization task force
over the attempt to consolidate the state advisory committees, the
administration used the commission's enforcement reports to complete
its reorganization, and the commission gave the administration credit
for a "newly rekindled level of commitment to effective employment
opportunity enforcement." The commissioners saw "enthusiasm and
determination" among federal officials newly appointed to the agencies,
but that was no substitute for action. They also found problems in the
standard of performance before these appointments, and as a result
there had been "little actual progress since 1975." They again, as they
had done since 1970, recommended the consolidation of all equal
employment enforcement at the EEOC. After the reorganization plan
was announced, the commission praised it and Carter thanked Chairman Flemming because "the assistance of the Commission on Civil
Rights was vital to development of this plan."[60]

Under the reorganization, implemented in 1978, EEOC chair
Eleanor Holmes Norton made major improvements at the agency,
which the commission encouraged and applauded, as the EEOC
became the lead employment discrimination agency in the federal government. The Labor Department's Office of Federal Contract Compliance Programs (OFCCP) received all of the contract compliance
programs spread out in executive departments across the government.

Between 1978 and 1980 the OFCCP expanded from 68 full-time
staff members to 1,304, and the EEOC went from 267 to 3,433. At the
EEOC, Norton emphasized class-action lawsuits against major employ-

ers and issued *Uniform Guidelines on Employee Selection Procedures*, a set of rules rooted in *Griggs v. Duke Power Co.* (1971) and other Supreme Court cases and based on disparate impact theory. Employers had to validate hiring tests before they could use them. But if they followed the guidelines, they were insulated against discrimination lawsuits. OFCCP required employers to file affirmative action plans with their bids for government contracts.[61]

The illness of John Buggs, the commission staff director, led to his resignation in early 1978, which gave the commission an opening to recommend Louis Nunez, his deputy, as the first Puerto Rican to hold the post. The commissioners were impressed with Nunez's "in-depth understanding of the issues." He had also "functioned as an administrator in such a manner as to command the respect not only of the commission but also members of our staff." In addition, he had shown the "ability to represent the commission effectively within the executive and legislative branches and with the public. His character is above reproach." Nominating him would provide continuity and "imaginative" leadership.

The White House staff, eager to name a Latino, even though he had originally been a Nixon appointee, did not even consider anyone else and accepted the commissioners' choice of Nunez. The personnel director, Arnie Miller, told the president in the memo seeking his approval that "Nunez is a Puerto Rican from New York. He would be your first Puerto Rican appointment in a major civil rights position."[62]

Carter had paid no attention to filling the vacancies that existed on the commission itself. The commission had operated with five members since Rankin had left in 1976, and the White House continued to leave his post vacant. Howard Glickstein warned White House staffers repeatedly that "failure to fill that vacancy is an indication of the low priority placed on civil rights." In January 1979, Republican congressman Floyd Spence of South Carolina pointed out that the "South should be represented on the commission." Alabama Democratic senator Donald Stewart told Carter he was "surprised to learn there were no southerners on the commission. The race question divided our region for a century. In recent years, our people have begun to come together and have made remarkable strides in solving our problems." The commission is intended to "promote unity." He thought "the viewpoints of a person from the south would be advantageous to their work." Assistant to the president for Congressional Liasion Frank Moore responded that their suggestion would "receive every consideration."[63]

When the White House decided to make appointments to the commission in the election year of 1980, it looked in other directions. First, the personnel office arranged the resignation of Commissioner Manuel Ruiz, a Nixon appointee, and Commissioner Frankie Freeman, an appointee of Lyndon Johnson, appointing them to other positions. Ruiz became a special advisor to ambassador-at-large and coordinator of Mexican affairs Robert Krueger, which, Carter told him, fit with his "varied experiences as an international lawyer coupled with your dedication to human rights." Freeman was appointed inspector general for the Community Services Administration, a full-time position that reflected her interests. Carter told Freeman she had "been unwilling to tolerate compromises when the dignity and worth of the individual have been at stake."

In an attempt to boost his flagging political fortunes, in April 1980 Carter decided to name three new commissioners: Blandina Cardenas Ramirez, Jill Ruckelshaus, and me. The president also designated me as vice chair once my appointment was confirmed by the Senate.

I had left my post as assistant secretary for education after helping the president to keep a campaign promise to establish the Department of Education and returned to teaching. Thirty-three-year-old Ramirez, already an experienced teacher and researcher in multicultural education from Del Rio, Texas, and educated at the University of Texas at Austin and the University of Massachusetts at Amherst, had worked for Vice President Mondale in the Senate before Carter appointed her as head of the Administration for Children, Youth, and Families and the Children's Bureau in the Department of Health, Education, and Welfare.

Forty-year-old Ruckelshaus, an ardent feminist from Indiana, had served as an assistant for women's issues to Anne Armstrong, the special counsel to the president in the Nixon White House, and was the wife of William Ruckelshaus, who had been the first EPA administrator and was associate attorney general during Watergate. We were easily confirmed as commissioners by the Senate.[64]

My first venture as a commissioner came when rioting in Miami's Liberty City black neighborhoods broke out, in May 1980, after four police officers were acquitted of charges that they murdered Arthur McDuffie, a thirty-three-year-old insurance executive who was beaten to death. Several days of violence and an estimated $100 million in property damage resulted. I went to Liberty City, where I met with several local leaders; Janet Reno, the state prosecuting attorney; and local citizens, then reported my impressions to Chairman Flemming.

In July 1980, the commission issued a thirty-page statement on "police practices and the preservation of civil rights," and Flemming encouraged local leaders to "come out of those board rooms and luncheon clubs" and take strong action to protect civil rights. The commission urged Congress to enact legislation to make it more possible for federal prosecution and civil suits against police officers who engaged in abuse or misconduct injuring citizens. We also asked for additional staff for the Justice Department offices that dealt with civil unrest, the Community Relations Service, and the criminal section of the civil rights division, which would bring cases under appropriate circumstances. We also recommended that the FBI collect statistics on shootings of civilians by police officers, just as it already collected data on assaults on officers by civilians.

In addition, Chairman Flemming announced that the commission would hold hearings in the Miami area to explore the underlying causes of the racial discontent. Flemming pointed out that the Dade County Department of Public Safety had few African American or Hispanic police officers. President Carter commended the commission "for its demonstrated ability to respond to current crises thoughtfully and persuasively." The commission hearings on the issues began in December 1980, soon after the election of Ronald Reagan.[65]

The commission had fared well during the Carter administration, despite the seeming lack of appreciation for its value beyond its contribution to reorganization and response to the Miami riots. The additions to the commission's jurisdiction and the budget increases of the Nixon years continued. For fiscal year 1980, beginning on October 1, the commission's budget reached $11.23 million, and for fiscal year 1981 it again rose, to $11,988,000. Louis Martin recommended that the president support another increase for fiscal 1982. They needed to ensure that the "commission's activities be sustained and that the problems of its traditional constituencies not be diminished as it takes on the new responsibilities of discrimination based on age and handicap."[66]

Much of the private discontent with Carter among those at the commission and the Leadership Conference on Civil Rights coalition arose from his seeming lack of passion for the issues and his deliberate style. In the end, the commission criticized his lack of leadership and negative rhetoric but gave the Carter administration high marks for the diversity of his appointments and the enforcement that his appointees undertook.

The commission staff had very good relationships with the Carter enforcement agencies, except for having to push the Justice Department to support affirmative action in the *Bakke* case, and a minor dispute with

HUD's African American secretary, Patricia Harris, over the annual enforcement report. Harris took the criticisms of the weakness of HUD's fair housing enforcement personally. The staff met with her, and she angrily reminded them of her long involvement in civil rights. They explained to her that these were structural problems that they had reported on before and that needed to be fixed. Otherwise, positive responses to commission recommendations were the rule.[67]

The Carter White House staff operated with the same lack of clarity about the commission's role and its independence as had existed in previous administrations. Some staffers regarded the commission as a nuisance because of its importance despite its lack of enforcement powers and because of its independence and ability to deflect administration efforts to control it, such as the failed effort to downsize the state advisory committees. However, since Carter perceived his role as being the steward of the laws enacted by his Democratic predecessors, and the commission considered itself the protector of those laws, they had little reason for conflict. Staff Director Nunez saw the overall White House attitude as "caution and benign neglect." On December 11, 1980, during the transition to the Reagan presidency, White House chief of staff Jack Watson wrote Flemming that "it has been a pleasure and a privilege to know and work with you over the past four years. Your wise counsel to the President and to me were very much appreciated."[68]

CHAPTER VII

"A Pocket of Renegades"

ARLY IN 1981, Edwin Meese III was riding high. Congenial,
"always ready with a one-liner like his boss of almost twenty
years," Meese was "affable in manner but with a determination
of steel." He behaved with the confidence of someone who had known
and worked for the former governor, now president, Ronald Reagan for
years. Meese made his reputation as a tough deputy district attorney
breaking up the Free Speech Movement protests at Berkeley, in his
native Alameda County. Then Governor Reagan hired Meese for a
lower-level legal post, from which he worked his way up to chief of staff.
Now, "hulking and rumpled, with a florid face and an outline of jowls"
and as counselor to the president, he had policy as his domain.

Everyone in the administration knew that Reagan and Meese shared
perspectives, along with the same "easygoing, folksy style and disdain
for personal confrontation." Reagan valued Meese's advice, and Meese
thought with the president's mind and spoke with the president's voice.
However, their shared ideological consistency sometimes created problems when their plans went awry. Despite repeatedly reminding correspondents of his lack of personal bigotry, Reagan sought to extend the
race-polarizing strategies that Republicans had used since the Nixon
presidency. Such strategies worked to drive the wedge deeper between
the Democratic Party and Northern white working men who felt
threatened by efforts to remedy long-standing employment discrimination by hiring blacks and women. Adding this constituency to anti–civil
rights Southern whites, the Christian right, and economic conservatives, and a few blacks who would provide political cover, Reagan tried
to create a new conservative majority. To help with this, Meese, sporting
his wide tie that featured Adam Smith, the advocate of limited government, began implementing their shared objective: turning back the
clock on civil rights.[1]

After the inauguration, Chairman Flemming sent the traditional congratulatory letter to President Reagan, explaining the mission of the commission as "an independent, bipartisan agency" and describing the studies the commission had undertaken. Not unexpectedly, there was no immediate response,[2] as in earlier administrations.

It soon became apparent to Meese that the Civil Rights Commission presented an obstacle to the president's plans. He thought, however, that the panel could be manipulated to make it useful. The commission, having concluded its hearings in cities around the country on police practices that violated civil rights, issued the report *Who Is Guarding the Guardians?* Replete with suggestions for improvements in police-community relations, the report garnered media coverage that displeased the White House. The criticisms of police abuse angered Meese, a former prosecutor who reportedly liked to "unwind at night by listening to the police band on his radio." The commission also finished work on guidance to employers, publishing *Affirmative Action: Dismantling the Process of Discrimination*, in draft in January 1981 for public comment. To Meese, the commission's actions signaled that the commission's independent criticism threatened the anti–civil rights shift that the White House had in mind.

To rein in the Civil Rights Commission, Meese set about to have Reagan simply appoint new commissioners who would endorse their plans and persuade the civil rights community to accept them. In September 1981 the media reported that the White House wanted to appoint Rev. Edward Hill, an African American fundamentalist minister from Los Angeles. Hill announced that he had turned down the post of commission chairman. It would take time away from his work and his opposition to gay rights and the ERA, and his association with Jerry Falwell's Moral Majority might generate controversy.

Then Meese turned to Clarence Pendleton, Jr., San Diego Urban League director since 1975, to lead the commission in a new direction. Pendleton, an African American, had been recruited by Mayor Pete Wilson to head the city's Model Cities Program when Meese was a professor at San Diego State. Slightly overweight and mustachioed, with an easy smile, Pendleton was always seen in monogrammed shirts with gold cuff links, a handkerchief in his breast pocket, and impeccably tailored suits. Through his ties with Wilson and Meese, by 1980 he had become a Republican, and he was the only local Urban League director to support Reagan for the presidency.[3]

Meese and Pendleton talked about redirecting the commission as part of a change in national policy on race. As White House personnel

Reagan's commission chairman,
Clarence Pendleton, 1982.

decided on new leadership at the commission, they ignored an obvious problem: the posts they planned to fill were already occupied. Unlike those who served in other political positions, which change hands at the beginning of an administration, the commissioners, given the commission's history and its mission, had no expectation that they would, or could, be involuntarily replaced.

The decision to change the commission leadership without consultation with the commissioners led Reagan to actions that by the end of 1983 had inflicted lasting damage on the Civil Rights Commission as a force for progress on equality of opportunity and ending long-entrenched discrimination. The president forced resignations from some commissioners and drew widespread public attention when he fired me and two other members of the United States Commission on Civil Rights, Murray Saltzman and Blandina Cardenas Ramirez. We insisted on the enforcement of remedies for race discrimination that had been endorsed by the Congress and the courts since the civil rights movement, and the president was unwilling to tolerate an independent commission watchdogging his steps. Reagan targeted me, in particular, telling a reporter I served at his pleasure and I was not giving him very much pleasure. We were dubbed a "pocket of renegades that needed to be cleaned out," according to *Rolling Stone*. The president nearly "cleaned us out."[4]

On October 24, 1983, the news was consumed with the October 23 tragedy in Lebanon when a delivery truck broke through a barbed-wire fence at the U.S. Marine barracks and killed 220 marines and 21 other U.S. service members who were there as peacekeepers between warring factions. On October 24, adding to the urgent news, the U.S. invasion of the Caribbean island of Grenada took place. On that same morning, while the media were distracted, Reagan fired us.

Two hours before the Judiciary Committee's scheduled consideration of the congressional bill to preserve the commission's independence and prevent our removal, the president had his personnel director, John Herrington, send identical letters to me, Ramirez, and Saltzman, saying your "appointment as a Member of the Commission on Civil Rights terminates, effective today." The White House apparently hoped the story would be ignored amid the news of events in Grenada and Lebanon. At this juncture, Ronald Reagan ripped through the carefully constructed White House public rationale prepared to explain his actions. He spoke his mind despite the staff talking points. He complained that he did not like the criticism coming from the commission.[5]

Meanwhile, Reagan's staff director, Linda Chavez Gersten, ordered the "fired" commissioners not to enter the commission building, even though it was open to the public. Saltzman told the press that the commission's independence and credibility had been so compromised that he did not believe it could survive. Ramirez stated: "I know what this Commission has done for minorities," and "I think what the President has done is fundamentally bad for my country. . . . I am outraged. . . . I'm angry." I said that the White House action was a "sign of their great frustration."[6]

For weeks we had wondered if Reagan might fire us. Scary times had

Linda Chavez and Clarence Pendleton watch President Reagan
sign Civil Rights Commission legislation.

Blandina Cardenas Ramirez *(left)* and the author at a press conference
announcing their suit against President Reagan after he fired
the commissioners in October 1983.

become scarier for us, and we were in a quandary about what to do. I
developed a disk problem that left me walking with a cane for weeks;
physicians finally determined that it resulted from stress and did not
require surgery. A few weeks earlier, I was on an airplane to Washington
and happened to be sitting across from former Republican senator
Edward Brooke, from Massachusetts, the first African American senator
since Reconstruction. I told him I was worried. I assumed the White
House was planning to fire us, and we had prepared, but I didn't know
whether to actually sue or not. He said something like "you're always
making speeches telling people to use whatever comes to hand in the
cause of justice, so the decision should be easy." After that it was easy:
we met with lawyers from the NAACP-LDF and MALDEF to plan a
response if we were fired.

Now we were in a confrontation with the president of the United
States. Ramirez and I held a press conference the day we were fired. And
with MALDEF and the NAACP-LDF alerting the press, we held it in
the lobby of the commission office building. I announced that we were
suing the president and asking for an injunction against his attack on the
independence of the commission. The press gave us wide attention,
even with the news from Grenada and Lebanon. I appeared on televi-

sion and radio programs to explain the issues and asserted repeatedly that the law had created the commission as a watchdog—not a lapdog. A White House congressional lobbyist responded that Reagan fired us because they "didn't have the votes to get rid of us."[7]

A media flurry erupted, and it seemed I appeared on every talk show and news program. I always focused on the need for the commission's independence—wherever it led. On November 11, 1983, after extended debate in the Congress, in a bipartisan effort and after hard negotiations with Ralph Neas of the Leadership Conference, Elaine Jones of NAACP-LDF, Althea Simmons of the NAACP, and others, Senators Howard Baker, Bob Dole, Joe Biden, and Arlen Specter announced an agreement with Ed Meese, who was with the president in Tokyo. The commission would be reconstituted as an eight-member hybrid bipartisan presidential-congressional agency, with half of the members appointed by Congress and half by the president. Dole told the civil rights advocates that Ramirez, Ruckelshaus, and I would be reappointed by Congress, with Pendleton, Mary Louise Smith, Morris Abram, and John Bunzel appointed by the White House, leaving one Republican congressional appointee to be decided.

Meanwhile, in court before U.S. district court judge Norma Holloway Johnson, we lost, at first, in our attempt to obtain a temporary restraining order against our firings. My disappointment was palpable. I groaned audibly. Then one of our lawyers reminded me that losing a temporary stay did not mean we would be denied a hearing of the issues. At the subsequent hearing, MALDEF and NAACP-LDF presented affidavits from former commissioners Flemming and Griswold saying they had never thought a president could fire commissioners.

Ralph Neas *(right)*, with his ever-present yellow legal pad, and Benjamin Hooks, executive director of the NAACP and leadership conference chair.

Elaine Jones, Washington office director of the NAACP-LDF. She later became director-counsel of the NAACP-LDF.

A former commissioner, solicitor general, and dean of the Harvard Law School, Erwin Griswold came to the hearing, offering to testify if needed. Former staff directors Bernhard and Glickstein also submitted affidavits. A key affidavit from Secretary of State Edmund Muskie, who signed our certificates, said the certificates had printed pro forma boilerplate stating that appointees served at the pleasure of the president. However, the law under which an appointee functioned controlled the term of office. The law governing the commission gave the president no power to fire a commissioner except for misbehavior in office. Further, we argued that the commission's watchdog function made it imperative that the president not fire commissioners for criticizing his policies, which was the reason the administration gave for our firings.

Shortly before the Senate acted to approve the compromise, Judge Norma Johnson granted a preliminary injunction to bar our dismissals. Johnson said Congress intended the commission to be "free from any control or coercive influence by the president or the Congress." At the end of her fourteen-page opinion, the judge concluded: "The public interest strongly favors the issuance of a preliminary injunction in this case. The work of the Commission is vital to the continued protection and advancement of civil rights in this country." Johnson concluded that "you can't fire a watchdog for biting." She issued an injunction based on her judgment that if a trial were held, we would win. Surprised and outraged, the administration filed a notice of appeal.[8]

After a protracted debate in Congress, Ramirez and I were reinstated. However, the president gained control of the commission, which never fully recovered. Over two years of conflict had taken place since the Meese-Reagan assault on the commission had first come to public notice in June 1981. On that date, the press reported the administration's interest in an appointment to please women's rights advocates. Mary Louise Smith of Iowa, a longtime feminist and the first woman chair of the Republican National Committee, told the press she would be willing to serve to advance the ERA.

Then, on November 16, 1981, the president announced his intention to nominate Pendleton to replace Flemming as chairman. He also expressed his choice of Mary Louise Smith as vice chairman to replace Horn. Reacting to his selection, Pendleton told the press of his admiration for Meese and San Diego mayor Pete Wilson. He explained that Meese strongly desired to have the president replace commissioners with appointees who would support his policies. For almost two years thereafter, until Reagan gained control in November 1983, the commission felt under siege.

When they heard the news of new appointees, commission staff worried about the stature of the agency, observing that Pendleton seemed unqualified for a post that had been held by Hannah, a former high-ranking federal official and president of Michigan State University, Hesburgh, the president of Notre Dame, and Flemming, who had been appointed to a cabinet-level post in every Democratic and Republican administrations since Herbert Hoover.

But White House staffers believed they had a public relations coup—a black chairman for the first time in the history of the commission, someone black to attack civil rights advocates and support the administration's turning back the clock.[9]

Commissioners were totally unnerved when the White House moved quickly to make the changes Meese orchestrated. The call to Flemming and Horn to leave came from a "an unnamed staff person," while we met at the commission, leaving us quite stunned. Flemming had asked to meet with the president and would have resigned as chairman if asked, but he was not given the courtesy. We could not believe that someone so well respected for his long years of public service could be so ill treated.

As we considered how to respond, Flemming reminded us that Nixon had appointed him to replace Father Hesburgh. Neither Nixon nor Reagan had the authority to fire a commissioner, but the president could certainly designate a chair. He also told us he would not have accepted the appointment from Nixon if Hesburgh had not resigned. We discussed whether he and Horn should protest loudly and insist on staying. However, Flemming told us he would announce that the firing was illegal, but would then go quietly. He urged us to stay and hoped that after changing the leadership, the administration might leave the commission alone. Horn, who had supported John Anderson during the campaign but was otherwise a stalwart Republican, agreed to go quietly as well and without public objection. However, since each commissioner, including the chairman, has only one vote, the commission continued to act independently until Reagan gained control in 1983.[10]

Meanwhile, Pendleton's public statements, while he awaited Senate confirmation, quickly underscored his unsuitability for the post. He told a reporter who asked about the commission's widely publicized affirmative action report, which conflicted with Reagan's policy, "Whatever the Administration's policy is in this respect, I have no choice but to support that policy, which must have come up through some previous advice." Clearly Reagan's choice as commission chair demonstrated no awareness of the function of an independent commission. Not surprisingly, throughout his tenure Pendleton assumed the role of spokesperson for administration policy.[11]

The affirmative action report led the special assistant to the attorney general, John Roberts, who became chief justice of the Supreme Court in 2005, to write a "blistering critique." Roberts rejected any support for affirmative action, saying it failed because it "required the recruiting of inadequately prepared candidates." He attached a suggested "innocuous reply" for his boss, Attorney General William French Smith, telling him he did not need to read the report. However, the report helped Meese to conclude that the president had to move as quickly as possible to replace commissioners with his own people.[12]

Reagan's assault on the commission was just more bad news for dispirited civil rights advocates after the mostly cooperative relationships of the Carter years. President Reagan's actions justified the foreboding that civil rights supporters had felt in August 1980 when candidate Ronald Reagan announced his campaign for president in Philadelphia, Mississippi, where three civil rights workers, James Chaney, Michael Schwerner, and Andrew Goodman, had been murdered in 1964. Reagan pledged that if he was elected, his administration would defend the principle of states' rights. The irony of the setting that he chose in which to articulate these ideals could not be overlooked. If Reagan had his way, federal interventions, such as the one that found the bodies of these three buried in an earthen dam, would no longer threaten state sovereignty. The next day, Reagan traveled to New York City, where he soothingly told an Urban League audience, "I am committed to the protection of the civil rights of black Americans. That commitment is interwoven into every phase of the programs I will propose." From the first days of his candidacy to the final days of his presidency, Ronald Reagan communicated on civil rights matters with misdirection and deception.

Reagan's biographers say he had no particular interest in the subject of race discrimination. His letters to correspondents emphasize his lack of personal bigotry, but not much else. If Reagan himself was disinterested, his attorney general and other officials adopted policies that undermined the civil rights measures for which so many had fought and died.

President Reagan named William Bradford Reynolds, a corporate lawyer with no previous civil rights experience, as assistant attorney general for civil rights, and the administration unabashedly opposed both civil rights laws and the Supreme Court decisions that affirmed them. Reynolds flat out refused to enforce laws intended to remedy race discrimination. He spent his time in public debate demonizing African Americans and canonizing white males, attacking remedies for discrimination in court and in the media. The administration's very rhetoric disheartened those who had experienced discrimination and deterred them from even bothering to come forward. For the first time since Eisenhower established the Civil Rights Division, the number of complaints filed with the Justice Department diminished steadily.[13]

The number of discrimination issues investigated by the Civil Rights Commission increased. Individuals brought forward many problems that the commission insisted on addressing through strong federal enforcement of existing civil rights laws, which supported considering race and gender in hiring, promotion, and admissions decisions, to avoid continuing discrimination. The commission also criticized administration budget cuts in education and other programs designed to overcome the effects of illegal discrimination. By maintaining its traditional emphasis on protecting the disadvantaged, the Civil Rights Commission did what it had done in every administration: it evaluated the president's actions and made recommendations to overturn those that subverted the cause of equality of rights. But the Reagan-Meese administration's furious reaction to commission criticism was a debilitating assault on the commission's independence.[14]

When Reagan entered the presidency, it was difficult to mount an effective counterattack defending civil rights. Some of the militants of the 1960s had gone mainstream, starting businesses or becoming elected or appointed officials. Others had become black conservatives, forsaking the civil rights movement. At key advocacy organizations, new leaders soon took the helm. The longtime leadership in the NAACP had been

William Bradford Reynolds, assistant
attorney general for civil rights
in the Justice Department.

replaced by former Republican FCC commissioner Benjamin Hooks, who took up the
NAACP mantle after Roy Wilkins retired in
1977. With that position, he inherited the
chairmanship of the Leadership Conference
on Civil Rights coalition. In 1981, Ralph
Neas, a white Republican and former staffer
to liberal Republican senators Dave Duren-
berger (Minn.) and Edward Brooke (Mass.),
became the executive director of the Leadership Conference.

Althea Simmons, a longtime activist, ran the NAACP's Washington office, and the NAACP Legal Defense Fund opened a Washington
operation for the first time, with Elaine Jones, a staff attorney and the
first black woman graduate of the University of Virginia School of Law,
as the head. Jones was known for having successfully argued *Furman v.
Georgia* in 1972, in which the Supreme Court abolished the death
penalty.

New organizations and leaders also sprang up, reflecting the expansion of professional rights advocacy. Judith Lichtman of the Women's
Legal Defense Fund and Marcia Greenberger of the National Women's
Law Center, Raul Yzaguirre at La Raza and Vilma Martinez at the Mexican American Legal Defense and Education Fund, Margaret Fung at
the Asian American Legal Defense and Education Fund, and Patrisha
Wright at the Disability Rights Education and Defense Fund became
key members of the Leadership Conference coalition.

The president's overall anti–civil rights agenda energized Washington advocates and their grassroots membership across the nation. They
persuaded Congress to deflect threats to gut the strongest tools the federal government had for disciplining rights violators, such as cutting off
federal funds to discriminators. They also persuaded Congress to ward
off the administration's attempts to reinterpret Section 504 of the Rehabilitation Act of 1973 in a way that would no longer protect disabled
persons. And they pressed successfully for the passage of legislation that
tried to preserve the commission's independence.

The activists pointed to the commission's reports, which showed
remarkable progress since 1964, when the Civil Rights Act became law.

However, the reports had demonstrated that laws and law enforcement were still needed: in higher education admissions, government contracts for women and minority entrepreneurs, programs for women on campus, disparate treatment of refugees and new immigrants, mortgage lending, credit availability and charges—in almost every area of American life.

The advocacy groups, all of them members of the Leadership Conference, opposed the nominations of Smith and Pendleton. They understood the danger of creating a commission that would be not a monitor and a critic but a partner with the administration in redirecting civil rights policy. However, because of Smith's well-known advocacy of a variety of women's causes and political experiences, they focused most of their fire on Pendleton's nomination. For civil rights advocates it was an example of how they could no longer rely on the assumption that any black appointee would support the civil rights laws. Race as a predictor of behavior or unqualified kinship became politically unreliable. But without the support of Horn and Flemming they could not quickly mount enough grassroots opposition, and Pendleton and Smith were both confirmed in March 1982.[15]

Though civil rights leaders could not defeat Reagan's first assault on the commission, they developed more effective resistance to the administration's goal of packing the commission with Reagan policy supporters when the White House announced the appointment of B. Sam Hart, an African American evangelist from Philadelphia. Hart would replace Jill Ruckelshaus, a liberal Republican, ERA supporter, and former special assistant for women's rights in the Nixon White House. Hart would satisfy the Christian right constituency left unattended by Hill's refusal of Reagan's offer of the chairmanship. Ruckelshaus, like Flemming, was told that the president wanted people on the commission who supported his philosophy and who had worked in his campaign.[16]

A torrent of criticism flooded the White House, condemning the idea of further firings at the commission and the replacement of Ruckelshaus with Hart. Twenty-seven members of the House of Representatives, including Republican Hamilton Fish of New York, wrote in opposition. In contrast, a supportive letter from Gordon Jones, executive director of United Families of America, said the commission had been "in recent years" an "active participant in the battle for social revolution." Hart would, in Jones's view, "be a voice of reason and sanity in what is often a strident area of the political and social debate."[17]

Much to the chagrin of the White House, both of Pennsylvania's senators, Republicans Arlen Specter and John Heinz, complained that they had not been consulted, the usual process for handling nominations requiring Senate confirmation. Every administration has gaffes in selecting appointees, especially in the first term, because of inexperienced staff work. But this was particularly sloppy, since the selection of Hart seemed to emerge wholly from conservative religious groups with the endorsements of Strom Thurmond and other conservatives in the Senate, without a thought of the home state senators, Heinz and Specter.

Specter wrote to the president on February 11, 1982, to say he objected to the procedures followed and wanted from now on to know of any appointments of Pennsylvanians. As for the "significant criticisms" of the nomination, he did not know whether they were valid or not, but he "intend[ed] to find out." Specter also told the press that although he was a Philadelphian and had been involved in politics for years, he had never heard of Hart. Despite these reactions, Reagan told reporters that although there had been procedural problems, he stood by the Hart nomination. "I am quite confident of his quality and ability for that job."[18]

Hart owned Philadelphia radio station WYIS, which aired a syndicated radio program titled *Grand Old Gospel Hour.* He served on the board of the National Religious Broadcasters (NRB). On the day after the announcement of his appointment, while in Washington for a convention of the NRB, Hart told a press conference that he agreed with Reagan's view that the IRS should not withhold tax exemptions from private segregated schools. He detailed his opposition to the Equal Rights Amendment and his belief that gays were homosexuals by choice: "They have chosen that way of life and have to accept the consequences." He said he agreed with Reagan's goal, which he understood as a desire to make the commission more conservative.[19]

Hart might have survived the attacks on his appointment but for the surfacing of negative information about his financial affairs. He owed back taxes and rent payments on property in a Philadelphia suburb, with some of the taxes more than two years past due. His radio station had defaulted on a $100,000 federal Small Business Administration loan, and he owed repayments to a Pennsylvania minority loan program. On November 7, 1981, two weeks after the offer of a commission post to Hart, the SBA deferred payment on the loan. Also, after being informed of his nomination, Hart registered to vote for the first time in his life.[20]

When Heinz and Specter noted his lack of "personal political activity," Hart responded that he "was indeed embarrassed" about it, but "he became discouraged because the candidates he supported were losing." In Hart's view, "since the outcome of elections represent God's will" he would have been voting "contrary to God's will." Heinz said that Hart's stance on this issue would cause "unmitigated hell."

After mounting difficulties, and an unsatisfactory meeting with Specter, Hart asked the White House to withdraw the nomination. In a February 26, 1982, letter to the president he blamed "contributing factors" for his withdrawal, specifically "phone calls and harassment of the press." He expressed hope that the administration would find a nominee who would "create less controversy."[21]

At the commission, we ignored Pendleton when he suggested we fall in line with the administration's policy since there was no way we could resist a sitting president. We instead, unsuccessfully, tried to make him accept the role of an independent commissioner.

To complete the planned takeover of the commission, the president made what the Meese-led White House staff regarded as a brilliant strategic decision, but it turned out to be a drastic mistake. Reagan announced a disastrous trio of appointments to replace the remaining holdovers. I was speaking at a university in Ohio when someone came to the podium and slipped me a note with the news. By the time I arrived in Washington later that afternoon, I had recovered sufficiently to face the claque of reporters and photographers who were waiting at the gate to gauge my reactions. I expressed sadness that the president was still bent on undermining the commission's independence.

The president named Congressman James Sensenbrenner's (R-Wis.) anti-abortion candidate, Robert Destro, to replace me. Destro, a young lawyer, was one of the new Reagan Democrats who came to the fore in the 1980s. His appointment would please the president's "pro-life" constituency. Destro was general counsel for the Catholic League for Religious and Civil Rights in Milwaukee.[22]

In addition, the president selected Guadalupe Quintanilla, an assistant provost at the University of Houston, in order to replace Ramirez with another Hispanic. He also named Constantine Nicholas Dombalis, dean of the Sts. Constantine and Helen Greek Orthodox Cathedral of Virginia in Richmond, as a clergy replacement for Rabbi Saltzman.

The public uproar began when Dombalis told reporters that he felt "in full concurrence" with President Reagan's statements on civil rights but also assured the press that he knew of no commission policies with which he disagreed. Since the president and the commission were so far apart, Dombalis's statements left the reporters dumbfounded.

Fired-up civil rights groups successfully argued the lack of experience of Dombalis and Quintanilla. Meanwhile some senators on the Judiciary Committee made it clear that they regarded attempts to replace any commissioners involuntarily to be a strike against tradition and a threat to the commission's independence. They would not permit the nominations designed to remove me, Saltzman, and Ramirez to move forward to confirmation. In the meantime, as we continued our work at the commission, we irritated the White House further, with help from Mary Louise Smith. Smith, furious over the president's attempt to replace her fellow women's rights Republican activist, Jill Ruckelshaus, with B. Sam Hart, agreed with us as we approved reports that were in the pipeline by a 5–1 vote, over Pendleton's opposition.[23]

In addition to undermining the commission, attacking remedies for discrimination, and opposing the continuation of voting rights safeguards, the president decided to support segregated private education. As incited civil rights supporters expressed outrage, Meese became even more devoted to gaining control of the commission.

In December 1981, after appeals from segregationists Republican House Whip Trent Lott of Mississippi and Senator Strom Thurmond, of South Carolina, a Bob Jones University trustee, Reagan instructed Treasury Secretary Donald Regan to give segregated Bob Jones University a tax exemption, which had been denied to segregated white-only schools since the Nixon administration. When Treasury officials announced the policy shift on January 8, 1982, alarmed civil rights organizations made undoing the change their highest priority.[24]

At the Justice Department's Civil Rights Division, several career attorneys resigned in protest over assistant attorney general Brad Reynolds's complicity with the policy redirection.[25]

Unbowed despite the administration's ongoing efforts to replace us, the commissioners held a press conference denouncing Reagan's actions and rejecting the president's legal conclusion that the IRS lacked authority to deny segregated institutions a tax exemption. The administration stubbornly refused to argue in support of the no-segregation policy challenged by Bob Jones in the court. The Supreme Court asked William Coleman, former Ford administration transportation secretary and chair of the board of the NAACP Legal Defense and Educational Fund, to take on the task. The Reagan administration lost when the Supreme Court held 8–1 that the IRS had the power to end tax exemptions when they involved discrimination based on race.[26]

While the Reaganites plotted to remake the commission, we continued to send reports and statements to the administration and to Congress emphasizing the need to enforce civil rights laws. When we agreed to send a letter to agencies objecting to the administration's refusal to apply Title IX broadly and fight sex discrimination in colleges and universities, Pendleton dissented.

When we asked the president, Congress, and the Justice Department to make greater efforts to end school segregation, even if housing patterns required busing, again Pendleton disagreed. He also balked when we asked fire and police departments, which had excluded black and Hispanic employees, to make amends by meeting minority hiring and promotion goals. Despite our explanations that goals were necessary "due to the entrenched nature and pervasive extent of race and national origin discrimination," he refused to agree.[27]

However, he did join us in approving reports that did not conflict with administration policy or criticize its enforcement efforts. He supported a report detailing minority unemployment over a decade, which showed that hiring bias existed "virtually everywhere, at every age level, at every educational level, at every skill level." The report strongly contradicted arguments by some economists and sociologists that factors such as poor education and training, geographical location, and the absence of a work ethic accounted for the persistently higher unemployment rates among minorities.[28]

Pendleton also joined a statement deploring intimidation and violence of racial and religious bigotry in America in January 1983, which asked that Congress pass legislation requiring local law enforcement agencies to track hate crimes so that better measurements would exist.[29] The statement praised Reagan for statements he had made condemning bigotry and violence and asked only that his words be matched by government actions showing a deeper commitment to civil rights.[30]

Pendleton also agreed when we sent a letter to Reagan, similar to the one I had persuaded the commission to send to President Carter, asking for a speedy resolution of the status of Haitian refugees and objecting to the limitations imposed on judicial review in asylum cases of refugees.[31] Pendleton also joined us in approving a report on disadvantaged women and their children in poverty, in which the commission expressed alarm about a growing concentration of poverty among families headed by black and Hispanic women.[32]

Much to the chagrin of commission members, Pendleton was quite anxious to let the public know he was a policy advisor and spokesman for the president. He used the issuance of the commission's 1982 report of hearings in Miami after the 1980 riots to reinforce his contacts with the

White House. The commission focused on ways to improve conditions for a "black community, once vibrant and economically viable, that has been isolated and excluded from the explosion of economic growth occurring all around it in the last two decades."

The commission asked the public and private sectors in Miami-Dade County to work together to relieve the economic and racial isolation of the black community. The commission also recommended that the school system address the dropout problem. To prepare students for work, Miami-Dade County needed a consortium of inner-city high schools to provide vocational education. Given the importance of the large Spanish-speaking population, the schools needed to teach functional Spanish as an employment skill. However, the report recommended that private employers use bilingual requirements only when needed. When Pendleton issued the report at a press conference in Miami, he disagreed with the commission entirely. He stated that he preferred the Reagan administration's tax-cut free-market economic development approach instead of the precise solutions recommended by the commission.[33]

Unknown to the commissioners, Pendleton pressed for a meeting with the president to discuss the Miami report, while the White House staff busily concocted ways to use him and the commission. The report got immediate attention, but not because it revealed the dire plight of blacks. African American special assistant Melvin Bradley was aware that since Miami's large Cuban population had voted Republican, South Florida was "an administration priority." He suggested that the White House should express "sensitivity" to the problems identified by the commission but should not perpetuate "the previous pattern of creating expectations that are impossible to satisfy or promise the unachievable" for blacks.[34]

As for Pendleton's meeting request, African American White House staffer Steven Rhodes circulated a proposed draft reply to Pendleton that was silent on the requested meeting but urged "Penny," as Meese and other White House staffers called him, on as "part of the drive to overcome blind criticism of the Administration's legislative and regulatory reform programs by civil rights groups." Rhodes wanted the president to say he wanted the Civil Rights Commission to eliminate "waste of human resources caused by illegal discrimination" and to enforce his commitment to civil rights.

Senior officials Chief of Staff James Baker, assistant to the president Richard Darman, and Meese thought this approach "inadvisable."

However, Meese, who reflected Reagan's views, noted, "We have a goal of enhancing Pendleton's stature as a civil rights spokesman for the administration." In order to accomplish this purpose, he thought they should give Pendleton a meeting with Reagan, where he would "receive a verbal charge, from WH [the White House] then release [a] statement." The Miami report as a meeting topic would satisfy this objective.[35]

For the meeting, in late June 1982, the president was joined by Edwin Harper, an assistant to the president for policy development, Meese, staff secretary Craig Fuller, and African American staffer Melvin Bradley. Pendleton had sent over his own agenda items, urging the president to maintain his economic recovery program, as "one of the most effective weapons in the fight for civil rights for all Americans." Also he recommended that the White House "develop, distribute, and market a civil rights policy that produces positive results. It must contain a racial 'safety net' that allows people to believe that they will not perish en route from a color conscious to a color-blind society." He also recommended that the president "convene a minority summit at Camp David to discuss public policy from our perspective."[36]

The president made no commitments at the meeting, but afterward an elated Pendleton not only announced to a commission meeting the president's acceptance of his proposals, including a summit at Camp David, but informed the press. On August 11, 1982, Pendleton followed up with Harper, asking about "the current status of" his recommendations. Mel Bradley worked on a response that would placate "Penny" without making any real White House commitments. He suggested that the president tell him they preferred "informal consultations with individuals or small groups of individuals," not a "plenary session of the minority group leadership on a one-time basis."[37]

When the White House began to receive press inquiries about Pendleton's statements that they were preparing for a summit, Reagan discussed the proposed letter with Meese and then decided not to send anything. Instead, Harper had a breakfast meeting with Pendleton to bring him into line. Pendleton still had not figured out that the administration was not seeking his advice but only using him, so he continued to tell the press that he expected a minority summit at Camp David to occur imminently.

Commissioners, including Mary Louise Smith, became increasingly disgusted with Pendleton's disregard for the commission's independence and with his public behavior. Meese and the president did not see

Pendleton's behavior as a problem. They were pleased with his advocacy of their policies as they made plans to change the remaining membership of the commission. When the commission's report criticizing Reagan's 1983 budget for civil rights was released, Steven Rhodes suggested to the senior staff that the president might say something to end "serious perception problems" about his civil rights policies. In the meantime, Pendleton was assigned to lead the White House's aggressive public attacks on the budget report.

Counsel to the White House and OMB director Michael Horowitz eagerly sought the assignment of helping Pendleton develop strategy and arguments for his speeches. Horowitz suggested that Pendleton explain that national defense and other matters took priority over civil rights enforcement funding. Further, Pendleton should insist that expenditures are not "a necessarily valid index of commitment to civil rights concerns." Horowitz assured Pendleton that their arguments would play well and told him the "stakes are too high to permit the Commission to remain a predictable purveyor of badly researched and often indefensible conventional wisdom."

Also, to distract the commission from its work of monitoring government civil rights protections and complaints, he told Pendleton he should have the commission focus on management and administrative issues, such as the EEOC's long-standing problem with vendors, bill payments, and contractual relationships. Horowitz was vigilant about keeping Pendleton on the administration's agenda. In September 1982, when the chairmen of thirty-three state advisory committees publicly criticized Reagan for firing Flemming and for "severe reductions in operating funds" of the civil rights agencies, Horowitz wrote talking points for Pendleton and the White House staff to use in rebuttal.[38]

The president enthusiastically responded as Pendleton publicly supported White House policies and made it appear that these were also the views of the commission. From Meese's domain, the assistant to the president for policy development, Edwin Harper, waxed ecstatic over the standard pro-Reagan speech that Pendleton repeated around the country, beginning immediately after his confirmation in 1982.

Pendleton's speech offered praise of Reagan and a mix of standard conservative criticism of civil rights leaders and existing social policies. He thundered that "equality of opportunity does not mean equality of result." Further, minorities should understand that "the social programs of the 1960's were a disappointing failure," according to conservative writers Charles Murray and Hoover Institution economist Thomas

Sowell. Pendleton also repeated again and again the falsehood that there must be proof of "intention to discriminate in order to validly prove a civil rights violation."

Pendleton told audiences that it was unfair for employers to be required to give valid reasons for their choice of employees and that the burden should be on the person complaining. He claimed that affirmative action makes it "dangerous" for employers to have "protected classes on the payroll because salaries and promotions might result in costly legal proceedings." Consequently, employers would hire only the "Super"-qualified and "leave behind the less qualified or disadvantaged minorities" in order to avoid a lawsuit. Celebrating Reagan's policies, he advised African American audiences, "Stop beating up on President Reagan." Instead they should "ask for more budget cuts so business can thrive. Join in supporting tax cuts and deregulation and getting rid of the minimum wage, and occupational licensing."[39]

Although the commission passed a resolution reminding Pendleton that his "public expressions of the Commission's views on Civil Rights Positions and Policies" should be consistent with policies approved by the commission, he ignored the resolution and continued to assert his own personal views as if they were those of the commission.[40]

When Pendleton sent the first speech to Harper, he circulated it to the president's civil rights appointees in the Justice Department, the Equal Employment Opportunity Commission, throughout the government, and to advisors outside the administration. Reagan Democrat and Vanderbilt professor Chester "Checker" Finn, who had decided to keep pounding the White House until it replaced the entire commission, told Harper the speech was "extraordinary." Pendleton was "obviously a good man" but, Finn opined, the commission "continues to be a disaster." He thought they ought to nominate people like Midge Decter, wife of Norman Podhoretz of *Commentary* magazine and a major player in her own right in the neo-conservative movement, Thomas Sowell, and political scientist, former president of San Jose State, and Hoover Institution fellow John Bunzel. He saw these individuals as "both sensible and confirmable." In the meantime the White House should "keep encouraging Pendleton."[41]

Pendleton and Meese worked closely together. Shortly after Pendleton and Smith were confirmed, in 1982, the commission staff advised us that the White House had refused for months to send documents needed to produce an analysis of how much diversity existed among Reagan's appointees. The report would be a follow-up to one produced during the Carter administration. The staff also had requested, to no avail, routine information about policies from the departments and agencies, which they needed to monitor their work. In early 1983 we decided to inform the administration of our disappointment in writing if the materials were not forthcoming. Then, when Congress was successful in obtaining documents from the Environmental Protection Agency concerning a lack of enforcement and we still had nothing, we decided to become more aggressive.

Once the commission's vote to subpoena the materials appeared in the press, Meese instructed the White House staff to cooperate with Pendleton to bury the issue. Recognizing the commission's authority, in March 1983 the White House counsel's office advised senior staff that indeed the "Commission does have statutory subpoena power" and nothing suggested "the Commission may not subpoena information from Executive branch departments and agencies."[42]

As the press continued to follow up on the controversy, Meese briefed the president, after which we received the entire list of full- and part-time appointments and the information on enforcement that we had requested. The personnel data showed that except for a refusal to submit to the commission's independent authority, the administration had had no reason for failing to respond to our requests for information on appointments. They had managed to find minority conservatives other than Pendleton and Clarence Thomas to fill a number of sensitive posts. The executive branch appointees, along with judges, marshals, and attorneys, showed an increase in females, as African Americans and Latinos held about the same number of posts as in the Carter administration. There was a slight increase in Asian appointments, but no Indians except eight part-timers in jobs that did not need Senate confirmation. Cabinet secretary Craig Fuller told Pendleton he "trusted that it [the list] will be treated as confidential and not released in its present form," and that it should be understood to satisfy all of the requests to the White House. But, more significantly, the information the agencies submitted showed what we expected—enforcement had declined.[43]

White House planning for the removal of the remaining commissioners collided with the expiration of the commission's authorization on November 29, 1983. The commission proposed a fifteen-year extension and six-year terms for commissioners, which would overlap and extend beyond any particular administration, thus preserving the idea of an independent watchdog commission. It also proposed a nationwide ability to subpoena documents, although not with the authority to compel people to come to Washington to testify.

The White House staff discussed how to proceed without accepting the importance of commission independence. Michael Horowitz and OMB staffer Michael Uhlmann agreed to insist on the president's authority to remove commissioners. They ignored history, which showed that presidents did not believe they had such power. With the White House puzzling over whether to make a proposal, Don Edwards's House Judiciary Subcommittee prepared for hearings on a bill that essentially contained the commission's proposals.[44]

After the nominations of Destro, Dombalis, and Quintanilla were returned by the Senate with no action in December 1982, "Checker" Finn weighed in again with White House staffer Ed Harper. He wrote: "Clarence Pendleton by his lonesome hasn't been able to make repairs." He alleged that the commission made civil rights issues out of things that were not. "Next thing we know, they'll be issuing reports on Administration foreign policy, Social security policy and the proper use of gas tax revenues." He wrote to Harper that he did "not understand why you [the administration] must endure Mary Berry, or several of her colleagues." The president needed commissioners who would use the commission's "watchdog" function to keep issues from being brought into the "civil rights orbit," rather than a group that examined administration policies. Harper thanked him and said, "The issues you raise, with respect to the Civil Rights Commission, have not fallen off the radar screen."[45]

After much weighing of the probability of success, Meese, on behalf of the president, finally settled on a dream team of confirmable nominees, all Reagan Democrats, in March 1983. After renominating Robert Destro, Sensenbrenner's choice from the Catholic League for Religious and Civil Rights, they selected John Bunzel, described by the White House press office as "one of the first public figures in the early 1970's to oppose preferential treatment," an "early supporter of the civil rights movement," and former president of San Jose State. Morris Abram, the third nominee, was a partner in a major New York law firm who had been president of Brandeis University, co-chair of the White House Conference on Civil Rights from 1967 to 1968, and chairman of the United Negro College Fund. The White House described him as a Carter supporter who "broke with him [Carter]" over his "misguided civil rights policies" to support Reagan's election and his policies.

The White House press office announcement in May 1983

204 AND JUSTICE FOR ALL

explained that these individuals were "recognized authorities and scholars in the field of civil rights" who "share the President's policy views."
The president had chosen Linda Chavez Gersten to be staff director.
He believed her work with the president of the American Federation of
Teachers and on the staff of Representative Don Edwards (D-Calif.),
chairman of the House Judiciary Subcommittee on Civil and Constitutional Rights, before she became a Reaganite gave her the experience
needed. She "is a conservative Democrat who supports the Administration's programs." The staff briefing memo further explained that her
nomination would offer "the political advantages of nominating a Hispanic woman with ties to organized labor . . . who is at the same time
strongly committed to the President's civil rights policies." The White
House announcement insisted the nominees were all "very impressive"
and would "be a credit to the President."[46]

Pendleton told the press that he had asked the White House staff to
replace Saltzman, Ramirez, and me. He had said, "I'm Chairman over
there but I can't get anything done because of them, the other Commissioners. You need to appoint more conservatives over there. . . . If I'm
going to be appointed to a political position in which I am ideologically
compatible with the administration, then I need some support."[47]

In announcing the new nominees, the White House staff followed
the guidance circulated by Horowitz in a devious memo on "communi-
cating our position to the press." The memo defined the problem as
persuading reporters to accept the White House spin. Staff should
abandon their standard explanation: "The administration is tired of
being criticized by the current Commissioners we plan to replace—We
desire to appoint 'our own people.'" Horowitz advised that this
approach led the reporters to believe that the president's intentions
threatened the commission's independent ability to monitor the executive branch. Rather, Horowitz wrote in his memo to White House
political operatives, they should influence the press to produce stories
about how qualified the president's appointees were and avoid the independence issue.

Further, Horowitz suggested, the staff should also persuade the press
that the real issue was that the commission had "uncritically" accepted
"quotas [and] busing," which most Americans rejected. Opponents had
effectively advanced the label "quotas" (which had been used historically by elite universities as a ceiling on the number of Jews they would
admit) to undermine public support for affirmative action. Whether
employers voluntarily set goals to include women and minorities to

achieve diversity or make up for past hiring discrimination, or a court ordered specific targets when an employer was found to have intentionally refused to hire women and minorities, such affirmative action was denounced as a quota.

Used most often with reference to African Americans, quotas embodied the complaint that blacks obtained jobs or admission to elite educational institutions when the places should have gone to whites who were "more qualified" by some particular measure, such as a standardized test score. Whites with lower scores who were admitted or hired went uncontested because the complaint was race discrimination. Civil rights opponents decried the admission of more blacks instead of whites as "reverse discrimination." The commission had consistently supported goals and targets for admissions and for hiring to make up for past exclusion and temporary minimum quotas when ordered by a court after a finding of discrimination. Evidence of the further perpetuation of discrimination had little effect on the public debate. Affirmative action became preferential treatment for less-qualified blacks using a quota. Democrats, who had a large African American constituency, resisted the argument, but the issue became a potent political weapon for the Republicans.

If the busing and quotas points proved ineffective, Horowitz advised, the staff should support the president's assault on the commission by circulating the falsehood that the president was concerned about "a noticeable decline in the scholarship, quality and fairness of the Commission's work in recent years."[48]

Bent on using every possible political and public relations advantage, the White House staff decided that though the nomination papers of the staff director accurately described her as Linda Chavez Gersten, they would drop Gersten, her married name, to emphasize the naming of a Hispanic. They "elected *not* to use Gersten in the press Release," and she became known simply as "Linda Chavez" from that day forward.

When the White House announced the new nominees at a White House photo opportunity on May 25, 1983, the press duly noted the statements that these nominees opposed quotas and busing. The press noted that the White House brought staff director Chavez center stage. In addition to her projection as a Hispanic, she helped to soften the image of the other, all-white-male appointees.

The press, not going along completely with the White House spin, also reported Press Secretary Larry Speakes's comment that "the President did what he wanted to do," and noted the commission's disagreements with the White House over police-community relations, school desegregation, and affirmative action. Our complaints that the White House had withheld documents we needed to monitor enforcement of civil rights laws also were reported, and the press pointed out that the president's firing of commissioners created a conflict over the independence of the commission.[49]

Despite White House efforts, the nominations ignited a firestorm because of Pendleton's performance as chairman and because of smoldering discontent over the assault on the commission's independence. Most of the correspondence and public statements from advocacy groups and individuals lamented the effort to "compromise the Commission's independence." Senators Lloyd Bentsen (D) and John Tower of Texas (R), in addition to their concern about the absence of a Hispanic among the commissioner nominees, objected to the White House's "unashamedly and overtly" replacing commissioners with appointees who would not fairly evaluate but rather always support the administration's policy, which had never been the role of the commission. The White House staff's planned reply cited the qualifications of the nominees, their "independent views," and the administration's commitment to not just fifteen years as suggested by the commission but a twenty-year reauthorization.[50]

Ramirez and I had no intention of leaving and would not acquiesce to what we regarded as Reagan's illegal attempt to gut the commission. We sensed that Reagan might fire us. We decided to resist to defend the commission's independence. Although Saltzman, advised by the president of his congregation that we could not win a legal fight, said he would not join us, we decided to sue the president if fired, which led to the November 1983 decision in Judge Norma Johnson's court.

The White House staff generally ignored negative letters, but they worried over how to respond to Rev. Jesse Jackson's denunciation of the "wholesale replacement" of commissioners. They did not want to give Jackson grist for continued publicity, which they knew he could obtain. Jackson told the president his actions "would undermine its [the commission's] moral authority and credibility which have resulted mainly from its bipartisan independent status." He asked for a meeting with the president, which would include other civil rights organizations, to discuss the matter.

White House staffers worked on a reply for the president, which John Roberts in the counsel's office reviewed in an effort to find a way to address the independence issue. Staff comments went back and forth until, in a senior staff meeting a week later, it was decided the letter should be signed by White House counsel Fred Fielding instead of the president. During this time Jesse Jackson continued his public criticisms of the administration's plans.[51]

When the negative publicity grew in intensity, some White House reporters accepted the spin that the OMB's Horowitz and the press office promoted, painting the commission replacements as a slight misstep rather than a calculated decision orchestrated by Meese (as reflected in White House files and confirmed by Pendleton's boasts). They reported the explanation of one unidentified senior administration official that "we fumbled the ball," attributing the mistake to "a new personnel director John Herrington who pushed the appointments through before we had thought out the political impact."

The White House files confirm the correctness of the stance taken by Leadership Conference executive director Ralph Neas, who tried to have the press focus on the changes as a political decision mulled over for a long time by senior staff, prodded by outsiders taking potshots at their slowness in moving, and endorsed enthusiastically by the president. Neas explained the staff disaffection with commission reports. He concluded, "The civil rights struggles of the 1980's will focus primarily on issues involving equal economic opportunity—jobs, fair and affordable housing, and discrimination against women in insurance, pensions and other economic areas." The commission had followed this understanding in developing its future agenda. These economic issues were among the ones that the Reagan commissioners would most want to control.

Even though some reporters gave the administration a pass, White House frustration grew when Pendleton's rhetoric and the touting of the nominees' credentials had little effect in Congress. Longtime members on the oversight committees, familiar with the work of the commission and hearing protests from their constituents, ignored the falsities coming from the White House.[52]

The gathering storm in Congress focused on the assault on the commission's independence. An outraged House Judiciary Committee oversight chairman Don Edwards (D-Calif.) said, "The independence of the Commission is its reason for being. It has irritated Lyndon Johnson and Jimmy Carter as much as Ronald Reagan. They need to be independent."[53]

Jerris Leonard, who had been assistant attorney general for civil rights during the Nixon administration, underscored Edwards's view. He told reporters that former presidents "had as much trouble with the Commission as William Bradford Reynolds, the current civil rights assistant and this administration are having."[54]

State advisory committee members, led by Tom Pugh in Illinois and Mattie Crossley in Tennessee, objected to the wholesale removal of commissioners as an "assault on the Commission's independence and integrity." Congressman Parren Mitchell called it the "political rape of the Commission." One hundred and sixty organizations in the Leadership Conference, without the thirty Jewish groups that did not want to oppose the appointment of Abrams, asked the Senate to reject the nominees. They called Reagan's actions subversive of the "Commission's independence and integrity." The civil rights leaders felt that the president must be denied a commission that, contrary to its legal purpose, would become part of the administration instead of a watchdog.[55]

At the commission, we complained to the White House that contrary to well-established practice, the commission had been given no opportunity to recommend a staff director to the president and had not been consulted about appointments. The commission's general counsel office concluded that the president had no power to remove commissioners involuntarily. Pendleton's repeated statements that he had urged the White House to replace the four incumbents because he needed more support in moving the administration's agenda undermined the White House's late-breaking argument that they were not intent on undermining the commission's independence.[56]

In preparation for the confirmation hearings, at the Justice Department Theodore Olson, assistant attorney general for the Office of Legal Counsel, prepared an argument supporting the power of the president to remove commissioners. Olson argued that Congress did not explicitly deny the president removal power and there were no terms in the statute. Since the law would presume against an inference of life tenure, the president could remove commissioners. At the White House counsel's request, he also prepared an argument to prevent Congress from passing legislation to prevent removal, which they could use in case the administration had to testify. They believed they were strongly armored to win the fight.[57]

OMB's Horowitz continued to help. This time he produced an error-laden "Historical Background of the Commission," which argued that the commission had never been independent and that presidents had shown before they could replace commissioners. His guidance concluded: "The real sources of controversy are the issues of RACIAL QUOTAS and FORCED BUSING." The president's highly qualified nominees are "independent-minded Democrats."[58]

At the confirmation hearing on July 13, 1983, the president became the issue. Senator Joseph R. Biden, Jr., of Delaware, the ranking Democrat on the committee, said that the nominees had "impeccable" credentials and would probably be confirmed, but that he would vote against them. "You are not the issue," he told the nominees. "The question at stake is the independence of the Commission." Senator Howard M. Metzenbaum, Democrat of Ohio, said that any nominee, "regardless of his or her qualifications, comes before us tainted by the President's act in firing the five Commissioners" appointed by President Gerald R. Ford and President Jimmy Carter. The Speaker of the House, Democrat Thomas P. O'Neill, Jr. (D-Mass.), and 157 members of the House of Representatives urged the Senate to preserve the commission's independence by rejecting the president's nominees.

Senators Paul Laxalt (R-Nev.), Thurmond, and Hatch went to discuss the rejection of the nominees with President Reagan after the hearing. Reagan wrote in his diary after the meeting: "The Dems are being vicious & unprincipled. Orin [Orrin Hatch] has been working too hard—he is very emotional on thin edge."[59]

The chairmen of twenty-one House committees and subcommittees with jurisdiction over civil rights objected to Reagan's actions. The House approved a five-year extension of the commission with language prohibiting the removal of commissioners except for neglect of duty or malfeasance in office. On July 19, 1983, eighteen Republican members of the House abandoned the administration. They told Reagan that to protect the commission's independence they were introducing an amendment to the reauthorization, establishing terms for the members, retaining the members in office on the effective date of the legislation, and permitting removal only for "inefficiency, neglect of duty, or malfeasance in office."[60]

Matters went no better in the second confirmation hearing, on July 28. Supporters of the president hinted, as segregationists did to attack earlier civil rights activists, that I should be replaced because I seemed sympathetic to communism. They cited my historical writings and a speech I made after returning from a trip to China when I was in the Carter administration. Democratic Senate staffers immediately told me of the comments and asked if I had a response. I spent hours compiling accurate information on my writings and speeches. I also included accurate information about the China mission, and about the egregious harassment I had experienced from the KGB while on a previous mission to the Soviet Union, which, when put in the record, squelched the tactic. After Democrats and some Republican senators vehemently expressed opposition to the wholesale removal of commissioners, Congress recessed. For years after that, Chavez misquoted the speech and asserted falsely that I quoted from Mao's Little Red Book constantly, which I, according to her, carried in my purse. Not only had no one ever heard me quoting Mao or seen me with his Little Red Book, which I did not possess, everyone who had ever seen me knew I never carried a purse. That did not keep her false statements from appearing in Wikipedia.[61]

After the recess, the objecting senators asked Majority Leader Howard Baker (R-Tenn.) to bypass the Judiciary Committee and move reauthorization to the floor, since committee chairman Orrin Hatch (R-Utah) refused to advance the commission's extension until Reagan's nominees were confirmed. The senators who opposed Reagan made it clear to Hatch that Bunzel and Destro could not be confirmed so long as the president insisted that Abram replace me, which meant none could be confirmed. Senator Specter, who must always balance the desires of his Philadelphia area constituency with more-conservative voters in Pittsburgh and western Pennsylvania, in an attempt to find a compromise, proposed that the commission would be reauthorized permanently and commissioners would serve six-year fixed staggered terms. Five of the current commissioners could serve until the end of their terms, and since Saltzman had already served longer than that, he would be replaced by Abram. The idea, which was dependent on Saltzman's voluntary resignation, died in its inception. Abram objected that since he and the other nominees had said they opposed us because we were in favor of quotas, if he agreed it would appear that he had accepted a quota—"a Jew for a Jew."[62]

With the nominations unresolved, Reagan appointed Linda Chavez as staff director. Since a vacancy existed at the end of the congressional session, he could use a recess appointment until the end of the next congressional session. The president also sent his nominations back to the Senate and urged Republicans to support their confirmation. Senator Charles "Mac" Mathias (R-Md.) refused, saying that "the dismissal of incumbent members" was contrary to "settled practice" since the Eisenhower administration. He told the president, "Your nominees are indeed capable and honest, but so are the incumbents." If the personal characteristics "are in balance, then the damage to the independence of the Commission becomes the deciding factor to me."[63]

Chavez did not wait for confirmation to begin moving on the Reagan agenda. She and Pendleton asked the commission to support the administration in siding with white firefighters in Memphis who argued that African Americans just recently hired under a court order to end their long exclusion should be laid off before whites as the last hired. Mary Louise Smith joined the rest of us in refusing to agree."[64]

The Senate Judiciary Committee arrived at a compromise that would let Reagan add commissioners by expanding the commission by two and providing staggered terms. The White House, according to media accounts, hoped "at least to get rid of Berry, the most outspoken holdover."[65]

With the firings declared illegal by Judge Johnson and a compromise worked out in Congress, the White House knew they had lost. The president had to sign the bill passed in the Senate and the House, a bill characterized by Congressman Don Edwards as "a workable compromise." As one of the key negotiators, Biden asserted, "Never again will this president, or the next president, or any other president, be able to fire a Commission member because that member differs with his views." Much to Biden's chagrin, the seeming victory quickly evaporated.[66]

The White House knew the president had to sign the bill to moot the case, thus avoiding a possible negative decision in the higher courts. The Justice Department, stung by its loss in court, wanted to include a "constitutional reservations" section in the signing statement, deeming the legislation "probably unconstitutional."[67]

This time, however, the White House staff bowed slightly to pragmatism. They took into account Director of Communications David Gergen's view that the Justice Department statement sounded "negative in tone and conveys the impression that we want to curtail the powers of the Commission." Gergen insisted that the signing statement created an "opportunity to put this controversy behind us and take a positive step forward in the President's commitment to civil rights and equal opportunity." Consequently, in his November 30 statement, Reagan simply reaffirmed his "commitment to equal opportunity as the central mission" of the commission and predicted that the commission's "best years are yet to come." Nevertheless, he noted that the Justice Department had reservations about the constitutional implications of the legislation and "appended" their reservations.[68]

Even so, the abandonment of any pragmatism or spirit of compromise came swiftly. OMB director David Stockman raised the difficulty of deciding on appointees in view of Meese's agreement that Smith and Ruckelshaus would stay. He found that "the bill poses real risks" for the president. "If at least five members of the new Commission do not support a changed Commission direction, an impasse could occur over your statutory designees for the Chairman, Vice Chairman, and Staff Director, since, as noted above, the bill requires those three designees to have the concurrence of a majority of the Commission's members."[69]

At this point Meese and the president acted in bad faith, betraying the trust of the senators who believed they had protected the commission. Knowing that Smith and Ruckelshaus could not be relied on to support Pendleton, Reagan decided to violate the agreement by not reappointing them. Instead, he appointed Esther Gonzalez Buckley, a high school science teacher from Laredo, Texas, the Webb County Republican chair, after making sure she would vote to confirm Pendleton and would follow administration policy. The administration then agreed with Republicans in the House to appoint Destro instead of Ruckelshaus. They had their five votes to confirm Pendleton as chair and Chavez as staff director.[70]

Reagan had made good on his boast to Pendleton, who had come in to see him on November 15, 1983, after the president's return from Tokyo. Reagan wrote in his diary that Pendleton complained about the "so-called compromise to keep me from Making new appointments," but Reagan told him: "The boys are playing games but I think I can snooker them."[71]

The White House actions infuriated members of Congress and their constituents. The president had essentially opted to appoint members who could not survive Senate confirmation in place of Smith and Ruckelshaus, who had been confirmed by the Senate. Meese, it appears, lied publicly on December 1 when he stated that "at no time during the negotiations was there discussion or agreement to particular personalities or individuals." He said that Dole agreed with him, but it was Dole who had said Ruckelshaus and Smith would be reappointed, and Dole did not confirm Meese's statement. The United Press International wire service story, which was tucked away in the White House files, noted that Meese's "statement conflicts with accounts of key senators and civil rights leaders." These senators and leaders insisted that Smith's reappointment had been part of the agreement.[72]

Civil rights groups announced that they felt they had been "betrayed" and "double-crossed" by President Reagan and other Republicans. African American, Hispanic, and women's organizations expressed their dismay that two distinguished Republicans, Jill Ruckelshaus and Mary Louise Smith, had been discarded. The agreement had been announced on November 12, and the White House did not begin to deny it until December 1. Kathy Wilson, chair of the National Women's Political Caucus, said, "I'm a Republican, a woman and a feminist, and I feel double-crossed." The Leadership Conference's Neas asserted, "The White House has accomplished the goal it has been seeking for six months—to pack the Commission."[73]

Some Republicans vented their anger at the abandonment of Smith, who had given such long and dutiful service to their party. Her home state senator Republican Charles Grassley, who disagreed with her about almost everything, including her support of abortion rights, said he was "extremely disappointed." Smith had "gained national stature as a Republican leader." While "extremely sensitive to civil rights issues, she has avoided extremes of both the right and the left politically" and is a "moderating force." He also objected that neither he nor other Republican leaders in his state were consulted, even though they had been consulted upon her original appointment. He asked the president for reconsideration. Iowa Republican congressman Cooper Evans was also "disappointed" and thought it did "serious political damage" to Reagan and "other Republicans who must run for Federal office in 1984, particularly in Iowa."[74]

Ruckelshaus was angry at the whole chain of events. She had tried to get the White House staff to understand that firing commissioners created more problems than it solved. We would be given greater visibility and a platform to denounce their actions with more publicity. She was particularly incensed at the treatment of Mary Louise Smith, a role model and an icon for Republican women. The press reported Ruckelshaus and other Republican women as proclaiming, "I want my party back" at a conference of women legislators in San Diego. Republican activists distributed a "sign-up telegram of Support for Mary Louise Smith's Re-appointment" signed by forty-four legislators at the conference. They asked that the president "recognize the long-time support and effort of Mary Louise Smith in behalf of all Republicans" by reappointing her.

White House staffers developed an all-purpose response, stating the president's philosophical commitment to equal opportunity "under which individuals are judged on their merit, not their race or sex." His

appointees shared that approach. This did not mean, however, "any criticism of Mrs. Smith and her record of service to the Republican party
and the nation." The letter did a disservice to Smith and Ruckelshaus,
who simply thought Pendleton, with his bombast and exaggerated criticisms of civil rights leaders, should not chair the Civil Rights Commission. They regarded him as an embarrassment to their party. When I sat
next to Vice President George Bush all evening at a Joint Center for
Political Studies dinner that I moderated, where Barbara Bush received
an award, I asked him about the president's treatment of Mary Louise
and Jill. He laconically replied, "What happened to Mary Louise was
unfortunate but Jill is a good girl and she'll land on her feet."[75]

The civil rights groups were adamant that Ramirez and I accept
appointment to the commission again even though we would be completely outvoted. The whole episode had taken a toll. Nonetheless, both
Ramirez and I reluctantly agreed to stay. Speaker of the House O'Neill
appointed me, upon the recommendation of Majority Leader Jim
Wright (D-Tex.), and President Pro Tempore of the Senate Strom
Thurmond (R-S.C.), upon Senator Robert Byrd's (D-W.Va.) recommendation, appointed Ramirez as the two Democratic congressional
appointees. Senator Howard Baker appointed Tennessee labor and
human rights commissioner Francis Guess, a pro–civil rights moderate
Republican. "The appointment of Mr. Guess, regardless of his qualifications, will not remedy the grievous damage that has been inflicted upon
the independence of the Commission," said the Leadership Conference.
As the "reconstituted" commission began its work, Pendleton thanked
the president and told him he could not "wait" for the first meeting so
he could begin to reevaluate "mandatory busing and quotas."[76]

Before the first meeting, NAACP-LDF staffer Phyllis McClure said
she expected "a redefinition of what civil rights issues and what legal
precedents are." I foresaw "a complete abandonment of the Commission's normal fact-finding procedures," including hearings, in order to
reach a predetermined result.[77]

If the Democrats had not controlled the House and if some moderate Republicans had not remained in both houses, no compromise at all
would have occurred. The betrayal of the compromise reflected the
power of the right in the Republican Party and the passing of the liberal
Republicans. Smith and Ruckelshaus faithfully reflected the aspirations
of the modern women's rights movement, but the Reaganites saw that
period as past. In a perversion of identity politics, they hoped that
Pendleton and his crew could lead women and minorities to embrace
conservative anti–civil rights Republican philosophy.

In pursuit of these objectives, the commission became simply another lobbying arm for the White House. Meese implemented Reagan's devastating blow to the commission's ability to function. The commission was no longer a civil forum in which commissioners from different perspectives would reason together and reach mostly unanimous recommendations across ideological and partisan lines. It had become yet another venue for political jockeying.

CHAPTER VIII

Speak First, Investigate Never

HOLDING A PRESS CONFERENCE at their first meeting conducted at the luxurious resort Hunt Valley Inn just outside
Baltimore, Maryland, in January 1984, the reconstituted commission celebrated their triumph. Chairman Pendleton, exulting in
Reagan's capture of the commission, told the reporters that now the
commission supported President Reagan's civil rights policies. Ramirez
and I, he said, were just "sore losers" for complaining that the commission had become an "outhouse public relations arm of the White
House" after their takeover.[1]

Under Pendleton and Chavez, traditional procedures and fact-
finding were for the most part abandoned. Instead of investigations and
hearings, they issued reports and policy statements in collusion with the
Reagan White House to support the civil rights retrenchment. These
pronouncements were prepared by contractors hired from conservative
think tanks or by political staff who had usurped the roles of the civil servants. The reconfigured commission abandoned the agency's sentinel
responsibility—to monitor the administration—because, as Chairman
Pendleton said, "we are part of the administration." The polarization on
the commission reflected the national disagreements over civil rights.
The Reagan commissioners had made up their minds and brooked no
objections. Commission members traded political barbs and fought with
each other; the collegial, amicable debates were gone. So, too, was the
commission's independence.[2]

The new commission performed exactly as President Reagan and the
White House staff had planned. It urged a rightward political drift of
the country and reinforced the decline in government efforts to combat
discrimination and advance equal opportunity. In its zeal to turn back
the clock, however, it overreached and consequently failed to undermine the civil rights laws completely.

The Reagan administration's strategy included appointing African

Americans, Latinos, and women who would help to undermine the civil rights laws. Their appointments, sometimes to jobs such appointees had not held before, led to many firsts but in reality to a bleak agenda for progress. Pendleton and Chavez, Michael Williams at the Department of Education, Clarence Thomas at the Department of Education and then the EEOC provide just a few examples of the new climate. At the commission, the White House strategy of appointing Chavez to fill a quota for a Hispanic to take a leadership role, ironically in attacking quotas, made the work of opposing Reagan harder. As the *Financial Times* put it, "The spotlight has now turned to Miss Linda Chavez, the commission's Staff Director, an articulate Hispanic, who claims as a goal the establishment of a colourblind nation."[3]

Ramirez and I consistently opposed redirecting the commission's policy in the absence of changes in the laws. We demanded that the Reaganites at least adhere to established government procedures. In this effort, we had an occasional ally in Francis Guess, a black Republican from Tennessee with civil rights experience. After Guess observed the behavior of his colleagues, his shame led him to do what he could while remaining loyal to the GOP. Ramirez and I were "seeds . . . that would later grow to entangle the commission in turmoil under Reagan," predicted James Reston, Jr., in *Rolling Stone* in 1986.[4]

The Reagan administration's efforts to downplay discrimination in employment, facilitate segregated education, and ignore the laws they were entrusted to enforce did not go unopposed. The Leadership Conference coalition worked hard to maintain the hard-won victories of the civil rights movement. The Women's Legal Defense Fund and the National Women's Law Center vowed to protect Title IX's prohibition of sex discrimination in education. Working with other civil rights groups, the women retained the federal government's authority to cut off funds to institutions that discriminated on the basis of race, disability, sex, or age. That authority came from an early Civil Rights Commission recommendation, first enacted in the Civil Rights Act of 1964 and included in every subsequent anti-discrimination law. The NAACP and NAACP-LDF worked to gain a new fair housing law that would add strong penalties to the weak 1968 provisions passed after the assassination of Martin Luther King, Jr. Karen Narasaki, of the National Asian Pacific American Legal Consortium, led the successful fight to enact a redress law for the World War II Japanese American internment.[5]

Against the racial screeds of the administration, which drew white Democratic votes, creating a sustainable Republican majority, the civil rights groups won a surprising number of victories. They beat back Reagan's nomination of Robert Bork to the Supreme Court. The NAACP, labor unions, and international human rights organizations worked with the Congressional Black Caucus to impose sanctions against South Africa that helped to destroy the apartheid regime. The Mexican American Legal Defense and Education Fund (MALDEF) and the National Council of La Raza, helped by the other civil rights groups, won amnesty for undocumented immigrants already in the country, in the Immigration Reform and Control Act of November 1986. Ironically, after the complacency of the Carter years, the need to fight Reagan actually strengthened the civil rights coalition.

In the House of Representatives, some opponents of Reagan's takeover of the commission wanted to abolish it, but others feared some of their constituents had not focused enough on the public debate to understand the closure of a civil rights agency. Divided over how to respond, the opponents settled for oversight and evaluation of the commission's management practices. It is usual for the General Accounting Office to find management problems when they review an agency. This time it was even easier to find widespread "irregularities in the personnel practices, travel records and financial management of the commission" since the takeover. The Reaganites paid practically no attention to procedure and management. They were interested only in promoting the administration's policies. On the basis of the GAO findings, Congress incapacitated the agency, cutting the budget from $11.5 million to $7.5 million.[6]

Traditionally, the commission's January meeting served as a planning session to discuss future work. Instead, ushering in a long, cold spring, the Reagan appointees were bent on establishing their credibility and announcing their views. Recognizing that the public valued the commission's much-discussed independence, they sought to declare themselves free of allegiance to the White House. In a public relations move, at odds with White House files replete with strategic agreements between the commission and the White House staff, Bunzel proposed a statement falsely declaring the commission to be independent, to which the White House, when asked by the press, chose not to respond. Bunzel was addressing press reports on Pendleton's visit to Nebraska to intervene in a controversy between some Christian fundamentalists and education officials over their operation of a school without a certification charter. Although Pendleton saw nothing wrong, and indeed rushed to help the White House on any occasion, Bunzel wanted interested observers to believe that a commission majority chosen because of its ideological agreement with the administration just happened to "independently" support the White House.[7]

The White House developed some sensitivity to handling the independence issue. When Pendleton scheduled a meeting with Reagan in the summer of 1984, the press office expressed "concerns about Penny arriving in the West lobby—press visibility etc.," given the criticism that the commission was "simply a public relations arm of the White House." The press office staff thought, however, that "the symbolism of getting him in through the back door (and then through the west basement) is somewhat troubling." Senior staff decided that the press should be told that the president and Pendleton discussed reports and other initiatives of the commission in the first term and "the prospects of continued economic growth that would lead to improved employment opportunities for minorities."[8]

Further distancing themselves from commission work in progress, at the Hunt Valley meeting the Reaganites rejected the staff's draft on the employment of Eastern and Southern Europeans. They blamed the need for a fuller discussion of the "adverse" effect of affirmative action. They then canceled a report on the negative effect of student financial aid cuts on minority students. After that came the elimination of a standard survey on the status of women and minorities, which was replaced by a report on the decline of race and sex discrimination.[9]

These first steps were just the beginning. Over the next few months, the Reaganites scheduled pro forma public proceedings to hear selectively from experts before announcing the conclusions they already had reached. They hired contract employees to replace civil servants in order to have predetermined reports produced. They stacked the membership of the state advisory committees with soul mates who had no record of interest in civil rights. They completely ignored their responsibility to monitor federal enforcement agencies.

When they proposed to look at the negative effects of affirmative action in higher education without convening hearings, soliciting public comment, or conducting field investigations, Ramirez and I dissented strongly. After announcing that they neither agreed nor disagreed with previous commission positions, they denounced a federal court order finding discrimination in the Detroit Police Department even though the federal district court found that African Americans had been deliberately excluded from hiring and promotions for years. The percentage of black police officers in Detroit reflected the city's majority black population after the hiring practices changed, but those hired were not promoted. Therefore, the judge ordered promotion from two separate promotion lists until the discrimination was remedied. Although the Supreme Court left the decision standing, the Reagan Justice Department echoed the denunciations issued by the Reagan commissioners. Ramirez and I dissented because the commission, after carefully studying the issues, had always supported a court's order for this type of penalty when blatant discrimination was found.[10]

Our dissent noted our agreement with the Supreme Court that "when appropriate findings [of discrimination] have been made by judicial, legislative, or administrative bodies with competence to act in this area," government may take race—and sex, for that matter—into account to remedy past discrimination. We also complained about the Reaganite commissioners' propensity to "speak first and investigate later." They seemed to believe that commission decisions were only a matter of philosophy, instead of the result of hard investigative work and analysis.[11]

The White House staff, feeling elated along with their appointees, at

Chairman Pendleton and the author, in her role as commissioner, arguing over commission report, April 11, 1986.

having taken over the commission, refused to respond to criticism even from local Republican leaders. When Jose Nunez, chairman of the Republican National Hispanic Assembly of Colorado, complained that their actions made it hard to "win minorities and women over to the party," they sent him a bland acknowledgment. In their view, the appointment of Chavez and Pendleton was proof of their commitment to equity for women and minorities.[12]

After Hunt Valley, Ramirez and I devoted ourselves to issuing strong dissents to their reports and statements in order to reinforce the existing civil rights laws as best we could. In doing so, we aided the civil rights coalition in discrediting the commission. In addition to dissenting, I consulted frequently with civil rights leaders to keep abreast of their efforts and to share with them our plans.

The Reaganite commissioners, in their back-channel public relations manipulations with the White House, insisted on suppressing anything that disclosed contradictions to their public commitment to Martin Luther King, Jr.'s color-blind society and the claim that it had been abandoned by the civil rights community. In pursuit of this theme, the commission occasionally pushed the administration to take actions reinforcing their stance.

In April 1984, White House files reveal, commission Vice Chair Morris Abram urged the president to publicly admonish his Department of Education for threatening his alma mater, the University of Georgia, with a funds cutoff because they used a graduation test that discriminated against African Americans seeking to graduate. As a leading opponent of special efforts to assist minorities, he was embarrassed when the episode was widely reported in the media, and Governor Joe Harris was resisting this "overreaching." Abram wanted the president to affirm the administration and the commission's view that "the use of racial preference as a remedy for discrimination is an abhorrent practice."

Abram also objected that the Department of Education was "recommending the set aside of monies for scholarships only for black students." Ignoring the university's long history as a legally segregated, taxpayer-supported institution that refused to admit blacks, Abram wanted the president to reverse the policy in their shared interest in a "colourblind" policy and "educational excellence."

The White House staff, including OMB's Horowitz; the assistant attorney general for civil rights, William Bradford Reynolds; and Secretary of Education Terrell Bell worried over deciding on a response. They did not want to appear to condone segregation of a higher-education institution after the Bob Jones tax exemption debacle. However, they did not want to appear less committed to color blindness than their commission.

Upon reading their draft reply to Abram, the assistant White House counsel, John Roberts, thought they should fudge the issue to avoid appearing to criticize their education secretary. Though "hotly and angrily disputed by Michael Horowitz," the letter was "too hostile in tone." It "conveys the impression that the President knows there is no actual discrimination at Georgia despite the word of his education secretary when the president had no opinion on the subject." Roberts would say instead, "If true, such a denial of equal opportunity to individuals will need to be corrected." His revision, he suggested, "makes the point without overkill."[13]

However, after considering staff and Education Secretary Bell's views, Chief of Staff Baker decided they should pacify Abram but not entangle the president, who should not sign the letter. John Svahn, assistant for policy development, sent the letter, telling Abram the issues were being handled consistently "with the principles of equal opportunity and educational excellence" and advising him to talk to Bell rather than relying upon the newspapers, which spread "more confusion than enlightenment."[14]

The collusion between the commission and the White House went into high gear when I asked that the agenda for a commission meeting include press accounts that Reagan had been endorsed for reelection by the Ku Klux Klan. I wanted a discussion about whether the Klan had misinterpreted the administration's policies as agreeing with their own views as a way to force honest commission consideration of the Reagan civil rights enforcement record.

But Chavez and Abram worked with Chief of Staff Baker's office to foreclose any discussion and to head in a different direction by attacking the Democratic candidates in the presidential race.

At the May 1984 meeting, with press that had been alerted, Abram announced that, without my knowledge, he had referred my agenda request to the president for a response. Reagan's reply, said Abram, "repudiated support from the Klan or any groups having similar views." I objected that I did not understand how a memo I had sent to the staff director as an agenda item ended up in the hands of the president and became the subject of a letter from Reagan.

White House files reveal that Baker staffer James Ciconni was told to draft the letter after Abram and Chavez gave them my memo. They agreed that "it is preferable to send the letter to Abram than to Berry." That way I would be caught by surprise. He thought they should be prepared to release it if there were further press questions. But whatever they did, they should "have something in Abram's hands before the commission meeting."[15]

Abram and Bunzel first cut off any discussion of my agenda item on Reagan and the Klan endorsement by distributing the Reagan reply. Then they executed the other part of the plan. For the first time in the history of the commission, and without any authority to do so, they threatened to take "action" against individuals for expressing their opinions and for their associations. They expressed concern about Democratic presidential primary contender Jesse Jackson's association with Louis Farrakhan and voted to tell Jackson that if he "has not repudiated the sentiments and endorsement of Louis Farrakhan before our next meeting," we would discuss his behavior and take action against him. They made the same demand of Vice President Mondale. Needless to say, the commission had no power to actually take action against anyone for his or her views. They were blatantly misusing the commission for political purposes. Embracing the independence argument, they sent Mondale an objection to his statement that if he were president he would "fire the new Commissioners and hire those who were fired."

The Reagan commissioners had achieved their objectives, but in the process they reinforced the belief of civil rights advocates that Reagan had eroded the commission's independence by making it just another political arm of the White House.[16]

The Reagan years, with increased polarization and lack of leadership on opportunity issues, saw an increase in racial violence. The commission, unlike in previous years, held no hearings in local communities or any investigations of the issues. We did, however, unanimously issue a statement analyzing and denouncing bigotry and violence against Asian Americans, a statement that did not mention the Reagan administration's inaction in this area.

The report was instigated by the death of Vincent Chin, a Chinese American, and the subsequent treatment of those responsible. Chin was attacked by two white autoworkers in Detroit on June 1, 1982, one of whom beat him to death. Incorrectly thinking that Chin was Japanese, the assailant blamed Chin for the ailing auto industry.

After Chin's attackers were given only probation and fines in court, Asian Americans mobilized and the civil rights movement demanded a federal investigation into a possible civil rights violation. In June 1984 the alleged murderer was convicted in federal court of violating Chin's civil rights, but his conviction was later overturned. After a civil damage award, he fled the state.[17]

Ramirez, Guess, and I tried repeatedly during the Reaganite hegemony at the commission to stimulate investigations into racial violence, but with no success. I proposed in December 1986 that we ask federal agencies for reports on how they were addressing what appeared to be an increase in racial violence. This was after the beating of three African American construction workers on December 20 in Howard Beach, a white section of the New York City borough of Queens. They were assaulted by a gang of white youths wielding baseball bats and tree limbs. One of the black men, Michael Griffith, twenty-three, died when he ran into the path of an oncoming automobile while fleeing his attackers. New York's governor, Mario Cuomo, after meeting with black leaders, had appointed a special prosecutor to investigate the beatings, allegations of police brutality, and charges of a cover-up by investigators.

Instead of the discussion I asked for so that we could determine whether and how the commission should proceed, in January 1987 the majority proposed a national assessment of racial incidents done by the SACs in their states. I found that ridiculous given that the SACs, as a result of budget cuts, had no staff support. Besides, the Reagan SAC appointees lacked credibility.[18]

When their proposal for SAC investigations was reported in the press, Leadership Conference on Civil Rights chairman and NAACP executive director Benjamin Hooks wrote to Congressman Don Edwards, the commission's oversight chair, calling anything the commission did suspect because it was a "propaganda arm" of the White House, "a sham and a national disgrace." Pendleton announced that the study could not be done because only Maryland kept crime statistics by race and religion. He said he opposed a commission investigation or a national commission report because the issues were not that serious. He explained: "Suppose you find out there's more incidents. So what? What do you do? Let's speculate that out to the point where, yes, everybody is beating everybody else. No public policy is going to change that."[19]

The commission was proud of its continued partnership with the administration. When the Supreme Court in the Memphis case *Firefighters v. Stotts* found that a lower court may not order an employer to lay off employees with greater seniority in preference to those with lesser seniority, even if the new employees were hired only as a result of an order ending discrimination, the commission expressed the same air of celebration reported at the Justice Department, agreeing with Assistant Attorney General Reynolds that it was a "slam dunk" for the administration and the end of affirmative action. The staff quickly prepared and issued a "report" called *Towards an Understanding of Stotts* to explain the validity and morality of the decision.[20]

Cardenas and I, of course, dissented. Then, when the Supreme Court decided *Johnson v. Transportation Agency*, supporting affirmative action in a sex discrimination case, I suggested that the commission issue a "Toward an Understanding of Johnson" statement, replicating the one they had issued praising the Court for appearing to reject affirmative action in the *Stotts* case. In *Johnson*, the Court upheld an affirmative action plan adopted by the Transportation Agency of Santa Clara County, California, in the face of a challenge by a white man who had been passed over in favor of a white woman. Both sought a job dispatching road crews, a position that had never been held by a woman. The court said an employer may sometimes favor women and minority-group employees to remedy "a conspicuous imbalance" in the employer's workforce.

Reagan political appointee deputy general counsel Neal Devins produced a memo criticizing the Court for preferences against white men, filled with misleading statements. The commission decided that commissioners could issue their own individual statements on the matter. Guess, Ramirez, and I issued a joint statement that the case "gives careful approval to much needed voluntary efforts to improve the employment status of women in a gradual way."[21]

On affirmative action, in addition to court decisions, the policy shifts under way at the enforcement agencies occurred with the support of Reagan's Civil Rights Commission. Clarence Thomas, who was first appointed to head civil rights enforcement at the Department of Education and then to head the EEOC, gutted the use of goals and timetables to achieve diversity and ended the use of class-action lawsuits that relied on statistical evidence of discriminatory effects, all in order to make it easier for employers to hire without worrying about penalties for discrimination. The EEOC was supposed to require federal agencies to prepare affirmative action plans with goals and timetables. William Bennett, director of the National Endowment for the Humanities, made known publicly his refusal to submit an affirmative action plan to the EEOC, with Thomas's acquiescence. After a congressional hearing and wide publicity over these developments, I asked that staff gather information on the dispute, to no avail.

Then the Reaganites planned a forum on affirmative action in order to seduce civil rights advocacy groups to make presentations, after which the commissioners, claiming fairness and balance, would issue an anti–civil rights position. I consulted with the civil rights leadership about how to defuse these plans. The NAACP and other civil rights groups appeared at the April 1985 proceeding, only to denounce the commission and stage a walkout. They asserted, loudly, that the commission lacked a serious agenda. Sure enough, the commission predictably reiterated its opposition to affirmative action.[22]

A few weeks after the April 1985 affirmative action forum, the commission showed its lack of interest in diversity of appointments and commitments to civil rights by completing its six-months-long "purge" of the SACs by removing pro–civil rights members, even though they served as volunteers. As a result of the forty-nine-state purge, only one position held by a white male in North Dakota remained unchanged. Of the new chairmen, thirty-three were white men with, in a new departure for the commission, no previous civil rights or advisory committee experience. The actions served to reinforce the hypocrisy of the Reaganites' merit-based color-blind society.[23]

The height of the Reaganites' manipulation occurred with a report on comparable worth, the doctrine that women and men should be paid on the basis of intrinsic worth of jobs as a means for eliminating sex-based wage discrimination. At Hunt Valley, Ramirez and I, at first not wary enough, in the spirit of collegiality, supported the Reaganites' proposal for a consultation of experts on the subject. We knew that, according to established procedures, no position would be taken until after a field investigation or a public hearing with sworn witnesses. We soon discovered expectations had changed.

Chavez, without waiting even for the consultation of experts, told the media that the concept of comparable worth, was "a fundamentally radical one that would alter our existing marketplace economy, by having courts and bureaucracies replace individual and collective bargaining." The White House agreed.[24]

When Chavez's memo to the commissioners describing plans for the consultation appeared in the *Washington Post*, Terry Hart Lee, the president of Federally Employed Women, wrote to the president complaining that the National Academy of Sciences in 1981 had already reported that the wage gap is partly due to discrimination and that closing it would help to reduce the "feminization of poverty." If the commission pursued a study, she hoped it would have a "more objective, unbiased attitude than is evident" in Chavez's memo. She also hoped the commission would not be used for "taxpayer-supported proofs for far Right ideology."

Continuing their relationship, the White House asked Chavez to suggest a reply. She recommended: "The President believes the commission will prepare a balanced report which examines all viewpoints of the Comparable Worth theory." After the consultation, she sent the papers to the White House for review before they were printed, while the recommendations were being written. Scholars whose studies supported comparable worth participated, apparently not believing the warnings of civil rights advocates that their work would be cited only to prove balance in the predetermined report.

Without official notice, Pendleton and Chavez released the papers at a press conference in November 1984 with conclusions and recommendations. Pendleton declared comparable worth "the looniest idea since looney tunes," and Chavez emphasized the radicalism of the idea. They knew that the State of Washington case, then in the federal courts, promised to be the defining decision on the subject. The commission not only had failed to engage in field investigations or to have public comment, but had not even discussed the papers. I told the press, "This is a political preemptive strike" to support the Reagan administration's opposition to comparable worth without a fair hearing.[25]

By the June 1985 meeting, the civil rights community was worried about how to rescue the endangered State of Washington comparable worth case. Congresswoman Mary Rose Oakar (D-Ohio) asked the commissioners to testify on the commission's report. Pendleton declined, pleading not enough notice, but I testified to the procedural irregularities and explained where some of the scholarly papers had been taken out of context. The committee asked the GAO to analyze the report, and the agency found it error-ridden and "shoddy."

Then Pendleton announced a press conference to respond to the GAO study. Bunzel and Abram, seeing that the Pendleton commission had inflamed the public debate but not gained new supporters for an anti–civil rights posture, suggested postponing any press conference until everyone had read the report and the staff responses to it. It was not just comparable worth that caught reporters' attention; Pendleton received widespread publicity for calling black leaders "new racists" who had "led blacks into a political Jonestown" by supporting the Democratic Party, just as surely as Jim Jones had induced his followers to suicide by drinking poisoned Kool-Aid. In September the federal appellate court decision in the Washington case against comparable work cited the commission's comparable worth "study."[26]

After the papers were printed, the Reaganites issued a formal report with findings and recommendations, as if they had held a fact-finding investigation. Chavez, knowing she had the votes, stated it was "a fair and balanced consultation." Ramirez and I dissented. Guess abstained because, as Tennessee commissioner of labor, he dealt with compensation issues.[27]

We had not been able to save comparable worth, but the civil rights community was able to save legislation repudiating the Supreme Court decision in *Grove City College v. Bell* (1984) limiting the power of fund cutoffs to education institutions that discriminated on the basis of race. When the case was first decided, Ramirez and I failed to persuade the commission to denounce the decision as inconsistent with the principle of "no federal funds to support discrimination," which had been originally established by the commission. After the Supreme Court decision, Reynolds suggested that the ruling might be applied to statutes on race and disability.[28]

Destro wanted to support cutting off funds only to hospitals, as a way of advancing his agenda of forcing hospitals not to permit abortions or the implementation of a "right to die" policy. To entice his colleagues, he inserted in a proposed commission statement language decrying the use of racial quotas, but we refused to join in "throwing red meat to the anti–affirmative action wolves." No final vote occurred.[29]

When I introduced a resolution asking Congress to review the impact of the *Grove City* Supreme Court decision on other civil rights statutes, the commission majority tabled it to await a memorandum on the commission's jurisdiction, although the commission had previously discussed the subject, and jurisdiction had already been determined. The Court said that when sex discrimination existed in a program within an institution federal funds could be cut off for that program but not for the entire institution, as had been the rule in the past. Then I worked very hard, along with the civil rights groups, to support the Civil Rights Restoration Act overturning the *Grove City* decision. I suggested that the commission should support the act to make sure that taxpayer funds were not used to support discrimination on the basis of race, sex, age, or disability. Destro did not want to vote, as he was conflicted because of his desire to preserve fund termination as a weapon against hospitals in decisions involving terminally ill newborn infants, which had become a major public discussion. However, he did not want to defund for discrimination based on race or sex.[30]

While the debate in Congress continued, the Reaganites arranged for a panel of "experts" on the *Grove City* case and the Civil Rights Restoration Act. Destro abandoned his anti-abortion and "right to die" issues, and they decided to simply support the administration's position that the civil rights statutes should be interpreted as narrowly as possible. If funds went to a college for student aid, the institution could discriminate everywhere on campus except in the student aid office.[31]

The administration's policy shifts, decimation of the SACs, and projection of African American and Hispanic faces without civil rights consciousness elicited widespread criticism. On May 25, 1985, Republican Denice Wheeler, "a conservative Mormon" who chaired the Wyoming Commission for Women, complained to Reagan about appointments to that state's advisory committee. She told him, "One of our most prejudiced and ill-informed legislators," former House Speaker Russ Donley, had been appointed to the SAC. She included news clippings describing Donley's various statements and activities. He was quoted as saying, "There may not be a point in this state" in having a civil rights committee. He said he might have been appointed because he "isn't much on comparable worth," since studies showing that women are paid substantially below men are "phonies." Ms. Wheeler told Reagan that she thought "manipulation" of committees would not make civil rights problems go away. In one week, Donley had made "a laughing-stock of our party." She hoped, in vain, that they could "correct the mistake." The White House believed in its people and, not caring who criticized them, ignored her.[32]

Verna Carson, a California NAACP regional director, reminded the president that in California he had very different African Americans, "the exact opposite of Clarence Pendleton," working for him. Robert Keys, for example, Reagan's director of community relations, had struggled "to enlighten" Reagan when he was governor, "despite the influence of several persons" close to him. Keys, she recalled, was very "unlike some of those around you now who lead the negative input." She thought he should "fire" Pendleton, whom she saw as "a disgrace to you and your administration," and reach out to African Americans "with the same emphasis that you are reaching out to the Russians. The Russians did not vote for you either." The staff did not respond to her letter.[33]

Black conservatives, though, urged the commission and the president on. Walter Williams, a self-described conservative black professor of economics at George Mason University, wrote Reagan to "commend" Pendleton for the "courageous steps he has taken in the highly politicized areas of race and sex discrimination." He thought Pendleton discussed issues that "most Americans have wanted raised a long time ago." Also, his position is supported by "mainstream America both black and white." Reagan thanked Williams for his letter, which "truly brightened my day." Reagan told him, "I called Clarence Pendleton when the latest press assaults occurred and told him of my whole-hearted support. I'll relay your words to him and know he will be very proud and pleased." He continued: "I share your view, we must have a totally color-blind citizenry and I pledge to you that is my goal."

No wonder that, with Reagan's repeated encouragements, Pendleton ignored my private attempts to persuade him to tone down his remarks. I told him they would eventually create problems for him. He responded during one of these discussions that I did not understand: "Look, white people take care of me."[34]

With her mission at the commission accomplished, shortly after the comparable worth report, Chavez went to the White House as deputy assistant to the president for public liaison, carrying with her, according to Pendleton, the "tribute" of several commissioners. Max Green, her special assistant, without any visible qualifications for the position, became acting staff director by a procedure that remains obscure. He then joined Chavez as special assistant for liaison with Jewish groups in the White House.[35]

Chavez pursued a successful career as a conservative Hispanic opponent of civil rights. Effectively using her commission experience—identified wrongly at various times as former chair, former commissioner, or former director of the commission on Civil Rights instead of staff director—she became president of the Center for Equal Opportunity, an author, and a political commentator in the media. She also lost a bid for the Senate from Maryland, where the goal of comparable worth was important for many federally employed voters. The Center for Equal Opportunity describes its CEO as seeking to "block the expansion of racial preferences."[36]

Disgusted with the Reaganites, the congressional oversight subcommittee, chaired by Don Edwards (D-Calif.), asked the GAO to audit the commission because of complaints from civil service staff that Pendleton misspent money on personal items. Numerous articles written by Jay Harris in Gannett newspapers and *USA Today* in 1982 and 1983 had already detailed Pendleton's questionable financial dealings while he was head of the Urban League in San Diego, but the White House and the Senate committee that confirmed him ignored the subject. According to press accounts, he had left the Urban League as a result.[37]

At the November 1985 meeting the Reagan commissioners discussed the burdens created by the GAO audit. At the same meeting, they concurred in the White House nomination of Alfred Latham as staff director. Latham, an attorney with a law degree from Vanderbilt, served as chief counsel to member Patricia Diaz Dennis, an anti-union Reagan appointee on the National Labor Relations Board, who later became an FCC commissioner.[38]

After the GAO concluded its audit of the commission, Edwards held hearings in April 1986 on the waste, abuse, and potential fraud that the audit had revealed. Utah Republican Orrin Hatch, the oversight chair in the Senate, complained to Edwards that the audit covered only the reconstituted commission. He ignored the fact that the commission's Republican appointees had initially requested an audit for the pre-Pendleton years but then retreated when they saw it would interfere with their policy work. Hatch wanted the hearing delayed until the completion of an audit covering the earlier period. After Edwards ignored Hatch's ploy, Hatch raised questions about the objectivity of the audit. The GAO, accustomed to being accused of bias, was unfazed by his complaints.[39]

The GAO concluded that the allegations that it had been asked to investigate were true. The commission had hired larger numbers of non-career employees and consultants mainly to prepare the research studies. Most of the consultant appointments examined by the GAO had irregularities, including the absence of any information showing that the people hired were qualified for the work.

The GAO found that the chairman and his female special assistant, Sydney Novell, were billing almost full-time for part-time positions. The GAO noted that the Small Business Administration had an investigation under way of the chairman and his special assistant's business dealings, but had not completed the work. Pendleton's travel vouchers showed that other sources paid for 45 of the 117 trips he took over four years. He did not, as required, identify the sources so that staff at the commission or the GAO could determine whether they were improper.

The GAO found that Pendleton engaged in illegal lobbying by telling audiences to "attempt to defeat the Civil Rights Restoration Act of 1985," for example. On state advisory committees, the GAO reported that the rechartered committee membership and the chairs had become almost devoid of minorities. The chairs, who controlled the SAC meeting agenda and relationships with headquarters, were overwhelmingly white and male. The GAO also found that the SACs had ceased issuing reports or holding fact-finding meetings.[40]

The GAO reported that Staff Director Chavez denied that she used the commission car and driver for unofficial purposes. However, employees attested that the driver transported the staff director from home to work, an impermissible use under the funds appropriated by Congress.[41]

When Pendleton testified before the House Oversight Committee on the GAO report in April 1986, he denounced it as "unfair" but said he would let Latham, as the agency's chief executive officer, answer the committee's questions. Morris Abram chimed in to complain that the GAO found only one example "that any law was broken." He also asserted that the audit resulted from "partisan political purposes," primarily because the "social engineers have lost their monopoly of the commission."

However, controversy that Abram did not expect erupted when Congresswoman Patricia Schroeder (D-Colo.) disclosed that among the consultants hired were Abram's son and friends of his. Schroeder pointed out to Abram that one of the friends had bragged that he did no work during the summer he was employed at the commission.[42]

A few days later, Roger Wilkins, Pulitzer Prize–winning journalist and nephew of longtime NAACP executive director Roy Wilkins, wrote Abram, whom he knew, to tease him about the widely publicized episode. Wilkins reminded "Morris" that he had attacked affirmative action in an interview in the *Washington Post* as "among other things, a way for civil rights leaders to obtain good jobs for their children." Now "viewed in that context, your exchange with the Subcommittee last week about the employment of your son and his friends at the Civil Rights Commission of which you are Vice Chair was most interesting."[43]

Instead of accepting Wilkins's comments, Abram replied by accusing Wilkins and others of preferring to "excoriate" him and his children rather than debating the issues. He then launched into an extended discussion of how the personnel department cast the net wide and came up with these "talented" persons—"they hail from Harvard and Columbia, Brookings and the Urban Institute." Then he complained about "martial tactics that target innocent young men in the prime of their career," saying the criticisms reminded him of "Joseph Welch's response to [Senator Joseph McCarthy's] indiscriminate salvos against a young member of Welch's staff: 'Have you no sense of decency?' " Wilkins, in a short handwritten note, replied: "Oh Morris—Come off it! Besides, Welch stood on a platform of decency, not a pompous pillar of self-righteous racist bullshit."[44]

In his testimony before the congressional committee, Staff Director Latham complained that the "GAO would have this subcommittee and the public believe it is unable to determine whether these esteemed professors," hired as consultants, "possessed the necessary background to render advisory services to the commission." Besides, any problems were the fault of commission career employees. Essentially, the GAO exposed both the Reagan commission's practice of using non-career employees who could do the work that the White House agenda required and the distain of the Reagan commissioners and their employees for the details of administration and management. The GAO findings did nothing more than form a basis for cutting the budget. But the budget cuts undermined the new agenda setting that the Reaganites had begun.[45]

As public criticism of the Reaganite management of the commission and Pendleton's rhetoric increased, and congressional willingness to fund the commission eroded, the Reagan commissioners began to consider abandoning the enterprise. Bunzel first thought of creating a new public image by jettisoning Pendleton. But Pendleton angrily rejected the suggestion that he resign. When the whole matter became public, White House counsel explored for the president whether Pendleton could be legally forced out by the commissioners. They concluded that there existed "no case law on the power of commission members to remove a chairman, either to strip him of his rights as chairman or to remove him from the commission entirely." However, they believed that under the reconstituted structure, the "unique constitution of the commission complicates the question and precludes a certain answer."[46]

The White House became very concerned when the House subcommittee decided in July to defund the commission as of December 31, 1986. In mid-July Max Green, now a White House staffer, wrote to Patrick Buchanan that the House provision would pass but he hoped the president would appeal to Senator Warren Rudman (R-N.H.), the Senate subcommittee chair. When Will Ball, from legislative affairs, checked with Rudman, he found him "very heated in his criticism of the commission, its chairman, and its operations." But Rudman said he would try to work out "something reasonable" in conference. Ball noted that "the commission does have some supporters, for example Nathan Perlmutter of the Anti-Defamation League of B'nai B'rith." He thought the Senate "was unlikely to act unless there is White House leadership." He thought that Congress proposed to defund the commission but not to remove its legal basis for existence, so that it could be "put back in gear if the next President is someone who is responsive to the civil rights establishment."[47]

On July 30, 1986, Pendleton asked to meet with the president to discuss the defunding, but the staff was divided on whether the president should become involved. White House personnel director Robert Tuttle reacted positively because the "commission is under attack by the left. I believe that a meeting with the President and chairman Pendleton would give the President an opportunity to restate his support for the commission." However, cabinet secretary Alfred Kingon saw the issue as "a funding problem with Congress not necessary for Presidential involvement." Policy development assistant John Svahn, wanting to show support for Pendleton, asked, "How can you not accept it's the bad guys who are after him? I'll talk to Penny."[48]

As the funding dried up and the criticism mounted, the Reaganites followed Chavez's lead in leaving the commission. Abram resigned three years before his term expired to accept the largely ceremonial post of chairmanship of the Conference of Presidents of Major American Jewish Organizations, "perhaps the most important position in the Jewish community." He asked for a photo opportunity with the president, and Max Green recommended a fifteen-minute meeting, given his "stalwart support." Reagan thanked Abram for his continued "pursuit of a color-blind society."

Abram did not abandon the cause. He wrote to the president shortly after he left in late July 1986, lamenting congressional budget cuts as a "pre-emptive strike against what ultra-liberals fear will be myth-destroying truths in several monumentally important reports," which the commission would produce. One report would show the unimportance of race discrimination in employment. Civil rights leaders had "a vested interest in killing this report." Other studies on busing for integration, voting rights, and affirmative action would show the "practical bankruptcy" of civil rights policy.[49]

He advised Reagan to pursue the line of claiming that before he fixed the commission, scholars regarded it as a "joke." The president should insist that the Reagan group had made the commission "again a model of scholarly excellence and integrity." He naturally did not mention such matters as the hiring of his son and his friends, or consultants who had no obvious qualifications for the work they did. He also took no responsibility for the gutting of the SACs or his own willingness to have the independence of the commission eroded by the firing of commissioners.[50]

When one of the reports that Abram cited, showing the unimportance of race discrimination in the economic status of black men, came before the commission, I read into the record research that the consultants had omitted showing race was still a factor. Guess and I also pointed out that the Reaganites had complained that the commission, before the takeover, had done work on social and economic issues. They responded to our complaints by voting to release this wholly economic analysis to the public. However, the report did not lead the interested public to abandon the quest to end race discrimination in employment, as Pendleton and the other Reaganites had hoped.[51]

Those left among the Reaganites responded to the prospect of budget cuts by proposing a reorganization to decimate the regional office civil service staff so they could keep funds to hire consultants and produce biased reports at headquarters. Guess joined me in the losing proposition that they keep the regional staff and reestablish a monitoring function in the Washington office.[52]

Congress followed through on reducing the commission's budget from $11.8 million to $7.5 million, instead of a complete defunding. Senator Frank Lautenberg (D-N.J.) told the media that they based the appropriation on the GAO study and that the commission failed to monitor federal government civil rights enforcement. Noticing the plans of the Reaganites, Congress included earmarks specifically allocating the funds mainly to the regions and included restrictions on the number of days commissioners could work, with the chairman permitted only 125 billable days, to reinforce the law under which he served in a part-time capacity. They also limited the use of consultants and contractors. The chairman told the press, "It's a matter of getting rid of Pendleton." Furthermore, by reducing the commission's budget, "there will be a lot of money left over, because people are leaving now."

Latham, recognizing the complete lack of credibility of the enterprise he managed, but insisting that he was hobbled by Congress, left, and his special assistant, Susan Prado, who lacked any relevant qualifications, became acting staff director. In leaving, Latham wrote Reagan that after three and a half years service at the NLRB and then the commission, he wanted to return to private practice. "It is clear the commission is being punished for its principled, independent positions and scholarly studies on such issues as racial preferences and comparable worth." He took particular pride in the report on the economic status of black men.[53]

In accepting Latham's resignation, Reagan called him part of the "select group" of people they had appointed on the principle "find the best people in every field and give them the freedom and support they need to implement sound policy initiatives."[54]

As the edifice crumbled and the prospect of more consultant studies disappeared, Bunzel announced in November that he would not accept reappointment when his term expired in December. He wrote "Penny" that he would leave with "mixed feelings." In his letter to Reagan, he took no responsibility for the commission's problems. He complained that "bitter railing" at the Reaganite commissioners had started from the beginning and continued because "the commission has been caught up in an unrelenting struggle for power and control." The civil rights lobby had fought hard "to maintain a philosophical majority" and lost. If the commission succeeded, it would "alter the framework of national debate on civil rights questions . . . leaving them without a widely acceptable agenda and the national standing to which they had grown accustomed."

He had hoped the commission "could become a forum for a much needed debate on many of the difficult questions that have divided thoughtful people around the country." However, "so fierce has been the level of rhetoric that polemical skills have too often replaced careful and respectful consideration of the issues." The commission, "sad to say, has become a little Beirut on the Potomac." He also thought it had "lost its credibility." Under Pendleton's chairmanship, "the crisis of credibility and confidence has deepened." Unhappily, "the best days of the commission are over."

Ralph Neas, of the Leadership Conference on Civil Rights, told the press that he agreed with Bunzel's conclusion but not his reasoning. The Leadership Conference coalition wanted the commission abolished because it had become "a sham, a national disgrace, a perversion of what it was intended to be. It has abandoned its independence and has become a morass of mismanagement."

Bunzel papered over his own complicity and the facts. The commission had maintained its independence even under pressure before the Reagan takeover. Its studies had aided the civil rights groups as they demanded enforcement, but over the years they did not always agree. The commission supported adding sex to the commission's jurisdiction, for example, despite the NAACP's concern. The commission also insisted that the minority language protections in the Voting Rights Act had to be a part of any reauthorization, despite similar objections.

Bunzel accepted Reagan's encroachment on the commission's independence by firing commissioners so he could be appointed. He also agreed with the abandonment of the commission's sentinel responsibility and supported the hiring of ideologically biased consultants and the displacement of the advisory committee volunteers. The commission declined in credibility during his tenure, but he bore as much blame as anyone else. Reagan accepted his resignation with a simple letter of appreciation.[55]

In September, Reagan appointed Murray Friedman, the Middle Atlantic States director of the American Jewish Committee in Philadelphia, as Abram's replacement as vice chair, after Pat Buchanan's demand that they give a seat to Linda Chavez failed. This time Abram did not repeat the objection he had made when Senator Specter suggested he replace Saltzman to settle the conflict over appointments in Reagan's first term. He had called the idea of "a Jew for a Jew" an unacceptable "quota."[56]

Buckley accepted reappointment for six years as Bunzel was leaving. Reagan appointed William Barclay Allen, regarded as a reliable black conservative, who was professor of government at Harvey Mudd College and Claremont Graduate University and his appointee as a member of the National Endowment for the Humanities board, to replace Bunzel, but not until four months had passed.

The budget cuts and earmarks led to cuts in the career staff at headquarters and the disappearance of the consultants. But the waste in which they had engaged had continuing consequences. They had contracted to spend $550,000 for a school desegregation report, which Guess, Ramirez, and I had attacked as biased and useless when it was first proposed. The idea was to demolish all support for the importance of desegregated schools. Not only was the cost exorbitant, but the contractor said he had no expertise in school desegregation. The study presented to the commission broke no new ground and repeated what scholars had already published. Further, the Reaganites refused to require their researchers to undertake a new field investigation to observe some school systems. With Bunzel, Abram, and Chavez gone, the remaining Reaganites decided to dispose of the issue by publication of the report with a statement that it did not represent the commission's views.[57]

The exodus from the commission and the budget cuts occurred just in advance of the September 1987 thirtieth anniversary of the agency. Pendleton wanted the president to acknowledge the anniversary with a commemorative statement. Mel Bradley was asked to propose a schedule for a presidential announcement with Pendleton, but he told senior staffers that he found the idea counterproductive. The administration had stressed economic opportunity with African Americans, not its civil rights policy, which was controversial. The administration had not received positive responses on civil rights from blacks, and an event like this would "provoke cat-calls from the opposition." Pendleton, already feeling anxious over the departure of Bunzel and Abram as well as the budget cuts, felt rejected.[58]

Congress remained unhappy with the commission, and Pendleton wondered if it would follow through on defunding in October 1987 as the fiscal year came to an end. Edwards wrote to the president complaining that since 1985 the commission had been without a staff director for twenty out of thirty-one months. He thought "the problem is obvious, there also has not been a Deputy Staff Director, usually a career position." If rehabilitation was to occur, the commission needed a professional staff director "to transform it back into the valuable agency it once was." The White House responded with thanks for his views.

Pendleton responded to the letter from the White House, telling Edwards that the budget cuts made it hard to keep staff. "As long as the commission must operate in this climate of uncertainty I will not recommend to the President that he appoint a permanent Staff Director." He insisted that "despite the severe impediments of Congressional micro-management, the commission has performed admirably."[59]

As 1988 began, in the fourth year of the Reagan disruption, the Republicans organized a panel to show Congress that the agency had support from groups that liked the anti-affirmative action, anti-European ethnic, and anti-"right to die" work of the commission. These included the conservative reincarnation of CORE, the Hudson Institute, the National Italian American Foundation, and the Spina Bifida Association of America. Congress was not impressed, and none of the major civil rights organizations appeared. The agency had to absorb another $250,000 budget cut.[60]

The commission scheduled a forum on the Fair Housing Amendments Act of 1988, for which the Realtors appeared but the Lawyers' Committee for Civil Rights Under Law and the Coalition of Citizens with Disabilities, although invited, did not. When Allen asked whether we could subpoena them, the commission's general counsel pointed out that we subpoenaed witnesses only for hearings and it had to be done ten days in advance. Allen introduced an emergency motion to subpoena for forums and briefings as well as hearings. Despite the absence of a quorum and the conflict with the law under which the commission operated, the Reaganites passed the resolution.[61]

Friedman tried to change the climate of opinion and gain credibility for the agency in a letter published in the *New York Times* expressing optimism that the commission might "be moving in a more useful direction." He pointed out that with the change in membership, six commissioners had voted to send a telegram to Reagan asking him to sign the Civil Rights Restoration Act, which he vetoed. Congress subsequently passed it over his veto. This and other developments, Friedman wrote, led him to hope that a "Progressive conservative or centrist" thrust might be developing on the commission.[62]

However, Pendleton continued to raise hackles, which depressed efforts to reinvigorate the commission. In December 1987 we approved a proposal to undertake a study of the civil rights implications of AIDS, including public health policies and initiatives to control AIDS in the Department of Health, Education, and Welfare. I objected to a footnote in the proposal that disapproved of homosexuality and called it an "abomination." I denounced the note as "completely out of place" in a serious discussion of law. Destro insisted that seeing homosexuality as sin was "a real part" of the debate over civil rights and AIDS.[63]

But I was not wary enough. I should have been suspicious when, after announcing conclusions on comparable worth—and affirmative action, for example, without bothering with fact-finding—the Republican appointees suddenly wanted a hearing. As we prepared for it, I became worried that even though I had voted in favor of the inquiry, I had made a grave error by doing so and had put rights at risk. I remained bothered by the dispute with Destro over the footnote's depiction of homosexuality.

When civil rights advocates pointed out the possible problem to congressional leaders, they responded by suggesting that the commission should not spend $218,000 on the study. They thought that much of what the agency proposed would duplicate the work of the Presidential Commission on AIDS. They urged the commission either to reconsider its project or to narrow it to complement the efforts of the president's commission.

In a January 1988 letter to Pendleton, Senators Kennedy, Lowell Wicker (R-Conn.), Tom Harkin (D-Iowa), and Robert Stafford (R-Vt.) agreed that the commission should be aware of discrimination against individuals with AIDS but thought "the commission could best complement the effort of the Presidential Commission by targeting its

Protesters from the New York chapter of ACT-UP wearing
clown masks at commission hearing, May 1988.

resources upon monitoring whether actual cases of discrimination are
being remedied under current law." Pendleton responded that "while
the Presidential Commission may touch on areas concerning civil
rights . . . we are the civil rights commission." He thought they "would
agree that if Rosa Parks were forced to sit in the back of the bus today,
you would rather have her complaint investigated by a civil rights body
than by the Department of Transportation."[64]

At the May 1988 hearings, a group of protesters wearing clown
masks and shouting, "Shame! Shame!" repeatedly interrupted the first
of the three-day proceedings. The protesters objected when the commission did just what they had suspected it would do all along. The day's
hearings focused on transmission routes of the disease, with an emphasis on homosexuality, which had already been throughly covered by
researchers and the Presidential Commission on AIDS. The protesters
left voluntarily after being asked several times to quiet down. The commissioners "have no business being here except to study the issue of discrimination," said Duncan Osborne, a leader of the AIDS Coalition to
Unleash Power of New York, which staged the hour-long protest. But
Pendleton replied, "If we didn't study transmissibility . . . someone
would say we're doing sloppy work."[65]

Pendleton became increasingly distraught as first Chavez and then

Abram, Bunzel, and Latham left the commission. He remained especially angry at Bunzel's effort to force his resignation and at the letter he
sent to Reagan upon leaving. He complained to me: "I carried water on
both shoulders," for their redirection of civil rights and then these two,
Abram and Bunzel, "turned on me." His exuberance was drained away
at the failure of the effort to change policy despite Reagan's leadership
and what he regarded as his colleagues' inability to see that his colorful
remarks and attacks on black leaders were important in changing attitudes. Galling also was that Ramirez and I, the "sore losers," were still
standing. When Pendleton died of a heart attack in California on June
5, 1988, President Reagan issued a statement the next day that he had
"lost a loyal friend and a compatriot deeply committed to my administration and its fight against discrimination wherever it exists." At the
June commission meeting, acting chairman Friedman presided, noting
the memorial service that day at four o'clock at Howard University.

Congressional Republicans wanted to take the opportunity to reinvigorate the commission and take anti–civil rights positions with a less
problematic leader, but they failed to do due diligence before making a
choice. Observers of the commission had already seen signs of the
wacky behavior of William Allen, in addition to his insistence on trying
to subpoena individuals to make presentations in a forum where counsel
told him subpoenas were impermissible.

Allen brought a California parent, Mary Amaya, to a commission
meeting, insisting that she tell us about his desire to have the Department of Justice investigate the state's education policy of not requiring
IQ tests for particular black children. He gave no notice of his plans and
had not asked that the issue be placed on the agenda. We had no staff
analysis of the issue, and he contravened the procedure of refusing to
permit spectators to interrupt commission meetings with demands to
speak. Otherwise, meetings would be impossible. If he had asked staff
to prepare for the issue and then placed it on the agenda, we could have
discussed it.

Not vetting Allen properly, the White House, upon the recommendations of Senator Hatch and other Republican senators, designated
Allen as chair. The Republican appointees voted to confirm him. Hatch
thought he would "be a strong force in building respect for the commission." Knowing Allen was a committed opponent of abortion and of
stern penalties for race discrimination, key Republican senators told
Reagan that he would "greatly enhance the credibility" of the commission.[66]

By the September 1988 meeting, the first for Allen as chair, Susan

Prado had left and the Midwestern regional director, Melvin Jenkins, served as acting staff director. A number of Asian Americans, including Congressmen Robert Matsui and Norman Mineta, wrote to the president asking for an Asian American appointee for the open position created by Pendleton's death. Senator Spark Matsunaga recommended a founder of the Organization of Chinese Americans, an internationally known mineral economist, Kung-Lee Wang. But Reagan followed the recommendation of Governor George Deukmejian and others and appointed Sherwin Chan, on August 13, 1988, to fill the unexpired term of Pendleton until November 29, 1989. Already an appointee to the board of governors of the California Maritime Academy, Chan, an engineer at the Northrop Corporation, had also been appointed to the President's Committee on the National Medal of Science.[67]

As the Reagan administration neared an end, the president, in a letter to fellow Republican and NAACP executive director Benjamin Hooks, described some of his accomplishments. He pointed out how Clarence Thomas, the head of his EEOC, had litigated more cases and "9.7 million in back pay and other monetary benefits, a rise of twice as much." Complainants who benefited from EEOC's voluntary complaint settlements increased by 53 percent. "The figures for investigations, settlements etc. show similar gains for our nearly 2 yrs here."

In addition, the lowering of inflation meant that "even people at the poverty level of earnings have several hundred dollars more in purchasing power." "Yes," he knew black unemployment remained "exceptionally high," but "all the political demagoguery in the land, couldn't hide that the recession was caused by high interest rates" before he took office. His program was "not yet in place when the bottom fell out." He knew the recovery would benefit everyone. He asked Hooks to understand that he had no "trace of bigotry or prejudice" in his heart, mainly because his "father and mother saw that they never got a start."[68]

Hooks replied, saying he was "delighted" to receive the letter and congratulating the president on his accomplishments, but he noted Reagan's effort to give tax exemptions to segregated private schools, and the other policy shifts about which the civil rights coalition had complained. He also told him the appointees to the EEOC and the Civil Rights Commission "were so unqualified that this organization publicly opposed them." The commission "warned of people who were totally unsuited for the position to which they had been appointed, or were known to have previously stated their opposition to the very tasks they were to discharge."[69]

In an effort to protect the president's legacy, the White House communications staff prepared a report on the Reagan record. They hoped the record would "help Administration spokesmen responding to such charges." The record's civil rights section described the administration's success in having "returned the federal government to its proper role of assuring that no person is denied opportunities because of his or her race, sex, religion, national origin, or other factors irrelevant to character and ability." They had "opposed quotas, which merely constitute new forms of discrimination." The record nowhere mentioned the appointees to civil rights posts who neglected their responsibility to enforce existing laws. Neither did it mention the failure of their commission to hold any hearings or issue any report at all in a principal area of its responsibility, analysis of the funding levels, efficiency, and effectiveness of civil rights enforcement agencies.[70]

Pendleton's rhetorical support of the low taxes, economic approach to uplift, and denunciation of government programs has remained a conservative Republican staple and is routinely echoed by black conservative apologists. He was a victim of his own eagerness to gain publicity through using colorful language to attack civil rights leaders. Instead of leading African Americans to reject the liberal civil rights vision, as the Reaganites had hoped, Pendleton reinforced their commitment. Reagan succeeded in accelerating the steady erosion of public support for penalties for discrimination against African Americans. However, during his eight years in office the groups in the Leadership Conference on Civil Rights essentially defeated his reactionary civil rights policies, which had been promoted by Pendleton and his crew.

When Reagan became president, he and his senior staff did not want an easy transition at the commission. If that had been their goal, they could have discussed resignations with the sitting commissioners, as other presidents had done, and avoided much of the controversy. Flemming and Horn were the type of public servants and staunch Republicans who certainly would have voluntarily resigned, and those of us who were left offended by Reagan's breach of the commission's independence and his disrespect might have followed their lead. But the Reaganites wanted a fight to please their constituency and a transition to a new civil rights reality. They left behind a dysfunctional agency with a new structure and a depleted budget that made it difficult to achieve anything useful. They left an appointment process and a pattern of ideological appointees that made it well nigh impossible to gather bipartisan support for any recommendations on the most controversial issues.

The commission that Reagan inherited was the independent conscience of the government on civil rights questions. Its fact-finding and open debate and discussion educated the public on contentious issues. The harm done to the commission by Reagan only reflected and symbolized the harm done to the public and those who sought remedies for long-standing patterns of discrimination. The commission had become a political agency, suffering perpetually from lack of resources, a new structure, and ideological appointees, a situation that almost guaranteed disunity.

CHAPTER IX

"Mickey Mouse Agency"

O NE DAY IN MARCH 1989 Pendleton's replacement, Chairman William Allen of the U.S. Commission on Civil Rights, was arrested at gunpoint on the White Mountain Apache Reservation in Arizona. Allen was attempting to take a fourteen-year-old Apache girl, Lalita Altaha, from a school bus. At Allen's invitation, national television covered the incident. The police recovered the girl and questioned Allen, who identified himself as a federal official, before releasing him. Allen belonged to an organization devoted to Native American adoptions. They believed poor Indian children were better off with more-affluent parents. Allen wanted to return Lalita to a white couple who claimed they had adopted her, and he stopped the bus after the school principal would not release her to him. Her natural mother and the tribe complained to the police that Allen was kidnapping Lalita.

The white couple, after befriending Lalita's mother when Lalita was an infant, had taken the child away and "adopted" her. The tribe searched for the adoptive parents and received a court order in 1982 proclaiming that the "adoption" was non-consensual and therefore illegal, and that she should be returned to her family on the reservation. The federal Indian Child Welfare Act gave the tribe review power before an Indian child could be adopted, rather than leaving the adoption decision to the birth parents. Congress passed the act because of complaints that some poor Indian children had been taken by whites, who came and established a friendship, then falsely claimed the parent had approved an adoption and took the child away. The tribe would pursue a national search to find the child and to gain his or her return to the parents in the courts, which often took years, as in Lalita's case.[1]

Allen and his fellow adoption advocates decided they would use vigilante self-help to "rescue" children from poor tribal surroundings and return them to the white "parents," instead of just trying to change the policy. When the commissioners asked Chairman Allen to explain his

William Allen, appointed chair
upon Pendleton's death.

behavior, he passed it off as if he was
simply acting in aid of a child in
distress and as if he had been trying
to learn how Indian tribes handle
custody battles. The commissioners
then asked Allen to apologize publicly for his "injudicious" behavior.
Instead he struck out angrily at us
for questioning him, suggesting "the
time has come for us all to go."[2]

At a Senate Committee on Indian
Affairs hearing on May 19, 1989,
Allen, instead of showing remorse,
went on the attack, complaining that
"Congress failed Lalita Altaha" by passing the Indian welfare law that
kept her from being taken from the tribe. The Senate committee made
it clear that they found his behavior inappropriate, especially given that
he used his official capacity as chairman of the Civil Rights Commission
to force the capture of the child.[3]

House oversight chair Representative Don Edwards said he did not
know whether the commission could survive this most recent blow,
especially since the House was in a "budget-cutting mood." Neas, of the
Leadership Conference on Civil Rights, said he was even more persuaded following this incident that the commission was now nothing
more than a "sham."[4]

The White House knew the president could not respond to the public outcry by simply firing Allen, or even taking away his designation as
chair, after the battles over the commission's independence of the Reagan years. Consequently, President Bush asked Allen to resign his chairmanship voluntarily. For more than six months, Allen refused. Ramirez,
Guess, and I were dumbfounded. We had wondered about Allen's idio-
syncrasies, including speaking with a British accent though he was from
Florida, and ceremoniously removing his jacket to display a belt with his
suspenders. We had also corralled him when he tried to subpoena witnesses illegally, but the most recent episode was simply unimaginable.[5]

Then, as if the White Mountain incident was not enough, Allen gave
an incendiary speech titled "Blacks? Animals? Homosexuals? What Is a

Minority?" at the Homosexuality and Public Policy Implications conference. The sponsor was the California Traditional Values Coalition, a group formed by 6,500 evangelical churches in California. In his speech Allen asserted that "express laws for minority groups, or the appearance of making express laws for minority groups, is the beginning of the evil of reducing American blacks to an equality with animals and then seducing other groups to seek the same charitable treatment." He thought this "fatal pattern" had "reduced certain contemporary homosexuals to pursue the identical barter of the precious right of American citizenship to determine one's own course for a like equality with animals." His language contradicted a fundamental premise of the commission's work—the pursuit of equality of rights.[6]

Further, all of the commissioners agreed that he should not have used commission resources to deliver the speech, since we had no policy on the subject of homosexual rights. We also condemned the speech title as "thoughtless, disgusting and unnecessarily inflammatory" for a chairman of a commission, speaking in his official capacity. Angrily declaring that the White House and the commissioners were "too reticent to contribute to the debate on civil rights," Allen resigned as chair but indicated his intention to stay for the remainder of his term as a commissioner, meaning he would remain on the commission for three more years.[7]

A few days later, President Bush rejected several gracious replies drafted by his staff and replied tersely, "I accept your resignation as Chairman of the United States Commission on Civil Rights effective immediately." Allen was later replaced with Bush appointee Arthur Fletcher.[8]

After two terms with Ronald Reagan as president and after Pendleton as commission chair, it was hard for civil rights advocates to imagine anything worse, but William Allen's behavior was only one of the challenges that plagued the struggle for civil rights during George Herbert Walker Bush's administration. Other blacks who undermined civil rights like Pendleton sprang up all over the Bush administration, in Congress and finally at the Supreme Court with the confirmation of Clarence Thomas as an associate justice. The Reaganite color-blind society theatrics had taught us not to trust black or female appointees, who were just as likely to spout anti–civil rights rhetoric as the white men they served. Even as child care needs went unmet and the death toll from AIDS, hunger, homelessness, and racial violence climbed, the president dithered. Meanwhile, his vice president, Dan Quayle, made news criticizing a fictional television reporter for becoming a single mother.[9]

In this climate, and with a divided commission, civil rights advocacy groups led the way in fighting discrimination. Attorney General Richard Thornburgh, a former Pennsylvania governor, and a low-profile John Dunne, appointed assistant attorney general for civil rights, went along as the White House denounced "racial quotas" repeatedly and deliberately invoked this "catch phrase," implying unfairness to whites in favor of unqualified blacks, to undermine the passage of an urgently needed new employment discrimination bill. In the states the Steel Belt rusted as a recession and unemployment grew, with black unemployment twice as high as that of whites. Reagan's deficit and tax cuts exacerbated class and racial tensions. Klansman David Duke ran a nearly successful race for governor of Louisiana against Edwin Edwards, who would later uphold the state's tradition of governors' becoming convicts. Duke's popularity with voters in and out of the Pelican State underscored the visibility of white supremacy in American politics.

Bush's soothing calls for a "kinder and gentler America" with a "Thousand Points of Light," perversely brought more victims of injustice seeking justice. Individuals filed more complaints of discrimination against employers, police officers, rental agents, schools, and real estate brokers than they had since the beginning of the Reagan administration. In 1990 the Department of Justice received 9,800 civil rights complaints, well over the 7,500 received in 1986.[10]

While African Americans filed the majority of race discrimination complaints, there was a spike in complaints from Hispanics, as well as Asian Americans. Interracial conflicts between minority groups constituted an even more disturbing development. A series of violent and deadly racial clashes in the Miami metropolitan area during the 1980s between blacks and Hispanics dramatically displayed this trend. Repeated episodes of racial tension and violence between Korean merchants and black customers in south central Los Angeles and other cities around the country increasingly fueled tensions.[11]

In the months before Bill Allen stepped down as commission chair, the Republican appointees continued their dysfunctional refusal to discuss the substance of reports or debate the issues, ordinarily ending the proceedings by noon. No one suggested ascertaining the president's views on civil rights policy or direction, as the commission had done in the past. The Reagan assault on the commission and on civil rights in general had made it clear that the Republican appointees were expected to implement Reagan-Bush policies as they developed—not act independently or offer constructive suggestions. Everyone also knew that the Republican appointees would have the access they needed to the White House staff, since the White House was pulling their strings. By this time, the commission had veered so far away from independence and nonpartisanship that one of the Republican appointees even suggested that the commission staff should be divided, similar to congressional staffs, into those working for Republicans and those working for Democrats.

But considering Allen's behavior, the remaining Republican appointees did not want to be seen as always voting with him. He was the lone dissenter when we voted, 7–1, to approve a resolution stating that *Runyon v. McCrary*, a 1976 Supreme Court decision that prohibited private non-religious schools from refusing to admit students solely on the basis of race, should not be overruled. The Court based its decision on the heart of federal civil rights law. In 1866, Congress, implementing the Thirteenth Amendment, had outlawed the use of race in contracts.

After Allen resigned as chair, Vice Chair Friedman stepped in as acting chair. Friedman projected a calm and deliberate manner, while maintaining his ideologically conservative positions. In a speech on October 24, 1989, which he sent to the White House and distributed widely, he said that with a "moderate administration in office" he thought it time for "civil rights groups to enter into dialogue with the White House." He noted that "some of the most controversial and sometimes abrasive figures who dominated discussion in the civil rights field are gone from the scene."[12]

In fact, there were few signs of healing or any relief from dysfunction. With the controversy involving Allen behind them, the Republican appointees quickly reverted to type. They decided to take up the report on the economic status of black women over our objections to the misleading use of data and the absence of comparisons with Latino, Asian, and white women that the majority had promised us when the study was first approved. When they insisted on voting, Ramirez and I absented ourselves in protest, leaving a quorum. Francis Guess then announced that he had fallen ill. With no quorum, the Republican appointees ordered the staff to include some comparative data and publish the study as a "staff report" and "an exploratory investigation," which did not require the commissioners to vote.[13]

As the commission was about to expire again, the oversight committees in Congress, chaired by Senator Orrin Hatch and Congressman Don Edwards, disagreed about the terms of reauthorization. I worked with Senator Paul Simon of Illinois, the ranking member on Hatch's Senate Judiciary Subcommittee on the Constitution, to develop a proposal that would solve some of the dysfunction of the commission. Because the commission was "too important to let die, or to let it continue with as little credibility as it has had in recent years," Simon proposed replacing the unworkable structure with seven commissioners, with Congress appointing four and the president three.

Hatch responded that he agreed with the White House on a straight six-year reauthorization. He did not like reducing to three the appointees for the president, and he disapproved of Simon's idea of annual reports on "the impact of federal fiscal policies, programs and activities on minorities and women." In Hatch's view, this was not "a fit subject" for the commission. He had not complained about the Reagan commission's attempt to highlight the impact of social and economic policies, while downplaying discrimination, in separate expensive time-consuming reports. However, he now insisted that the commission should not look at social or economic or spending policies and their effect on minorities and women. Instead, he said, the commission should "address discrimination issues—as they affect all Americans."[14]

The White House knew it wanted to reauthorize the commission and use the slots vacated by the expiring terms of Friedman, Destro, and Guess to place their clamoring position-seekers. The White House particularly disliked Edwards's House bill, which extended the agency for only six months. Chief of Staff John Sununu wrote to Hatch and Edwards that "such a proposal is totally unacceptable to the President." With a six-months reauthorization, the White House felt that the commission could not attract good people and would be a "hollow gesture" and a "disservice to the cause of civil rights." President Bush wanted the six-year reauthorization passed.

The White House used its support of a six-year reauthorization to appeal for support from African Americans. In November 1989, the president met with Jesse Jackson, Benjamin Hooks, and other black leaders to talk about the commission. His talking points included describing the problems with the commission as resulting "not from the commission's structure or mandate, but from conflicts among commission members." He told the leaders that he would push a six-year reauthorization and would appoint members "who will work together constructively to advance the cause of civil rights." However, he did not work very hard to gain congressional approval. The six-month extension passed, and Bush signed it on November 28, 1989, extending the agency only until September 30, 1991. The staff planned to relocate its office above the local YWCA headquarters to save money.[15]

Behind the scenes, the White House worked on finding a place for Arthur Fletcher, a friend of the president and a liberal Republican. Fletcher, who had known Bush since the Nixon administration, thought he deserved a cabinet secretary appointment, but the president ended up offering him only the part-time commission chairmanship.

After college in Kansas, where he played football, Fletcher became the first African American to play for the Baltimore Colts. After a short career in professional football, he became politically involved in Kansas when Fred Hall, a liberal Republican running for governor, asked him to manage his black community campaign. After Hall won, he rewarded Fletcher with a job overseeing the building and maintenance of Kansas highways. The job, which Fletcher held in the 1950s in the midst of a boom in highway building, gave him a firsthand look at exactly how lucrative government contracts were obtained.

Fletcher left Kansas after some white business leaders attacked him for awarding contracts to blacks. His family eventually settled in Washington State, where he organized a community self-help program in East Pasco that caught the attention of President Nixon, who gave him an appointment as a Department of Labor assistant secretary. Since his days implementing the Philadelphia affirmative action plan to require contractors who received federal funds to hire blacks in the Nixon administration, Fletcher had briefly served as president of the United Negro College Fund and as a business consultant.[16]

Bush considered Fletcher for HUD secretary, but instead named another former pro football player, New York congressman Jack Kemp. Another option, the post of administrator of the Small Business Administration, went to Congresswoman Patricia Saiki of Hawaii, who became the first Asian American to lead a federal agency. The president appointed Elizabeth Dole as secretary of labor, and when she left after one year Congresswoman Lynn Martin of Illinois filled the post.

For Fletcher, appointment to the commission, a small, battered agency with less than one hundred employees and no enforcement power, was bittersweet at best. Although disappointed and feeling mistreated, Fletcher told President-elect Bush after meeting with him in December 1988 that he "would consider it an honor and a privilege to serve" as commission chairman and, further, that he would accept the offer "on the spot if and when extended." After all, he had been a "member of the Bush team" since the 1970s.[17]

In early February 1989, when Fletcher thanked Bush for inviting him and his wife, Bernyce, to dinner and a movie, he reaffirmed his willingness to be the chair of the commission after personnel director Chase Untermeyer called him to determine his interest. As the "Father of the Philadelphia Plan," Fletcher, who became known as the person who coined the term "affirmative action," told Bush he objected to the *Richmond v. Croson* Supreme Court decision, striking down a minority contract set-aside program, and thought matters might worsen. His appointment, Fletcher said, would send a "pro civil rights signal."

At the commission, he could lead in "planning and carrying out the research that would point the way toward launching the final phase of the nation's equality of opportunity revolution." This would reduce discrimination substantially by the year 2000, which could be "a legacy of the Bush administration." Bush responded, "When the time comes to name a new Chairman of the Civil Rights Commission, I'll be proud to have an old friend and loyal trooper in that important post."[18]

Allen refused to leave, and Sherwin Chan resigned to create a vacancy for Fletcher, who had the votes of the other Republican appointees but needed at least a vote from me or Ramirez to gain confirmation. We both agreed to vote yes in order to show support for his chairmanship. I had known Fletcher's work on civil rights since the Philadelphia Plan and Nixon's subsequent rejection of his efforts. When he arrived at his first meeting as chair, I expressed my pleasure at having an appointee who had a commitment to civil rights. Allen voted no in opposition to being displaced by Fletcher. "For a rise in Blood Pressure check Bill Allen's dissent," personnel director Untermeyer told Bush, when one year later, the commission confirmed Fletcher's nomination.[19]

White House press secretary Marlin Fitzwater announced that Bush appointed Fletcher because he wanted to restore the commission "as an effective institution. We have felt that it could be stronger and more forceful in representing the concerns of minorities and others and we expect it to operate in that fashion." In answer to a press question, he said Bush and Fletcher would have a short meeting and photo op to "talk about the future of the commission. The President will emphasize his support for the work of the commission and his interest in seeing that it's an effective institution."[20]

Civil rights groups "praised" Fletcher's selection. The Leadership

Conference's Neas, however, worried about the other "right-wingers" on the commission. In May the president named Charles Wang of New Jersey, president of the China Institute in America and executive director of the Chinese-American Planning Council, a social service agency in New York, as his second appointee, so that there would be an Asian American commissioner. Following the tradition of having the leadership from different political parties, Bush designated Wang, a supporter but a Democrat, as vice chair.[21]

The president had wanted to name Fletcher earlier when Allen became embroiled in the White Mountain Apache "kidnapping episode," but it took months to achieve Allen's voluntary resignation as chair even though he stayed on the commission. Allen finally left when his term expired in December 1992. Almost immediately after his appointment, Fletcher became ill and unable to attend meetings. He had his second triple bypass operation in March and took about six weeks to recuperate.[22]

During the Fletcher years, the commission was still divided between anti–civil rights ideologues and commissioners who were committed to preserving and extending the gains of the 1960s. The commission, therefore, became stalemated. Nonetheless, individual commissioners made their own contributions. Arthur Fletcher helped to gain the enactment of the Civil Rights Act of 1991 and Bush's eventual signing of the bill after he first vetoed it. Compared to the early years, the prestige level of commission appointees continued to decline as the ideological divisions persisted. To replace Destro, Friedman, and Buckley, Bush and the Congress appointed conservatives who disagreed with the chairman he appointed. By the end of George H. W. Bush's administration, the commission had reduced its loud denunciations of existing civil rights policy, but it had accomplished little.

Bush appointed a Latino, Wilfredo Gonzalez, who had already been appointed as the associate administrator of the SBA's Minority Small Business and Capital Ownership Development, as staff director. Gonzalez had been a fellow in the Department of Health, Education, and Welfare in 1976 and had served in the Peace Corps as a volunteer. My dear friend Antonia Pantoja, founder of ASPIRA, the leading training and advocacy organization for Puerto Rican youth, knew him well and assured me that he would focus only on management. In the pattern of earlier staff directors, Gonzalez maintained ties with several low- or mid-level staff at the White House but made no apparent effort to penetrate the upper echelons.

After Francis Guess's term expired in December 1989, Senator Dole appointed Russell Redenbaugh, a founding partner and director of Cooke and Bieler, a financial investment firm in Philadelphia. Redenbaugh, a wealthy, well-connected free marketer who had been blinded in an accident when he was a teenager, was the first openly disabled commissioner, but he had not been involved in disability rights advocacy. A nephew of Republican senator Jake Garn, he seemed to have a direct pipeline to the *Wall Street Journal* editorial page. He had wanted an appointment to the Federal Reserve Board, which would have been more suited to his interests, but Dole told him the commission was all that was available.

Dole advised Bush on February 8, 1990, that Russell will bring "a firsthand knowledge of the real life experiences of people with disabilities" to a commission that Dole thought had "lacked a disability focus since its inception." Ironically, the commission had done cutting-edge work on disabilities. Further, upon his appointment as a commissioner, Redenbaugh immediately upset disability rights advocates by challenging the need for key civil rights protections for the disabled.

Redenbaugh was distinctly out of step with the disability rights

President George H. W. Bush with Arthur Fletcher after appointing
him commission chairman, February 1990.

movement. Two disabled advocates for persons with disabilities, wheel-chair-bound Evan Kemp, Jr., named by Bush as chair of the EEOC, and Justin Dart, a successful businessman whose grandfather founded Wal-greens drugstores and whose father was a member of Reagan's kitchen cabinet, worked with Patrisha Wright and the Leadership Conference on Civil Rights to pass the Americans with Disabilities Act, which Bush signed on July 26, 1990. The bipartisan bill reflected the protections for the rights and opportunities of the disabled that the commission had developed in its report *Accommodating the Spectrum of Individual Abilities,* published in 1983. It helped that Kemp was a friend and bridge partner of White House counsel Boyden Gray.

In applauding Redenbaugh's selection, Dole also expressed his per-sonal pleasure at Fletcher "of Kansas" being appointed: "Art [Fletcher] is a true leader who will be a tremendous asset." Republican House Minority Leader Robert Michel appointed Carl Anderson, vice presi-dent of the Knights of Columbus, who had worked as a congressional staffer and on the White House Office of Public Liaison staff. Anderson had also served on the Native Hawaiians Study Commission.[23]

The Civil Rights Act of 1990 presented the first big civil rights test for Bush. He had approval ratings in some polls of almost 70 percent among blacks, a level not achieved by a Republican president since Eisenhower. Many said cynically that he won this high level of approval simply by not being Reagan. White House staffers debated whether their political goal of maintaining conservative support for the next election required opposition to the bill, introduced in Congress by Sen-ator Ted Kennedy and Congressman Augustus Hawkins (D-Calif.). It sought to modify or overturn five 1989 Supreme Court decisions that civil rights groups saw as "turning back the clock" on protections against job discrimination. After originally taking the position that no remedy seemed necessary, the administration submitted counter-legislation to modify two of the court decisions.

The administration's bill would undo the Supreme Court's *Patterson v. McLean Credit Union* ruling, which narrowed the ability of minorities to win monetary damages for job discrimination. The bill would also restore the burden of proof to defendants in cases where employers' hir-ing practices had a discriminatory impact. Under a 1971 Supreme Court ruling in *Griggs v. Duke Power Co.* the employer had the burden of prov-ing that a hiring practice was required by business necessity. The Court, in *Wards Cove Packing Co. v. Atonio*, overturned that ruling in 1989. Also, in 1989, in *Price Waterhouse v. Hopkins*, the Court had decided that when an employer had mixed motives for making an employment decision only one of which was sex discrimination, the employee's complaint is invalid if the same decision would have been made without the sex discrimination.

The Court had also restricted the use of a law that prohibited race discrimination in contracts, saying that it outlawed only an original hiring decision and not any actions taken thereafter, even if the actions were discriminatory. In *Martin v. Wilks*, the Court let white firefighters in Birmingham, Alabama, sue to overturn a consent decree years after a lower federal court approved it, even though they were notified of the consent decree beforehand and had a chance to object. Meanwhile, attorneys for the civil rights groups prepared an analysis of both bills that addressed these court cases to present to Attorney General Thornburgh and Bush.[24]

On May 14, the White House asked African American leaders, including Fletcher, to meet with Bush. In addition to the heads of major civil rights organizations and their lawyers, he invited what the White House described as "conservative blacks who did not emphasize civil rights," such as Robert Woodson, the president of the National Center for Neighborhood Enterprise. The meeting, which the White House called "a listening session" for Bush, would be followed by meetings with other groups, including "Hispanics, Jews, Roman Catholics, the disabled, Asians and women."

Although Bush asked Congress to pass a bill, after the Supreme Court decisions, broadening protection against job discrimination, Thornburgh threatened to urge a presidential veto of the Kennedy-Hawkins legislation, characterizing it as requiring quotas. Fletcher said he did not agree. By this time the label "quotas," signifying some unfair, unjustified advantage to blacks over whites, had been used effectively by Republican conservatives and served to inflame much of the public against any civil rights measure to which the term was applied.[25]

"The major hang-up, is whether it would produce so-called quotas," Fletcher said after the ninety-minute meeting. He insisted that the Kennedy-Hawkins bill had goals, not quotas. "You're talking to the person who wrote the Philadelphia Plan, who put goals, targets and timetables in the first plan that was ever issued 20 years ago," Fletcher said. "A quota is a flat number that has to be satisfied irrespective of whether the person can do the job. . . . All businesses pursue goals."

Woodson, downplaying the need to remedy discrimination, commented that the president should forget both the administration proposal and the congressional bill. Using a standard conservative tactic of minimizing discrimination issues by directing attention solely to other major problems in black communities, Woodson said Bush should "go back to the drawing boards and really construct legislation that addresses the critical needs of people whose brains are being blown out in these inner cities, whose families are in crisis."[26]

On May 21, 1990, Paul Craig Roberts in the *Washington Times* suggested that Bush "set himself up for this bill when he replaced Civil Rights Commission Chairman William Allen, a black who opposed quotas, with Arthur Fletcher." Fletcher's responsibility for the Philadelphia Plan, which he describes as requiring goals and timetables in government construction contracts, should have been enough to prevent his appointment as chairman. Roberts, trading on the now well-nigh-public acceptance of the badness of anything labeled "quotas," explained in the article that in his view, "goals and timetables" are a euphemism for quotas.

Therefore, according to Roberts, Justice Byron White's June 1989 majority opinion in *Wards Cove* correctly decided to take away the burden of proof from employers when employees alleged discrimination and when a statistical imbalance existed in the workforce. Roberts felt that the congressional legislation should be vetoed because it would restore the burden of proof to employers, who might decide to avoid any penalties under the new law by using racial quotas.[27]

The negotiations continued over the summer as Fletcher did everything he could in the media and with other black Republicans to persuade Bush to support the Kennedy-Hawkins bill. To no avail, they argued that a presidential veto could trigger an angry response from minorities and hurt Republican efforts to recruit African Americans as GOP voters.

In July the commission tried to shore up support for the bill in a report that examined "the provisions of the Civil Rights Act of 1990 from both a legal and a policy perspective." The report, endorsed by Fletcher and Wang, who consistently followed the lead of the chairman, Ramirez, and me, concluded that "the President should sign the legislation." We based the report on all of the prior investigations and reports the commission had produced. Even though the law already clearly limited the use of "quotas" to egregious cases, we decided to make a recommendation that gave a nod to those who kept characterizing the act as a "quota bill."

We suggested that Congress might want to add language stating that in the absence of a court order they did not intend to "promote employment quotas, nor will the use of quotas be condoned as a means of avoiding liability." We particularly noted our approval of new language in the bill that permitted women and religious minorities the same opportunity, previously available only to racial and ethnic minorities, to collect money damages for proven discrimination.[28]

Commissioner Buckley, feeling caught in the disagreement between a Republican chair and the other Republicans, abstained. In dissent, Redenbaugh, Anderson, and Allen held fast to the Reagan use of quota language to inflame public debate. They cited a number of "technical problems," but said their dissent was "unqualified" because of the report's "insouciance about quotas." Anderson also produced a separate statement objecting to the report.[29]

Anderson surreptitiously cooperated directly with the White House in resisting the bill, while Fletcher, reflecting the commission majority view, was trying to persuade Bush to sign it. Anderson kept deputy White House counsel John Schmitz informed of his recommendation to the commissioners to avoid issuing a statement. He suggested we should instead produce a study of employment practices and "how much discrimination is there" creating "barriers," not just to employment but to the "formation of new, minority owned enterprises." He recommended that this should all take place "without casting an eye at the legislative calendar."

When Anderson asked us to endorse the president's bill, he attached a letter from Abram to the president, which he described as "circulating in Washington." Abram's letter to the president characterized the bill as a "quota bill" that Bush should oppose. When we rejected Anderson's efforts, in his separate dissent he quoted from Abram's letter to Bush, saying that if he were still practicing law, he would love the bill because as a "quota bill," "while it may enrich some lawyers, it will impoverish the principle of equality for all Americans."[30]

Ramirez and I noted that the fallout from the Supreme Court decisions was not "abstract" but real. In just one year hundreds of people had their race discrimination claims dismissed by courts and administrative agencies. Consequently, we hoped for urgent enactment of the civil rights bill.[31]

In early October Bush proposed a compromise that would allow race discrimination for "legitimate community or customer relationship efforts." The president did not give any examples of when discrimination would be appropriate. Fletcher was apoplectic as he told the media that Bush's proposal would "take us back to the 1940s. I cannot believe anyone sincere about civil rights could have proposed such language. The Chamber of Commerce has had the President's ear on this." On

October 16, the Senate passed the Kennedy-Hawkins bill 62–34, without Bush's suggested language. The House followed suit, passing the bill on October 17 by 273–154, but the White House reiterated the president's intention to veto it.[32]

Former Ford administration transportation secretary William Coleman, a leading lawyer and chairman of the board of the NAACP-LDF, met with Bush for one last attempt at persuasion and left feeling "reassured." Civil rights leaders and women's rights advocates marched at the White House on Friday, chanting, "Sign the bill." They sought a meeting with President Bush, but press secretary Fitzwater said it "probably would not be that helpful" and unless Congress changed the bill Bush would veto it.[33]

On October 19, 1990, Neal Devins, who had served as a Reagan appointee in the Office of the General Counsel at the commission, attacked the Bush appointees for supporting the civil rights bill. Pointing to Fletcher and Vice Chairman Wang, he groused that Bush's record of appointments suggested that his principal civil rights agenda was "appeasement" of the civil rights community.[34]

Fletcher was sensitive to the need to support Bush's agenda when he could do so in good conscience. Consequently, he was pleased when the commission agreed to support the president with a statement that balancing the budget might retard economic growth and adversely affect "the economic well-being and civil rights protections of historically disadvantaged groups." He thought this commission action supporting a policy of the president might help his campaign to persuade the president to sign the civil rights bill. Fletcher forwarded a copy of the press release to Bush, saying the commission had convened an emergency meeting to discuss the issue.[35]

The efforts of civil rights advocates, including Fletcher, failed. Bush decided to stick with the conservative opponents. On November 21, 1990, Bush vetoed the Civil Rights Act of 1990, and the Senate voted 66–34 to override, failing to gain the required two-thirds majority by one vote. Kennedy called the veto "tragic and disgraceful." It meant that "when the chips are down, the White House is against civil rights." Neas noted that Bush had joined "Andrew Johnson and Ronald Reagan as the only presidents to veto a civil rights bill." Fletcher told the press that we were on record as strongly disagreeing with Bush's stand. *Boston Globe* columnist Derrick Jackson pointed out that "none other than David Duke," the former Grand Wizard of the Ku Klux Klan, who had just lost a U.S. Senate race in Louisiana but won 44 percent of the vote in a "rabid campaign against affirmative action," came to the Hill to praise the failure to override the veto. Duke proclaimed, "The President and the Congress are getting my message." As civil rights advocates and the supporters in Congress prepared to reintroduce the legislation in the next Congress, Bush's ratings among African Americans receded to Reaganesque levels.[36]

On women's rights concerns, Bush also decided to stick with his conservative base. While Vice President Quayle flogged fictional television character Murphy Brown for becoming an unwed mother, the increased numbers of women in the workforce meant that child care had become a major issue that divided people who believed only in traditional families in which mothers stayed at home from those who saw day care and parental leave as essential. President Bush tried unsuccessfully to strike a balance between those who were interested in child care services and parental leave and those who were opposed.

The commission report on *A Growing Crisis: Disadvantaged Women and Their Children* (1983) had placed commission policy firmly on the side of supporting increased child care services. After a great deal of wrangling in Congress, on November 5, 1990, President Bush supported a limited child care service bill including the block grants, tax credits, and proposals to fund before- and after-school child care proposals. After all of the discussion and controversy, the child care bill promised only the most minimal help for parents trying to balance jobs and children. In addition, the administration kept delaying implementation, projecting a start date of no earlier than sometime after September 1, 1991. The parental leave bill, watered down to a family and medical leave bill, and without pay for time off, passed the Congress in June 1990. Bush vetoed it as promised, and the House tried and failed to override.[37]

Despite differences, Fletcher continued to have warm relations with the Bush White House staff because he knew the president personally. This relationship insulated him from criticism when complaints were received about his civil rights advocacy. Even after Fletcher opposed Bush on the civil rights bill, Bush reinstated his name on a list of invitees to a Black History Month celebration after staff had removed him from the list. When an observer remarked on Fletcher's support for the president at a SAC forum, the president replied in a handwritten note, "I was not surprised. Simply delighted." He then forwarded the correspondence to Fletcher with a handwritten note: "Art, very nice." Bush also kept track of Fletcher's accomplishments and wrote to congratulate him on being tapped as a distinguished professor to create the University of Denver's Institute for Corporate Social Policy on June 13, 1991.[38]

Bush greatly appreciated Fletcher's support of his nomination of Clarence Thomas to the Supreme Court. The commission traditionally did not take positions on nominations, but individual commissioners were free to express their own personal views, as I had done in opposition to Robert Bork. Fletcher acknowledged publicly that he had some differences with Thomas on civil rights; however, he believed that the Supreme Court appointment would give Thomas the security to express support for civil rights. "In fact, I'm inclined to believe that he will probably be free for the first time in his life," said Fletcher. "He will be the freest black American in the country, free to do whatever he wants to do, whenever he wants to do it, however he wants to do it and explain it." Fletcher said that he studied the issue for three weeks and believed Thomas knew that he had personally benefited from *Brown* and affirmative action, and had been "fortunate enough to ride them both all the way to the top." Fletcher also insisted that Thomas would not forget his African American experience once he gained confirmation.[39]

Even though I had studied Thomas's record over the summer and shared my views with civil rights advocates, I did not become involved until UCLA law professor Kimberlé Crenshaw called one morning during the confirmation hearings and told me of Anita Hill's allegations of sexual harassment. Female members of Congress were pressing the Senate Judiciary Committee on her behalf. I went to Capitol Hill for a news conference with women lawyers Patricia King, Marcia Greenberger, Barbara Arnwine, and others to denounce the Senate for not hearing from Anita Hill after Senate investigators apparently leaked to the press that she had charged Thomas with sexual harassment. We were "outraged that the Senate is not taking seriously the allegations of sexual harassment by a black woman. Black women have historically been put in this position."

Anita Hill's testimony was heard in the end, but discounted. Thomas deflected her allegations and went on to confirmation, propelled, in part, by his inappropriate use of the "high-tech lynching" analogy to portray himself as a victim of racism, when racism had nothing to do with Hill's accusations. The committee neglected to seriously consider his weak enforcement, anti–civil rights record as a government official at the Equal Employment Opportunity Commission and the Office for Civil Rights in the Department of Education.[40]

In the next round of commission reauthorization, as the six-month extension neared expiration on September 30, 1991, Senator Simon wanted a six-year bill, but the House had passed Edwards's bill for a two-year reauthorization. A *Wall Street Journal* editorial on September 23, 1991, charged that Edwards wanted to take reprisals against the commission for Fletcher's support of the Clarence Thomas nomination. Edwards replied that the commission had done no work in the twenty-two months since the last reauthorization. He said, "The divisive rhetoric is gone and fiscal management has improved but virtually no fact-finding has been done in the past two years—no hearings, no consultations, and only one report on work already in progress. The commission has been given a couple of years to demonstrate that it is able to tackle current problems and make a real contribution." He saw problems "involving such matters as Asian and Hispanic new immigrants, minority set-asides and how affirmative action was working." If the commission would not undertake these studies and investigations, "some other organization must be found or created to carry out its mandate."[41]

Redenbaugh, who likely used his connections to inspire the editorial, responded to Edwards's letter in the *Wall Street Journal.* He attributed Edwards's action to anger over the commission's work on economic issues, such as urging enterprise zones and a zero capital gains tax rate "on behalf of America's disadvantaged." At the time Redenbaugh had been pushing the commission to support these economic concerns, using another standard conservative Republican claim that such measures would help poor blacks. We agreed with some of his ideas but not as a substitute for monitoring the enforcement of civil rights. Redenbaugh asserted that the commission had begun to debate whether affirmative action would do more good if based on economic conditions. "This is a point Judge Thomas made in his confirmation hearing," Redenbaugh explained. "This is the debate we are joining and Don Edwards is trying to stop that debate." In fact, Edwards had long-standing reasons for being dissatisfied with the commission unrelated to the Thomas nomination.[42]

Fletcher became increasingly discontented with the budget and comparative unimportance of the commission he had been given to chair when Bush denied him a more significant post. In August 1991 he toured six U.S. military bases in Germany, where he said he found evidence of pervasive race discrimination. The commission could not pay for travel abroad and did not have the resources in any event, so he went on the tour, from August 7 to 19, as a guest of the NAACP. He reported at a commission meeting of finding "endemic" discrimination in the hiring and promotion of enlisted personnel and civilian employees and among employees' children at schools. He complained that black children in Defense Department schools were punished more severely than white students, given unequal access to extracurricular activities, and given less-challenging academic work. He said blacks who wanted to sing in the choir were told to start their own gospel choir. In one school teachers called black children who excelled "little chocolate fluffs." Still, he asserted, "there is reason to believe that blacks do better in the military than they do in civilian life." He found that those discriminated against were afraid to complain for fear of retaliation. He wanted a commission follow-up, but we had no funds.[43]

In the House debate, Wisconsin Republican congressman James Sensenbrenner, in sparring about Edwards's short reauthorizations sponsored a bill to stop financing the commission. He thought the agency no longer contributed to the mainstream debate, and said, "It's time for Congress to bite the bullet and say, 'Enough is enough.'" A conference committee would resolve the difference between a two-year reauthorization and the Senate's compromise vote for four more years. The staff had declined to 77 from nearly 300 in the 1980s, and the budget from $11.6 million to $7 million over the course of five years. Fletcher told the *New York Times*, "There is no way we are going to monitor agency after agency with a Mickey Mouse organization like we have now." Further, he stated, "I don't mind being put on a short leash. But I gave them a counter-proposal: fully staff us; give us $10.5 million to $11 million over the next three years. At the end of that time, if we haven't done our jobs, put us out of our misery."[44]

Fletcher and Gonzalez recommended, and the commission agreed, that we should ask for whatever budget we thought we needed despite the cuts and hostility of the Congress. The request, sent to OMB in September 1991, asked for $16,382,000. It pointed out that in 1983 the commission had 256 full-time positions, 171 in headquarters and 85 in the regions. In fiscal year 1991, the commission had decreased to 79 full-time permanent positions and 28 in the regions.[45]

I believed the commission should request full funding, but I also agreed with Edwards's objections to the commission's budget request because of the absence of fact-finding and investigative work. With the Republican appointees in control, the commission had failed to evaluate the work of any federal enforcement agency. Monitoring and fact-finding had formed the heart of commission activity before Reagan gutted the agency and political appointees burrowed into the commission's civil service.[46]

The divided commission did not weigh in when Michael Williams, an African American lawyer and Bush's assistant secretary for civil rights in the Department of Education, announced offensive new student financial aid rules in December 1990. He would forbid colleges receiving federal funds from offering scholarships designated for minorities unless they had proven evidence of past discrimination. Williams said he had told the sponsors of the Fiesta Bowl they could not offer $100,000 in such scholarships to schools participating in the bowl.

Williams admitted that his statement conflicted with a federal policy of the previous year upholding similar minority scholarships in Colorado. Schools used the scholarships to increase their enrollment of black and Latino students from funds given by private donors. The commission, before the Reagan takeover, supported minority scholarships. David Tatel, a Washington lawyer who ran the Office for Civil Rights in the Carter administration, said minority scholarships given by donors had long been permitted under the Civil Rights Act of 1964, so long as minorities and non-minorities had access to the institution's overall scholarship program.[47]

The White House responded to press criticism by denying any knowledge of Williams's actions. Then curiously, on December 13, Lauro Cavazos, the country's first Hispanic cabinet member, resigned as secretary of education. On December 14 Bush said he had asked for a quick "readout" from his staff. They were trying to decide whether to tell Williams to back off. Many conservative Republicans agreed with giving scholarships as a benign way to promote opportunity.[48]

After the review, Williams announced that colleges could award such scholarships so long as the money came from private donations designated for that purpose or from the Patricia Roberts Harris and National Science Foundation (NSF) graduate fellowships, established by Congress. Schools could not use operating funds for minority scholarships and would have four years to adjust their activities. State and locally financed scholarships remained untouched as a constitutional issue.[49]

The policy issued "an invitation for lawsuits and complaints filed with the Education Department by people who wish to undermine the programs and affirmative action," I told the press. I saw "a wholesale assault on these programs and people shouldn't be fooled." Sure enough, conservatives announced plans to challenge in court any minority scholarship program. John Scully, counsel for the Washington Legal Foundation, which had earlier filed a complaint against minority scholarships at Florida Atlantic University, said, "They [the Education Department] are just caving in to political pressure" and announced that he would litigate.[50]

When asked about the policy during his confirmation hearings for secretary of education in February 1991, Lamar Alexander told the committee he would completely reverse Williams's actions. Once in office, he rescinded the policy, ordered a six-month study, and announced that the scholarships could continue in the interim. In September 1991 the commission completed a review of targeted minority scholarships and, on the basis of our legal analysis, urged their support. In December 1991, Alexander announced that colleges could use such scholarships open to all but with race as a plus factor to increase diversity, as allowed under the *Bakke* Supreme Court decision.[51]

While the Congress and civil rights advocates worked on the Clarence Thomas nomination and other issues, they also concentrated on passing a civil rights bill in 1991 to overcome Bush's veto of the 1990 act. Within the Leadership Conference on Civil Rights, Ralph Neas, Marcia Greenberger, Judith Lichtman, and Elaine Jones were the key players. The commission was already on record with recommendations and support. After considerable negotiations in which Senator John Danforth, Republican of Missouri, played a major role, Bush decided to accept the slightly revised bill. He claimed that new language allowing businesses to defend themselves against charges of unintentional discrimination settled the quota issue. Danforth and White House counsel C. Boyden Gray agreed to accept a reiteration of the language from *Griggs v. Duke Power* that the court had overturned in *Wards Cove* in 1989, which had, in part, stimulated the call for legislation. After an employee showed discrimination, the new language left the burden of proof on the employer to show that he did not engage in unintentional discrimination on the employee. Again, however, it did not define the "business necessity" that employers could assert as a basis for what appeared to be discrimination.[52]

The other major issue that Danforth and Bush administration officials settled concerned the new provision under which women, religious minorities, and the disabled who won discrimination lawsuits could claim damages, in addition to back pay, just as racial and ethnic minorities could. The agreement included a sliding scale of punitive and other damages with a cap ranging from $50,000 to $300,000, depending on the size of the business. In announcing the compromise, Bush stated, "I can simply certify it is not a quota bill; it is a fair bill, and it's going to hit a lick against discrimination in the workplace. And I couldn't be more happy."[53]

However, White House counsel Gray unhappily fielded criticisms from conservatives. He published an opinion-page column in the *Wash-*

ington Post saying, "Contrary to a rapidly congealing press myth, President Bush did not 'cave' or 'surrender' on quotas in the new civil rights bill." He asserted that a legislative compromise became possible "only after the Democrats beat a total retreat on quotas, thereby paving the way for the president to make concessions on other, less fundamental, issues." Civil rights lawyers, former Urban League president Vernon Jordan, and Ford administration transportation secretary William Coleman responded on November 18, 1991, that the bill had in fact restored the law to its meaning before the five 1989 Supreme Court decisions, with improvements on damages. Most important, with Senator Danforth leading the charge, the Congress had passed a bipartisan bill. The president helped to put civil rights back where it belongs "as part of a national consensus." They were dismayed because Gray's column "attempts to rip that consensus apart just as it was forming again," which "ill serves the President and the country."[54]

Bush signed the bill, but the attempt in Congress to add remedies for congressional employees who experienced discrimination, which the commission supported, did not pass. Instead, the bill established a new fair employment office within the Senate as the first step in an administrative process for complaints filed by Senate employees. House employees already had a complaint apparatus.

Bush had to quell a last-minute dispute when White House counsel Gray circulated a draft memo, the night before the signing ceremony, that appeared to tell agencies and departments, despite the new law, to stop enforcing affirmative action in federal government hiring. Bush disclaimed the memo and in his signing statement, praised affirmative action and said "nothing in this bill overturns the government's affirmative action programs."[55]

Bush's signing statement alleviated some tensions but created new anxiety because it used a misleading legislative history, submitted by Senate Minority Leader Robert Dole (R-Kan.), that left loopholes for employers to engage in discrimination. The history was apparently written in close consultation with the White House counsel's office. Following a policy embraced by the White House in the Reagan years, Bush's signing statement permitted arguments for neglecting enforcement or arguing in court later against the bill's agreed-upon provisions. If the tactic worked, businesses could claim a practice was necessary for business purposes and thereby defeat discrimination charges despite the new law. Fletcher found the signing statement a ridiculous attempt to curry favor and placate conservatives. Legal experts differed on whether the White House could persuade the Supreme Court to use the distorted legislative history.[56]

Fletcher was jubilant when Bush signed the Civil Rights Act of 1991. In his eagerness to capitalize on it, without consulting the commission he asked Bush to issue an executive order to move the issue "out of the White House and into the hands of our independent, nonpartisan" Civil Rights Commission. The order would say: "Every Interpretation of Title I of the Civil Rights Act of 1991 by any federal agency shall, prior to issuance or promulgation, be submitted for review to the United States Commission on Civil rights. All federal agencies shall cooperate with the commission in the conduct of such a review." Fletcher faxed the memo to the president on November 23 and then called to discuss it with the president, but a staffer talked to him instead. Counsel Gray replied to Fletcher for the president that "because the commission is not an agency within the executive branch, I don't think the process you suggest would be feasible. Offering to take on this difficult task, however, is a wonderful example of your generosity, and that of your fellow Commissioners."[57]

In January 1991, Ramirez and I gained the support of our conservative Republican colleagues in a needed long-term project, racial tensions in local communities. We cited renewed Ku Klux Klan activity, the police response to disturbances by vacationing African American college students over the Labor Day weekend in Virginia Beach, Virginia, and the shooting death of Yusef Hawkins, a black teenager, by a group of white youths in the Bensonhurst section of Brooklyn. Just as concerned, Francis Guess, who, though a Republican, often sided with us, commented that "the rhetoric of racism in this country has shifted to the point where [Black Muslim minister Louis] Farrakhan appears as a moderate—and that frightens me." He expressed a particular concern about statements from the political right. Guess cited the taunts shouted by whites in Bensonhurst when African Americans marched in the neighborhood to protest the shooting of Hawkins. Guess said, "The rhetoric is back where it was in the 1930s and 1940s. We thought it had gone away but it hasn't." The commission agreed to our proposal, and over the next few years, we held hearings on racial tensions in affected communities.[58]

The fallout from the Rodney King beating in Los Angeles fell within our racial tensions emphasis. On March 3, 1991, Lake View Terrace resident George Holliday videotaped the police beating King, an African American man whose automobile they had pursued in a high-speed chase. The commission responded by surveying local governments to ascertain whether they had implemented our recommendations for improving police-community relations and preventing disturbances in the commission's 1981 *Who Is Guarding the Guardians?* report.[59]

After the trial in the King case, the long-standing problems of police-community relations and the Justice Department's ineptness in alleged police cases came glaringly into public view. Between 1982 and 1991 the Justice Department conducted 720 investigations of police and sheriff's departments. Only four cases resulted in indictments, and only three cases, one involving the Border Patrol, resulted in convictions. The commission held hearings in Los Angeles as part of the racial tensions series and reported on festering police-community relations, despite obstructions to the hearing process and denials from police and sheriff's departments.[60]

After a Simi Valley jury acquitted Sergeant Stacey Koon and officers Laurence M. Powell, Theodore J. Briseno, and Timothy E. Wind in the beating of Rodney King and triggered the Los Angeles riot, President Bush suggested the impossible—that the acquittals might be reversed on appeal—showing his ignorance and bad advice about the judicial process and the unwillingness of his Justice Department to bring a federal prosecution.

The president held a meeting on May 1, 1992, with civil rights leaders to consider responses. Accompanied by Vice President Dan Quayle, Missouri governor John Ashcroft, the chairman of the President's Commission for Urban Families, his two highest-level African American appointees, Constance Newman, director of the Office of Personnel Management, and Louis Sullivan, secretary of Health and Human Services, as well as Fletcher, the president met in the Roosevelt Room with an array of civil rights leaders. They included Benjamin Hooks, executive director of the NAACP; John Jacob, president of the National Urban League; Raul Yzaguirre, executive director of La Raza; Dorothy Height of the National Council of Negro Women; Bush aide Thaddeus Garrett; and Rev. Edward Hill, pastor of Mt. Zion Missionary Baptist Church in Los Angeles, whom Reagan had proposed for commission chair. The leaders suggested a blue ribbon race relations panel to investigate the issues, but Bush rejected that idea on May 1, 1992. Perhaps the staff recalled how the Kerner Commission went much beyond what Johnson expected.

Fletcher offered the assistance of the commission and suggested the importance of the federal Community Reinvestment Act.

Nothing specific occurred. The president first blamed the Great

Bush at a meeting with civil rights leaders after
the Rodney King riots, May 1, 1992.

Society for the rioting, then decried casting blame, or the idea that
money could solve the Los Angeles problems, but rather asked for "an
honest, open national discussion about family, about values, about public policy, about race."[61]

The commission, continuing its attention to racial tensions, held the
January 21, 1992, meeting in Washington, D.C., at Carlos Rosario
International Public Charter School, where we conducted a hearing on
grievances of Hispanics concerning the District of Columbia government, which had paid little attention to the Hispanic community. The
hearing occurred after riots in the Mount Pleasant area, ignited by
claims of police abuse. We recommended improved police-community
relations, including the hiring of Spanish-speaking officers, and improvements in public services in the Latino community.[62]

As the 1992 election approached, the Congress reauthorized the
commission for one year at a budget of $8.27 million and prohibited the
creation of new regional offices. The administration had requested
$10.2 million. The appropriations bill approved only $7.776 million,
with the ban on new regional offices. Bush signed both bills.[63]

After Bill Clinton defeated Bush in the election, on November 22,
1992, Fletcher told the White House that in the next two months the

six-year terms of four commission members would expire. Carl Anderson had already written to Constance Horner, former Health and Human Services deputy secretary and director of White House personnel, asking to discuss the appointments and the "programs for the future" with her before Fletcher's letter.

Bush naturally wanted to appoint his supporters to any post that did not require Senate confirmation before he left office. Bush asked Horner to prepare a list of appointments "I am free to make between now and January 20. I have in mind certain people I want to accommodate." On November 6, she gave him a list "per your request of appointment options available to you," noting that some would be "an honor" even though they would expire when Bush left.

She told Bush they were assigning office seekers to temporary positions in agencies and inserting White House staff into civil service positions "carefully, legally, and with prudent attention to maintaining both the reality and the appearance of propriety." Fletcher recommended that they reappoint Buckley and keep staff director Wilfredo Gonzalez. Gonzalez had been the subject of a scathing letter about his dereliction of duty addressed to Bush and faxed over to the White House by Anderson on December 14, 1992. Civil servants wrote that he bought new furniture, including "a grandfather clock," and used commission services for the last year and a half to find a job. They also wrote, "It is common knowledge that he is not at the office or working for the agency most of the time. When he is there he comes in late and leaves early."

Horner, another Reagan Democrat turned Republican, had been director of Vista, director of the Office of Personnel Management, and associate director of the Office of Management and Budget before becoming deputy secretary of the Department of Health and Human Services. Bush had switched from pro-choice to anti-abortion as his party tilted rightward, and Washington gossip had it that she was appointed to HHS to please anti-abortion advocates who worried about Secretary Louis Sullivan's reliability on the issue. Repeating recommendations made unsuccessfully in the Reagan years by Pat Buchanan and other conservatives, Congressman Henry Hyde put forth Linda Chavez and Abigail Thernstrom as commissioners, but to no avail. Horner selected herself for one of the White House commission appointments. The president suggested Morris Abram again for the second seat. Horner told the president, "He has declined" but "has recommended a number of alternatives we are considering."[64]

Bush appointed Robert P. George, a Princeton political philosophy professor and anti-abortion advocate, whom Horner referred to as "Robbie," to the other position. With Anderson, Horner, and George, who were sworn in on January 20, 1993, just before the inauguration of the new president, the commission had three strong anti-abortion advocates.[65]

When Blandina Cardenas Ramirez's appointment expired on January 16, 1993, she decided not to accept reappointment. She was tired of the commission wars and eager to return to higher education in Texas. Senate Democrats appointed Cruz Reynoso, a distinguished lawyer and the first Hispanic justice of the California Supreme Court, to replace her. The son of Mexican immigrants and a graduate of Boalt Hall, the University of California at Berkeley's law school, he gained national recognition as deputy director and director of California Rural Legal Assistance, where he fought for rights of the poor from 1968 to 1972. After serving as a jurist with the Third District Court of Appeals of California in Sacramento, he served as an associate justice of the California Supreme Court from 1982 to 1987. When my appointment expired on December 12, 1992, Speaker of the House Thomas Foley (D-Wash.) reappointed me. Fletcher, Wang, Redenbaugh, and Anderson had appointments expiring in 1995.[66]

After Abram, Pendleton, and Bunzel left, Anderson quietly pursued the conservative agenda and Allen had tried to do so until he was discredited. The Republicans challenged the liberal Fletcher only infrequently, because though he was a fast-disappearing relic in the party, he was a Bush friend. Fletcher knew civil rights issues and wanted a robust commission. Baffled and embarrassed by the rejection for the Labor appointment and the insufficient commission resources, Fletcher remained disconsolate. The civil rights groups heralded him as a Republican supporter of affirmative action, and the president invited him to social events, but he was not able to influence policy as he had hoped.

The commission's past work on disabilities and penalties for employment discrimination helped to gain the passage of the Americans with Disabilities Act of 1990 and the Civil Rights Act of 1991, both of which the president signed. The president's conservative constituency, including members of the commission, remained unable to defeat the civil rights coalition in the struggle to preserve and advance protection against discrimination.

CHAPTER X

Here You Come Again

A T PARAMOUNT HIGH SCHOOL in Boligee, Alabama, in the heat and humidity of the cafeteria, with no air-conditioning, "the crowd grew as still as the July air when the Rev. Levi Pickens stood up on his one leg to speak." Pickens's Mount Zion Baptist Church, founded right after Reconstruction, had been mysteriously burned to the ground. There, in the heart of Black Belt Alabama, in a tiny, one-traffic-light town of about four hundred people, mostly black, Pickens expressed astonishment "at what's going on. Every time you turn on your TV you hear about a fire." Mount Zion was one of three churches that burned in Boligee, among nine African American churches that had burned in Alabama. Pickens had no detailed recommendations: "We have a problem," he said. "We need to admit we have a problem. We need to have enough love in our hearts to solve our problem." More than 162 small rural African American churches were burned down in 1996, all under suspicious circumstances that fire investigators called arson.[1]

No matter the causes of the fires or that a few white churches were torched as well—African Americans reacted with the knowledge that church burnings by the Klan and other white supremacist groups had been a favorite way to terrorize blacks since Reconstruction. In Mississippi, Alabama, Louisiana, Tennessee, and North and South Carolina, where the ghosts of civil rights martyrs stalk the land and the flames of burning churches are etched in memory, they feared the rise of another reign of terror.

The forum in Boligee marked the commission's third visit to the area since 1968. Before the fires, the communities remained racially divided, but race relations seemed relatively quiet. The SAC forums offered an opportunity for residents to speak, to listen to national and local investigators, and to allay some of their fears, despite what had occurred and the fact that they lived amid images of the Confederacy, still sustained and defended. I was there as commission chair appointed by Clinton in

Above: Rev. Levi Pickens, pastor of Mount Zion Baptist Church in Boligee, Alabama, whose church was burned and rebuilt, September 1996.
Below: Arson investigators sort through the remains of a sanctuary on the grounds of Matthews-Murkland Presbyterian Church in Charlotte, North Carolina, Friday, June 7, 1996. The black church had burned the previous day.

1993. The only commissioner who was a Republican appointee to attend the forums was Carl Anderson, the political director of a religious organization, the Knights of Columbus.[2]

Now we sat in the Paramount High School cafeteria, as wet from perspiration as the water glasses on the table. Not enough had changed in the county since 1968. Northern reporters who covered the forum were unprepared for the rot of Southern rural poverty and the persistent racism that we all observed. The public school where we held our forum was 99.9 percent black. The private academy, to which whites had fled after 1965, remained 100 percent white. They had exercised their "freedom of choice" to avoid attending school with blacks.[3]

An old Alabama woman complained that the Civil Rights Commission had been there "30 years ago and you've come again and again and you promise to come back but little changes." She was correct. As quickly as the fires attracted attention, they subsided, and concern about the poverty and Jim Crow in the communities we visited disappeared.[4]

Investigators failed to find out who set the majority of the church fires. President Clinton's National Church Arson Task Force reported that racism was behind some of the blazes, but others at African American churches and other houses of worship were motivated by a wide array of factors, "including not only blatant racism or religious hatred, but also financial profit, burglary and personal revenge."[5]

Of the cases that the task force closed, it concluded that one-fifth were racially motivated. Arrests were made in about 35 percent of these cases, compared to the average arrest rate of 16 percent in arson cases generally. In 1997, when I went back to the areas on which the task force had reported, I found African Americans generally still upset, although some Northern white churches were helping in the rebuilding. There had been new incidences of arson in some places. At many of the sites where we had held forums, the story was the same as that in Alabama, where only five of the twelve black church fires had been solved. In addition, two more had occurred in the week before my 1997 visit. In Boligee, Alabama, where Northern volunteers helped Rev. Pickens to rebuild, the black church arsons were never solved.[6]

We continued to follow up on the plight of poor rural African Americans after the church fires. We urged Agriculture Secretary Dan Glickman to take action on the long-standing complaints of black farmers about discrimination in receiving loans and advice from his department's programs that had led to the loss of their land. We had followed up on this issue since the commission's 1982 report on the subject and

Agriculture had used the study to develop an enforcement plan even as the black farmers geared up to sue. Reynoso and I also went to Agriculture to meet with Glickman, who said he was working on the issue, about which he had known nothing before he became secretary. Eventually, the department established a new, strengthened civil rights office, as the commission recommended, and hired one of our civil service employees to manage it. The farmers sued and eventually received some small compensation.[7]

One of the racial and ethnic tensions hearings we had held years before permitted us to go back to the Mississippi Delta area in the spring of 1997 for what ended up as a heated and heavily attended four days of hearings on public education, the economy, and voting rights. We found 50 percent of the residents living below the poverty line, unemployment 30 percent above the national average, and widespread segregation, as we had seen elsewhere in the rural South during the church fires forums. African American children attended public schools, and whites went to the private academies, which as Mayor Paul Artman, Jr., of Greenville pointed out, drained their families' incomes, making it difficult to support anything else. The poor pay made it impossible to keep or hire good teachers. Andrew Mullins, Jr., special assistant to the chancellor of the University of Mississippi, noted that sometimes "it's just a choice between a warm body and nobody."

The Mississippi riverboat casinos, which were supposed to jump-start the economies in the region, had not seemed to help the poor African American population in any measurable way. The few who worked in them had very low pay, and not enough were employed to make a difference. On voting, black witnesses testified of the harassment they faced when they tried to register to vote. We had successfully conducted the hearing, but knew we would not be able to gain approval of the report anytime soon from our Republican colleagues, most of whom did not even bother to attend. Deeply rooted poverty and inequality still pervaded the region.[8]

As a result of the congressional legislation enacted after the Reagan assault on the commission, the agency remained fractured and evenly divided along ideological lines until well into Clinton's second term. Using SAC forums made it possible to afford a podium to those, like Rev. Pickens, who felt harmed by what appeared to be civil rights violations. However, because these forums were not official hearings, we were unable to use our subpoena power, which would have allowed us to elicit even more information. It was not until 1999, when terms expired and the majority of the commissioners were Democrats, or Independents like me, instead of Reagan Bush Republicans, that we were able to pursue the monitoring and investigations that the commission needed to do and on which the commission had built its reputation. Finally, for a brief period, a majority committed to civil rights came into existence on the commission, for the first time since Reagan's takeover.

When the commission systematically returned to monitoring the federal government, holding hearings, and making recommendations, the reaction from the right was unrelenting. As commission chair beginning in 1993, I had to fight Congress after the Republican takeover and withstand constant attacks by Fox News Channel, the *Wall Street Journal* editorial page, and conservative columnists in other newspapers, instigated mostly by the remaining Reagan Bush commissioners. The unfair criticisms further poisoned working relationships at the commission and made it more difficult to focus on ways to attack discrimination.

That I became chair of the commission at all was almost a miracle. Although I was by then its longest-serving member, my relations with Clinton were not always amicable, from the time I first met him at Camp David during the Carter administration. Although the commission still had no specific jurisdiction over issues of sexual orientation, commissioners acting as individuals took different positions. I supported gay rights and criticized Clinton for his handling of the issue of gays in the military. My Republican colleague Robert George testified in *Romer v. Evans* as an expert witness in Colorado's losing attempt to prohibit cities and towns from taking any legal action to protect homosexuals from discrimination based on sexual orientation. I was pleased when the United States Supreme Court declared the law unconstitutional, finding the attempt to ban legal protection for homosexuals a denial of equal protection under the Fourteenth Amendment.[9]

When Clinton, shortly after taking office, was pushed by conservative Republicans and Democrats, as well as the military, to continue the exclusion of gays from the military, I opposed their efforts. The Servicemembers Legal Defense Network asked me to persuade Coretta Scott King to hold a press conference as part of its effort to influence Clinton to adopt a broad non-discrimination policy. Mrs. King had earlier criticized discrimination against gays, but she had not objected to a conditional policy that would discharge anyone whose sexual orientation became known, since Clinton set up a six-month review before announcing a decision.

Trading on a relationship born of many struggles, I asked Mrs. King for her help. She told me that "some of the men who had been with Martin" advised her to "stay out of it." However, she firmly believed Dr. King would have stood up for gays because of his unconditional belief in human rights. She finally said if I would come to stand with her, she would hold the press conference. I went to Atlanta, where Rev. Joseph Lowery broke ranks with the other "men who had been with Martin," to stand with us. Before the cameras, Mrs. King read a wonderfully supportive statement, recalling the debate over the role of Bayard Rustin, a gay man and a well-known civil rights organizer, in the 1963 March on Washington, Mrs. King said, "Like Martin, I don't believe you can stand for freedom for one group of people and deny it to others." I chimed in that the president should not issue a keep-quiet-about-it policy, which would essentially make liars out of gays in the military. Clinton issued the unsatisfactory "Don't Ask, Don't Tell" policy in July 1993, and I criticized him publicly.[10]

Early on, I had also criticized the president for refusing to support his nominee, Lani Guinier, to head the Civil Rights Division in the Justice Department. Clinton withdrew her name after Reaganites assailed her as a "quota queen" for her views on voting rights. Moreover, I had also criticized the president for not adopting a receptive stance for Haitian refugees and for being weak on affirmative action. Indeed, there were so many issues about which I disagreed with the president that it was only because of intense pressure on Clinton from disgruntled members of the Congressional Black Caucus that my designation as chair materialized. In addition, the Senate and House oversight chairmen, Paul Simon and Don Edwards, along with the Leadership Conference on Civil Rights coalition, proposed a leadership slate to the president including me as chair; Cruz Reynoso, distinguished professor at UCLA Law School and the first Hispanic on the California Supreme Court, as vice chair; and Stuart Ishimaru, a lawyer on Edwards's congressional staff, as staff director.[11]

Instead of waiting for Clinton to act on the commission appointments, Fletcher and the other four Republican appointees asked him to nominate Wang as chairman and Bobby Doctor as staff director. Wang, though a Democrat, was named to the commission by Bush. Doctor was a career civil servant at the commission who was head of the regional office in Atlanta. He became staff director, appointed by Fletcher at the end of Bush's presidency. Counting votes, the Republicans decided Clinton had no choice but to keep Doctor because the commission statute required five commissioners to confirm Clinton's nominee.

The White House ignored the Republicans' attempt to remain in control of the commission and vetted the names put forth by the civil rights groups. I know from talking to Clinton staffers that there were some who objected to my appointment because of my criticisms of the president. As chair, I would have a larger platform for denouncing the administration's positions. White House personnel director and Clinton confidant Bruce Lindsey asked me directly if, as chair, I would criticize Clinton. I assured him that if the president did nothing to undermine civil rights, he had nothing to fear from me. I was also questioned at length by the White House counsel's office about news articles in which I criticized some of Clinton's actions. I was forced to explain— once again—the independence of the commission. I was exercising my responsibility as a member of a watchdog agency. I kept saying that I believed Clinton appreciated an independent commission.

Less than a year into the Clinton administration, African Americans were keenly dissatisfied with the president. They had voted for him, despite concerns over his actions. He had made a special trip back to Arkansas during his campaign to witness the execution of Ricky Rector. He made a show of his anti-liberal bona fides by attacking the views of a participant, Sister Souljah, whom Jesse Jackson had invited to appear at his Rainbow/PUSH convention, in Jackson's presence. At that time Jackson was, by any measure, the nation's most popular black leader. As the 1993 Congressional Black Caucus meeting and dinner approached, Clinton had angered many blacks in Congress by his concessions to conservatives on the federal budget. The caucus refused an invitation to meet with the president the day before Clinton was scheduled to speak at the annual dinner. The White House decided to placate the CBC by assembling the administration's leading African American officials onstage at a news conference at the Democratic National Committee headquarters.

At this press conference, Alexis Herman, assistant to the president for public liaison, made the most of the announcement of my nomination as chair of the commission. The nomination, she said in florid prose, "continues in the tradition of demonstrating our commitment to pursue an active agenda of civil rights and to continue to pursue our partnership with the African-American community." When Clinton went to the dinner that night, he received an ovation from a placated CBC, rather than boos and hisses.[12]

However, I still had to overcome the objections of the Republicans on the commission. They decided to vote against my confirmation as chair unless Bobby Doctor became staff director. But in their calcula-

tions the Republicans discounted Stuart Ishimaru, who had been proposed by the civil rights group and Democratic leaders in Congress.
Further, Ishimaru's boss, Don Edwards, wielded significant clout as
oversight chairman. Edwards threatened to defund the commission if
they refused to support the White House slate.[13]

Redenbaugh, who considered himself quite adept at calculating the
odds to maintain influence, became key. After I promised him I would
be fair and make sure all commissioners had a chance to express their
views, he agreed to vote for me and Reynoso. He reasoned that Clinton
would not nominate anyone else and I would be grateful for his support,
so he decided to vote for us. Wang, a Democrat, made a similar calculation and voted for the candidate advanced by the Democratic president,
but Fletcher abstained, thus denying us the five votes needed. Therefore, the appointment process was stalled.[14]

It was Alexis Herman who talked Fletcher into changing his mind,
although I reminded Fletcher that I had supported him when he needed
my vote to become chair. Herman knew how bitterly disappointed he
had been when he was denied the position of secretary of labor and
rewarded, after all his years, with a "Mickey Mouse" small agency like
the commission. She would have the president appoint him to the Pennsylvania Avenue Development Corporation, where he could pursue his
interest in economic development contracts for minorities. He stepped
down as chair but stayed on the commission. He agreed to vote for us,
and Reynoso and I were confirmed in December 1993.

Left unresolved was the designation of the staff director. While the
Republican appointees seethed, Clinton went ahead with the Ishimaru
nomination. Fletcher would not vote for Ishimaru because he worked
for Edwards, who had refused to recommend a budget increase for the
commission while Fletcher was chair. Fletcher also objected to Ishimaru, as a Japanese American, because he somehow reminded him of
Japan's perfidy in World War II. Ishimaru, a native-born American who
joked that he even preferred pizza to sushi, was dumbfounded. Not willing to abandon Ishimaru, the president was forced to appoint him as
acting staff director.[15]

The president's action set off an explosion at the commission. The
Republican appointees, having failed to maintain control through their
own staff director, retaliated. George successfully sued against the
appointment of Ishimaru as acting staff director. Judge Royce Lambeth
ruled that the president could not name an acting staff director without the agreement of a majority of the commissioners. Otherwise, he

could use an acting appointment to thwart the concurrence requirement indefinitely. This meant that, contrary to commission practice,
Fletcher's earlier appointment of Doctor as acting staff director also was
improper. According to Judge Lambeth, no one could nominate a staff
director or an acting staff director except the president with the agreement of a commission majority. Therefore, the agency would, practically, have either a confirmed staff director or none.[16]

Then the Republican appointees argued that Lambeth's opinion
meant Clinton should nominate Doctor because he had their five votes.
I had known Doctor since I was first appointed to the commission and
had helped him to obtain a position again after the layoffs occasioned by
the budget cuts in the Reagan era. As acting staff director he reinforced
Fletcher's sour mood by maintaining that the commission could not do
its work because of inadequate resources, instead of encouraging greater
effort. He refused to accede to the president's preference for Ishimaru.

The stalemate after the court decision forced us to find a compromise. We were in a fix with Karen Narasaki and others in the Asian
American civil rights groups who had Clinton's agreement to name an
Asian American. He had followed through by naming Ishimaru, even
though he lost the court challenge. We floated names of several other
qualified candidates but could not find support for their confirmation.
After much discussion in the spring of 1994, we finally settled on Mary
Mathews, the assistant staff director for administration, a civil servant
with an MBA and admittedly very little knowledge of civil rights matters, whom the Republicans agreed to confirm. Doctor returned to his
regional director's job in Atlanta.[17]

Cruz and I wondered whether we would accomplish much with a
staff director who was somewhat beholden to the Republicans. On civil
rights issues, we could count on Fletcher's vote, and Wang would follow
our lead since he had no particular concerns. But all that would accomplish was a 4–4 tie. On management and our ability as an investigative
agency to conduct research, we faced a slashed budget and a demoralized staff. The only advantage we had was Mathews's promise after she
was confirmed that she would manage the agency on a nonpartisan
basis.

For the next six months, relations with Congress were smooth. We
achieved a small budget increase with Edwards's help. But the midterm
elections of 1994, in which Newt Gingrich (R-Ga.) became Speaker
of the House, broke that brief interlude. Congressman Henry Hyde
(R-Ill.) became chairman of the Judiciary Committee; Charles Canaday

(R-Fla.) assumed the chairmanship of the House Judiciary Committee Subcommittee on the Constitution, displacing Edwards. Mathews and I called on him in his House office in January 1995, as a routine courtesy. He and his staff, clued in by the Republican commissioners, listened while we talked and then ushered us to the door.

When we met with Congressman Hal Rogers (R-Ky.), the Appropriations Subcommittee chair, he displayed a complete lack of understanding of the commission's role. He demanded to know how we could cut our budget even more—perhaps by having the federal agencies detail staff to help us perform our work. He became irritated when I responded that we could not very well have agencies that we monitor help us to evaluate their own work. Clinton kept recommending increases, at my insistence, even though the civil rights coalition had given up on the commission after Ishimaru lost the staff director's position and we became divided 4–4. The coalition preferred to have the president use his influence on increasing the Justice Department enforcement budget, where they had some success in the Congress. This was wise because the commission's Republican appointees, relying on Republican control of the House, insisted that the commission would receive no budget increase until they had a staff director who did their bidding.

After the Republican takeover of the House, California congressman Julian Dixon, our Appropriations Subcommittee senior Democrat, told me it was all he could do to keep the budget from being chopped further. As a matter of strategy, the civil rights groups wanted those of us who were Democratic appointees to stay on the commission to prevent the production of bad reports. But their political posture was to continue their condemnation of the useless and dysfunctional commission created by Reagan.

Adding to our woes, freely available media forums in the *Wall Street Journal* editorial page and the *Washington Times* were entirely open to the Republican appointees. We, on the other hand, had difficulty even getting letters to the editor published to correct errors in those two papers. Indeed, we had trouble gaining access to any other media unless we were criticizing Clinton.

The commission, with an evenly divided membership, struggled to accomplish some productive work until we gained a majority in 1999, more than halfway through Clinton's second term. Our consistently positive relations with the relevant White House staff, most of whom I had known since we served in the Carter administration, gave us enough

access to push recommendations. Staffers alerted me to anything that
affected civil rights and asked for the commission's views. They understood our independence, and I was willing to give advice based on what
I perceived to be consistent with commission policy, and to express my
personal opinions. They also wanted to keep me informed in the hope
that I would not criticize them unnecessarily in the press. I do not recall
any occasion where a civil rights decision was announced that caught me
unawares.

Instead of writing letters, beyond transmittal of reports to the White
House, I usually called a staffer I knew if I wanted to discuss some particular recommendation or complain about some problem I thought
needed attention. On unusual occasions, perhaps twice during Clinton's
tenure, I would fax a letter to the president and receive a reply. Given
our experience with Reagan, I was more concerned about protecting the
commission's independence than having Clinton's approval. I was more
interested in ensuring that the agencies enforced civil rights and that
bad policy was avoided.

I also talked to Clinton directly, while sitting next to or across from
him at small dinners and at informal meetings about civil rights issues.
On social occasions, I sometimes harassed him about such matters as the
persistent Haitian refugee problem and the exile of the elected Haitian
president Jean-Bertrand Aristide, a former Catholic priest. Reynoso
also talked to the president on such occasions.[18]

Cruz and I were able to give advice, based on the commission's work,
on a presidential response to a summer of 1995 Supreme Court decision
that race-based set-asides in government contracts would be unconstitutional in most circumstances. Given the continued minuscule share of
taxpayer-supported contracts awarded to minority contractors, despite a
policy to remedy the disparity dating from 1978, the entire civil rights
coalition was in despair.[19]

George Stephanopoulos, displaced by Dick Morris's ascendancy as a
Clinton advisor, volunteered to work on a new policy for the president
that would withstand legal scrutiny. He had Christopher Edley, who had
returned from OMB to Harvard when his leave expired, serve as a special counsel and write the report. Edley and Stephanopoulos consulted
widely with experts and civil rights leaders as they developed ideas.
Clinton received a steady flow of briefing papers and held informal discussions, some of which Reynoso and I attended, to discuss the issues.
The four commission Republican appointees, despite the commission's
long-standing support for minority contracts, opposed the measure.

Discussion during dinner with Bill Clinton as he developed a policy
to permit the continuation of affirmative action, July 1995.

The Democratic Leadership Council conservatives pressured Clinton to abandon the set-asides instead of finding ways to continue them.

At one small working dinner near the end of the process, I told the president that beyond the policy issues, given his rhetorical emphasis on his race relations history, the public would find a statement in opposition to be ridiculous. At the National Archives on July 19, 1995, Clinton made his "Mend It, Don't End It" speech, preserving most of the policy. The contracting agencies would first use race-neutral approaches in selecting awardees, including, instead of race, such factors as social disadvantage. They would need to justify the use of race as a plus factor. After the agencies made sure their procedures were in compliance, they continued to award contracts.[20]

Cruz and I also thought the commission needed a way to hear from experts and aggrieved persons on issues that would have been the subject of the hearings that we could not hold because of the 4–4 split. After consulting with the staff director, we persuaded the other commissioners that the commission should hold informal public briefings on issues whenever any commissioner desired, without the necessity for formal agreement. The timing of such briefings would depend on scheduling opportunities handled by the staff director. The others agreed because the opportunity to propose briefings and witnesses was available to any commissioner. With the briefings on national issues and reports generated by the state advisory committees, we would be able to shine a spotlight on issues and hear from the public even if not under optimal circumstances. The state advisory committee reports on church fires were conducted in this way.

The Republican appointees supported a report produced by the staff to renew an annual review of funding for civil rights agencies that the commission had produced routinely before the Reagan disruption. They voted for it because while it revealed that enforcement agencies had experienced their deepest cuts during the Reagan administration, it also explained that funding levels increased during the George Bush administration at a greater rate than during the Clinton administration. However, the Bush increases occurred because the overall workload of the enforcement agencies increased as more civil rights laws were adopted, including the Civil Rights Restoration Act of 1987, the Fair Housing Amendments Act of 1988, and the Americans with Disabilities Act of 1990. The new laws permitted persons who would not have been covered before to file complaints when they suffered discrimination.

We found that most of the enforcement agencies tried to exercise their responsibilities but simply lacked sufficient resources. Clinton requested small increases, but not enough money. We hoped our report would insulate the EEOC, Justice, the Office of Federal Contract Compliance in Labor, and the Civil Rights Offices in the cabinet departments from cuts and maybe even help them garner an increase from the Congress. The administration knew we were correct, and the civil rights organizations pushed for more funding, but the Clintonites did not appreciate the political fallout from our criticism of their minuscule budget request. Despite complaints, Clinton, pressed by the civil rights coalition, began to ratchet up increases, especially for the Civil Rights Division of the Department of Justice.[21]

The Republican appointees, working with congressional staffers and their constituencies, did everything possible to make life miserable for Staff Director Mathews and to harass me so that the commission could achieve nothing productive. Then the congressional oversight House chairman, Canady, would complain that we were not being productive. When we were productive we were attacked.

In the fall of 1995 we prepared for a hearing on racial and ethnic tensions in Miami focused on immigration and anti-immigration legislative and constitutional attempts. The staff were so accustomed to the General Counsel's Office issuing subpoenas routinely to all witnesses at our hearings, as had been done since 1957, that they never considered how the opposition to our efforts might mislead the public about our procedures. The commission issued subpoenas to protect witnesses who were afraid to testify or who risked their employment, and also to avoid drawing distinctions between willing and unwilling witnesses at hearings. Each witness would be told that it was a blanket process and did not imply his or her unwillingness. The subpoenas covered persons and relevant documents. They were approved in a blanket way for each hearing by the commission when it voted to have a hearing and they would be prepared by the General Counsel's Office and signed by autopen for the chair.

Three South Florida anti-immigration activists who were not on the staff's list asked to testify. They wanted Florida voters to approve four constitutional amendments that would make English the state's official language and ban illegal immigrants from receiving most social services and from attending public schools. They also wanted to require school officials to report suspected illegal immigrant children to federal immigration authorities.[22]

Suspecting nothing, the civil service lawyers told them they would receive subpoenas and put them on the witness list. When the subpoenas were issued, the anti-immigrant activists went public with complaints to their congressmen attacking the commission and me, in particular, for compelling them to testify. They lied to create a fuss, claiming that staff had harassed and intimidated them by threatening them with subpoenas. They also falsely accused the staff of requesting materials that intruded into the privacy of their organizations. We quickly realized that the anti-immigrant activists had staged the episode.

Soon the Florida affiliate of the ACLU was thinking of taking the case. I realized that no one in the ACLU would remember that the organization was a principal supporter of subpoena power for the commission when it was established in 1957. It agreed then that the power was needed "to put the facts on top of the table." I believed that if the matter played out in the press the way they were positioning it, it would pose a real threat to the continued existence of the subpoena authority.

I wrote to the activists and released to the public a letter withdrawing the subpoenas. I explained that we had been willing to include them at their request but could manage without their testimony.[23]

However, the Republicans achieved a temporary public relations coup. An editorial in the *St. Petersburg Times* bought the argument that we were prying into the private affairs of an organization unnecessarily, saying we were right to come to Florida but not to "pack a crowbar."[24]

Our oversight chairman, Florida Republican congressman Canaday, announced hearings, sent a steady stream of questions to the commission about the matter, and threatened to take away the subpoena power. Canaday's staff managed to tie up the commission staff answering questions, which delayed other work, and then complained publicly about the delays. However, the furor soon died down, and we had kept the subpoena power.[25]

Working relationships at the commission did not improve even after Clinton appointed two new commissioners when Fletcher's and Wang's terms expired. In December 1995, the president appointed Yvonne Lee, a San Francisco activist on aging and other justice issues. I persuaded the widely respected former federal appeals court judge A. Leon Higginbotham, Jr., to accept an appointment on November 30, 1995. After a distinguished career as a federal judge, Higginbotham served as public service professor of jurisprudence at Harvard University's John F. Kennedy School of Government and was counsel to the law firm of Paul, Weiss, Rifkind, Wharton, and Garrison. President Clinton had already awarded him a Presidential Medal of Freedom. But having two distinguished jurists on the commission did not help. We still had a 4–4 ideological split, and sadly, the Republican appointees had no more respect for the judges than they had for me or the staff director.[26]

The Republicans were not finished with us after the subpoena gambit. They insisted on formally reviewing Mathews's work for her personnel file, in order to force her to leave. They had no right to review her because, as a presidential appointee, she served at the pleasure of the president. However, as an outstanding career civil servant she did not want her record smeared, no matter how bogus the process. She also resented the discussion of the issue at commission meetings open to the public.

The Republican appointees had essentially made her life miserable when they saw she would not follow their lead. She cooperated fully with me and tried to manage the agency as best she could, given the lack of resources, but they wanted her to delay the work we tried to do and then have Congress complain that we did no work. The situation was made worse by the continued hostility of the civil rights groups that had been promised an Asian American appointee as staff director.

When a disgusted Mathews retired in December 1996, we were left

Judge A. Leon Higginbothan, distinguished jurist, lawyer, and
scholar, receiving the Medal of Freedom in 1995 from
President Clinton with Hillary Clinton.

with no staff director and no hope of five votes to approve any new
appointee. The only person who could appoint a deputy staff director
was the staff director, and under the rules she could not appoint a
deputy staff director if four commissioners objected. In the absence of
any other strategy before Mathews left, she appointed Gerri Mason
Hall, a career civil servant working as personnel director, to become acting deputy staff director. Our counsel advised that we did not need a
majority vote to name an acting deputy staff director, and the Republicans did not object. When Hall eventually left, we continued to concoct
acting deputy positions until we had the votes to confirm a staff director.

At the instigation of the Republican commissioners, the oversight
committee decided to have the GAO and the Office of Personnel Management audit the agency. Not surprisingly, the GAO found an array of
minor management deficiencies that needed remedying. A major finding was the failure to rewrite the volumes of administrative instructions,
governing the day-to-day management of the agency, which had not
been rewritten since the 1970s. Reagan staff director Chavez did not
rewrite them because, according to Pendleton, with the budget cuts,
they did not want to take precious staff time away from their work. We

did not rewrite them for the same reason. The staff spent a great deal of time responding to the GAO letter, and we devoted staff time to rewriting the instructions. However, our oversight subcommittee held a hearing in order to garner press coverage of the "bad management," to score political points.[27]

In addition to the congressional conflict, we confronted angry SAC chairs when the Republican appointees refused to vote to accept reports from the Illinois, Indiana, and Michigan state advisory committees. They insisted that the SACs rewrite the reports to present a "balanced" view, which really meant opposition to affirmative action. Reports could be printed and disseminated only if they were "accepted" by the commission. The chairs pointed out that the reports reflected the views of people in their state, expressed in forums open to anyone who wished to speak on the subject. In addition, they reminded the commission that the committees, composed of volunteers, were the "eyes and ears" of the commission and not reflectors of the commission's preferences. When the four Republicans refused to relent, the chairs found resources to have their reports printed privately and released through the media. I apologized publicly to the SACs for the 4–4 standoff. This unprecedented commission action violated the very principle on which the SACs were established. If they were forced to report what commissioners wanted, there would be no reason for their existence.[28]

When former Mississippi governor William Winter wrote to Clinton in 1997, asking him to begin an initiative on race, the White House staff shared Winter's letter with me and asked my opinion as the idea developed. Some commissioners wanted me to propose that the commission undertake the initiative. I have no idea as to whether I could have persuaded the president to let the commission undertake the task, but I did not try. The president had in mind serving his political needs, and what we produced might conflict with his goals. Our band of pro–civil rights commissioners did not like the possibility of being instructed by the president to prepare a report on any subject where the expected result was preordained, given our concerns about the commission's independence. Also, we agreed that the agency had been deeply wounded both fiscally and by the presence of a 4–4 split, as well as the Republican appointees' hostility and refusal to behave in a collegial manner. We were too divided to produce a consensus. After a great deal of discussion, the president settled on appointing a committee, chaired by historian John Hope Franklin, to hold public forums around the country to help encourage better race relations and make recommendations to the White House.

Some of our internal problems at the commission were solved when the president appointed Ruby G. Moy as staff director on June 20, 1997. Moy, who was Chinese American, had worked for Alexis Herman in the White House before she become secretary of labor. The White House staff thought she satisfied the desire of the Asian American civil rights community for an Asian American staff director. She had no civil rights experience, but was a politically seasoned operative. Moy had been on the staff of Congressman Frank Horton, a New York Republican, from 1973 to 1992, managing his Washington and district offices. We had enough votes for confirmation because Redenbaugh, who so much wanted to force Mathews out, was willing to vote for Moy. Since she admittedly knew little about civil rights, he mistakenly expected her to embarrass the administration.[29]

Showing her political savvy, Moy responded to an op-ed in the *Washington Post* from Reagan-era commission staff director Linda Chavez, who used her Center for Equal Opportunity to attack anything designed to enhance opportunity for African Americans and me in particular. She used Clinton's announcement of his race commission to explain how the commission "has simply outlived its usefulness."

Moy said, "Clinton has demonstrated his support by seeking budget increases for the commission. If he intended to do away with it, he would not have appointed me as the new staff director." She also noted that the "President did not turn to the commission to serve as his advisory board for a national dialogue on race because he wanted personal advisers. The commission is an independent fact-finding agency that conducts its own investigations and reports to the President and Congress." She also pointed out that the commission's responsibilities "go considerably beyond race" and include responsibility for age, disability, sex, and national origin. Moy also noted that Chavez had overlooked examples of mismanagement, identified by the GAO, that had transpired when she was staff director in the 1980s and that she had not remedied.[30]

Even with the divided commission, we were able to obtain enough votes to publish studies, so long as they did not take a position on penalties for discrimination against African Americans. These included a report on students with disabilities and enforcement of Section 504 of the Rehabilitation Act of 1973 and the enforcement of Title VI and the *Lau* remedies for students with limited English ability. We also published the Miami racial and ethnic tensions report. We recommended that any legislation making English an official language should take into account the inadequacy of language education and the difficulties facing

English-only speakers who did not know Spanish when seeking jobs in Miami. We also pressed the Haitian refugee issue again and emphasized the lack of economic development as contributors to the riots that occurred after the police shootings. George and Redenbaugh concurred, and Horner and Anderson dissented. We held hearings on schools and religion in New York and Seattle, at the behest of the Republicans, who thought the rights of individual students to engage in silent prayer and otherwise practice free exercise of religion were violated. At the hearings, we took extensive testimony but heard no evidence of any official effort to undermine free exercise of religion.[31]

We also published two reports on the Americans with Disabilities Act, one on local government compliance and the Justice Department's coordination of compliance by federal grant-making agencies, and the other evaluating the EEOC's enforcement of the employment non-discrimination provisions of the Americans with Disabilities Act. We praised the EEOC for processing an increasing number of complaints despite a stagnating budget. But the EEOC had not developed policy statements on complex issues like reasonable accommodation, which employers and disabled people needed. Though the Justice Department had developed effective outreach and technical assistance programs, it had failed to monitor ADA compliance at the agencies that it supposedly coordinated.[32]

We tried mightily but could not persuade the Republican commissioners to actually review and debate reports or to try to find consensus. In the general lack of cordiality in commission proceedings, Judge Higginbotham began to regret his participation. On December 14, 1998, he died, after a long battle with heart disease. Even during his final days and when he became ill at a commission meeting, I was appalled when the Republican appointees showed a studied indifference toward his condition and appeared to have no respect for his contributions or reputation.

Horner and George left when their terms expired in December 1998, giving us a majority, which was extended when Clinton and the Democrats in Congress made new appointments. Reynoso and I resigned our congressional terms simultaneously with our acceptance of Clinton presidential appointments. After my reappointment, I recommended the appointment of a Native American, for the first time in the history of the commission. Senate majority leader Tom Daschle appointed Elsie Meeks, a Lakota Sioux businesswoman from South Dakota, who had run unsuccessfully for governor, to the Senate

Democratic vacancy left by Cruz Reynoso's becoming a presidential appointee.

I asked Minority Leader Dick Gephardt to appoint Harvard law professor Christopher Edley, Jr., who was partly responsible for the successful "Mend It, Don't End It" policy. I had known Edley since we both served in the Carter administration. His father, who was executive director of the United Negro College Fund, and I became friends when I headed federal education programs. Edley Sr. and I spent almost twenty-four hours straight together figuring out how to rescue black colleges from an administration proposal to cut off their student loan funds because of a high default rate. Gephardt appointed Edley on May 4, 1999, to the vacancy left when I moved to a presidential appointment.[33]

Having a majority did not insulate us from sharp attacks from the two Republican appointees, megaphoned by their media. With the attacks, the dysfunctional structure, and congressional oversight in their hands, extraordinary efforts were required to achieve anything positive. We had to be able to withstand withering personal attacks to keep doing the work. But we felt rewarded because ordinary people gained a hearing and some responsiveness from their government despite our weakness and fractiousness.

One of the issues where we achieved some traction was on alleged police abuse. On February 4, 1999, eight days before the Senate vote on Clinton's impeachment, Amadou Diallo was killed by police in New York City. Diallo's body absorbed nineteen of a barrage of shots fired by four white police officers in the vestibule of his apartment building for no apparent reason. The commission first asked Attorney General Janet Reno to investigate the shooting, focusing on our consistent concern with episodes that exacerbated bad police-community relations. We thought that "only by demonstrating a wholehearted commitment to finding the truth" would "public concern about police community relations be alleviated." Reno replied that she had begun an investigation with the involvement of the FBI and would keep us apprised of the results. I also wrote the president, explaining that through constant engagement we were "fed up" with the persistence of unaddressed "alleged police misconduct." He quickly replied: "Janet is on it."[34]

We puzzled over whether we should respond to the demands of civil rights groups that we go to New York to investigate police-community relations. We had been monitoring police-community relations in New York City since the Abner Louima incident in August 1997, and our

Mamadou Diallo holds the kickplate from the front door of an
apartment building shot through with bullet holes, February 4, 1999,
in New York. Diallo said the holes were made when police officers
fired forty-one bullets at his nephew Amadou Diallo.

state advisory committee and Representative José Serrano (D-N.Y.), the
ranking member of our Appropriations Subcommittee, had asked us to
conduct hearings after the Diallo shooting. We reflected on the commission's consistent experience with the media and police, first attacking
any criticisms and then retreating when we were shown by events to
have been correct. The most recent experience was our report on the

Los Angeles police covering improper police behavior, the handling of complaints against police officers, and the adequacy of procedures for selecting and training officers who train fellow officers in the field. We recommended best practices used in other departments to heal police community relations.[35]

When the commission released the report on Los Angeles in May 1999, the police immediately attacked its charges of abuse and corruption as outdated. The *Los Angeles Times* editorialized in support of the police argument. Thereafter, incontrovertible evidence of the truth of our report surfaced, leading to a succession of police chiefs and other officials, hired and fired, who claimed to deal with the problems. It was not until November 2000, however, that a *Los Angeles Times* news story noted that "the Civil Rights Commission 18 months ago cited abuses at the Police Department and the Sheriff's Department—months before the Rampart scandal shook the LAPD with evidence of police corruption. That scandal triggered an agreement this week between the city and the Justice Department that gives the federal government unprecedented oversight powers in forcing reforms at the Police Department."[36]

We decided that despite the probability of the usual criticism, we would investigate the New York Police Department, the use of deadly force, and police-community relations. Having no funds to pay an adequate permanent staff, the staff director hired a small woman-owned public relations firm, McKinney and Associates, to conduct the commission's media outreach and public information. The commission's legal staff collected information and interviewed witnesses, and then, on May 26, 1999, we held a hearing in New York focused on the Diallo incident and other complaints about alleged police abuse, which was titled "Police Practices and Civil Rights." In a packed hearing room, we listened to and questioned Mayor Rudolph Giuliani, police officials, officers, and the individuals who asked to speak in a forum lasting until the early-morning hours.

At first Mayor Giuliani's administration welcomed our police practices hearing. He recalled cooperating with us during the Wall Street and immigration hearing in 1996. The report on that hearing included data and analysis of the disparate opportunities offered to women and some people of color in the financial services industry. We assured him that we understood the tough work of crime fighting and the need to exercise restraint when appropriate. I said, "We all want to be protected from abuse or criminal behavior." However, "at the same time it is better for both the police and for residents that the police are respected and

Above: New York mayor Rudolph Giuliani testifying in May 1999 at commission hearings on the New York Police Department. *Below:* Protesters outside United Nations headquarters after acquittal of police officers in Diallo shooting death, February 27, 2000.

that they carry out their duties in a way that is not itself a source of abuse."[37]

The audience at the hearings hissed and booed Giuliani, and protesters against him and the police gathered outside. Weeks later, when we made our recommendations, he expressed fury at our conclusion that the police engaged in racial profiling when determining whether to make an arrest. Instead of contending with the supportive data from the police department which we subpoenaed and analyzed in the report, Giuliani focused on a $250 contribution I had made to Hillary Clinton's Senate campaign and described the investigation as a "political operation of the Democratic Party." Since I was a part-time government official, no rule or policy prevented me or any other commissioners from making contributions to campaigns. The civil service staff prepared the New York report with the help of a law firm they engaged. As with every commission report, I had only one vote in deciding whether to approve it. I pointed out that "we have no intention of publishing the report without seeing the comments of the mayor, the police chief and all of the other people who testified at the hearing," all to no avail.[38]

In the 250-page report, published in August 2000, we praised the police department for several efforts to improve its relationship with minorities. However, we characterized the department's overall approach to race relations as flawed in everything from training to promotions. *The New York Times* noted, "Even though its findings are largely critical, the draft report is restrained in its language, and there are several discussions of disputed issues in which the commission acknowledges that statistics support the Police Department's version of events. For instance, although critics have suggested that psychological screenings were being used to block minority candidates from the Police Department, the commission found that the statistics did not support that contention." The Giuliani administration issued a detailed rebuttal of the findings, which we published in the report.

The racial profiling section of the report, based on NYPD data from 1998, indicated that 51 percent of the people stopped and searched by the police in Staten Island were black. Most of them were never charged with anything. African Americans constituted only 9 percent of the island's population. Throughout New York City, African Americans were stopped well above their proportion in every community. Police commissioner Howard Safir complained that we did not take into consideration "many factors, including who the victims describe, what the demographics of crime are in this city and who the criminals are in individual instances." The police data showed, however, that descriptions of who might have committed the crime did not affect the race of the persons stopped.[39]

Our most controversial recommendation naively suggested the need for an independent prosecutor when police are accused of crimes, since local district attorneys "must work with police on a routine basis." We did not reckon with the iconic status of the Manhattan district attorney, Robert M. Morgenthau, who thundered that the commission erred in never seeking information about his record, which included the prosecution, even when it failed, of many brutality cases. Some critics accused us of making a personal attack on Morgenthau's integrity and his office. The report merely stated a reality of how police and prosecutors interact and suggested the need for precautions. Some noted the decline in police killings and thought that should have been highlighted instead of the racial profiling data concerning arrests. After the furor died down, the police quietly implemented some of the best-practice ideas that the commission recommended that were already in use in other communities, with better police-community relations achieved without weakening their crime-control efforts.[40]

In the spring of 1999, in addition to the New York hearings, the commission also held consultations with experts and briefings in Washington on such subjects as the crisis of the young African American male in the inner cities. We covered employment, the criminal justice system, and inadequate education and motivational programs and activities in a report issued in early 2000 that suggested solutions. Clinton appointed Victoria Wilson, a senior editor at Alfred A. Knopf publishers in New York, to the vacancy created by Higginbotham's death. With a majority of commissioners, we were able to seriously consider the reports we asked the staff to prepare.[41]

We also decided to continue to accept requests from our state advisory committees that we educate ourselves by meeting with them in their states, making site visits and hearing from local people about their concerns. Commission proceedings would also give greater visibility and clout to the committees as they tried to influence local officials. The Republican appointees objected. They wanted a national media platform to attack us in Washington in order to pursue their political agenda of making us appear inefficient and ineffective, characterizing the commission as a body that achieved nothing.

Having a majority, we were able to respond when our South Dakota State Advisory Committee became very concerned about the treatment of Native Americans in the criminal justice system. They had monitored the issue for years, but reports of the deaths under suspicious circumstances of at least fifty-seven Native Americans near the Pine Ridge Reservation and allegations by the tribes that the FBI did nothing in response caused the committee to ask for our help. In December 1999 we went to Rapid City, South Dakota, to hold a forum with the SAC. Native Americans also complained that while the reservation prohibited alcohol use and sale, Indians became drunk in the town of White Clay, Nebraska, across the border. Many would drive home in the dark, contributing to a high rate of accidents and accidental deaths.

The bodies of two Sioux men, Wilson Black Elk, Jr., and Ronald Hard Heart, were found in a grassy ravine north of White Clay. Authorities suspected foul play but made no arrests in their deaths. In one egregious case, twenty-two-year-old Robert "Boo" Many Horses was found dead in a garbage can in Mobridge on June 30. A judge dismissed manslaughter and assault charges against four youths who allegedly dumped his body in the garbage can, ruling that the evidence was insufficient. The local authorities announced that Many Horses died of alcohol poisoning.

After a site visit to facilities and homes on the reservation, commissioners sat with the SAC at a crowded, daylong forum where the testimony went on for hours into the night. Native American families drove for miles from across the state and some camped out to attend. A wheelchair-bound, ninety-year-old Sisseton, South Dakota, grandmother said she was assaulted by a town and tribal police officer. A sobbing Wagner, South Dakota, couple said local authorities refused to investigate the alleged sexual assault of their thirteen-year-old daughter at the hands of a non-Indian. We need "justice today, not tomorrow, today," the Wagner mother said. "You've got to do something about it." As testimony continued, I left the chair to go over to the couple, as they cried out loud, and I tried to console them. I asked them to provide information to an FBI agent waiting nearby.

Because they knew the commission majority might vote to hold formal hearings where they could be subpoenaed, the officials from the FBI and local government came to testify. The Native Americans expressed amazement, saying they had tried and could obtain no answers from any responsible official. The SAC included the allegations and responses in their report, *Native Americans in South Dakota: An Erosion of Confidence in the Justice System*, published in March 2000. The FBI thereafter reported that following its investigations some of the murders had been solved but others were still unresolved.

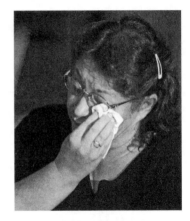

Peggy Redday at the commission's Native American Forum, December 1999.

Lakota Sioux Elaine Holy Eagle of Rapid City, South Dakota, cries as she reads a statement at the commission's Native American Forum at Pine Ridge, December 1999.

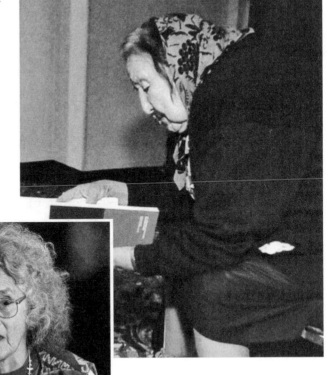

Esther Moves Camp of Pine Ridge at the December 1999 Forum.

Darlene Renville Pipe Boy testifies at the Forum.

The local press coverage of our South Dakota investigation was the most extensive and objective we had ever had. However, South Dakota's governor, William Janklow, called the report "garbage" and "fiction," and said we had "bad-mouthed" the state. Such a public outcry against his remarks ensued that he ordered a study of the justice system. But, to his dismay, the state-funded study released almost two years later, in November 2002, confirmed the SAC's findings. The study showed inequities at every point in the administration of justice. Native American arrest, prosecution, and incarceration rates were the highest in the state. Even for the same crime, Native Americans received more severe punishment. Because of such experiences, Native Americans expressed deep mistrust of the whole system.[42]

We decided to visit White Clay, two miles from the Pine Ridge Reservation, where alcohol is banned, and found a town that existed only as a liquor emporium, selling four million cans of beer a year, mostly to residents of Pine Ridge. The town profited from beer and alcohol sales to reservation residents, who walked or drove across the state line. Sheriff Robbins, of Sheridan County, Nebraska, whose jurisdiction includes White Clay, told us that two men who committed suicide—one of them a Pine Ridge resident who was serving eleven days in jail—were depressed. Robbins said, "Alcohol doesn't work in the Native American system like in other ethnic groups," which adds to the problems created by unemployment and idleness. The county had no short-term detoxification center. Although merchants who sold alcohol to someone already drunk could have their license suspended, Nebraska law allows retailers to keep operating if they paid a penalty of $50 a day.[43]

We also met with White Clay business owners at the Fireside Inn, one of the other businesses on the town's main street. A number of Native American men sat along the street, drinking from bottles in paper bags. The street was littered with discarded cans and bottles of beer not permitted on the reservation. The business owners told us they did not see racism in White Clay, which drew sneers from the Indians crowded into the room.

A few months after the SAC forum, I traveled to Nebraska to join Commissioner Meeks for a meeting with Governor Mike Johannes to ask him to do something about White Clay. We wanted more detoxification centers, a policy where individuals who were obviously drunk would be able to sleep before going home, or more emphasis on the availability of counseling services in White Clay. He understood the problem but seemed at a loss as to how to deal with it. We hoped the positive publicity about our site visit and the meeting with the governor might have a shaming effect. However, White Clay remained an attraction for Native Americans who drank excessively, and no action was taken to control the problem.

The commission decided to play a role when Texas, after a negative affirmative action court decision, and California, after a referendum, both outlawed affirmative action in admission to their colleges and universities. The commission had long supported taking into account racial diversity as one factor when admitting students, but by this time the long public relations campaign by conservatives to label such programs as unfair preferential treatment, "quotas," and reverse discrimination against whites, despite the small number of blacks in elite public higher education institutions, had taken a toll. At the same time leaders in all fields of endeavor knew that including blacks and the rapidly increasing and underrepresented Latino population in such institutions was necessary in order to achieve a quality education for everyone and for the future development of the national economy. Further, persons in these populations constituted a larger share of the taxpayers who funded public institutions, including colleges and universities.

California and Texas had adopted plans in which the top 10 percent of graduates from every high school could attend some flagship institution in the state. Florida had implemented such a plan without any legal force to do so. In 2000, entering the debate on protecting affirmative action in higher education, we analyzed the impact of percentage plans, irritating those on all sides who had embraced them, to determine their effectiveness as a solution to the lack of diversity in higher education and as substitutes for affirmative action. We determined by a 6–2 vote, with Redenbaugh and Anderson dissenting, that such plans "may succeed as an effective public relations strategy" and "could gain broad appeal because they focus on the goal that everyone should have an equal opportunity to learn in higher education." However, "they are no substitute for strong race-conscious affirmative action in higher education." We also criticized Florida governor Jeb Bush because he failed to offer remedies for his state's acknowledged inadequate public education, which undermined the ability of victimized students to prepare for college.

We found that the plans successively included minority students but not the same students or as high a number as under affirmative action, especially in Florida's flagship institutions. The plans did nothing for graduate and professional education, and they depended wholly on the perpetuation of rigid racial segregation in the public schools. Only because the public schools remained segregated did drawing 10 percent from each high school result in black and Hispanic students among those admitted to Florida's elite universities. Our assessment, I told the press, was "not a scorched earth condemnation of what is being done." With effort, Florida might "arrive at something that would work."[44]

As the Clinton administration came to an end, the commission, despite the lack of resources, had stuck to a determination to produce substantive work. The commission completed the publications in the series on racial and ethnic tensions hearings from Miami, New York, Los Angeles, Chicago, and the Mississippi Delta. Compared with the previous period, when no reports were issued between 1993 and 2001, we issued twenty-four reports based on fact-finding with recommendations.

During this period, not once after the 1994 Republican takeover did the House Oversight Subcommittee ask us to testify on any issue or our own work in a public hearing. The only hearings that the subcommittee held publicized management problems, and even then they would not permit us to discuss our productivity.

Nevertheless, career civil servants in the enforcement agencies and the advocacy groups, as well as local police departments and federal agencies used our work to improve their efficiency and value. The commission had survived and had renewed its participation in the public debate on achieving equal opportunity and diversity.

CHAPTER XI

"You Can Forget Civil Rights in This Country"

ECRETARY OF STATE KATHERINE HARRIS of Florida appeared at commission hearings in early 2001 "suited up for business." Heavily lipsticked, with her skin "plastered and powdered," masklike, hair falling over one eye, Harris was subpoenaed to refute claims of discrimination in the 2000 election. She had the audacity to deny all responsibility for the voting problems. Instead, she declared a "silver lining." Everyone should be pleased because there had never been "a more extensive voter education scenario in the history of our country than I think what we have incurred in the last five weeks, an extraordinary lesson in civics."

After listening to Harris's repeated excuses and refusal to give a straight answer, Commissioner Victoria Wilson excoriated her efforts to blame everyone except herself. Wilson told Harris she felt "like I'm on this merry-go-round called denial." The Bush administration discontent with the Civil Rights Commission began that day in Tallahassee, when the commissioners courageously held hearings to listen to official and unofficial complaints that called into question George W. Bush's election to the presidency. In the end, Bush struck back by undermining the fragile independence that the commission had tried to reestablish in the Clinton years.[1]

The commission conducted the early 2001 investigation despite a staff funded at minimal levels by congressional Republicans. The commission was the only government agency to investigate what happened in Florida. It was one of the most important responsibilities undertaken by the commission in its history. We heard from more than one hundred people—qualified voters and poll workers who testified under oath about problems they had faced during the election in more than thirty hours of testimony. Commissioners grew impatient as every elected

The author questions Florida governor Jeb Bush
at Tallahassee hearings.

Florida governor Jeb Bush reacts to a question
posed by the commission in Tallahassee
regarding his personal involvement
in the state's election process.

state and county official made excuses for the flaws and blamed others for the mistakes.[2]

Governor Jeb Bush, brother of the president who benefited from any election wrongdoing, pointed to his secretary of state, Katherine Harris, and the county supervisors of elections as the culprits. We asked the governor if he would exercise his authority to appoint special investigators to look for election law violations in the recently concluded election. He insisted that his responsibility was not with past mistakes but to look ahead and propose new laws to fix problems. He reminded the commission of the bipartisan task force he had appointed to look into the new approaches.[3]

After days of hearings, broadcast gavel to gavel by C-SPAN, and extensive news coverage that included all of the American networks, and BBC, Japanese, and Swedish television, among others, the glare of publicity failed to bring even one official confession of malfeasance or error. In an election where 54 percent of the rejected ballots cast that were not counted belonged to African Americans, no public official admitted to wrongdoing or even negligence.

More worrisome, the press, orchestrated by James Baker and company, shifted the focus. Butterfly ballots, hanging chads, malfunctioning equipment—all the process issues—became the newfound religion. Politicians, following Governor Bush's lead, began to call for reforms to fix the process. The real story of denial of democracy to eligible voters who were declared ineligible to vote—what we at the commission called the "No Count"—was all but lost.[4]

We were in Florida on January 11–12 and February 16, 2001, because on election day and the days thereafter, citizens complained to the commission about violations of the right to vote in the 2000 presidential election, most of which centered in Florida. The law under which the commission operates mandates that "the Commission shall investigate allegations in writing under oath or affirmation relating to deprivations of the right to vote because of color, race, religion, sex, disability, or national origin."[5]

The commission sent civil service staff lawyers to Florida to conduct a preliminary investigation. They observed a forum, convened by the NAACP, at which witnesses claimed various abuses as they tried to vote. The complainants were quite willing to state their charges in writing and to affirm them.

The lawyers also interviewed Republican and Democratic Party leaders and local election officials and returned with a recommendation that a substantial basis existed to support a further inquiry into whether voting rights had been compromised. At the December 2000 meeting, we decided, unanimously, that the commission had to go to Florida to look into irregularities in the presidential election. At that point the Republican appointees were loath to appear unwilling to investigate. They knew the commission report would not affect the outcome of the election.

Commissioner Wilson called me the day after the election to insist on an investigation. Also, civil rights groups wanted us to hold hearings right after the election, but we could not do so until after the Supreme Court decision in *Bush v. Gore*, Bush's appeal from a Florida state supreme court decision favoring Gore. But the commission could not organize a formal hearing in an instant. Subpoenas require notice, and our procedures required additional investigation before a hearing could take place.[6]

When we opened the hearings in Tallahassee, Florida, on January 11, 2001, the eight commission members included Meeks and Edley, appointed by Democrats in Congress; four presidential appointees, including two Independents, myself and Wilson; and two Democrats, Reynoso and Lee. There were two Republican appointees, Redenbaugh and the newly appointed Abigail Thernstrom, who had first sought an appointment to the commission during Reagan's first term. Thernstrom replaced Carl Anderson, who left when he became the Supreme Knight of the Knights of Columbus. Thernstrom had appeared widely in media and in print attacking long-standing civil rights laws. Thernstrom, describing herself as a voting rights specialist, who had given expert witness testimony, and a "social scientist," was another example of the continued influence of Linda Chavez on the Republican backward turn on civil rights. Thernstrom served on the board of Chavez's inaccurately named Center for Equal Opportunity, which was devoted to squelching efforts to include more African Americans in higher education, employment, and other pursuits from which they had been historically excluded. Thernstrom's appointment to the commission, like others since Reagan's assault, was designed to keep the commission from effectively monitoring civil rights enforcement.[7]

Witnesses described the shameful saga of vote suppression in the 2000 election, which began in 1998 when Katherine Harris took over as Florida secretary of state. Like many others, the state had a complicated system of accountability and responsibility for elections that dated back to the nineteenth century after the Civil War. In the 2000 election a spotlight was shone on its defects. Each of the sixty-seven counties chose its own voting system and was responsible for conducting the

Leon County elections supervisor Ion Sancho at Tallahassee hearing.

elections. The county supervisors were charged with conducting elections fairly, with controls and audit procedures in place to reconstruct the count in case of protests under the rules in the code and with the assistance of the secretary of state.

However, the secretary of state was responsible for technical assistance, setting overall standards and rules, and certifying counts. The secretary of state was charged with creating and maintaining a central voter file, providing voter education assistance to the public and technical assistance to county supervisors, maintaining uniformity in the application and operation of the election laws, and providing training to all state agencies to ensure the proper implementation of the laws, including the National Voter Registration Act of 1993 (the Motor Voter Act), and maintaining a fraud hotline and providing election fraud education to the public. The governor had to see that the secretary of state faithfully executed the laws and was responsible for appointing special officers to investigate alleged violations of the election laws.

When Katherine Harris became secretary of state in 1999, she "cleaned out the institutional memory" from the elections division, one county supervisor testified. She put in place a new director, Clayton Roberts, who lacked experience and familiarity with the problems that already had developed.[8]

Clayton Roberts, director of the Florida Division of Elections, to whom
Florida Secretary of State Katherine Harris *(center)* shifted blame
for any election problems, Tallahassee hearing, January 2001.

Vice Chair Cruz Reynoso questioning Roberta Tucker at
Tallahassee hearing, January 2001.

Secretary Harris, who had only had a short time to devote to our hearing since her staff said she had to catch a plane, told us she had no responsibility for the problems in the election. She had followed "best management practice" by delegating operations to her division directors. Therefore, Clayton Roberts had the "day to day responsibilities for implementing the duties outlined in the Florida Elections Code." When she described her role as only "ministerial," the general counsel, Edward Hailes, recalled that Charles Canady, general counsel for the governor, told the commission that Harris bore responsibility for the overall implementation of the election. He asked where in the statute she found a description of her election duties to the public and the county supervisors as "ministerial." Harris took refuge in a vague assertion that some case law seemed to point in that direction.[9]

Vice Chair Reynoso reminded Harris that her delegation of duties did not relieve her of ultimate responsibility. He asked her about testimony from county officials that she "provided no guidance to local agencies, the local counties, in terms of the standards to be used on the recount." When she denied their charge, he asked, "What standards do you provide?" She asked Roberts to reply, who, bemused, answered that parts of the law seemed inconsistent and needed clarification.[10]

Reynoso asked Harris about complaints from the supervisors that they had repeatedly requested funds for voter education to ensure a smooth election. They had warned her office that thousands of newly registered voters were likely to swamp the polls in November. Harris claimed she asked Governor Bush for $100,000, but Governor Bush claimed he received no such request. Harris's testimony indicated that she seemed to take seriously only one part of her responsibilities. She spent $51,000 on billboard and pamphlet warnings about voter fraud and nothing on voter education.

In Florida ex-felons could vote only if their rights were restored in a time-consuming legal process. Harris expressed ignorance about the purge of the voter rolls that had incorrectly identified persons as felons and excluded them from the polls, even though the work was contracted for by her office. The explanations of George Bruder, vice president of ChoicePoint, the contractor responsible for the felon purge, pinpointed the ineptness and lack of concern in Secretary of State Harris's office.[11]

Bruder testified that after the state decided to make sure no felons were on the rolls, they gave his company the contract to purge the rolls. However, he said, state officials instructed the company to include not only ex-felons' names but names with similar spellings in compiling the list of those persons who should be removed from the rolls. Further, "there was a parameter set by the state that included not to look at [just] the last name and to include 90 percent of that last name to make a match rather than 100 percent." The state then sent the list of more than 57,000 names, which necessarily contained mistakes, to the counties to use to purge their rolls. The company received $4 million for the error-filled list. But Bruder said they did the work they were asked to do and that any fault lay with the county supervisors of elections and the secretary of state.[12]

In addition to the ChoicePoint felon purge of legal voters, the commission heard a great deal of testimony about "mysterious missing voter registration cards" for some of the 600,000 people who registered under the Motor Voter Act permitting registration at driver's license bureaus. Students at Florida A&M University, a historically black institution, told of registering at the Department of Motor Vehicles and discovering on election day that the department had failed to submit their registrations to the board of elections. The director of the department gave

George Bruder, vice president of ChoicePoint, the state's contractor for the felon purge from the voting rolls.

sworn testimony that there simply was no procedure for assuring that the registrations were ever submitted.[13]

Entering the polling place and actually voting was a problem for some of the registered voters who came forward to testify. After Roberta Tucker and John Nelson testified concerning the presence of state highway patrol officers, either on the way to or at their polling places, Vice Chair Reynoso asked Tucker why she called the NAACP to complain instead of a state agency. Tucker replied that it was a civil rights issue. The road where she was stopped was in "a predominantly black community," and "that's the route most of them have to take to go to that voting poll." Furthermore, she knew that state procedure required the patrol to announce driver's license checkpoints in the media, but she had not seen or heard any announcement for this road.[14]

Rev. Willie Whiting told the commission, after listening to Tucker and Nelson describe highway patrol checkpoints on election day, "most of us in Florida have always had the highest respect for the Florida Highway Patrol." Even when they gave him a speeding ticket, he "felt good about it." He always "saw them as being professionals." But now "that's been tampered with, so I'd like for you to tell them that."[15]

Colonel Curt Hall, director of the Florida Highway Patrol, explained that "while some policy violations occurred," no one "was unreasonably delayed or prohibited from visiting their voting precinct as a result of that checkpoint." The checkpoint was not pre-approved or announced to the media as required. He did not see any reason to stop the policy of having checkpoints on election day.

Commissioner Wilson, pointing out that Whiting had "a very strong feeling of admiration for the Highway Patrol" before the election and that he "was very disappointed," asked Hall if he would try to "rectify that impression." Hall answered, "We would certainly do that.[16]

From the first panel, Thernstrom badgered the witnesses, already reeling from the abuse they had suffered while trying to vote, with questions about whether they knew of other incidents. She implied falsely that only a pattern and practice would be of real value, not their individual cases. She told Nelson, Whiting, and Tucker, "We need to establish a record of a pattern of irregularities here. Isolated incidents, you know, are isolated incidences." I countered, explaining to the confused witnesses that our authority to act covered individual cases whether or not the person who complained of other instances.[17]

Thernstrom elicited the response she wanted from a witness who had problems exchanging a registration card that included her first

At the hearing in Tallahassee, January 2001, Rev. Willie Whiting
tells the commission of feeling "sling-shotted back to slavery"
when the poll worker at his precinct accused him (falsely) of being
a convicted felon who was ineligible to vote.

Roberta Tucker, a local registered voter, tells the commission's
Tallahassee hearings, January 2001, of her fears at a Florida Highway Patrol
checkpoint set up on the only main road leading to her polling place.

name incorrectly. After all of her efforts, she still received another incorrect card. When she went to the polling place she saw workers give non-black voters who had registration problems affidavit ballots attesting to their identity, but when she requested one she was turned away. Thernstrom prefaced her question to this witness with a warning: "You have made a charge of racial discrimination at the polling place, which is obviously a very serious charge . . ." Now "do you believe that in general black voting was suppressed in the state of Florida, and if so how do you square your own story with the huge, and you know, very welcome, turnout." The witness nervously backed off, saying, "It was not about racial."

I asked the witness if she would consider it unfair if Florida officials knew heavy turnout was expected and did not make sufficient preparations, especially "in the particular precincts where there were a large number of African American voters." She answered, "Yes, very unfair."[18]

I also asked her, "Even if no one in your precinct did anything to you because of your race, if there were an overall approach that made the resources not available in those particular precincts so that you got treated the way you were treated, you would consider that unfair as I understand your testimony?" She answered, "Yes."[19]

Dr. Frederick Shotz, who was confined to a wheelchair, told the commission that when he arrived at the polling place "the disabled person's parking space was occupied" by a car with no permit to park there. "But nobody at the poll cared about that." He also found the voting machines at an inaccessible height from the wheelchair. Even more outrageous, he thought, was what happened to "a group of people from Palm Beach, with physical disabilities." They "had arranged for a bus to transport them from their condominium to their polling place. When they arrived, they discovered that the polls were on the second floor of the building with no elevator." They returned home, unable to cast a vote.

Felix Boyle, a Miami resident, found that his polling place "had become a construction site. So it looked like a medieval labyrinth. It was sulfuric odors from standing waters, orange cones, barriers, deep pits, broken concrete." He could not find a place to vote. As he started to leave, a passerby directed him around the corner, where he found a "smashed cardboard box with 'Vote Here' written in green crayon." This was the polling place, at a different address from that on his card.[20]

Commissioner Redenbaugh tried to undermine the hearings with

During the Tallahassee hearings, January 2001, John Nelson, a local registered voter, recalls that Florida Highway Patrol cars were parked outside his polling place on election day 2000. Although he was frightened, he went inside, where a poll worker demanded for the first time not just his voter registration card but two pieces of identification.

Witness Felix Boyle, holding photograph of his inaccessible polling place.

the false notion that unless what happened to an individual was shown to be intentional, no discrimination existed. He asked witnesses, "Is it your view that you were prevented from voting as a consequence of mismanagement or inefficiency, or is it your view that it was in some way intentional and discriminatory?" However, when he asked Boyle, "Is it your view that the location of the polling place may have been intentionally selected to discourage turn-out," Boyle surprised him by answering, "Yes, I do."[21]

Poll workers confirmed the testimony of the voters who complained and offered even more detail. Palm Beach County poll worker Millard Suid said his most important problem on election day at the Boynton Beach Waterworks Department site was that "the gate's on automatic timer. It closed at 6:15 p.m.," but the polls were supposed to close at 7:00. "It was a disaster." His deputy came running in when the gate locked to say they had a problem, having "turned away thirty or fifty people who could not vote." No telephone had been installed in the polling place. Several cars honked horns and waited. Using his own phone, Suid called the police to reopen the gates. When they arrived at 6:45, countless voters had left after finding the gates locked. Then the poll workers thought they only could accommodate voters until closing time.[22]

Poll workers and prospective voters agreed that nothing had been done to address the confusion, from the widely discussed butterfly ballot to other ballots that were also confusing. One ballot from Duval County, Commissioner Wilson observed, "looked more like a take-out menu from a delicatessen than a ballot designed to make it easy for Americans to vote." Wilson said if she had seen that ballot on election day, with time pressure and people waiting their turn, despite the fact that she had voted in eight presidential elections, she would have left without voting at all.[23]

County supervisors complained of a lack of resources for everything from telephones to poll workers and sample ballots. They also confirmed the inaccuracy of the felon purge lists they received. They blamed the secretary of state for giving them no guidance on how to conduct counts and recounts, and problems with voting equipment.[24]

Although no one, from the governor on down, ever admitted responsibility for the problems in the election, the Florida legislature clearly heard the criticisms from around the world. The day before the commission's May 2001 meeting, the legislature agreed to reforms that were a direct response to complaints of witnesses at the commission hearings. We commended the legislature, while reiterating that we would return to Florida to monitor the process until reforms were actually made.

After reviewing the testimony, sending additional questions and receiving answers from a number of witnesses, conducting supplemental research in areas of law, and reviewing more than 118,000 subpoenaed documents, General Counsel Edward Hailes's staff produced a draft report at the end of May. Thernstrom and Redenbaugh refused to review and discuss the report in detail or to help find compromise language where we differed in order to present the public with a consensus document. They were following a pattern pursued by Republican appointees since Reagan took over the commission and anti–civil rights ideology became the hallmark of Republican appointees. At our meeting in June 2001, we approved the draft report by a vote of 6–2, with Redenbaugh and Thernstrom dissenting. We charged Harris and other officials with "injustice, ineptitude and inefficiency."

Beyond the problems with voting procedures, machines, ballots, and the count that had dominated public discussion, we found that a "no

Commissioner Russell Redenbaugh attacks Felix Boyle's testimony about an inaccessible polling place, Miami hearings, February 16, 2001.

Commissioner Victoria Wilson at Tallahassee hearings, January 2001,
contending with Katherine Harris.

count" plagued Latino and Haitian voters needing language assistance, the disabled, and many African American voters. They were simply denied the right to even cast a vote. We put the draft on our Web site, as we waited until June 29 for dissents before printing the report.[25]

Commissioner Wilson filed a concurrence, in which she noted: "In times of crisis, it is to the U.S. Commission on Civil Rights that people have turned. And it is the Commission that has risen above the general state of fear, inertia, and politics and has willingly moved toward the flashpoint, in an effort to sort out truth from distortion." She was convinced after listening to the hours of testimony that while we could not prove conspiracy, the confluence of circumstances provided enough to be "unsettling."[26]

Fox News, the *Weekly Standard*, and the other media on the right, our two Republican appointees, the White House, and congressional Republicans went on the attack immediately. Their first attempts to rebut the report foundered. Charging us with partisanship failed because we criticized county supervisors, some of whom were Democrats, along with Harris and Governor Bush, for the problems. Harris's response that the report made "bald assertions that directly contradict the evidence" gained no traction, except among her political supporters, because too many people had seen her casually disinterested testimony during the hearings.[27]

The evidence that blacks had been excluded from voting—the "no count," we called it—was also difficult to refute. The "no count" resulted from problems identified in the testimony; the tainted felon purge, the Department of Motor Vehicles failure to send in registrations, the unexplained denials of people on election day who had voted before, and the jammed phones all contributed. A study conducted by Allan J. Lichtman, a history professor at American University and an expert on elections, which found an array of disparities, clinched the case. Lichtman said that when he had been asked to determine whether there were disparities, he was skeptical. But he was "amazed and shocked" at the evidence. He said ballots cast by blacks were rejected at a rate of 14.4 percent and those cast by non-blacks were rejected at a rate of 1.6 percent. This reality accounted for the 54 percent of Florida ballots that had been rejected as improperly marked, cast by African Americans.[28]

Under the circumstances, our recommendations seemed justified to anyone who had observed the hearings, and not the least bit radical. We asked for uniform voting procedures throughout the state, increased training for poll workers, adequate communications between the polling places and the clerks, voter reminder cards, the provision of accurate polling place information to voters, and the processing of Motor Voter registration cards before the election. We also wanted a clear provisional ballot requirement made available at every polling place on election day so that challenged voters could vote and have their registrations reviewed before the count, and better technology, made equally up to date in all polling places.[29]

Our reasonableness did not ward off Thernstrom's insistence that any faults lay with the voters, who she said, without evidence, probably were less literate, poorer, and first-time voters. She and Redenbaugh cited potential fraud as more of a problem than disenfranchisement. But they concentrated their fire on our inability to conclude that what happened was done intentionally. No matter that Thernstrom and Redenbaugh knew that if a statistical analysis showed a connection between a voter's race and the likelihood that his ballot would be rejected, there was a violation of the 1965 Voting Rights Act and there was no need for a showing of intentional discrimination to prove a violation. They assumed the public would believe that it was not a problem to operate a system that kept people from voting so long as no one could prove you did it intentionally. I explained, "If I ran over you at ninety miles an hour and killed you, it doesn't matter whether I intended to or not. I still killed you." The conservative media continued to spin their argument that because we did not prove intentional disenfranchisement, no discrimination occurred.

The Republicans, led by Thernstrom, also tried to squelch discussion of our findings by raising process questions. She claimed I had leaked the report before giving them an opportunity to read it. I was amazed at how even the mainstream media simply reported what they said without ever actually checking with the civil service staff. If reporters had inquired, they would have discovered that all of the commissioners received the report at the same time.

The media games included White House spokesman Ari Fleischer's June 27, 2001, response to a questioner who asked if the president planned "to take action" toward me for the Florida report. Fleischer stated that "many questions have been raised about whether that report was accurate and whether the motives for that report were political." The implication was that the president would remove me as chair.[30]

While the media skirmishing proceeded, Senator Christopher Dodd (D-Conn.), chairman of the Senate Rules and Administration Committee, held hearings to consider election reform. Our recommendations became part of the discussion. At the hearings, I had to sit next to Thernstrom, called as a witness by the Republicans on the committee, as she lied about the release of the report and the publication of her dissent and kept smearing black voters as particularly prone to errors and emphasizing the lack of any intent to disenfranchise.[31]

When Thernstrom tried to rebut Allan Lichtman's study, she had to contend with Senator Charles Schumer (D-N.Y.). Schumer forced John Lott, who accompanied Thernstrom as her expert, to utter "a defeated 'yeah' " to the question of whether "a greater percentage of black and Hispanic people are turned away than, or don't get to vote, than white people?"[32]

I blasted back at Thernstrom when she told the committee that the commission staff had refused to let her have access to data she had asked for so she could check Lichtman's work. The staff had responded to her that she or her assistant could find the data on the Internet and had given her the site. I had brought with me the entire set of exchanges between Thernstrom and the staff, and with Chairman Dodd's approval had placed them in the record at the beginning of the hearing. I lost my composure absolutely at her repetition of the slur of our staff, who had put in backbreaking hours of work under the most stressful circumstances. I told her the facts were in the record and I did not mind attacks on me, but she should not lie about the staff.[33]

Thernstrom's flaunting of her "expert," in defiance of commission policy, had already infuriated the general counsel and the commissioners, except Redenbaugh, who joined her in opposition to the report. She first announced blithely at a commission meeting that she had Lott write a one-hundred-page report for her to use as a dissent for herself and Redenbaugh. Since 1957, the commission statute had forbade using uncompensated services. Also, any consultant must be screened and hired by the civil service staff and the staff director. Commissioners have no authority to hire anyone to produce commission work. She violated the rules. When she wanted her dissent published, Vice Chair Reynoso objected that she illegally produced it and therefore we should not include it in the report.

General Counsel Edward Hailes explained to commissioners that career staff had researched the issue and found that Congress designed the prohibition to "make sure persons who might have a particular interest in some phase of the problem," if employed by the commission, would be employed on an "impartial basis," essentially by the career staff and not by political appointees.

When the staff director hired Allan Lichtman as a consultant, he followed the procedures required for employing and screening experts. Not surprisingly, Vice Chair Reynoso interpreted the law and facts correctly. Individual commissioners had no authority to hire experts to produce commission work, and in any case, the procedures had not been followed. We could not publish the dissent unless all portions prepared by the volunteer were removed.[34]

After a great deal of debate, with the press eagerly awaiting to report on the infighting, I knew from experience that if we did not publish the dissent, the press, instead of focusing on Thernstrom's illegal behavior, would characterize the result as suppressing her freedom of expression. I thought I saw a way out. When we testified before Dodd's committee, she had introduced her dissent for the record. I asked my colleagues to permit the inclusion of the Senate testimony in the appendix to our report. That way no one could say we were suppressing it. We could publish it along with other Senate testimony, providing a "fig leaf" over her illegal behavior. They agreed reluctantly, and the commission published the dissent.

To undermine the report, Thernstrom told the media repeatedly thereafter that I had refused to publish their dissent. It was not until more than a year later, after continuous repetition of this lie in the press, that Peter Carlson of the *Washington Post* actually looked at the report and wrote in an article that the dissent was in fact included. Even after Carlson's article, Thernstrom continued to peddle the lie that for partisan reasons, I had suppressed her freedom of expression. Commissioner Wilson's warning to her that if she continued to lie to the press about the report she would call her on it publicly had no visible effect.[35]

The importance of the commission prohibition against commissioners' hiring consultants became very apparent in the case of Thernstrom's expert. John Lott, an American Enterprise Institute resident scholar, when "engaged" by Thernstrom, used a pseudonym for three years to defend himself against critics in online debates and to attest to his expertise. Mary Rosh defended Lott over and over as a meticulous researcher and not "driven by the ideology of the left or right." She even "gushed" over classes she had taken with him, describing him as "the best professor" she ever had. Mary Rosh *was* Lott. When caught, Lott admitted his misdeeds but also claimed his thirteen-year-old son wrote a review of his book purporting to show that more guns led to less crime, posted on Amazon.com as Maryrosh. Whether written by Lott or his son, Maryrosh gave the book five stars. Lott used the pseudonym to defend himself against critics who called his work on guns and on the Florida election misleading and inaccurate. A staffer at the Cato Institute, Julian Sanchez, tracked Mary Rosh back to John Lott. If the staff had been asked to hire Lott, he certainly would not have passed their employment screening.[36]

The staff director and the staff spent an enormous amount of time responding to the House Judiciary Committee Subcommittee on the Constitution, our oversight subcommittee, chairman Steve Chabot (R-Ohio) about the details of their management of the agency's small budget. He never asked about Thernstrom's illegal hiring of John Lott. His questions concerned operations that were the staff director's responsibility. But he directed his questions to me with a simultaneous release to the press in hopes of eliciting a "Berry mismanages" story. The staff director, Ruby Moy, answered the questions, but the time-consuming work undermined staff morale and impeded the substantive work, which was probably Congressman Chabot's intent. Since Congress has the powers of subpoena and of the purse, agencies must respond. Les Jin, appointed by Clinton in October 2000 after Moy retired, had been a civil rights lawyer in Chicago and had the approval of the Asian American civil rights groups. He cooperated fully with Chabot's subcommittee, but the questions kept coming.[37]

The Justice Department shared Chabot's disinterest in our Florida findings. During the hearings, we learned of e-mails and other data that could determine whether Florida officials intended their actions or set in motion a conspiracy. But the Justice Department ignored our request that it pursue the question of intent. Instead, Justice embarked on a voter integrity campaign to prove that Democrats were engaged in fraud in registering voters, in order to frighten organizers and thus suppress the Democratic vote. When we finally received a response, it came from a career civil servant's assurances that the information was being "carefully reviewed by career attorneys in the civil rights division."[38]

Civil rights groups used our report, despite the inattention of the Justice Department and the House committee, to win a federal case against Florida, enjoining the practices that had marred the election. In addition, the Senate used our report in crafting the Help America Vote Act.

The staff continued to monitor election reform, performing studies that aided in the process leading to the passage of the Help America Vote Act. We analyzed proposed reforms and refined our own recommendations for avoiding the problems we had found in Florida and in a survey of other states. We even held another briefing in Florida, at which county election supervisors told of their fears for the fall 2002 election. I encouraged the secretary of state's office to oversee the training of poll workers and establishment of communications to avoid a "mini-disaster." Jim Smith, the new secretary of state, along with county officials, made sure there were command centers, "war rooms," and rapid-response teams all over the state and the election ran relatively smoothly. The commission was pleased that Florida figured out how to run an election efficiently.[39]

When Congress passed the federal Help America Vote Act (HAVA) in 2002, for the first time since the Reagan administration the legislators took the views of the commission seriously. The law included many of the recommendations from our report on Florida and our subsequent report analyzing the election in other states. The legislation required provisional ballots and made funding available for training and voter education. It established the Election Assistance Commission, but rejected our recommendation that the commission require states to meet standards for machines and procedures as a condition of receiving federal funds.[40]

After HAVA passed, we monitored its implementation, hoping to avoid problems in the next presidential election. In April 2004 we held a briefing with experts and advocates to discuss voting equipment and the fall election. HAVA forced states to consider using electronic voting machines instead of punch cards to avoid the problems with ballots that Florida encountered in 2000. But the Election Assistance Commission had not begun to set standards for the equipment, and forty-one states had received waivers giving them until 2006 to have computerized voter registration lists. Because states had to replace punch-card and lever machines, voting officials nationwide were buying electronic machines, many using touch-screen technology.

Witnesses told us that technology alone would not solve the problem. Michael Shamos, a computer science professor at Carnegie Mellon University, explained: "They haven't rushed to educate people on how to properly use the machines, which is creating all kinds of problems." The use of computerized voting also created questions about security and reliability and paper trails. More than a dozen states were already considering issuing paper receipts.

Wade Henderson of the Leadership Conference worried that talking

Wade Henderson, president of the Leadership Conference on Civil Rights, tried to preserve an independent commission.

about continuing problems might discourage people from voting. His civil rights coalition was divided on the question of paper receipts. Disability rights advocates preferred touch screens, which were more accessible.[41]

In July 2004 we held a briefing on voting problems again. This time we considered reports that Glenda Hood, the new secretary of state in Florida, had put together another error-plagued list, ostensibly designed to purge felons from the state's voting rolls. The list had a methodological flaw virtually guaranteeing that voters who registered as Hispanics would not be purged, while thousands of blacks might be. Hood refused to testify, and since we had scheduled a briefing and not a hearing, she had not been subpoenaed. Her office announced that it had discarded the list after the mistakes surfaced. However, we remained concerned that discarding the list without replacing it also could lead to the unequal treatment of voters. Election supervisors in all of Florida's sixty-seven counties might err in removing the names of those who were ineligible to vote.

Accenture partner Meg McLaughlin, whose private company contracted with the state to help with the purge, did testify. Reminiscent of the ChoicePoint felon purge, she said they used the data given to them by the state. They did not know about the defects: "We were not provided with that information." But, "I would think we should have been."

Gracia Hillman, vice chair of the Election Assistance Commission established under HAVA, confirmed that her commission gave Florida $47 million with another $87 million due. Since Congress did not accept the Civil Rights Commission's recommendation to require compliance before the receipt of funds, they had no authority to even threaten to withhold funds when problems surfaced in any state. Congress had decided that states' rights required state control. States could get help, but without rigid requirements.

After hearing from an assortment of witnesses, we called for the Justice Department to investigate Florida's problems. We thought the controversy over the list might indicate more problems. Commission Edley emphasized, "This is not just about sloppy databases; it's not just about bureaucracies strapped for resources, it's about the possible deprivation of a civil right, possibly criminal." We continued to monitor developments in the effort to end discrimination in elections in Florida and elsewhere.[42]

The drama and press attention given to the 2000 election and the sniping over our report faded on September 11, 2001. Soon after the horrific deaths in the collapse of the World Trade Center towers and the Pentagon, backlash against some individuals identified or misidentified as the same nationality or ethnicity of the bombers demanded the commission's attention.

In Arizona, a Sikh gas station operator was beaten to death by an angry mob who thought he was an Arab. At least six bullets shattered windows of a North Texas mosque, but no one was injured. Even as political and religious leaders urged Americans not to condemn Muslims and Arab Americans for the 9/11 attacks, the government's wholesale roundup of suspects, especially in Michigan and Brooklyn, fueled fear and anger. The commission's hotline for reporting civil rights violations was overwhelmed with calls alleging official and unofficial abuse.

We used our National Complaint Line and SACs to track discrimination complaints and to direct those who called for assistance. We also asked our SACs to organize forums on the question of tolerance during the stress of terrorist attacks. Because President Bush, Mayor Rudolph Giuliani, Secretary of State Colin Powell, Attorney General John Ashcroft, and the United States Senate, among others, had condemned the targeting of Arab Americans and Muslim Americans, initially there were no politically motivated attacks on our actions. The hotline received a large number of claims of employment discrimination and police abuse, which we referred to the Equal Employment Opportunity Commission and the Justice Department, but they were slow to respond. I also made a widely shown public service spot asking for tolerance.[43]

The conditions for Arab Americans and Muslims were made worse by the tightening enforcement after 9/11. Other groups also suffered. Until 9/11, though denied immediate resettlement rights in the United States, Haitian refugees at least had the right to be released from detention while they awaited a decision on their petitions for asylum. A boatload of refugees arrived offshore on December 3, 2001. Their sailboat crashed within sight of the Miami coastline with 187 on board. The U.S. Coast Guard rescued 167 people. Two drowned, and 18 swam to shore. The Immigration and Naturalization Service (INS) had changed the hearing policy and kept them in detention, where they remained for months. The men went to Krome Detention Center and the women to a prison, the Turner correctional facility. They asked for political asylum. We went to visit the women to shed additional public light on their plight. I told the press that "it's a very tragic situation after a two-hour hearing and a tour of the prison where the female refugees were held."

They were "being treated as prisoners, but they haven't committed any crime."

The women complained that they could only wash their one garment, a prison uniform, every twenty-one days and guards frequently strip-searched them. They had been separated from their children and incarcerated for seven months. One woman said nothing, but wailed loudly the entire time. Sister Jeanne O'Laughlin, president of Barry University, cried as she told us that she had offered to house the women and take responsibility for them but had been refused. We negotiated better food, translators and interpreters, and phone calls home for the women with the local INS representative, but there was no change in the policy.[44]

While dealing with the aftermath of 9/11 and continuing our other substantive work, we also had to address another politically motivated attack on the commission's independence. So anxious was the White House to deflate our majority after the Florida election report that Bush decided to replace Wilson with Peter Kirsanow, a Cleveland labor lawyer, before Wilson's term expired. Kirsanow, whose practice focused on representing management, was chair of the board of the Center for New Black Leadership, a black conservative organization.

Bush's approval ratings were at an all-time high, since the September 11 terrorist attacks, and politicians, the media, and the public all expressed uncritical support for almost anything he did. The commission was almost alone in criticizing him. In response to Bush's demand for Wilson's slot, the commission general counsel advised us that unless she left voluntarily, she could not be replaced. Under the legislation passed after I sued Reagan, which was revised in 1993 to reinforce the length of terms, all commissioners served six years from the date of their appointment. We knew the appointment certificate that Wilson had been given mistakenly said she served at the pleasure of the president, but our counsel told us not to worry because *Berry v. Reagan* decided that the term of office is governed by the law, not by a mistaken certificate prepared by a clerk. Chabot weighed in to help the Bush administration by threatening that "any payment to Commissioner Wilson for her work as a Commissioner after November 2001 would be a willful misuse of appropriated funds for an unauthorized purpose."

The White House did not back off even though its Justice Department assistant attorney general, Daniel Bryant, seemed to agree with our counsel's interpretation of the law. Bryant copied me on a letter to Judiciary Committee chairman James Sensenbrenner telling him that the administration's language conflicted with the statutory language that "the term of office of each member of the Commission shall be six years" from the date of appointment. However, the Bush administration had decided Wilson's term ended on the date that the term of Judge Higginbotham (whom she succeeded) would have ended—on November 29, 2001.[45]

When Wilson refused to resign, White House counsel Alberto Gonzales decided to bully us. He called Commissioner Wilson directly, even though she was represented by counsel, but failed to scare her into submission. When he told me I had to have Kirsanow seated at the next commission meeting, I explained that we were an independent commission and according to the law Wilson had a six-year term. He then insisted that I follow the president's order to seat Kirsanow. When he persisted, I asked what he would do if I did not comply. Could I expect that he would send marshals to the meeting? He hung up abruptly, and the next thing I knew, the White House had told the press that I said marshals would have to drag me away. The *Wall Street Journal* editorial page described me as standing in the schoolhouse door, preventing Kirsanow's entrance, like George Wallace had prevented the desegregation of the University of Alabama.[46]

Gonzales followed up in writing that "actions blocking him [Kirsanow] from entering service following a valid appointment would," in his opinion, "violate the law." House Judiciary Committee members Congressmen John Conyers (D-Mich.) and Jerrold Nadler (D-N.Y.), who were "immediately involved with the drafting of the law," courageously released a letter to me on December 7, 2001, saying that the language "each commissioner shall serve six years from the date of appointment" meant we should continue to recognize Wilson. I had actually been present when members of the subcommittee discussed the language in the bill and knew that the language had been carefully selected to accomplish the purpose of a new six-year term for any appointee. And Wilson's term had not yet expired. We had no idea what Gonzales might do. When Wilson came to the meeting on December 7, 2001, she wondered if she might be forcibly ejected and taken to jail for resisting Gonzales's orders. Even though none of us had any idea what reprisals the White House might pursue, upon our general counsel's advice and a majority vote of the commission, I did not seat Kirsanow. He immediately sued Wilson to remove her from the commission.[47]

The commissioners voted to file a brief in *United States and Kirsanow v. Wilson* in support of our legal position and to await the outcome in the courts. Shortly thereafter, Wilson was notified that she would be subjected to an Internal Revenue Service tax audit, for the first time. Wilson had engaged her own lawyer, and the staff director enlisted corporate lawyer Theodore Wells for a nominal fee to represent us as interveners to protect the independence of the commission. He explained to Wells that our statute prohibited us from using pro bono services. We could not ask the Justice Department to represent us because they were supporting Kirsanow. Because the House was controlled by the Republicans, Nadler and Conyers, who were present at the enactment of the bill, could not file an intervention to protect their legislative interpretation.

Needless to say, the right-wing media and the Republicans in Congress and the White House publicized the case as if it were *Berry v. Bush.* Responding to an all-out attack on me for refusing to seat Kirsanow, Wade Henderson, executive director of the Leadership Conference on Civil Rights, pointed to the importance of the commission's work on the 2000 election and other issues. He begged the attackers to leave the Kirsanow matter to the courts, to no avail.[48]

Chabot's House subcommittee added to the public relations effort, threatening to remove me if I did not seat Kirsanow. Chabot warned that if I hired a lawyer with government funds, I would face criminal penalties. He knew I could not approve the allocation of funds for any purpose, since only the staff director controlled commission funds. But making the staff director the target would not have helped their effort to blame me. We hoped the courts would accept the words in the statute.[49]

In February 2002, Federal district court judge Gladys Kessler rendered a decision for Wilson in the district court, based on the plain meaning of the statute. After having served as a Carter appointee on the District of Columbia Superior Court, Kessler was appointed to the district court by Clinton. She said the language "the term of each commission member shall be six years" from the date of appointment had changed an earlier version that provided for interim and temporary appointments. We were relieved at the trial court's decision in Wilson's favor in the face of publicity condemning the commission's temerity in resisting a popular president's appointment.

Kirsanow appealed to the District of Columbia Circuit Court, where we had little hope of winning, given the three-judge panel with two Republican judges, Reagan appointees David Sentelle and former Bush appointee A. Raymond Randolph. But we hoped we would get at least one vote, from Clinton appointee David Tatel. Kirsanow's side agreed with our assessment. After not even bothering to appear in Judge Kessler's courtroom, expecting a favorable outcome, Kirsanow and his supporters crowded the appellate hearing. We were disappointed when Tatel joined the others in deciding that the statute could not mean what it said about commissioners' serving six years from the date of their appointment, despite the plain language. Before Congress passed the statute, anyone appointed to replace a resigned or deceased person served only for the remainder of their term, and the court could not believe that Congress intended to change the rule. Our lawyers pointed out that congressional appointees to the commission, including Reynoso and I, had served terms that ended, and then new ones started later, with no attention to who had occupied the position before or the circumstances of their leaving, but each time for a new six-year term. The court simply ignored these facts, and Wilson lost.

The commission endorsed Wilson's appeal to the Supreme Court, to give us some time to regroup as we awaited the inevitable rejection. The case did not fit the Court's discretionary standards for level of importance. Before Wilson left, to ease the pain of returning to a 4–4 tie, we made several rule changes to make it possible to produce some work. The most important change was to publish draft reports on the Internet for public comment before the commission acted on them. Although Wilson introduced the motion, the Republican appointees who had created such a stir with their complaints about leaks felt constrained to vote for it. This procedure made it possible to place the 2004 staff report on Bush's record on the Internet.[50]

The hard times worsened after Kirsanow took office, as we pursued our work on post-9/11 civil rights issues. We held a briefing on bioterrorism and health care and promoted the idea of an office of civil rights and civil liberties in the new Department of Homeland Security without too much contention. However, when we held a forum with the Michigan SAC in Detroit, sparks flew. We heard from Arab Americans, most of whom were Christians, about what they perceived as harassment since 9/11. Kirsanow chastised them for complaining, warning, "If there's another terrorist attack and if it's from a certain ethnic community or certain ethnicities that the terrorists are from, you can forget civil rights in this country."

According to Kirsanow, the Arab Americans "should understand that an attack might give rise to internment camps such as those used on Japanese Americans in World War II." The Arab Americans in the hearing room were outraged. Kirsanow explained his remarks to an astounded press afterward as only reflecting the public view, which would demand internment camps. An angry American-Arab Anti-Discrimination Committee and the civil rights coalition asked Bush to remove Kirsanow from the commission because he appeared to "be condoning collective guilt and seems open to the idea of mass internment of an entire community."

The Japanese American Citizens League's executive director, John Tateishi, said he expected "civil rights champions" to quell any such idea rather than predicting its occurrence. White House spokesman Scott Stanzel defended Kirsanow as simply emphasizing the importance of "ensuring the security of the American people . . . in guaranteeing their civil liberties."

Kirsanow's remarks stirred widespread national and international criticism directed at the entire commission. I did not attack Kirsanow; I urged him to apologize, but he refused. The commission released a statement reaffirming its commitment to protecting the civil rights of Arabs and Muslims and explaining that individual commissioners are entitled to their own personal views. Kirsanow, whose law firm promised to protect employers from union organizing, remained on the commission even after he accepted a recess appointment from Bush to the National Labor Relations Board in 2005. It appeared that he could not gain Senate confirmation for the post over Democratic senatorial objections.[51]

Aside from dealing with post-9/11 issues, we published a staff report updating our work on percentage plans, as the Michigan higher education case went before the Supreme Court. The staff collected data from the states of California, Florida, and Texas showing that percentage plans yielded much smaller numbers and percentages of black and Hispanic students than affirmative action. The staff director published it as a staff report because the four Republican appointees would not vote for it. One of the justices cited the study in the Michigan affirmative action law school case.[52]

We responded eagerly to requests from state advisory committees to hold forums and briefings away from Washington to consider local issues and to reinforce their work rather than always holding meetings in Washington. The Republican appointees refused, in most cases, to travel to the states for meetings. They seemed interested only in coming to Washington to engage in ideological squabbling for media consumption. They refused to go to Wilmington in September 2002, where we met with the SAC chairs from the surrounding states. We also heard testimony from Delaware residents about education, race relations, and other state issues.[53]

Commissioners went to Alaska to explore racial tensions between Alaskan natives and whites in the wake of several paintball attacks on natives. We also went to San Diego to hold a forum on immigration and border control. We visited patrol points and the fences along the border and investigated vigilante activity. More than 2,200 migrants, mostly from Mexico, had died trying to cross in remote desert areas since the mid-1990s when Operation Gatekeeper cracked down in urban areas. We also met with the National Congress of American Indians leadership, who had a scheduled convention in the city. They told us how much they appreciated the commission's work on Native American issues. We spent much of the meeting discussing their concerns about the erosion of Indian sovereignty.[54]

The Republican appointees voted in favor of work on American Indians. It did not conflict with their ideological agenda. We published the research report *A Quiet Crisis: Federal Funding and Unmet Needs in Indian Country* in 2003, and then held hearings in Indian country to produce *Broken Promises: Evaluating the Native American Health Care System* in 2004. Congress responded to the commission's work on the awful conditions and the federal government's failure to keep its promises by increasing the budget of the Indian health programs. The Congress of American Indians gave the commission an award in appreciation for the study.

Tensions on the ideologically divided commission remained. For the May 17, 2004, scheduled meeting, none of the Republicans appeared, with no notice that they would be late. After the meeting some of us planned to attend *Brown v. Board of Education* commemorative events elsewhere in Washington. The staff director had someone look for the Republican commissioners throughout the commission offices and reported that neither they nor their assistants could be found. We did not have a quorum and had no idea when—or whether—they would arrive, so Commissioner Edley and the audience decided to leave. The Republicans, except for Thernstrom, arrived after we had adjourned, with conflicting stories about their absence. No one explained why neither they nor their assistants had communicated with us. We could not reconvene an adjourned meeting on the same day, since public notice was required. The Republican appointees became furious and followed us to the staff director's office. Then Thernstrom arrived without any explanation. We discovered later that she had been on television at the exact time of the meeting and apparently decided not to tell us. Had I known, I am sure everyone would have agreed to delay the start of the meeting. They placed a press story that I had violated their rights by adjourning the meeting.

The Republicans decided to take control of the commission after our report on Bush's performance in December 2004, a report that was critical of the president. Bush was given credit for being clearer before 9/11 on racial profiling than Clinton and for assembling a diverse cabinet. But his funding requests for civil rights enforcement fell far short, his Justice Department retreated from enforcing voting rights or increased inclusion and diversity in higher education and employment. He also failed to promote the passage of election reform after the 2000 debacle, in time for the 2004 election. In addition, he successfully urged Congress to cut billions of dollars from programs to help low-income and disabled persons pay for housing through rent vouchers, and proposed nothing to replace these initiatives.[55]

The report faulted Bush for doing practically nothing to ensure the reduction of environmental hazards in minority and low-income communities, making a mockery of the hard-won 1994 executive order requiring action gained by the environmental justice movement. Shortly after the commission held public hearings to listen to advocates and Environmental Protection Agency officials who had no rationale for their neglect, EPA administrator Christine Todd Whitman resigned and went back to New Jersey.

The report detailed how Bush had expanded the discrimination that had long denied asylum to Haitian refugees in Florida, despite the generous policy for Cubans. He authorized federal agents to hold Haitians in detention indefinitely without bond until their cases were heard by an asylum court, with no firm date set for a hearing.

Bush also closed the White House Office for Women's Initiatives and Outreach and attempted to close the Women's Bureau at the Department of Labor. In addition, he embarked on an initiative to undermine the enforcement of Title IX's prohibition against sex discrimination in higher education, but retreated after overwhelmingly negative public reaction.

The report found that one of the most significant wrongs Bush inflicted was his attempt to redefine civil rights, to include the bogus claim that denying taxpayer money to religious programs is a denial of civil rights based on religion. This improbable and intellectually dishonest redefinition was used to provide a rationale for supplying religious groups with federal funds through Bush's Office of Faith-Based and Community Initiatives, even though doing so violated the separation of church and state and the free exercise clause of the First Amendment. The policy forced taxpayers, whether religious or not, to support religion despite their objections. In addition, under this program individuals who needed government-supported services, such as drug counseling, might find themselves forced to use a religious provider for those services. Some federally funded faith-based programs had already been found to engage in attempts to recruit new religious or political adherents through the programs.

Whatever the amount, small or large, of federal funds that actually went to faith-based programs, the very attempt to enshrine as civil rights a policy that served a particular religious view was "reprehensible," according to the commission report. The report concluded that "failing to build on common ground, the Bush administration missed opportunities to build a consensus on key civil rights issues and has instead adopted policies that divide Americans."

The commission staff submitted the report to the commission in October 2004. They followed the timetable the staff director had given the commission a year earlier and had repeated each month in a schedule of work distributed to each commissioner. The report was simultaneously released in draft for public discussion on the commission's Web site, as required under commission procedures for all reports. Nonetheless, the release of the draft for public comment outraged the Republican commissioners. They wanted the report assessing Bush's record to disappear. Commissioner Jennifer Braceras, who had advocated the abolition of the commission before her appointment by Bush in 2001, sought to squelch the report by having it removed from the Web site.[56]

When Braceras's motion failed on a tie vote, with Republican and Democratic appointees evenly split—we were adamant that the report, having been posted properly on the Web site, would stay there—Braceras moved to delay consideration of the report until after the election. We voted for the motion because this deviation from the timetable at least did not require withdrawing material that had validly been released to the public.

The Republicans complained to the press that the release of the draft was political. They charged that the staff just wanted to criticize the president before the election. While the staff might have believed it would be useful for the public to know the president's record before November, under commission procedures, the Republicans could have easily asked for a different timetable months earlier, but they did not. Of course, their complaints drew attention to the existence of the draft and stirred up conflict.[57]

The report was still in the public domain on the Internet and widely publicized in the media. After President Bush was reelected, he announced replacements for me and Reynoso effective in early December, even though our terms did not expire until January 21, 2005. The White House argued that we were serving out the terms of our predecessors, which ended in December. We had both decided not to accept reappointments so that the next president, whoever he was, could appoint our replacements. We believed that since the commission legislation, enacted in 1994, said that each commissioner upon appointment served six years, we could serve for six years. The commission's legal counsel advised us that what we regarded as the wrongly decided *Kirsanow* case was irrelevant because it concerned how to fill an unexpired term created because of the death of an incumbent, not when a full term ended.

Counsel noted that congressional appointees to the commission had been serving six years from the date of their appointment, no matter when their predecessors left. This meant that Congress interpreted the statute that it had passed just as we did. Reynoso and I had served on that basis as congressional appointees before we accepted presidential appointments in 1999. It made no sense to have one rule for congressional appointees and another for presidential appointees under the same statutory language.

Bush insisted that Reynoso's term had also expired and that he had replaced me with Gerald Reynolds, a Kansas City electric utility company lawyer. Reynolds served briefly at the Office for Civil Rights in the Department of Education, a post to which President Bush appointed him during a congressional recess in 2002. Reynolds had to leave that position after one year because the Senate refused to confirm him. He had also served as president of the conservative Center for New Black Leadership, which Kirsanow chaired. Civil rights groups objected to Reynolds's appointment. They insisted that our terms had not ended. They also noted that Reynolds had criticized civil rights organizations that achieved *Brown v. Board of Education* and the civil rights laws of the 1960s as being too concerned with discrimination. He also questioned the need for Title IX's emphasis on ending unequal educational opportunity for women. As continuing evidence of her importance to the Republican anti–civil rights efforts, Reynolds had worked as a legal analyst for Linda Chavez's Center for Equal Opportunity, another indicator of Chavez's role in the Republican anti–civil rights movement.[58]

At first, Reynoso and I ignored Bush's announcement that he had replaced us. Then, once we had denounced his action, two weeks later we sent him a letter resigning. I sent a copy of the report to the president, suggesting that he "embrace the core freedoms and values enshrined in our civil rights laws." The media speculated that we would sue, but we did not because our terms would have ended, in any event, on January 21. Staying another month by virtue of a court order would unnecessarily waste legal resources.[59]

Bush's manipulation of the appointment process dealt another blow to the commission's independence. This time, unlike Reagan, he had the full support of the Republican majority in Congress and in the federal courts. After a long hiatus, the commission, with the investigation of the 2000 election in Florida, had returned to its mission—listening, making recommendations, and acting in support of the struggle for opportunity for the historically disadvantaged. That period had apparently come to an end.

The commission had survived another very difficult period. The decline of civility that began during the Pendleton years worsened when I became chair. Substantive discussion of staff work or civil rights issues was often impossible. The Republican appointees rudely assaulted civil rights advocates directly. Bush showed contempt for the role of the commission by appointing commissioners who would undermine it. The diversity that civil rights advocates had long worked and hoped for led to the appointment of women and minorities who, ironically, actively opposed the commission's mission.

Since December 2004, Bush has kept his campaign promise to appoint judges with records like those of Antonin Scalia and Clarence Thomas, who had opposed most of the concerns of the civil rights movement. Bush appointed two conservatives to the Supreme Court, John Roberts, whose work in the Justice Department during the Reagan administration turned out to be a faithful reflection of his views twenty years later, and Samuel Alito. Alito served in the Reagan and Bush I Justice Departments while the retrenchment in civil rights enforcement took place until President George Herbert Walker Bush nominated him to the United States Court of Appeals for the Third Circuit in 1990. In the Justice Department he early advocated the use of signing statements, used by Reagan and Bush to argue that a president's intent when signing a bill should have as much weight as the language in the bill or the intent of Congress. Roberts and Alito have joined Scalia and Thomas in conservative opinions on civil rights since they were appointed to the Court.[60]

The Bush administration opposed affirmative action, gay rights, reproductive rights, and other human rights issues in court. The president and the right worked to "turn back the clock," and this time civil rights opponents had all three branches of the government under the control of the same party for most of this president's time in office.

The commission continued to work in a worsening environment for civil rights advocacy. Bush, like Reagan, appointed African Americans, Latinos, and Asians to high government positions, some that had never been held before by a person of color. However, these appointments apparently did not influence his civil rights policies in a positive direction. The commission was mostly ignored by civil rights advocates, who did not expect anything positive since its chairman, Gerald Reynolds, publicly stated that he did not know of any discrimination problems.

Bush's other African American appointee, named in December 2004, was Ashley Taylor, a partner at the Richmond firm of Troutman Sanders LLP, who served as the deputy attorney general for Virginia from 1998 to 2001 with responsibility for the health, education, and social services areas. Taylor, whose practice focused on employment law, commercial litigation, and matters involving governmental entities, quietly voted with the majority, which included Reynolds, Kirsanow, and Taylor, three African American conservatives.

Michael Yaki and Arlan Melendez, the two Democratic congressional appointees, have not moved the Bush commissioner to act in the cause of civil rights. Yaki, an Asian American, San Francisco lawyer and a former board of supervisors member and past district director in Congresswoman Nancy Pelosi's office, was appointed by the Speaker. Melendez, appointed by Democratic senator Harry Reid of Nevada, was chairman of Nevada's Reno-Sparks Indian Colony, a federally recognized tribal government representing 840 Paiute, Washoe, and Shoshone tribal members.

The Civil Rights Commission under Republican control betrayed the mission for which the agency was founded. It did not address immigration issues, the treatment of victims of the flooding in the aftermath of Hurricane Katrina, or the need to find ways to achieve diversity in education and jobs, given demographic reality. It ignored the opportunity to revisit the recommendations in the police report after the 1999 Diallo killing when the 2006 shooting of an unarmed Sean Bell occurred and the New York Police Department was assessing itself. Analyzing the impact of race could have been useful, particularly since two of the three police officers involved, all of whom were acquitted, were black. But Republicans have used the agency to undermine such attempts to address important concerns.

The commission has ignored its responsibility to hold hearings or conduct field investigations before making findings and recommendations. It has opposed congressional efforts to acknowledge the status of Native Hawaiians so they could gain financial benefits that Native Americans receive in other states. On the thirty-fifth anniversary of Title IX's mandate of gender equity in educational institutions, the commission questioned the interest of women and girls in sports. It made a point of signaling opposition to affirmative action in law schools after the Supreme Court approved the University of Michigan Law School's admissions policy. It asked the American Bar Association to stop asking law schools to support racial, ethnic, and sexual diversity in admissions.

The commission also announced that few if any benefits accrued to minority children from racial diversity in K–12 education in advance of the Supreme Court 2007 decision outlawing voluntary integration in the Seattle and Louisville cases.[61]

When blacks claimed disparate treatment of African American boys accused of attempted murder in the criminal justice system in Jena, Louisiana, beginning in 2006, the commission took no notice. Even as the complaints escalated into a major civil rights march with people from around the country massing in Jena in September 2007, the commission had no response to alleviate tensions and sort out the facts from rumors and misinformation. Congressional Republicans ceased their attacks on the commission after the Republican takeover, and the Democratic Congress elected in 2006 ignored the commission. Essentially, during Bush's second term, the commission was as ideologically driven as in the Reagan years, but it was unsuccessful in gaining attention in the public debate because the commissioners did nothing to gain public respect. Bush used gay and lesbian issues, changing the balance between church and state, and disingenuous civil liberties claims to inflame public debate and polarize Americans.

The commission's pronouncements on the race question based on no fact-finding were too predictably dismissive of laws designed to improve opportunities for African Americans, given its makeup and the obvious way Bush packed the commission. The proposed solutions con-

In Jena, Louisiana (Thursday, September 20, 2007), marchers protest attempted murder charges brought against black high school students involved in an altercation on school grounds.

sistently blamed the disadvantaged without positive recommendations addressing current needs or problems. The overwhelming congressional vote to reauthorize the Voting Rights Act in 2006, with almost no attention paid to wrongheaded objections from the commission, showed how irrelevant it had become.

Tragically, the commission's major role of hearing the grievances of those who are usually ignored has been abandoned. African Americans, Native Americans, women, gays, Asian Americans, and Latinos, especially those who want their complaints about wrongful discrimination heard, find the commission disinterested in their problems.

Despite the progress made toward diversity and inclusion in our society, including Barack Obama's political success, discrimination has not yet been eradicated. Further, the commission's authority needs to be augmented to include discrimination based on sexual orientation. In general, however, no matter who is president, a new and different commission would help to develop a nonpartisan consensus to move the nation closer to equality of opportunity for all.

The commission could be converted into a human rights commission devoted to the idea that all people have a right to be treated fairly

Gallup Indian Medical Center CEO Floyd Thompson *(center)* shows
commission members the waiting room of one of the hospital's clinics,
Thursday, October 16, 2003, Gallup, New Mexico.

because of their humanity, as suggested by former commission chair and
Notre Dame president Father Theodore Hesburgh during his tenure.
Given the continued contention and resurgence of conflicts over race
and other domestic issues, however, it might also be better to maintain
the commission's focus on civil rights in this country. To change it might
signal a belief that the work that needs doing is done or an abandonment
of the idea of further progress because the job is too difficult and the
issues intractable. The best approach would be a commission on civil
and human rights. The addition of human rights could make clear a
concern with the nexus between race, sex, disability, age, national origin, sexual orientation, religious discrimination, poverty, and civil liberties concerns. A civil and human rights commission could also monitor
U.S. compliance with the international human rights covenants to
which we are a party and encourage adoption of those we have not
approved. This would answer the complaints regarding the continuing
lack of self-criticism of our own human rights record by nations that are
reviewed in the annual survey of human rights abroad, issued by the
U.S. State Department.

The new commission will need the appointment of a combination of civil rights activists or experts and respected citizens of goodwill who may know nothing in particular about civil rights but who take seriously the responsibility of careful investigation and fact-finding when issues arise that cause conflict and who support longer inquiries to make recommendations for positive change. Perhaps such a group could help us gain a consensus on the balance between individual and collective responsibility in the quest for opportunity.

Ideally, the commission also needs the power to enforce its own subpoenas of witnesses and documents. The requirement for Justice Department enforcement permits presidents to influence, delay, or suppress investigations by having the attorney general refuse to represent the commission. The Congress should also include a provision giving individuals and private organizations the power to file suit based on the commission's findings if an enforcement agency refuses to act on the findings within a specified time period.

If creating a new commission is impossible, at the very least, the Civil Rights Commission legislation should be modified to state clearly that the date on which a member is appointed is the beginning date of that member's six-year term. This would prevent the kind of manipulation of terms that has been a recurring problem in recent years. Further Senate confirmation should be required for all commissioners selected. At least in this way the public would know who the nominees are and would have an opportunity to voice objections.

These changes would re-create a commission not unlike what the Civil Rights Commission was before the cynical manipulation begun by the Reagan administration. Such changes should be considered in order for us to move forward as a nation because as we become more diverse and more self-aware, the importance of equal opportunity and fair treatment remains critical.

As in the earliest days of the commission, there is still a great need for a governmental conscience armed with subpoena power and designed to "put the facts on top of the table" in the struggle to achieve liberty and justice for all.

Notes

Prologue

1. See, for example, United States Commission on Civil Rights, *Ten-Year Check-Up: Have Federal Agencies Responded to Civil Rights Recommendations?* Vol. 1, *A Blueprint for Civil Rights Enforcement*, September 2002.

2. United States Commission on Civil Rights, Report 1961, Justice, p. 166. The 1961 commission report contained five separate volumes, one each on voting, education, employment, housing, and justice. The reports are online at www.law.umaryland.edu/marshall/usccr.

3. Ibid.

4. Adam Nossiter, "U.S. Says Blacks in Mississippi Suppress White Vote," *New York Times*, October 11, 2006, p. A48.

5. Neil Lewis, "Justice Department Reshapes Its Civil Rights Mission," *New York Times*, June 14, 2007, p. A1.

Chapter I

1. The testimony is taken from the United States Commission on Civil Rights verified transcript of voting irregularities in Florida, pp. 26–27, 32, 36–37, 121, 131, 137, 149–152. Throughout this book "commission" means the United States Commission on Civil Rights unless otherwise indicated. The commission is hereafter cited as CCR.

2. Ibid.

3. Reynoso said he thought it "odd" that Whiting was told he could not vote even after the supervisor determined that the alleged "felon" was Willie J. Whiting and he was Willie D. Whiting. In fact, he was allowed to vote only after he created a disturbance and threatened to hire a lawyer. Even more puzzling to Reynoso and other commissioners was that, without any further identification, after his mention of a lawyer, the poll worker permitted him to vote. As Whiting put it, "I could be sitting here today as a convicted felon," having voted, given the process used. Whiting testimony, CCR transcript, pp. 54–56.

4. See generally Bettye Collier-Thomas and V. P. Franklin, *My Soul Is a Witness: A Chronology of the Civil Rights Era in the United States, 1954–1965* (New York: Henry Holt, 2000).

5. Report of the United States Commission on Civil Rights, 1959, p. 97.

6. Ibid., p. 94.

7. Anthony Lewis, "Dr. Hannah Is Appointed to Head Civil Rights Unit," *New York Times*, December 24, 1957.

8. Ibid.; John T. McQuiston, "John Hannah, 88, Who Headed Michigan State and Rights Panel," *New York Times*, February 25, 1991.

9. Sherman Adams, *Firsthand Report* (New York: Harper, 1961), p. 333, points out that Lois Lippman, who served on the secretarial staff during the campaign, was the first black on the White House office staff; Rabb was secretary to the cabinet.

10. E. Frederic Morrow, *Black Man in the White House* (New York: Coward McCann, 1963), p. 171–174; Adams, *Firsthand Report*, p. 333, points out that Wilkins was the first "Negro" to sit in a cabinet meeting. He sat in for Labor Secretary Mitchell, who was out

of town. *Time*, March 15, 1954; "Labor Post Goes to Negro, First of Race in Sub-Cabinet," *New York Times*, March 5, 1954, p. 10; "An Excellent Appointment," editorial, *New York Times*, March 5, 1954, p. 18; Catherine Cymone Fourshey, Review of E. S. Atieno Odhiambo and John Lonsdale, eds., *Mau Mau and Nationhood: Arms, Authority, and Narration* (Athens: Ohio University Press, 2003), in *JENDA: A Journal of Culture and African Women's Studies*, Issue 7 (2005). Beyond Kenya, there were connections that reached as far as the AFL-CIO leadership in the United States. George Meany, A. Philip Randolph, and J. Ernest Wilkins invited Tom Mboya to speak in 1956 and awarded a $35,000 grant to Kenya's Federation of Labor to build its headquarters in Nairobi.

11. "Negro Prospects Held Improving," *New York Times*, February 16, 1956, p. 20.

12. Morton and Roland, "Sketches of Civil Rights Appointees," *New York Times*, November 8, 1957, p. 20.

13. Anthony Lewis, "Dr. Hannah Is Appointed to Head Civil Rights Unit," www.flheritage.com/museums/collection/governors.

14. James R. Sweeney, "A Segregationist on the Civil Rights Commission: John S. Battle, 1957–1959," *Virginia Magazine of History and Biography* 105, no. 3 (1997): 287–316.

15. *Time*, February 9, 1962, cover; Theodore M. Hesburgh, *God, Country, Notre Dame: The Autobiography of Theodore M. Hesburgh* (New York: Doubleday, 1990); Morton and Roland, "Sketches of Civil Rights Appointees."

16. Foster Rhea Dulles, *The Civil Rights Commission: 1957–1965* (East Lansing: Michigan State University Press, 1968), pp. 34–35.

17. Commission Report, 1959, pp. 84–85.

18. Ibid.; Robert Burt, *The Eisenhower Administration and Black Civil Rights* (Knoxville: University of Tennessee Press, 1984), p. 235.

19. Commission Report, 1959, p. 100.

20. *Hannah v. Larche*, 363 U.S. 420 (1960).

21. Michael R. Gardner, *Harry Truman and Civil Rights: Moral Courage and Political Risks* (Carbondale: Southern Illinois University Press, 2002), pp. 14–15, discusses how "civil rights" as the term to use arose. Most people used the terms "civil liberty" or "human rights" to apply to the whole array of discrimination issues, but in the course of staff studies they decided to adopt the label dating from the acts passed after the Civil War: "civil rights." Truman issued Executive Order 9808 establishing the committee on December 5, 1946; Richard Bardolph, *The Civil Rights Record: Black Americans and the Law, 1849–1970* (New York: Thomas Y. Crowell, 1970), pp. 254–259; Mary Dudziak, *Cold War Civil Rights: Race and the Image of American Democracy* (Princeton, N.J.: Princeton University Press, 2000).

22. Gardner, *Harry Truman and Civil Rights*, pp. 44–45.

23. Ibid.; Genna Rae McNeil, *Groundwork: Charles Hamilton Houston and the Struggle for Civil Rights* (Philadelphia: University of Pennsylvania Press, 1983).

24. Gardner, *Harry Truman and Civil Rights*, pp. 51, 60–61, 190.

25. Burt, *Eisenhower*, p. 207.

26. Ibid.; Herbert Brownell, with John Burke, *Advising Ike: The Memoirs of Attorney General Herbert Brownell* (Lawrence: University of Kansas Press, 1993), pp. 218–219, 228; J. W. Anderson, *Eisenhower, Brownell, and the Congress: The Tangled Origins of the Civil Rights Bill of 1956–57* (Published for Inter-University Case Program, Inc., Kingsport, Tenn., by University of Alabama Press, 1964); Burt, *Eisenhower*, p. 207; 85th Congress, House Report No. 291, April 1, 1957, p. 8; *Congressional Record*, August 7, 1957, p. 12637 (daily edition).

27. Burt, *Eisenhower*, p. 209; Adams, *Firsthand Report*, pp. 336–338.

28. Until his death in 1874, Sumner was the most prominent opponent of slavery and supporter of the rights of African Americans in the Senate. Burt, *Eisenhower,* p. 209; Adams, *Firsthand Report,* pp. 336–338; Brownell, *Advising Ike,* p. 219; Burt, *Eisenhower,* p. 214; Taylor Branch, *Parting the Waters: America in the King Years, 1954–63* (New York: Simon & Schuster, 1988), p. 182 and notes there cited. Brownell submitted the legislation to Congress on April 9 and testified the next day before the House Judiciary Committee; 85th Congress, House Report No. 291, April 1, 1957, p. 8; *Congressional Record,* August 7, 1957, p. 12637 (daily edition).

29. Morrow, *Black Man in the White House,* p. 168; King's speech "Give Us the Ballot," in Clayborne Carson, ed., *The Papers of Martin Luther King, Jr.,* vol. 4, Symbol of the Movement, January 1957–December 1958. (Berkeley: University of California Press, 1992–).

30. Essie Mae Washington-Williams, *Dear Senator: A Memoir by the Daughter of Strom Thurmond* (New York: Regan Books, 2005); Dulles, *Civil Rights Commission,* pp. 14–15, Thurmond quoted; see also pp. 12–13 and notes there cited; *Congressional Record,* Senate, August 6, 1957, pp. 13848, 13374, 13725; "Thurmond Talks Hours on Rights," *New York Times,* August 29, 1957, p. 1; see generally Robert Mann, *When Freedom Would Triumph: The Civil Rights Struggle in Congress 1945–1968* (Baton Rouge: Louisiana State University Press, 2007) on the importance of the 1957 act to later legislation.

31. Pub. L. No. 85-315.

32. King to Nixon, August 30, 1957, William P. Rogers Papers, Series I: General Correspondence, Box 50. Dwight D. Eisenhower Presidential Library.

33. Mary Frances Berry, *Black Resistance, White Law: A History of Constitutional Racism in America* (New York: Penguin, 1994), pp. 14–43.

34. Dulles, *Civil Rights Commission,* pp. 21–23.

35. Ibid., pp. 23–26.

36. Ibid., pp. 26–27.

37. "Negro Prospects Held Improving," *New York Times,* February 16, 1956, p. 20.

38. www.math.buffalo.edu/mad/PEEPS/wilkins_jearnest.html. Wilkins, who after meeting with Eisenhower at the White House planned to announce his resignation from Labor for reasons of health, blurted out that his high blood pressure had nothing to do with it. He said he had clashed with his boss, Secretary James Mitchell, for giving leftist labor leaders too much say in department policy. He said nothing more, and Eisenhower, when asked, told a press conference that he had not been asked to resign. "Riddling the Ritual," *Time,* September 1, 1958.

39. "Civil Rights Aides Hear Eisenhower," *New York Times,* June 10, 1959, p. 18; "J. Ernest Wilkins, Member of Civil Rights Unit," *New York Times,* January 20, 1950, p. 35; Dulles, *Civil Rights Commission,* p. 22.

40. Dulles, *Civil Rights Commission,* pp. 27–31; Report of the Commission, 1959, pp. ix–xv, describes how the commission functioned, meeting on an average of once a month, and how dissents were handled as footnotes or statements at the end. They also implemented a suggestion in the Civil Rights Act of 1957 that they appoint state advisory committees.

41. Dulles, *Civil Rights Commission,* pp. 116–118.

42. Michael Janofsky, "A New Hope for Dreams Suspended by Segregation," *New York Times,* July 31, 2005, p. 1.

43. CCR, *Freedom to the Free* (1963), pp. 184–185 and notes there cited.

44. Burt, *Eisenhower,* p. 236; "Executive branch cooperation with the Commission on Civil Rights," February 27, 1959, Morgan Records, Box 6, Dwight D. Eisenhower Presidential Library.

45. Interview with Father Hesburgh, February 2006; Cheever Griffin, "Secrets of the Lake," *Notre Dame Magazine*, Winter 2000–2001.

46. Interview with Father Hesburgh, February 2006.

47. Report of the Commission, 1959, p. xiv.

48. Ibid., pp. 554–557.

49. Ibid., pp. 134–143.

50. Ibid., pp. 534–540.

51. Ibid., p. 540.

52. Ibid., pp. 545–546.

53. The paragraphs until the next note rely on Dulles, *Civil Rights Commission*, pp. 82–88.

54. Berl Bernhard, Oral History, p. 5; Wofford and William Taylor were the other 1954 Yale Law School graduates. Rocco Siciliano, an oil and gas labor lawyer, was assigned the civil rights portfolio after Maxwell Rabb left. He insisted on abandoning it when the press identified him as the staff member for minorities, as he didn't believe that would help his career. Branch, *Parting the Waters*, pp. 235–237.

55. The 1959 Report noted that the commission was not unmindful that other race and national origin groups had problems that required study; *Time*, "North of the Line, Too," November 24, 1958.

56. See generally Arnold Hirsch, *Making the Second Ghetto: Race and Housing in Chicago, 1940–1960* (Cambridge: Cambridge University Press, 1983); Thomas Sugrue, *The Origins of the Urban Crisis: Race and Inequality in Postwar Detroit* (Princeton, N.J.: Princeton University Press, 1996).

57. Hearings Before the United States Commission on Civil Rights, Los Angeles, California, January 25–26, 1960, and San Francisco, January 27 and January 29, 1960, p. 307; Los Angeles, California, January 25–26, 1960.

58. Ibid., pp. 308–309.

59. Ibid., pp. 325, 329.

60. Ibid., p. 331.

61. Ibid., p. 323; Dulles, *Civil Rights Commission*, pp. 118–121.

62. Hearings Before the United States Commission on Civil Rights, Los Angeles, California, January 25–26, 1960, San Francisco, January 27 and January 29, 1960, pp. 512–518, 780.

63. Hearings Before the United States Commission on Civil Rights, Detroit, Michigan, December 14–15, pp. 58, 402–403; Dulles, *Civil Rights Commission*, pp. 122–127.

64. Responding to black protests, Eisenhower's Justice Department sued Harrison County and the City of Biloxi, Mississippi, for denying blacks access to beach facilities. Federal funds had been used for the beach's anti-erosion project and seawall. Oklahoma civil rights leader Clara Luper led thirteen members of the NAACP's Youth Council, including her daughter Marilyn, in a sit-in at the Katz Drug Store lunch counter in downtown Oklahoma City on August 19, 1958, but it did not receive great national public notice. By the end of 1960 there were about 50,000 blacks engaged in direct-action campaigns, including sit-ins, walk-ins, and pray-ins. About 3,600 protesters were arrested. See *Bell v. Maryland*, 378 U.S. 226 (1964); *Garner v. Louisiana*, 368 U.S. 157 (1961); *Peterson v. City of Greenville*, 373 U.S. 244 (1963); *Bouie v. City of Columbia*, 378 U.S. 347 (1964); *Barr v. City of Columbia*, 378 U.S. 146 (1964); and Monrad G. Paulsen, "Sit-in Cases of 1964, but Answers Came There None," *Supreme Court Rev.*, 1964, p. 137; the whole issue was made moot by the enactment of Title II of the Civil Rights Act of 1964, insofar as the facilities in question are covered by the terms of that act; Burt, *Eisenhower*, pp. 254–255.

65. Dulles, *Civil Rights Commission*, pp. 93–99, covers the material until the next note.

66. Burt, *Eisenhower*, p. 250; Commission Report, Justice, pp. 62, 225, 176; only one victim was a minority, a Cree Indian. None of the officers served jail time. They received fines, suspended sentences, and probation.

67. The commissioner of education, Lawrence Gridley Derthick, formerly superintendent of Chattanooga schools, had insisted that federal impact aid, given to school districts since 1950 to offset the demands on public services from the presence of military personnel who do not pay taxes to state or local governments, be withheld from segregated schools. He had implemented this policy in Pulaski County, Arkansas, and also argued for the use of impact aid to obtain more desegregated schools, moving faster than the White House wanted. Commission Report, Education, 1961, p. 45; see also Record Group 12, U.S. Education Department, Division of Equal Educational Opportunity Records on Desegregation, Box 3.

Chapter II

1. Crymes was first denied a pension on the grounds that his disability resulted from his "own willful misconduct." After the officer was indicted, and the commission made inquiries, the claim was reviewed again. A full field investigation determined that Crymes "was innocent of willful misconduct in the shooting incident resulting in his severe permanent injuries," and he received a pension; CCR Report, 1961, Book 5, Justice, pp. 21–23; Crymes's statement in CCR files labeled "Document No. 7 Human rights in Alabama." The incident was brought to the attention of the commission by an interracial intercitizens committee in Birmingham, headed by Rev. Herbert Oliver, a black minister; conversation with Rev. Oliver, May 4, 2008.

2. Foster Rhea Dulles, *The Civil Rights Commission: 1957–1965* (East Lansing: Michigan State University Press, 1968), pp. 99–100, and Berl Bernhard, p. 7, Oral History, John F. Kennedy Library (hereafter cited as JFK Library). Manuscript materials cited in this chapter are in the JFK Library, FG 93, unless otherwise indicated. As the administration began, the staff had studies under way on the living conditions of Native Americans in the Southwest and a survey of discrimination against African Americans in sixteen Southern Black Belt counties.

3. Dulles, *Civil Rights Commission*, pp. 104–105; Nick Bryant, *The Bystander: John F. Kennedy and the Struggle for Black Equality* (New York: Basic Books, 2006), p. 473, says Kennedy missed "the great revolution of his age" because he did not want to be inconvenienced.

4. Bernhard interview, July 20, 2005.

5. Ibid.

6. Harris Wofford, Memorandum to the President, reminding him of Hannah's desires, July 1, 1961, FG 634, JFK Library.

7. Ibid.; Harris Wofford, *Of Kennedys and Kings: Making Sense of the Sixties* (New York: Farrar, Straus, and Giroux, 1980); Bryant, *The Bystander*, p. 473.

8. Wofford to Lawrence O'Brien, February 16, 1961, FG 634, JFK Library. Hannah had hired Johnson for Michigan State's programs in Nigeria. After being pushed, Carlton resigned voluntarily, telling the president, "You should be free to organize the Commission in keeping with your wishes and in that spirit I am tendering my resignation."

9. Dennis Hevesi, "Erwin Griswold Is Dead at 90; Served as a Solicitor General," *New York Times*, November 21, 1994.

10. Eric Pace, "Spottswood W. Robinson 3d, Civil Rights Lawyer, Dies at 82," *New York Times*, October 13, 1998.

11. Bernhard to Ralph Dungan, January 23, 1961, Commission on Civil Rights Organization and Procedures, Box 11; Wilkins to JFK and King to JFK, March 1, 1961, FG 634; Kennedy to Wilkins and King separately, March 21, 1961; U.S. Commission on Civil Rights, January 20, 1961–August 15, 1961, Executive Box 198.

12. Bernhard, Oral History, p. 8.

13. Dulles, *Civil Rights Commission*, pp. 99–103; Mike Manaton to Larry O'Brien, May 23, 1961, tells him Eastland objects to Griswold; his slot should have gone to a Southerner. Nominees for the Commission on Civil Rights; Hearings Subcommittee on Constitutional Rights, Committee on the Judiciary, United States Senate, 87th Congress, First Session, June 16, 1961, FG 634; Bernhard, Oral History, pp. 4–8. Hannah recommended Bernhard as one of the "Ten Outstanding Young Men in the United States" in 1962 as selected by the United States Junior Chamber of Commerce. He was also a recipient of the Arthur S. Flemming Award as one of the "Ten Outstanding Young Men in Federal Government" in 1960. Bernhard to Ralph Dungan, Special Assistant to the President, January 23, 1961; Wofford to the President, February 27, 1962, "Meeting with Dean Storey on Civil Rights Commission," Wofford files.

14. Bernhard, Oral History, pp. 8–9.

15. Although the commission ignored the administration's request to defer the District of Columbia hearing, it agreed when they asked for a delay in the reconvened Louisiana voting rights hearing. Part of the unstated problem was always the administration's worry about offending Southern senators. However, Justice pleaded that the commission should wait until after a mayoralty election, since their presence might help defeat the most pro–civil rights candidate. The commission agreed and held the hearing later because, as Bernhard put it, the timing was not crucial to the agency's independence. But "we never backed off from what we wanted to do. And I think this is a great credit to the Commission, also a credit to the reserve of the White House not to interfere." Dulles, *Civil Rights Commission*, pp. 36–43.

16. Ibid., pp. 127–128.

17. Ibid., pp. 127–131; Part I, Voting, Louisiana, 1961, pp. 63, 68–70, and hearing transcript there cited.

18. Dulles, *Civil Rights Commission*, pp. 108–109.

19. Ibid., p. 131. They agreed to have 10,000 copies made in order to distribute it widely after sending it to the president and Congress; Part I, Civil Rights, 1961, p. 1. In the education volume the commission objected but seemed somewhat bemused about whether the freedom of choice plans used to defeat desegregation were constitutional under some interpretation of states' rights; Education, Book 2, pp. 67, 97–98.

20. Justice, pp. 21–23. Bernhard to Bobby Kennedy, May 30, 1961, Bernhard Papers, JFK Library, Series I, CCR files.

21. Bernhard to Bobby Kennedy, May 30, 1961, files, Bernhard Papers, JFK Library, Series I, CCR files; Justice, pp. 21–23.

22. Bernhard, Oral History, pp. 19–20, 21; Hoover to Hannah, December 5, 1961, enclosing policy statement of 1946, "Scope of the Civil Rights Statutes"; Hoover to Hannah, January 8, 1962; Hoover to Bernhard, January 12, 1962; Memorandum from Hannah to Hoover, January 13, 1962, recapitulates request for cooperation.

23. Bernhard, Oral History, pp. 51–53. The commission had the bureau do name checks at first on witnesses, feeling that the operation was so "delicate" that they did not want to put known Communists on as witnesses. But that practice was abandoned. If staff received any information about a person that they thought might be "potentially dangerous," Bernhard would talk it over with the liaison from the FBI, but he never gave them written information on anyone; Taylor Branch, *Parting the Waters: America in*

the King Years, 1954–63 (New York: Simon & Schuster, 1988), pp. 859–862; Kenneth O'Reilly, *Racial Matters: The FBI's Secret File on Black America, 1960–1972* (New York: Free Press, 1989), pp. 73–74; John D'Emilio, *Lost Prophet: The Life and Times of Bayard Rustin* (New York: Free Press, 2003), pp. 298, 373; Jervis Anderson, *A. Philip Randolph: A Biographical Portrait* (New York: Harcourt Brace Jovanovich, 1973), p. 230; Daniel Levine, *Bayard Rustin and the Civil Rights Movement* (New Brunswick, N.J.: Rutgers University Press, 2000), p. 121. Interview with Berl Bernhard 7/20/05: according to Bernhard, Payne, the FBI agent sat outside his door for nine months watching. He was cordial; I asked Bernhard "Why did Payne tell you Martin King was a 'switch-hitter' and a 'pervert'?" He answered: "to get me to stop dealing with him; so I wouldn't have anything to do with him." Bernhard recalled that Payne let him listen to a tape ("I think") also. In Bernhard's oral history he says the agent showed him documents; V. P. Franklin, *Living Our Stories, Telling Our Truths: Autobiography and the Making of the African American Intellectual Tradition* (New York: Oxford University Press, 1996), pp. 309–311.

24. Dulles, *Civil Rights Commission*, pp. 111–113.

25. Ibid., pp. 140–141. Rankin joined in Storey's dissent and added a "personal comment." He did not see the Fifteenth Amendment as a mandate to "usurp" the power of each state over voting. He too thought the 1957 and 1960 laws went far enough.

26. Commission Report, 1961, Education, pp. 176–177, 181–185.

27. Commission Report, 1961, Housing, pp. 152–153. He believed that the Federal Home Loan Bank system, which made home mortgage loans throughout the country, could be regulated.

28. Commission Report, 1961, Voting, p. 96. The Justice Department also failed to protect Joseph Atlas, a black farmer from East Carroll Parish, Louisiana, where blacks outnumbered whites but not a single African American had registered to vote. After he testified before the commission, the local cotton gin and farm services supplier would not handle his cotton, and he could conduct no business transactions at all in the parish. The case ended with an agreement that the intimidation would stop, his cotton would be ginned, and he could purchase the goods and services he needed; Raymond Arsenault, *Freedom Riders: 1961 and the Struggle for Racial Justice* (New York: Oxford University Press, 2006).

29. Mary Frances Berry, *Black Resistance, White Law: A History of Constitutional Racism in America* (New York: Penguin, 1994), p. 150; Branch, *Parting the Waters*, p. 640; Burke Marshall, *Federalism and Civil Rights* (New York: Columbia University Press, 1964), discusses Justice Department attitudes.

30. Commission Report, 1961, Justice, pp. 162–163.

31. Ibid., p. 165.

32. Ibid., pp. 165–166.

33. Ibid., p. 168.

34. Ibid.

35. Dulles, *Civil Rights Commission*, pp. 107–109; Bernhard, Oral History, p. 49; Myer Feldman, deputy special counsel to Hannah, April 13, 1962, FG 634, JFK Library. They raised anew the politically motivated management investigation that they used to drive Tiffany away, the "unsoundness" of Rankin and Robinson on the race question, and the improbability of commission impartiality. The Southern senators registered their discontent by insisting on a reduction in Bernhard's salary ($22,500 under the statute) of $2,000.

36. William L. Taylor, *The Passion of My Times: An Advocate's Fifty-Year Journey in the Civil Rights Movement* (New York: Carroll and Graf, 2004), pp. 36–37; FG 634, General, JFK Library, contains numerous referrals and letters sent by Taylor on behalf of the

president on routine civil rights inquiries; Branch, *Parting the Waters*, pp. 586–587, and notes there cited; Bernhard, Oral History, p. 5.

37. Bernhard, Oral History, pp. 10–13.

38. Ibid., pp. 22–24.

39. Branch, *Parting the Waters*, pp. 685–687, 698–699.

40. Ibid., 698.

41. John Hope Franklin, *Mirror to America: The Autobiography of John Hope Franklin* (New York: Farrar, Straus, and Giroux. 2005), pp. 197–200.

42. Ibid.; *Freedom to the Free: Century of Emancipation, 1863–1963*, CCR, 1963, pp. 2–3. Storey announced the study and John Hope Franklin's role at a hearing in Phoenix in February 1962.

43. Bernhard, Oral History, pp. 53–55; Dulles, *Civil Rights Commission*, pp. 156–157. Martin also kept Sammy Davis, Jr., on the list despite White House staff worries over the political impact of his interracial marriage. The staff, however, managed to avoid a picture of Davis with the president; Branch, *Parting the Waters*, pp. 686–687, 694–695, 698–699; Franklin, *Mirror*, pp. 200–201.

44. Branch, *Parting the Waters*, p. 671.

45. Bernhard, Oral History, pp. 44–48; Harris Wofford to the President, July 11, 1961, FG 634, JFK Library.

46. Bernhard, Oral History, p. 48; Hannah to Speaker John McCormack and Vice President Lyndon Johnson, March 11, 1963, FG 634, 440, JFK Library; Dulles, *Civil Rights Commission*, pp. 192–193, 176–177.

47. Ibid.

48. Ibid.

49. John Dittmer, *Local People: The Struggle for Civil Rights in Mississippi* (Urbana and Chicago: University of Illinois Press, 1994), chapter 4.

50. Ibid., p. 195 and notes there cited.

51. Attorney General to Hannah, December 6, 1962; Hannah to Kennedy, January 2, 1963, in Hannah's files, p. 180; Dulles, *Civil Rights Commission*, quotes Hannah's response; Phillipa Strum, ed., *Civil Rights Politics and the Law: Three Civil Rights Lawyers Reminisce* (Washington, D.C.: Woodrow Wilson International Center for Scholars, 2006), p. 19.

52. Exchange between Hannah and O'Donnell, White House Central Files, December 17, 1962, from O'Donnell; December 23, 1962, from Hannah; Hannah correspondence, November 1959–April 23, 1963, Box 5.

53. Dulles, *Civil Rights Commission*, p. 181.

54. Bernhard, Oral History, pp. 24–27; Attorney General to Hannah, March 26, 1963, FG 90; Commission on Civil Rights, Hannah correspondence, November 1959–April 23, 1963, Box 5.

55. Dulles, *Civil Rights Commission*, pp. 181–182.

56. Bernhard, Oral History, p. 29; White House Central Files, United States Commission on Civil Rights, JFK Library; Hugh Davis Graham, *The Civil Rights Era: Origins of National Policy, 1960–1972* (New York: Oxford University Press, 1990), p. 185.

57. Bernhard, Oral History, p. 27.

58. Ibid.; Schlesinger, *A Thousand Days: Kennedy in the White House* (Boston: Houghton Mifflin, 1965), p. 953.

59. Branch, *Parting the Waters*, pp. 746–747.

60. Ibid.; Interim Report, pp. 1–5; Dulles, *Civil Rights Commission*, pp. 183–184; Hannah correspondence, November 1959–April 23, 1963, Box 5.

61. Bernhard, Oral History, p. 32.

62. Ibid.

63. Branch, *Parting the Waters*, pp. 822–823; Dittmer, *Local People*, pp. 165–166.

64. Dulles, *Civil Rights Commission*, pp. 189–192, 195.

65. Ibid., p. 209; quote on p. 210 from *New York Times*, September 29, 1963.

66. Dulles, *Civil Rights Commission*, pp. 210–211.

67. Hannah to JFK, October 10, 1963; JFK to Hannah, October 21, 1963, FG 634, FG 634A, Executive Box 199.

68. Hannah to JFK, October 28, 1963, FG 634.

69. Dittmer, *Local People*, p. 198 and notes there cited. The commission's 1963 report covered education, voting, housing, and employment, as usual, along with material on discrimination in health facilities and services, African Americans in the armed services, and the state advisory committees. It also included a section describing responses to the commission's recommendations. The report emphasized that Kennedy's newly issued housing executive order tracked the commission's recommendations dating from 1959. However, Executive Order 11063 covered only FHA and VA-insured mortgages, not conventional mortgage activities of federally assisted lenders. The commission thought that created a competitive advantage and remained convinced that there should be a comprehensive order covering all lenders. It determined to monitor the effects.

On voting, Rankin and Storey, persuaded by events and the investigations, changed their minds and joined the other commissioners in pointing out the inadequacies of the weak Civil Rights Act of 1957. Therefore they now supported not just a sixth-grade literacy requirement but the use of federal registrars.

70. Hannah to JFK, November 13, 1963, White House Central Files, FG 634. In thinking about a staff director, the president suggested Harold Fleming from the Potomac Foundation, and Hannah agreed that he should receive "serious consideration."

71. Ibid.

Chapter III

1. *Hearings Before the United States Commission on Civil Rights*, Vol. 2, *Administration of Justice*; "Declares Negroes Armed Themselves," *Jackson Clarion Ledger*, February 19, 1965, p. 1.

2. Roy Reed, "TV Widens a Crack in a Racial Wall," *New York Times*, February 21, 1965, p. 5; *Hearings Before the United States Commission on Civil Rights*, Vol. 2, *Administration of Justice*, Jackson, Mississippi, February 16–20, 1965, pp. 96–103.

3. *Hearings Before the United States Commission on Civil Rights*, Vol. 1, *Voting*, Jackson, Mississippi, February 16–20, 1965, pp. 155, 163; Beckwith was not convicted until 1994.

4. Hannah to Johnson, January 16, 1964; Johnson to Hannah, January 21, 1964, White House Central Files, Ex FG 634, Box 375, LBJ Library. Hannah told Johnson that his reported consultations with "Reverend Mr. King and various others . . . and our inability to contact you, resulted in a presumption that perhaps you were contemplating reconstituting the Commission." All manuscript materials cited in this chapter are in the LBJ Library unless otherwise indicated.

5. Ibid.; Foster Rhea Dulles, *The Civil Rights Commission: 1957–1965* (East Lansing: Michigan State University Press, 1968), p. 215.

6. Dulles, *Civil Rights Commission*, pp. 215–216; Hesburgh suggested they might involve themselves in the poverty programs. Rankin thought they could deal with trouble spots and make more suggestions on the role of the government. Griswold preferred

that they continue to educate the public. Hannah to Johnson, January 16, 1964; Johnson to Hannah, January 21, 1964, White House Central Files, Ex FG 634, Box 375.

7. Dulles, *Civil Rights Commission*, p. 217; Johnson named Robert Weaver, who had been New York State rent commissioner before President Kennedy named him administrator of the Housing and Home Finance Agency, to his cabinet, heading the newly created Department of Housing and Urban Development. Johnson nominated Thurgood Marshall to the Supreme Court and appointed seven black federal district court judges, who joined the two who had been appointed by President Kennedy. One of his judicial appointments was Constance Baker Motley, the first African American woman federal judge, and the other was A. Leon Higginbotham, who, when named to the Federal Trade Commission by President Kennedy, was the youngest person and the first African American appointed to a federal regulatory commission. Johnson also appointed Clifford Alexander as White House deputy counsel. The Southern president and longtime Washington power broker also named economist Arthur Brimmer as the first black member of the Federal Reserve Board.

8. Hannah to Johnson, October 15, 1965, reminds him that they have met only once, in February 1964, White House Central Files, Ex FG 634, Box 376; phone message from Whitney Young to Johnson, White House Central Files, Ex FG 634, Box 375; Frankie Muse Freeman, *A Song of Faith and Hope: The Life of Frankie Muse Freeman* (St. Louis: Missouri Historical Society Press, 2003), pp. 42–49.

9. Jonathan Rosenberg and Zachary Karabell, *Kennedy, Johnson, and the Quest for Justice: The Civil Rights Tapes* (New York: Norton, 2003), pp. 273–274. Rayburn died in office on November 16, 1961.

10. Ibid., p. 277.

11. Ibid., p. 279.

12. Dulles, *Civil Rights Commission*, pp. 216–218; Freeman, *Song*, pp. 90–93; oral interview with Freeman, May 2005; phone message from Whitney Young to Bill, White House Central Files, Ex FG 634, Box 375; "2 Civil Rights Nominees Backed by Subcommittee," *New York Times*, July 28, 1964; Gene Roberts and Hank Klibanoff, *The Race Beat: The Civil Rights Struggle and the Awakening of a Nation* (New York: Knopf, 2006), pp. 284–285, 351–352; Randall Miller and Stanley Harrold, *The Changing South of Gene Patterson* (Gainesville: University of Florida Press, 2002), pp. 146–147.

13. U.S., *Public Papers of the Presidents*, Lyndon B. Johnson, November 22, 1963–June 30, 1964, p. 808; *New York Times*, June 24, 1964, p. 1; *United States v. Price*, 383 U.S. 787 (1966); *United States v. Guest*, 383 U.S. 745 (1966); Kenneth O'Reilly, *Racial Matters: The FBI's Secret File on Black America, 1960–1972* (New York: Free Press, 1989), pp. 162 f.

14. Dulles, *Civil Rights Commission*, pp. 210–211.

15. As a result of a flap over a questionnaire distributed by the Utah State Advisory Committee, the legislation prohibited the commission from investigating the practices of private and fraternal clubs and religious organizations; ibid., pp. 218–222; Pub. L. No. 88-352, 78, *Statutes at Large of the United States* 241 (1964), Title 42, United States Code, Section 2000A.

16. CCR Minutes, September 2, 1964; Dulles, *Civil Rights Commission*, pp. 224–225; Lee White to the President, December 23, 1964, January 4, 1965, White House Central Files, Ex FG 634, Box 375.

17. Lee White to Attorney General, February 8, 1965, White House Central Files, FG 634, 135 Commission; Warren Huff, chairman of the Board of Trustees of Michigan State University, called the White House before they left Washington to say he wanted the record to show that the board "supported Dr. Hannah's efforts and were concerned

about his safety." He knew of the limitations of federal protection but hoped "there would be no incidents, or indeed, there would be no personal threats to Dr. Hannah, other members of the Commission and the staff." Lee White informed the attorney general that he told Huff he would alert Justice and knew that they had already alerted state and local authorities to the hearings.

18. Freeman, *Song*, p. 96.

19. WBLT was owned by Lamar Life Broadcasting, a subsidiary of a large insurance company. The owners and managers were active participants in the White Citizens' Council. In 1955 when they received a license and went on the air, the Citizens' Council started producing a syndicated TV forum that was featured on WBLT as part of their aim of using news and educational programming to maintain the color line. William G. Thomas, "Television News and the Civil Rights Struggle in Virginia and Mississippi," *Southern Spaces*, www.southernspaces.org.

20. Reed, "TV Widens a Crack in a Racial Wall," *New York Times*, February 19, 1965, p. 1.

21. Hearings Before the United States Commission on Civil Rights, vol. 1, Voting, Jackson, Mississippi, February 16–20, 1965, pp. 5–8, 153.

22. Ibid., pp. 155, 163.

23. Ibid., pp. 29–31.

24. Ibid., pp, 29–32, 153–175, 78; Freeman, *Song*, pp. 98–100.

25. Freeman, *Song*, p. 103. Panels of lawyers, business leaders, and ministers reported some recent improvement in racial attitudes and gave more hopeful testimony. They, however, conceded that whites who wanted to speak out for change had no real support or encouragement. In the portion of the hearing devoted to general law enforcement, the commission turned to the black church burnings and harassment and firebombing of black workers trying to unionize or to vote.

26. O'Reilly, *Racial Matters*, pp. 215–217. On July 11, 1964, Klansmen killed Lemuel Penn, a black educator from the District of Columbia who was on duty in Georgia as an army reserve lieutenant colonel while he was driving from Fort Benning to Washington.

27. The commissioners recommended that the voting rights bill include prohibitions on the use of poll taxes, literacy tests, and other devices used to discriminate. They also renewed their repeated request for federal registrars and poll workers to supervise elections. The terms of the Voting Rights Act were similar to those of the Lodge elections bill of 1890, which was labeled unconstitutional by its opponents. However, this bill was saved from the onslaught of Southerners by the Supreme Court decision in *South Carolina v. Katzenbach* (1966), in which the act was determined to be a valid exercise of constitutional power under the Fifteenth Amendment.

28. Kennedy to Hannah, May 15, 1965, Hannah files, JFK Library.

29. Jocelyn C. Frye et al. "The Rise and Fall of the United States Commission on Civil Rights," 22 *Harvard Civil Rights Civil Liberties Law Review* 449 (1987).

30. *New York Times*, July 21, 1964, p. 1; September 27, 1964, p. 81; Arthur Waskow, *From Race Riot to Sit-in: 1919 to the 1960's* (Garden City, N.Y.: Doubleday, 1966), pp. 255–260; U.S. National Advisory Commission on Civil Disorders Report (Washington, D.C.: 1968), pp. 19–20 (hereafter cited as Kerner Report); U.S., *Public Papers of the Presidents, Lyndon B. Johnson, July 1–December 31, 1964*, p. 938; O'Reilly, *Racial Matters*, p. 235.

31. *New York Times*, August 13–15, 1965, p. 1; Governor's Commission on the Los Angeles Riots, *Violence in the City: An End or a Beginning* (Los Angeles, 1965).

32. *Congressional Record*, 89th Cong., 1st sess., 1965, pp. 20488–20489, 20490, 20793.

33. Dulles, *Civil Rights Commission*, p. 250.

34. Johnson to Hannah, November 17, 1965, White House Central Files, Ex FG 634, Box 375; *New York Times*, November 17, 18, 1965; Freeman, *Song*, p. 107.

35. "An Analysis of the McCone Commission Report," California State Advisory Committee Report, January 1966; Taylor to Hayes Redmon, January 26, 1966, White House Central Files, Ex FG 634, Box 375.

36. Ibid.; "Watts Riot Study Depicted as Weak," *New York Times*, January 23, 1966, p. 71.

37. "An Analysis of the McCone Commission Report."

38. Lee White to Johnson, December 4, 1965; White to Hannah, December 4, 1965; White House Central Files, FG 634, Box 375; FG 654, Box 20, LBJ Library.

39. Katzenbach to Taylor, December 4, 1965, White House Central Files, FG 634, Box 375; minutes of commission meeting, January 6, 1966, FG 654, Box 20, LBJ Library.

40. 79 Stat 437, 42 U.S. 1973 (1965); Mary Frances Berry and John W. Blassingame, *Long Memory: The Black Experience in America* (New York: Oxford University Press, 1982), p. 184.

41. Hannah to LBJ, October 15, 1965; Valenti to White, October 20, 1965; White to Hannah, October 25, 1965; White House Central Files, FG 634, Box 376. They did meet with the president in 1965; see Freeman, *Song*, p. 97.

42. McPherson to Watson, January 3, 1967, notation nothing else sent to files as of 2/7/67, White House Central Files, Ex FG 634, Box 375; Freeman, *Song*, pp. 108–109; White, a Kennedy holdover, left in 1966 and was appointed to the Federal Power Commission; the president's schedule in the LBJ Library files does not include a meeting with the commission in January. However, Staff Director William Taylor says they did meet, but the rewards were "primarily psychic"; Johnson did nothing; William L. Taylor, *The Passion of My Times: An Advocate's Fifty-Year Journey in the Civil Rights Movement* (New York: Carroll and Graf, 2004), p. 96.

43. Robert Semple, "Congress Is Cool to Rights Report," *New York Times*, February 22, 1967; "No Road to Integration," Editorial, *New York Times*, February 21, 1967.

44. Freeman, *Song*, pp. 108–109.

45. Office of the Commissioner of Education to Doug Cater, 4/5/67. Of the twenty negative ones, seven came from the Northeast, six from the Midwest, four from the South, and two from the West. Of the nineteen favorable ones, twelve were from the Northeast, four from the Midwest, and three from the West; Taylor to McPherson, April 12, 1967, White House Central Files, Ex FG 634, Box 375. Two independent commissions reported on the housing crisis during the Johnson years. However, the commission's annual reports made recommendations that were used in executive orders and legislation. Frye et al., "The Rise and Fall of the United States Commission on Civil Rights," p. 22 *Harvard Civil Rights Civil Liberties Law Review* 449 (1987).

46. *Congressional Record*, 89th Cong., 2nd sess., 1966, pp. 20754–20756; pp. 14765, 20825; pp. 16764–16766.

47. John Herbers, "Rights Hearing Focuses on Negro Ghetto in the North," *New York Times*, April 4, 1966, p. 17.

48. Commission on Civil Rights, *A Time to Listen . . . A Time to Act: A Report of the United States Commission on Civil Rights*, 1967, pp. 1, 18.

49. Ibid., pp. 20–21.

50. Ibid., pp. 43–44.

51. Ibid., p. 49.

52. Ibid., p. 92; Bill Taylor to McPherson, November 16, 1957, forwarding *Time to*

Listen, Time to Act, White House Central Files, Ex FG 634, Box 375; Robert Semple, "Hope for Negroes Found Dwindling," *New York Times,* November 23, 1967, p. 47; Paul Delaney, "Indians Criticize Long Neglect as Rights Panel Opens Inquiry," *New York Times,* November 15, 1972, p. 39. A suggestion that the commission devote more resources to Indian problems emerged from a staff meeting during this period, but no one took it seriously yet.

53. Taylor to McPherson, September 21, 1966, White House Central Files, Ex FG 634, Box 375.

54. Lee White to Morris Abram, president, American Jewish Committee, White House Central Files, Ex FG 634, Box 376. As early as January 1965, when New York lawyer Morris Abram, president of the American Jewish Committee, suggested to Johnson that the commission do "a study of the violent demonstrations of last summer in a number of cities in various parts of the country," White House staff rejected what they saw as a very bad idea. The commission could not be relied upon to give the president the findings he expected. Lee White responded to Abram, on January 21, 1965, telling him that requests, but not assignments, could be made to the Civil Rights Commission, "inasmuch as the Commission is an independent body and I would think its jurisdiction is fixed by the legislation under which it operates, and of course, by its own decisions."

55. Hannah to LBJ, November 1, 1967; Marvin Watson to LBJ, November 6, 1967, LBJ checked off that he would see them; White House Central Files, Ex FG 634, Box 375; "Senate Panel Backs Bill on Rights Unit," *New York Times,* October 6, 1967, p. 32.

56. Taylor, *The Passion of My Times,* p. 97. Persons convicted of violating the Fair Housing Act could be subjected to a $10,000 fine or not more than ten years' imprisonment, or both. However, contrary to the commission's recommendations, the Congress enacted weak enforcement provisions that made practically no dent in the housing discrimination problem. Congress did enact amendments and a new section to the civil rights criminal code to close loopholes, which had been pointed out by the commission and the Supreme Court, in cases arising out of the murders of the civil rights era in Mississippi and Georgia; Title 42, U.S. Code 3601 (1968), 82 Stat 81; see sections of U.S. Code in the Appendix.

57. Freeman, *Song,* pp. 119–123; Freeman reports that someone shot into her motel room one night in Montgomery but she was not hit. She did not report it to the police, saying, "This is Alabama. I just didn't want to do that." Commission report, Cycle to Nowhere, 1968, p. 32; "Rights Panel Finds Alabama Race Bars," *New York Times,* May 5, 1968, p. 46.

58. Taylor, *The Passion of My Times,* p. 96.

59. They considered E. Frederic Morrow from the Eisenhower administration, then with the Bank of America. However, in the absence of sufficient "supporting evidence that this is the type of man the President should have," the idea went nowhere. Faiss to James Jones, May 25, 1968, White House Central Files, Ex FG 634/FG 655, Box 376; Matthew Coffey to Bill Hopkins, May 24, 1968; William Hopkins memo for files, May 25, 1968; Macy to LBJ, January 9, 1969; White House Central Files, Ex FG 634A, Box 376. The president decided to appoint former Maryland governor Theodore McKeldin to the Griswold vacancy, but as the paperwork was about to go to the Senate, he withdrew; Claudia Deutsch, "Maurice E. Mitchell, 81, Leader of a College and Public Radio," *New York Times,* December 4, 1998.

60. Hannah to Johnson, October 3, 1968, White House Central Files, Ex FG 634, Box 376. As early as December 1965, Berl Bernhard, Washington lawyer and former commission staff director, who had been engaged to help organize the upcoming White House Conference on Civil Rights, had raised the issue of Latino problems with Lee

White and others. Bernhard told White, concerning Hispanics, that "the nature, extent and degree of problems they face is less well known." They faced different issues depending on where they came from and where they lived. "These differences involve not only language but difference in law, tradition, and culture. What is urgently needed is the same kind of objective and comprehensive study of these problems which the problems of the Negroes have received." The commission could perform such a study.

61. Rather could not think of a "Texan suitable." Dr. Garcia and Dr. Sanchez were "not broad enough on civil rights." She also thought that since the work was in Texas a non-Texan would be better. The commission's field office suggested some Californians who seemed better suited. Mary Rather to the President, October 11, 1968, White House Central Files, Ex FG 634, Box 376.

62. Macy to President, November 5, 1968, White House Central Files, Ex FG 634 Box 376; Joe Holley, "Hector Perez Garcia, 82, Dies; Led Hispanic Rights Group," *New York Times*, July 29, 1996.

63. "Migrants' Plight in Texas Denied," *New York Times*, December 13, 1968; "Mexicans in U.S. Voice Optimism," *New York Times*, December 16, 1968, p. 52.

64. The White House staff became irritated when Bill Taylor resigned as staff director so near the end of the president's term. Personnel director Macy wrote the president on August 22, "Although I object to resignations of Presidential appointees at this particular point in time, I am not inclined to fight this one as Taylor has committed himself and the administration might be better served by a new Staff Director anyway." But they wanted to announce a new appointment along with the resignation to avoid questions by the press. This meant they probably needed to select someone in government, preferably, at the commission. Macy to LBJ, August 22, 1968; Hannah to LBJ, August 23, 1968; White House Central Files, Ex FG 634, Box 376.

65. Faiss to Jones, September 6, 1968, White House Central Files, Ex FG 634, Box 376.

66. Freeman said she would only say that she dissented, without giving reasons. Macy offered the president three options: appoint a staff director, appoint an acting staff director, leave it alone and let Glickstein run things with just the authority of the commissioners. He recommended the third course. Macy to Reedy September 13, 1968; Reedy to LBJ September 6, 1968, with LBJ's notation; Hannah to Macy September 9, 1968, White House Central Files, Ex FG 634, Box 376. With no action by the White House, Hannah sent an explanation of the commission's actions to Macy on September 9. While they respected Glickstein as general counsel, they wanted the runner-up for the job, Sam Simmons, to be considered. Hesburgh had not returned from traveling abroad, Maurice Mitchell had not been confirmed, and Hannah chose to abstain. Patterson and Rankin voted in favor of Glickstein, which left Freeman voting against him alone. She asked Hannah to vote, which would have resulted in a tie, awaiting the full complement of members, or to use Hesburgh's proxy, but he declined. Hannah told Johnson the members thought they needed to move ahead after Holman refused the job and selected Glickstein as the best choice. He explained: "Needless to say the decisions were without prejudice to whatever he [the President] might wish."

67. The staff directors always worried about access and getting along with White House staffers. Without any discussion with the commissioners, the staff director's office continued to draft responses to routine inquiries for the White House, only occasionally crossing the line by signing letters on behalf of the administration. The staff director also sent along newsmaker items to the White House routinely, and a weekly report required of executive branch agencies that reported to the president, despite the agency's independence. Also, Taylor, like Bernhard before him, sent the same memo

required of non-independent officials to the White House when he left the city for a hearing, asking permission and indicating who would be on duty. White House Central Files, Ex FG 634, Box 375–376, contain evidence of this. See, for example, Taylor's telegram to Rabbi Stanley Relkin, Anne Arundel County League for Human Rights; the communications seemed gratuitous but questionable for an independent commission staff. There is no evidence that the commissioners knew about this cooperative relationship over the years. Taylor would write "the White House has asked us to respond," or on behalf of the White House, which was less problematic than "This administration believes, etc."

Chapter IV

1. Hearing Before the United States Commission on Civil Rights, San Antonio, December 1968.

2. Ibid., p. 6.

3. Ibid., p. 7.

4. Ibid., pp. 40–42.

5. Ibid., pp. 42, 44–45. Captain Allee did not want to testify because the San Antonio police reported a threat on his life. After Commissioners Freeman, Rankin, and staff met with him and refused to withdraw the subpoena, he testified along with other witnesses.

6. Ibid., p. 46; CCR Minutes, January 9, 1969, pp. 1–6. On Hesburgh's question about whether the harassed farmworkers were subjected to peonage, the Justice Department concluded that insufficient evidence existed. The CCR discussed follow-up to the San Antonio hearing, including a response to local Latinos who wanted the San Antonio field office kept open. Also, the president had asked Agriculture Secretary Hardison and Labor Secretary George Shultz to recommend whether farmworkers should be permitted to unionize under the National Labor Relations Act. The CCR had, also, written to Defense Secretary Melvin Laird to ask why, at Laughlin Air Force Base, children of dependents were bused across a poor, predominantly Mexican American school district to one that was about 50 percent Anglo. This meant the Anglo district received impact-aid funds allocated by the federal government to districts that educated dependent children to substitute for the tax revenue they could not collect. They suggested that Secretary Laird meet with HEW to find a remedy to such situations. CCR Minutes, March 1969, pp. 2–3.

7. Enforcement agency budgets increased overall from $75 million in 1969 to $600 million in 1973.

8. Craig Allan Kaplowitz, "A Distinct Minority: LULAC, Mexican American Identity, and Presidential Policy-Making, 1965–1972," *Journal of Policy History* 15 (2003): 192–222.

9. To the president-elect at Hotel Pierre, February 3, 1969, Ex FG 90/A, Richard Nixon Presidential Library. All manuscript collections cited in this chapter are from this library unless otherwise indicated. At their meeting on January 9, Hannah asked the staff to prepare comprehensive statements for those new cabinet members he knew personally, beginning with the Department of Defense and the Department of Health, Education, and Welfare (HEW), to bring them up to date on civil rights responsibilities in their departments; CCR Minutes, January 9, 1969, pp. 1–6.

10. Hannah to Nixon, January 23, 1969, Ex FG 90, Box 1, 1969–70, 1 of 2. He said, "The staff of the Commission and members of the White House staff established and maintained infrequent communication."

11. Hannah to Nixon, February 7, 1969. Ex FG 90, Box 1, 1969–70, 1 of 2. He suggested John Gardner, former HEW secretary and head of the National Urban Coalition, and a Republican, as the new chairman. However, if Gardner refused, the president should turn to Commissioner Mitchell. He also suggested that Nixon designate Frankie Freeman, "the Negro member of the Commission," as vice chairman, since in the past when that post went to a Republican chairman the vice chairmanship had always gone to a Democrat.

12. Moynihan to Nixon, February 12, 1969. On February 10 Moynihan wrote to Hannah to tell him he had been given responsibility for keeping White House staffers generally informed about the commission but that shouldn't interfere with his "direct relations with the President." "A short summary of matters you think we should be informed of would be most helpful both now and on a continuing basis." He had no recommendation about appointments, just having learned the commission was one of his areas, but he would have some soon. Ex FG 90, Box 1, 1969–70, 1 of 2.

13. Alexander Butterfield for President's File, Meeting with Moynihan and Commission, February 16, 1969; Meeting File, Box 77; H Notes, February 14, 1969, Civil Rights Commission, "our Mexican" and "strengthen staff with our people," Haldeman Box 40; Butterfield to Moynihan, February 14, 1969; Ken Cole to Haldeman, February 14, 1969; Ex FG 90, Box 1, 1969–70, 1 of 2.

14. Theodore Hesburgh, *God, Country, Notre Dame* (New York: Doubleday, 1990), pp. 206–207; from Nixon papers it was OEO, p. 94; Hesburgh to Nixon, March 6, 1969, FG 90; "Hesburgh Is Named Head of Rights Commission," *New York Times*, March 13, 1969, p. 38.

15. Garment to Erlichman, May 20, 1971; Ex FG 90, Box 1, 1969–70, 2 of 2; Tape 502-20, May 20, 1971, Oval Office; Tape 4-6, June 1971, Nixon Papers, National Archives and Record Service, College Park, Maryland. The killing of four students and wounding of nine at Kent State on May 4, 1970, was the most publicized incident of the period.

16. CCR Minutes, March 1969, pp. 2–3; April 15, 1969—"any problem with Steve Horn at Brookings as Vice Chairman of civil rights Commission to succeed Hesburgh"; FG 90, Box 40.

17. Moynihan to Hesburgh, March 25, 1969, White House Central Files, Subject Files, FG 90, Box 1, Gen (1969–70); Hesburgh to Nixon, March 28, 1969; Moynihan to Hesburgh, April 16, 1969; Ex FG 90, Box 1 1969–70, 1 of 2.

18. At the commission meeting on September 11, 1969, the staff noted the employment of a Puerto Rican attorney. Meanwhile, in a continuous effort to shape policy, commissioners accepted congressional invitations to testify. Frankie Freeman appeared to support the reauthorization of the Voting Rights Act, and Garcia presented the commission's support for education and other efforts to help migratory labor. Nixon's handwritten note on news summary, September 12, 1969, p. 2, Box 30; Ken Cole to Erlichman, September 15, 1969; Martin Castillo to Erlichman, September 20, 1969; Ex FG 90, Box 1, 1969–70, 1 of 2.

19. In the meantime, the commission had staff investigate a complaint from MALDEF about discrimination at Hill Air Force Base. They also discussed a protest by about five thousand local Latinos against the request of the Del Rio County Commissioners to remove Vista volunteers in the Mexican American community, who the county officials said had "done more harm than good" by helping the workers. The commission sent staff to observe the peaceful rally and to help reduce the potential for violence; "Rights Panel Urges Laws to Protect Mexican-American," *New York Times*, April 29, 1970; Hesburgh to Moynihan, June 23, 1969; enclosure Glickstein to Hamp-

ton, undated, Ex FG 90, Box 1, 1969–70, 1 of 2; Minutes, Commission Meeting, April 1969, p. 3; Nixon's handwritten note on news summary, September 12, 1969, p. 2, Box 30; Ken Cole to Erlichman, September 15, 1969; Martin Castillo to Erlichman, September 20, 1969; Ex FG 90, Box 1, 1969–70, 1 of 2.

20. Brown to President, August 28, 1969; Ex FG 90, Box 1, 1969–70, 1 of 2. Erlichman to Nixon, September 2, 1969, Ex FG 90, Box 1, 1969–70, 1 of 2.

21. Brown to President, August 28, 1969; Ex FG 90, Box 1, 1969–70, 1 of 2. Brown's memo was sent to the president, with a notation that he did not need to respond. Nixon noted, "I agree."

22. Jack Rosenthal, "U.S. Rights Panel Criticizes Nixon on Desegregation," *New York Times*, September 13, 1969; John Herbers, "Finch Forecasts Vast Integration in Next Two Years," *New York Times*, September, 14, 1969, p. 1; Michael Klarman, *From Jim Crow to Civil Rights: The Supreme Court and the Struggle for Racial Equality* (New York: Oxford University Press, 2004), p. 363, apparently believes the HEW account that desegregation was increasing enormously.

23. Hesburgh to Nixon, September 12, 1969; Garment to Staff Secretary Cole, September 23, 1969; Brown to Cole, September 19, 1969; Brown to Hesburgh, September 23, 1969; Ex FG 90, Box 1, 1969–70, 1 of 2.

24. Carlos K. Blanton and George I. Sanchez, "Ideology and Whiteness in the Making of the Mexican American Civil Rights Movement, 1930–1960," *Journal of Southern History* 72 (2006): 572.

25. Ruiz left notes in the Cabinet Room following President Ford's meeting with Dr. Arthur Flemming and Civil Rights Commission, March 12, 1975; Correspondence File, Central Files—Confidential File, FG 90, Gerald Ford Presidential Library. He described his deep sense of responsibility as a Mexican American when he was appointed to the commission. Laura E. Gomez, "From Barrio Boys to College Boys: Ethnic Identity, Ethnic Organizations, and the Mexican American Elite, The Cases of Ernesto Galarza and Manuel Ruiz, Jr.," Working Paper Series No. 25, Stanford Center for Chicano Research, May 1989, pp. 18–19, 22–23.

26. Michelle O'Donnell, "Arthur H. Fletcher, Civil Rights Advocate and Affirmative Action Pioneer, Dies at 80," *New York Times*, July 14, 2005; conversations with Art Fletcher.

27. CCR Minutes, January 14–15, 1970, p. 2.

28. Ibid., January 1970, pp. 2–4; Mary Frances Berry, *Black Resistance, White Law: A History of Constitutional Racism in America* (New York: Viking Penguin, 1994), pp. 187–188.

29. William Timmons to Congressman Augustus Hawkins and separately to Congressman John Conyers, December 15, 1969; White House Subject Files, FG 90, Box 1; Gen (1969–70), UPI wire story, October 25, 1982.

30. Clarence Long, "Between Civil Rights and Black Power in the Gateway City: The Action Committee to Improve Opportunities for Negroes," *Journal of Social History* 37 (Spring 2004), describes Green's activism.

31. Seth King, "Rights Commission Told U.S. Agencies Fail to Stop Racial Bias in Suburbs," *New York Times*, January 18, 1970; Richard Witkin, "Negroes an Issue in F-15 Contract," *New York Times*, January 31, 1970, p. 20.

32. Frankie Muse Freeman, *A Song of Faith and Hope* (St. Louis: Missouri Historical Society Press, 2003), pp. 128–131; *McDonnell Douglas v. Green*, 411 U.S. 792 (1973), 463 F.2d 337. The opinion also denounced Percy Green, who, laid off, had organized protesters to block access to the plant and filed complaints with the commission and the EEOC, as a troublemaker. He lost in the district court on May 13, 1969 (318

F.Supp. 846), and won a remand for a new trial on appeal. However, on remand in February 1975 the district court found that he was not rehired because of his participation in unlawful demonstrations, not because of his race, and also that since his layoff in 1964, the firm had substantially increased the number of blacks hired. *Green v. McDonnell Douglas Corp.*, 390 F.Supp. 501 (1075). Blacks were 72.5 percent of the laborers, 39.4 percent of the service workers, and less than 1 percent of professionals, officers, and managers.

33. Deputy Defense Secretary David Packard said the plan "pledges McDonnell Douglas to vigorous new action to insure equal opportunity in recruitment, hiring, training, transfer and upgrading of all personnel." Without giving any figures, it included targets in every job category for hiring and promoting blacks. "U.S. Clears McDonnell-Douglas of Bias Charges," *New York Times*, February 11, 1970, p. 78.

34. Freeman, *Song*, pp. 130–132; *McDonnell Douglas v. Green*, 411 U.S. 792 (1973).

35. "Rights Agency Asks Housing Guidelines," *New York Times*, February 20, 1970, p. 18; John Price to Erlichman, Price to Cole, April 7, 1970. The list included the state and local government report already issued, a two-part study on the federal government's structure and coordination of civil rights enforcement, a recurring report on school desegregation, a study of Mexican Americans and education, one housing report on site selection and a second on nondiscrimination policies of housing federal agencies, a study of students' views of racial attitudes, a report on whether minorities played a role in economic development policy in the South, civil rights problems of American Indians, race-related student protests, Mexican Americans and the administration of justice, and the recruitment of minorities in police and fire departments. Tod Hullin to Erlichman, April 23, 1970, Ex FG 90, Box 1, 1969–70, 2 of 2.

36. Jack Rosenthal, "Rights Unit Chief Hails Nixon Move," *New York Times*, May 23, 1970, p. 1.

37. The commission considered proposing that all federal funds should be withdrawn from all white suburban jurisdictions adjacent to communities with large concentrations of African Americans when federal funds financed the segregated housing. "Hesburgh Criticizes Lag in Rights Gains," *New York Times*, August 20, 1970, p. 22; Ben A. Franklin, "Rights Panel Expected to Urge Fund Curb on White Suburbs," *New York Times*, August 29, 1970, p. 10; Hesburgh Closing Statement, June 17, 1971. However, Steve Horn wrote to Garment, who passed the letter along to Erlichman, that the administration witnesses at the hearing had acquitted themselves very well. He thought a "further push" was needed at HUD and "and additional shove at the Veterans Administration." It seemed that the "civil servants have simply been doing things the old way for far too long"; Horn to Garment, June 23, 1971, Ex FG 90, Box 1, 1969–70, 2 of 2.

38. CCR, *Federal Civil Rights Enforcement Effort*, 1970.

39. He suggested Richard Nathan at OMB (who had consulted for the commission) to staff it. Everyone knew Nathan and he had "outstanding credentials in the area of human resources." Garment to Erlichman, August 25, 1970, copy to OMB Director Shultz, Ex FG 90, Box 1, 1969–70, 2 of 2.

40. Hesburgh to Garment, October 1, 1970, Ex FG 90, Box 1, 1969–70, 2 of 2.

41. Shultz to Garment, September 14, 1970, Nathan to Shultz, September 22, 1970, Shultz to Nathan, September 14, 1970; Garment to Cole, September 29, 1970; Garment to Shultz, October 5, 1970, Ex FG 90, Box 1, 1969–70, 2 of 2.

42. Erlichman to Shultz, October 6, 1970, and notes attached; Ex FG 90, Box 1, 1969–70, 2 of 2.

43. Enclosure in Brad Patterson to Erlichman, October 7, 1970, budget director Robert Mayo to John Mitchell and to Garment, March 6, 1970, enclosing budget examiner Luman Rensch's analysis; Ex FG 90, Box 1, 1969–70, 2 of 2.

44. Ibid.

45. Hesburgh's statements quoted from *New York Times*, October 13, 1970, p. 1; excerpts from report, p. 28; John R. Brown to Erlichman, October 13, 1970; Nixon on news summary dated October 12, 1970, p. 8, information on commission noted, October 22, 1970; Tod Hullin to John Brown. The subject of the commission was covered orally with the president at 11:30 a.m., Friday, October 23, at a meeting with Shultz, Erlichman, and the president; Ex FG 90, Box 1, 1969–70, 2 of 2.

46. Ibid.

47. CCR Minutes, November 9, 1970, p. 3; December 14, 1970, p. 3.

48. CCR Minutes, December 14, 1970, p. 2; Garment to Haldeman, Erlichman, Shultz, Moynihan, Herb Klein, December 16, 1970, Ex FG 90, Box 1, 1969–70, 2 of 2; Hesburgh to Garment, Haldeman Papers, December 16, 1970, Box 3.

49. Nixon to Hesburgh, February 24, 1971; David Parker to Hesburgh on behalf of "RN," March 10, 1971; Garment to Erlichman, March 15, 1971, Ex FG 90, Box 1, 1969–70, 2 of 2.

50. Alger to Ray Price, May 25, 1971; White House Central Files, Subject Files, Ex FG 90, Box 11; January 1, 1971–December 31, 1972.

51. CCR Minutes, April 4, 1971, p. 3. At this same meeting the commission decided to subpoena cabinet members if after they were invited they refused to come to a hearing voluntarily.

52. Chapin to Colson, May 26, 1971; Hesburgh to Nixon, June 8, 1971; Campbell to Erlichman et al., June 10, 1971; Hullin to Glickstein, June 10, 1971; Garment to Hesburgh, June 22, 1971; White House Subject Files, Ex FG 90, Box 11, January 1, 1971–December 31, 1972.

53. Hesburgh to Nixon, June 16, 1971; Garment to John Campbell, June 21, 1971; White House Subject Files, Ex FG 90, Box 11, January 1, 1971–December 31, 1972.

54. Glickstein to Nixon, July 8, 1971; Garment to President, July 13, 1971; staff secretary to Malek, July 14, 1971; Malek to Campbell, July 14, 1971; Nixon to Glickstein, July 22, 1971; John Campbell to Ken Cole, July 19, 1971; White House Subject Files, FG 90A, Box 23, 1971–1974. A reply to Glickstein required several drafts. Garment pointed out that his letter to the president was "warm and complimentary." This was pleasing "coming from a man who was, to begin with, an antagonist of the Administration gradually shifting to a more understanding and appreciative attitude in recent months." Malek agreed with Garment's proposed letter, but Campbell told Ken Cole he asked Mike Smith to review it and "to prepare one toned down in praise." The letter sent, signed by autopen, was warm, accepted his resignation with "regret" and offered "best wishes." Scott to Dave Parker, December 14, 1971, White House Central Files, Subject Files, Ex FG 90A, Box 1, 1971–1972.

55. CCR Minutes, August 29, 1971, p. 1. The commission also proposed, unsuccessfully, expansion of the existing power to subpoena within fifty miles of a hearing to nationwide subpoena authority.

56. John Herbers, "New Rights Study Finds Some Gains in Enforcing Laws," May 11, 1971, p. 1; "Slow Pace Toward Equality," *New York Times*, May 14, 1971, p. 40.

57. Paul Delaney, "Rights Panel Again Assails Efforts by U.S. Agencies," *New York Times*, November 17, 1971, p. 1; United States Commission on Civil Rights, "The Federal Civil Rights Enforcement Effort: One Year Later; Low Marks on Civil Rights," Editorial, *New York Times*, November 22, 1971, p. 38; Paul Delaney, "The Federal Agencies and Rights," *New York Times*, November 27, 1971, p. 35 — analysis of responsibilities and no measuring of performance results; Tinsley Yarbrough, "Tax Exemptions and Private Discriminatory Schools," in Tinsley Yarbrough, ed., *The Reagan Administration and Human Rights* (New York: Praeger, 1985), p. 110.

58. CCR Minutes, August 29, 1971, p. 1; interview with Carol Bonosaro, June 14, 2005; John F. Dean to Ken Cole, November 17, 1971; White House Central Files, Subject Files, Ex FG 90, Box 1, January 1, 1971–December 31, 1972; Hugh Davis Graham, *The Civil Rights Era: Origins and Development of National Policy, 1960–1972* (New York: Oxford University Press, 1990), p. 405; Buchanan to Cole, November 26, 1971, White House Central Files, Subject Files, Ex FG 90; Box 1, January 1, 1971–December 31, 1972.

59. Carlucci to Cole, January 8, 1972; Shultz to Erlichman, January 14, 1972; White House Central Files, Subject Files, Ex FG 90, Box 1, January 1, 1971–December 31, 1972; Franklin wrote: ("Women impt [*sic*] sees political risk to P in either case—tough call").

60. Commission Minutes, February 14, 1972, p. 6; March 13, 1972, p. 2; interview with Carol Bonosaro, June 14, 2005; on Sloan, see Kimberly Springer, *Living for the Revolution: Black Feminist Organizations, 1968–1980* (Durham, N.C.: Duke University Press, 2005), p. 135.

61. Freeman, *Song*, pp. 139–141.

62. Nixon's annotated news summaries, Box 40, April 13, 1972, Nixon Papers, National Archives and Record Service, College Park, Maryland.

Chapter V

1. CCR Minutes, May 8, 1972; Erlichman to Garment, July 6, 1972, White House Central Files, Subject Files, Ex FG 90, Box 1, January 1, 1971–December 31, 1972, Richard Nixon Presidential Library (unless otherwise indicated, manuscript collections cited in this chapter are in this library); "Civil Rights Panel Says Busing Foes Oppose Integration," *New York Times*, May 18, 1972, p. 8.

2. CCR Minutes, August 1972, pp. 4–5.

3. Tod Hullin to Cole with Cole's handwritten note, August 14, 1972; Cole to Ehrlichman, August 29, 1972; McFarland to Cole, September 15, 1972; Cole to Ehrlichman, September 18, 1972, White House Central Files, Subject Files, Ex FG 90; Box 1; January 1, 1971–December 31, 1972; "Rights Panel Given a Role in Sex Bias in Senate Measure," *New York Times*, August 5, 1972, p. 28.

4. Tape 109, October 27, 1972, 3:13–3:45, Nixon Papers, National Archives and Record Service, College Park, Maryland; Erlichman to Cole, November 13, 1972, September 18, 1971, White House Central Files, Subject Files, Ex FG 90, Box 1, January 1, 1971–December 31, 1972; Theodore Hesburgh, *God, Country, Notre Dame* (New York: Doubleday, 1990), p. 204.

5. John Herbers, "Hesburgh Quits Rights Panel at Request of White House," *New York Times*, November 17, 1972, p. 97.

6. Hesburgh to Nixon, November 16, 1972; Nixon to Hesburgh, December 20, 1972; Commission Minutes, December 19, 1972; Theodore M. Hesburgh, "The Commission on Civil Rights—and Human Rights," *Review of Politics* 34 (July 1972): 291–305. On another note, "Our reports have criticized individuals in high positions in government. Not in an effort to discredit them politically but to let them know and the public know that we view their performance in the field of civil rights as lacking."

7. Paul Delaney, "Hesburgh Is Pessimistic on Civil Rights Outlook," *New York Times*, February 26, 1973, p. 12.

8. Timmons to Wyatt, May 23, 1973; Dana Mead to Jerry Jones, July 17, 1973, White House Central Files, Subject Files, Ex FG 90, Box 1, January 1, 1973–August 9, 1974.

9. Horn, testifying in the House Appropriations Committee, discussed the response of federal agencies to the recommendations in the commission's enforcement reports. White House congressional liaison William Timmons responded to Congressman Wendell Wyatt, who pointed out his support for the administration during the questioning, congratulating him and "Al Cederberg" for "putting the Commission's statements in proper focus" at the hearing. Timmons to Wyatt, May 23, 1973; White House Central Files, Subject Files, Ex FG 90, Box 1, January 1, 1973–August 9, 1974; Paul Delaney, "Rights Units Says Nixon Still Lags," *New York Times*, February 10, 1973, p. 65; the report was completed in September but not issued until February.

10. William M. Blair, "500 Indians Seize U.S. Building After Scuffle with Capital Police," *New York Times*, November 3, 1972, p. 1; William M. Blair, "Indians Take Documents as They Leave U.S. Building," *New York Times*, November 8, 1972, p. 49; King to Commissioners Rankin and Mitchell, November 17, 1972; Frankin Muse Freeman, *A Song of Faith and Hope: The Life of Frankie Muse Freeman* (St. Louis: Missouri Historical Society Press, 2003), p. 142; Paul Delaney, "Indians Criticize Long Neglect as Rights Panel Opens Inquiry," *New York Times*, November 15, 1972, p. 39. New Mexico governor Democrat Bruce King severely chastised the commission for airing negative criticism about the plight of Indians. The governor wrote the White House and the commission, which included his letter in the report.

11. "Panel Finds Indians in Two States Face Job Curbs," *New York Times*, May 15, 1973, p. 16.

12. Richard Margolis, "Indians a Long List of Grievances," *New York Times*, November 12, 1972, p. E5; UPI, "Armed Indians Seize Wounded Knee, Hold Hostages," *New York Times*, March 1, 1973, p. 1; William K. Stevens, "Indians and U.S. Sign Agreement at Wounded Knee," April 6, 1973, p. 85; Andrew H. Malcolm, "Indians Sign Accord to End 68-Day Seizure of Town," *New York Times*, May 7, 1973, p. 1; Andrew H. Malcolm, "Occupation of Wounded Knee Is Ended," May 9, 1973, p. 97; CCR, *Report of Investigation: Oglala Sioux Tribe, General Election 1974*, staff report, October 1974.

13. James P. Sterba, "Navajo Leader Assails Federal Unit," *New York Times*, October 23, 1973, p. 8; CCR, *The Navajo Nation: An American Colony*, 1975, pp. 1–10.

14. CCR, *The Navajo Nation*.

15. Ibid., p. 1.

16. Ibid.; CCR Minutes, November 1972, p. 4, January 15, 1973, p. 7; Horn to Nixon, May 25, 1973, White House Central Files, Subject Files, Ex FG 90, Box 1, January 1, 1973–August 9, 1974; Freeman, *Song*, 142–143; James Streba, "Navajo Hearings Begin Today," *New York Times*, October 22, 1973, p. 10; James Sterba, "Policy Defended by Indian Bureau," *New York Times*, October 24, 1973, p. 13.

17. CCR, *The Navajo Nation*, p. 1; James Sterba, "Policy Defended by Indian Bureau."

18. CCR, New Mexico State Advisory Committee, *The Farmington Report: A Conflict of Cultures*, 1975.

19. Ibid., pp. 16–17.

20. Ibid., pp. 18–19.

21. Dan Frosch, "In Shadow of 70's Racism Recent Violence Stirs Rage," *New York Times*, September 17, 2006, p. 26.

22. CCR Minutes, January 15, 1973, April 9, 1973, p. 10.

23. The commission at first opposed Title IX for fear of diluting attention to race and national origin. Ibid., October 9, 1973.

24. Nixon had numerous meetings in which Flemming participated in the White

House Conference on Aging and Social Security. Flemming had served from May 1971 to June 1972 as the chairman of the White House Commission on Aging. Nixon had then appointed him commissioner on aging in the Department of Health, Education, and Welfare on May 25, 1973. In order for the president to appoint Flemming, one of the Republican appointees, of whom three remained on the commission, had to resign. Mitchell, an Independent, submitted his resignation when Hesburgh did, and it was accepted in December with the understanding that he would serve until the confirmation of his successor. Thereafter, Nixon announced Flemming's nomination. He attended a meeting as commissioner designate on March 11, 1974; Nixon to Maurice Mitchell, December 14, 1973; Jerry Jones to Nixon, January 15, 1974; White House Press Release, December 5, 1973.

A flap developed at the commission in July 1974 when staff went public with the charge that a report on the impact of *Brown* had been held and watered down by the commission. The staff said the commission wanted to avoid criticizing the Nixon administration. Instead of the report, the commission issued a press release in May announcing that it would publish a series of reports on the status of civil rights. Staff said the report was killed because of objections from Horn, who thought it too negative. "But we were honest in putting it together," said one staff member. Horn commented that others on the commission brought up the issue of negativity but he "agreed." Flemming said he agreed to delay the report.

A staff member said the report concluded that twenty years after *Brown* "segregation was intact and in some cases increasing both in the North and South." It charged "administrative nullification" by the Nixon administration, by giving funds to districts that did nothing to desegregate. This was nothing new and was factual. Flemming and Horn denied political considerations. Paul Delaney, "Rights Report Delayed by Panel's Clash with Staff," *New York Times*, July 14, 1974, p. 32.

25. Ford appointed a number of African Americans. Aaron Spaulding became the first black associate White House personnel director, and Weldon Latham became associate director of OMB; William Coleman, Secretary of Transportation, was Ford's one cabinet officer. Thaddeus Garrett and Richard Parsons were staffers for Vice President Rockefeller. Parsons was deputy counsel and associate director of domestic policy, and Garrett was domestic affairs adviser.

26. Flemming to Ford, August 19, 1774. Casselman to Hartmann, August 21, 1974; Warren Rustand to Flemming, October 7, 1974; White House Central Files, FG 90, Gerald Ford Presidential Library (the manuscript collections cited in the remainder of this chapter are in this library unless otherwise indicated).

27. Walker to President, undated (week before the election), and attachments October 31, 1974, White House Central Files FG 90.

28. *Adams v. Richardson*, 356 F.Supp. 92, 94 (D.D.C., 1973); *Adams v. Weinberger*, 391 F.Supp. 269 (D.D.C., 1975).

29. Scott to Rumsfeld, Cheney, Baroody, January 10, 1975; Geoffrey Shepard to Deputy Attorney General, January 13, 1975, White House Central Files, FG 90; John Robert Greene, *The Presidency of Gerald Ford* (Lawrence: University Press of Kansas, 1995), pp. 86–90.

30. "Panel Criticizes Ford on Busing," *New York Times*, December 23, 1974, p. 11.

31. Ibid.; Scott to Rumsfeld, Cheney, Baroody, January 10, 1975; Geoffrey Shepard to Deputy Attorney General, January 13, 1975; White House Central Files, FG 90; "Bias Seen in Use of Shared Funds," *New York Times*, February 14, 1975, p. 10.

32. CCR, *Desegregating the Boston Public Schools: A Crisis in Civic Responsibility* (1975). Judge A. William Garrity announced *Morgan v. Hennigan*, 379 F.Supp. 410 (D. Mass.,

1974), aff'd 509 F.2d 580 (1st Cir., 1974), cert. denied, 421 U.S. 963 (1975), imposing mandatory desegregation on some Boston public schools.

33. CCR Minutes, January 22, 1975, p. 3; February 12, 1975, p. 4; April 14, 1975, p. 2. Interview with Louis Nunez.

34. Commissioners to President, November 15, 1975, White House Central Files, FG 90.

35. Ibid.

36. Ford to Flemming, January 15, 1975, White House Central Files, FG 90.

37. Cole to agencies, February 3, 1975. Each agency replied in February or March. Ray Garrett, Jr., Chairman SEC, to Kenneth Cole, Jr., March 17, 1975, White House Central Files, FG 90.

38. Ernest Holsendolph, "3 U.S. Agencies Held Lax on Civil Rights," *New York Times*, January 23, 1975.

39. *The Voting Rights Act: Ten Years After.*

40. "Bias Seen in Use of Shared Funds, *New York Times*, February 14, 1975, p. 10.

41. Memo from Warren Rustand to Bill Casselman, Robert Hartmann, Ron Nessen, and Stan Scott, February 20, 1975, responses handwritten on copies, except Stan Scott to Rustand, February 25, 1975, White House Central Files, FG 90.

42. Notes found in the Cabinet Room following meeting with Dr. Arthur Flemming and Civil Rights Commission, March 12, 1975; correspondence filed White House Central Files, Confidential File, FG 90; Laura E. Gomez, "From Barrio Boys to College Boys: Ethnic Identity, Ethnic Organizations, and the Mexican American Elite—The Cases of Ernesto Galarza and Manuel Ruiz, Jr." (Working Paper Series No. 25, Stanford Center for Chicano Research, May 1989), pp. 18–19, 22–23.

43. "Hesburgh Urges Extension of the Voting Right Act," *New York Times*, March 7, 1975, p. 56; Ernest Holsendolph, "Rights Unit Backs Wider Voting Act," *New York Times*, April 10, 1975, p. 10.

44. Richard Madden, "Congress Passes 7-Year Extension of Voting Rights Act," *New York Times*, July 29, 1975, p. 1.

45. CCR Minutes, February 10, 1975.

46. CCR, *Constitutional Aspects of the Right to Limit Childbearing;* CCR Minutes, April 15, 1975, p. 14; April 14, 1975, p. 2. At Rankin's instigation, the commissioners discussed the commission's employee workforce. He perceived an underrepresentation of whites among clerical workers. The commission's staff director hired me, as a lawyer and an expert in legal history and a professor at the University of Maryland, to work on the report as a consultant.

47. Hugh Davis Graham, *The Civil Rights Era: Origins and Development of National Policy, 1960–1972* (New York: Oxford University Press, 1990), p. 207 and notes there cited.

48. Ibid.; CCR report, *Minorities and Women as Government Contractors*, May 1975; letter of transmittal and recommendations, pp. 110 ff., House Report no. 94-1719, p. 182b (1977).

49. "Action to Assure Job Rights Urged," *New York Times*, July 20, 1975, p. 12. In its 1975 report, *Twenty Years After Brown: Equality of Economic Opportunity*, the commission explicitly stated that the way to ensure that government contractors provide equal opportunity is to establish "goals and timetables . . . to measure progress in increasing minority employment." The report recommended that affirmative action be applied as a means of guaranteeing equal economic opportunity, stressing that "it is now time that specific operating goals, an implementation timetable, and monitoring procedures be established to insure the achievement of economic parity between all racial and ethnic groups and men and women."

50. "Rights Panel Asks Education Shift," *New York Times*, May 14, 1975, p. 22.

51. The commission released a study in January 1977 that analyzed age discrimination in a variety of institutions, ranging from community health centers to universities. Defining age discrimination as "any act or failure to act, or any law or policy that adversely affects an individual on the basis of age," the study forcefully discounted a number of usual justifications for age discrimination. Although some commentators criticized the report for its statistical methodology, Congress adopted the commission's recommendations in the 1977 volume of findings and recommendations in the 1978 amendments to the act. The commission's second report, describing the methodology, was not issued until the Carter administration. The Carter White House coordinated agency responses to the draft of the report, issued in 1979, through Nelson Cruikshank, counselor to the president on aging. Cruikshank recommended that the president award Flemming a second Presidential Medal of Freedom; Cruikshank to Greg Schneiders, Medal of Freedom, July 2, 1979. Flemming did receive a second Medal of Freedom from President Clinton in 1994. Pub. L. No. 94-135, 89 Stat. 728 (1975); United States Commission on Civil Rights, *The Age Discrimination Study* (1977) (hereafter cited as *Age Study*), Part I, *Summary, Findings, and Recommendations* (1977), Part II, *Detailed Analysis and Methodology* (1979). Stuart Eizenstat and Nelson Cruikshank to Heads of Departments and Agencies, January 31, 1978, FG 93, Jimmy Carter Presidential Library.

Chapter VI

1. United States Commission on Civil Rights (hereafter cited as CCR), Philadelphia 1979 Hearing Transcript, p. 124; "Dr. Ethel Allen Dies; Held Pennsylvania Job," AP wire story, December 1981.

2. CCR, Philadelphia 1979 Hearing, pp. 126, 129; Georgia A. Persons, "The Philadelphia MOVE Incident as an Anomaly in Models of Mayoral leadership," *Phylon* 48 (1987): 249.

3. CCR, Philadelphia 1979 Hearing, p. 209.

4. Ibid., p. 213.

5. Ibid., pp. 144, 246.

6. Ibid., p. 261.

7. Ibid., p. 35.

8. CCR Report, *Who Is Guarding the Guardians?* October 1981.

9. *Time*, April 19, 1976.

10. Ibid.

11. Hugh Davis Graham, "Civil Rights Policies in the Carter Presidency," in *The Carter Presidency: Policy Choices in the Post–New Deal Era*, edited by Gary Fink and Hugh Davis Graham (Lawrence: University of Kansas Press), pp. 202–203.

12. Giannini to Harriston, February, 17, 1978; Nunez to Miller, February 26, 1980. Staffer Ken Harriston asked the White House for a breakdown of the employment of minorities. Valerie Gianni, director of operations, responded. Nunez sent Arnold Miller, director of presidential personnel, a draft of the latest report in February 1980; FG 93, Jimmy Carter Presidential Library (unless otherwise indicated, manuscript collections cited in this chapter are in FG 93 in this library).

13. CCR Report, *Last Hired, First Fired*, January 1977, pp. 15–16, quote on p. 16.

14. CCR Report, *Last Hired, First Fired*; Philip Shabecoff, "Rights Panel Raises Job Seniority Issue," *New York Times*, January 19, 1977, p. 12.

15. Press Release, White House Press Secretary, September 20, 1977. After taking effect, the Mitchell legislation was challenged in court. The Supreme Court upheld the legality of the public works set-aside by a vote of 6–3 in *Fullilove v. Klutznick* in 1980.

16. Chairman Flemming, Vice Chairman Stephen Horn, Commissioners Frankie Freeman, Manuel Ruiz, Jr., Murray Saltzman, and Staff Director John Buggs to Carter, December 15, 1976; White House counsel Lipshutz, Civil Rights Commission, December 1976–August 1978.

17. Nunez to Schneiders, June 9, 1977; Schneiders to Nunez, June 13, 1977. Nunez included a note to Schneiders telling him that "Jack Nelson of the L.A. Times suggested I send you an advance copy of the report. I will call you next week to see if we can meet on it." Nunez wanted to discuss what improvements the administration might make as a result of the report. Schneiders asked a staffer to draft a response but said, "Don't mention meeting with him." The response, thanking Nunez for the report, said simply "If I have any questions, I'll be in touch."

18. Commissioners to President, June 13, 1977; Mitchell to the President, June 14, 1977, with enclosure to Powell; Kraft to Fran Voorde, June 16, 1977. Replies June 22 to Fran Voorde, McKenna, Jean Hurley for DPS meeting memo Mitchell; all in "Scenarios for Meeting with Civil Rights Commission."

19. Eizenstat to Flemming, October 3, 1977; Flemming to Mitchell, July 23, 1977; Flemming to Carter, July 11, 1977.

20. CCR Minutes, February 13, 1978; M. Gail Gerebenics through Richard Baca, General Counsel to Louis Nunez, January 23, 1978; April 17–18, 1978, p. 4. In agreement with the administration's position, they also decided to support an extension of the time for the ratification of the ERA. Congress granted the extension, but the ERA failed.

21. Flemming to Chisholm, May 16, 1978, reprinted in Subcommittee on Oversight hearing, pp. 237–238; Tinsley Yarbrough, "Tax Exemptions and Private Discriminatory Schools," in Tinsley Yarbrough, ed., *The Reagan Administration and Human Rights* (New York: Praeger, 1985), p. 111.

22. Flemming for the Commissioners to Carter, undated but before February 16, 1977.

23. Carter to Flemming, February 16, 1977. On February 15, 1977, Staff Director John Buggs sent copies of two commission reports released that day to the president. One, *Statement on Metropolitan School Desegregation*, concluded that in some areas "racially isolated schools" could be desegregated only by the use of metropolitan desegregation county-wide instead of limited to the boundaries of cities because of segregated housing. The *New York Times* reported, in March, that Drew Days, Carter's appointee as assistant attorney general for civil rights in the Justice Department, a former NAACP-LDF attorney, agreed with the commission that "metropolitan desegregation might, in some cities, require less busing than a plan confined to the central city." However, Days noted that the Supreme Court decision in the Detroit case made it clear that there must be proof of suburban involvement in segregation before suburbs could be ordered in metropolitan desegregation. The second report, *The State of Civil Rights 1976*, found that "federal civil rights enforcement efforts remain deficient and must be strengthened, and that economic progress, including full employment, is essential if we are to ensure equal employment opportunity for all Americans."

24. Eizenstat to Flemming, October 3, 1977; Flemming to Mitchell, July 23, 1977; Flemming to Carter, July 11, 1977.

25. The Carter White House staff kept telling civil rights advocates that the solicitor general at the Justice Department was making an independent decision about what position to take with no White House involvement implying it would be inappropriate. But Carter attorney general Griffin Bell took a copy of the draft *Bakke* brief to a meeting with President Carter, where White House counsel Lipshutz was sitting in. Carter gave Lipshutz a copy and also sent copies to Eizenstat and Mondale. Griffin Bell, *Taking*

Care of the Law (New York: Morrow, 1982), pp. 29–32; I am grateful to Bradley Patterson, *Ring of Power: The White House Staff and Its Expanding Role in Government* (New York: Basic Books, 1988), executive assistant to Leonard Garment during the Nixon years, for his help on this point.

26. "Rights Unit Hints It Opposes Bakke," *New York Times*, October 12, 1977, p. 16.

27. "Civil Rights Unit Lauds Decision in Bakke Case," *New York Times*, July 2, 1978, p. 18, CCR Minutes, January 14–15, 1980, p. 1. Antonin Scalia, "Commentary: The Disease as Cure: In Order to Get Beyond Racism, We Must First Take Account of Race," 1979 *Wash. U.L.Q.* 147, 156.

28. Berry and Blassingame, *Long Memory*, pp. 189–190; "Bakke Ruling Supports Rights Goal, Carter Says," *New York Times*, July 3, 1978, p. 26.

29. CCR Report, *Window Dressing on the Set*, August 1977, p. 74.

30. Ibid., p. 136.

31. Ibid., p. 85.

32. Ibid.

33. Ibid., pp. 72–73.

34. Flemming to Carter, August 8, 1977; Nunez to Mitchell, August 12, 1977; Commissioners to Carter, August 16, 1977, an acknowledgment came from the clerk; Louis Martin to Stuart Eizenstat, undated.

35. Tom Shales, "Unlocking Doors to Those Rooms at the Top," *Washington Post*, August 21, 1977, p. F1.

36. Haft to Costanza, April 28, 1977. However, she did not think Costanza should attend the meetings, since the task force "will report back" to them anyway. Regarding the commission as just another executive branch entity, she told Costanza, besides, "consistent with the President's wishes," they should not appear to be "riding herd" over the agencies. But if Costanza wanted to attend, she would be welcome.

37. CCR Minutes, August 15, 1977; October 11, 1977; Costanza to Flemming, October 19, 1977. The commission turned its attention to problems of Asian Americans in employment, issuing the report *Success of Asian Americans: Fact or Fiction?* in September 1980. It pointed out that the success of high-income Asian Americans was limited by the discrimination they still experienced.

38. CCR Report, *The Age Discrimination Study*, 1977.

39. CCR Report, *The Federal Fair Housing Enforcement Effort*, 1979.

40. CCR Minutes, July 14, 1975, p. 1. They substituted a report on women and girls in athletics for a study of medical experimentation on women and minorities. The experimentation issue arose out of public disclosure of the Tuskegee syphilis experiment from 1932 to 1972, in which 399 African American males were denied treatment for syphilis and deceived by United States public health officials. As part of the study, they were told they were being treated for bad blood.

41. CCR Report, *More Hurdles to Clear: Women and Girls in Competitive Athletics*, 1980.

42. Ibid.; CCR minutes April 17–18, 1978, p. 4.

43. Interview with Carol Bonosaro, June 14, 2005, Web site National Coalition Against Domestic Violence; Jimmy Carter to cabinet secretaries and Director of Action, Commission on Civil Rights and Community Services Administration, April 27, 1979; Linda Tarr-Whelan, deputy assistant to president for women's concerns to Lucy Edwards, February 17, 1980, asking for battered women reports. Weddington to Bonosaro, October 27, 1978.

44. Weddington to Flemming, August 10, 1979; Flemming to Weddington, September 11, 1979; General Accounting Office Report, "Training Administration, Use and Equal Opportunity," HRD-92-43, March 2, 1992, available at www.gao.gov.

45. CCR Minutes, March 18–19, 1980, pp. 2–3; Peterson to Bonosaro, September 19, 1977; hearing in Harrisburg, June 17–18, 1980; hearing in Phoenix, January 12–13, 1980; "Panel Finds Flaws in Immigration Laws," *New York Times*, September 14, 1980.

46. Freeman, *Song*, pp. 145–146; CCR Reports, *Window Dressing on the Set*, 1978, and *Puerto Ricans in the Continental United States: An Uncertain Future*, October 1976; David Vidal, "Puerto Rican Plight in U.S. Deplored," *New York Times*, October 14, 1976, p. 18.

47. National Puerto Rican Leadership Forum Web site; letter from Flemming to Bunny Mitchell, September 14, 1977; "Study of Puerto Rican Aid Urged," *New York Times*, May 23, 1978, p. A8; Flemming to Eizenstat, May 1978; Malson to Eizenstat, May 24, 1978.

48. Maxey to Carter, September 6, 1977; Kenneth MacDonald to Carter, September 15, 1977. The letters were left to Jim King in Personnel to handle as a simple question of replacements and acceptance of resignations.

49. Chairs Howard Brown (Delaware), Roy Littlejohn (District of Columbia), Marjorie Smith (Maryland), Grace Alpern (Pennsylvania), Ruth Charity (Virginia), James McIntyre (West Virginia) to Carter; chairs Peg Anderson (Iowa), Constance Menninger (Kansas), Paul Smith (Missouri), Michael B. Adams (Nebraska) to Carter.

50. Voorde to Watson; handwritten note of Watson, September 13, 1977; Buggs to McIntyre, December 7, 1977; McIntyre to Ted Nichols; mailgram, Nicholls to Commission, including McIntyre correspondence, November 15, 1977; his explanation is in the letter. White House scheduler Fran Voorde told Carter's chief of staff, Jack Watson, that Jim McIntyre suggested that the SAC chairs meet with OMB and the chairman of the commission, or with a White House staff member. At Watson's instruction.

51. Buggs to McIntyre, December 7, 1977; McIntyre to Ted Nichols; mailgram, Nicholls to commission, including McIntyre correspondence, November 15, 1977; Flemming to Carter, October 13, 1977.

52. Pettigrew to Ted Nichols, to John Rose, Jr., Chairman, Connecticut SAC, October 7, 1977; to Franklin Williamson, Chairperson, Phelps Stokes Fund and New York State SAC, January 16, 1978. Frank Moore to Charles Rangel, December 16, 1977; to Connecticut Republican congressman Ronald Sarasin, November 23, 1977; to Republican senator Clifford Hansen, November 7, 1977.

53. Seidman to Buggs, March 21, 1977.

54. Seidman to Gutierrez, April 14, 1977; Gutierrez to Eizenstat, July 15, 1977.

55. Costanza to Hamilton Jordan, December 7, 1977. She was concerned that no one had been appointed to fill the vacancy on the commission.

56. Testimony of Drew Days, Subcommittee on the Constitution, Committee on the Judiciary, U.S. Senate, December 15, 1977; press release, Senator Birch Bayh, December 15, 1977; president's memo to heads of department and agencies, August 26, 1977, pointing out that he had appointed a task force and wanted sex bias removed: "Where statutory revision or repeal is necessary, I will recommend to Congress that appropriate legislation be enacted. Where executive action will suffice, I will take appropriate steps to ensure that benefits and opportunities provided by the federal government are made equally available to all, regardless of sex." The president had mentioned the report in his memorandum to heads of departments and agencies of August 26, 1977, on the anniversary of the women's suffrage amendment.

57. January 9, 1978, p. 1; Hagedorn and Treen to Carter, October 3, 1978; Karen Mulhauser, executive director of NARAL, to Carter, September 12, 1978. NARAL took the position that the amendment advocated censorship of the work of the commission and established a "dangerous precedent" by interfering with the commission's discretion in deciding what to investigate under denials of equal protection. Treen and Hagedorn

argued that no court had found it a denial of equal protection to prohibit abortion. They were technically correct because *Roe* was decided on privacy grounds. Women's rights attorney Ruth Bader Ginsburg had argued such cases in the lower courts on equal protection grounds. However, the commission had never been bound by what courts decided and most often made recommendations completely contrary to existing law.

58. Eizenstat and Bob Malson to the President, October 11, 1978; an amendment proposed by Congressman Caldwell Butler of Virginia to explicitly outlaw lobbying by state advisory committees and the commission to defeat national or local legislation was stricken in conference. However, Louis Nunez had OGC prepare a memo that explained that by virtue of the commission's role, lobbying was already outlawed. The commission could educate and provide advice and testimony on matters that had been studied, but it could not lobby. Eileen Stein, General Counsel, to Louis Nunez, February 28, 1980.

59. CCR Report, *Civil Rights of Euro-Ethnic Americans: Challenges and Issues,* pp. 398–399; on employment, Leonard F. Walentynowicz, executive director of the Polish American Congress, recommended that for the census the "government direct that additional categories be created for groups such as Polish-Americans, Italian-Americans and so forth." He thought that instead of affirmative action, "blacks have a unique situation here—let's give them and anyone else who qualifies, extra help like we did veterans, a point system." But counting everyone and tracking progress would reduce "alienation and tension" and be fairer.

60. CCR Report, *The Federal Civil Rights Enforcement Effort—1977: To Eliminate Employment Discrimination: A Sequel;* Flemming to Carter, March 6, 1978; Carter to Chairman Flemming, April 11, 1978. The report made several recommendations for the reorganization: Uniform guidance must be given to employers, whether in private or public sectors. There must be consistency in the approach to investigating complaints. There should be a government-wide standard on what constitutes prima facie discrimination, whether under Title VII, Executive Order 11246, or any other authority, as well as a uniform standard on what is an acceptable affirmative action plan and what constitutes compliance. When more than one agency is involved with one employer, there should be joint investigations and review. There should be one final authority on equal employment matters for the whole government. The reorganization should be done without delay.

61. CCR Report, *Federal Enforcement of Equal Employment Requirements, 1987,* pp. 17, 73, 74.

62. Flemming to Carter, March 23, 1978; Buggs to the President, January 30, 1978; Carter to Buggs, February 3, 1978; Kraft and Miller to Carter, November 11, 1978.

63. Spence to Carter, January 19, 1979; Stewart to Carter, January 30, 1979; Frank Moore to Spence, January 30, 1979; Moore to Stewart, February 7, 1979.

64. In addition to working on the commission's abortion rights report, I had testified before the agency. At the March 1978 meeting, the commission heard testimony on whether the federal program to aid the education of disadvantaged students (Title I) was distorted by permitting the funds to follow the child to a private school. I testified in my capacity as assistant secretary for education. CCR Minutes, March 13–14, 1978. Biography, Blandina Cardenas, Office of the President, University of Texas Pan American, December 2006; Q&A with William and Bill Ruckelshaus, January 4, 2005, C-SPAN, the Indiana Law Blog, January 17, 2005.

65. Robert Pear, "U.S. Rights Unit Urges Easier Prosecution of Police," *New York Times,* July 10, 1980, p. A13; CCR Minutes, July 7–9, 1980, p. 1; January 11–12, 1981, p. 1; Jimmy Carter to Flemming, July 24, 1980; CCR Report, *Confronting Racial Isolation in Miami,* December 1982.

66. Eizenstat to the President, Enrolled Bill S 721, October 5, 1979; Eizenstat and Frank White to Carter, Enrolled Bill S 2511, October 10, 1980.

67. Interview with Louis Nunez, April 24, 2005.

68. Watson to Flemming, December 11, 1980.

Chapter VII

1. Jiron K. Skinner, Annelise Anderson, and Martin Anderson, eds., *Reagan: A Life in Letters* (New York: Free Press, 2003); see for example, pp. 330–340; Lou Cannon, *Reagan* (New York: G. P. Putnam and Sons, 1982), pp. 381–386; William Johnson, "The Push to the Right: Reagan's Alter Ego Meese Stands at Pinnacle of U.S. Law Enforcement," *Globe and Mail*, August 28, 1985; Christopher Alan Bracey, *Saviors or Sellouts: The Promise and Peril of Black Conservatism, from Booker T. Washington to Condoleezza Rice* (Boston: Beacon, 2008), describes the successful recruitment of black Reaganites.

2. Nunez to President, July 8, 1981; Reagan to Nunez, August 6, 1981; Flemming to Reagan, September 8, 1991; White House Subject Files, FG 93, Ronald Reagan Presidential Library (unless otherwise indicated, manuscript collections cited in this chapter are in this library); CCR Minutes, July 14–15, 1981. Flemming asked Reagan for the courtesy of an opportunity "to meet with you to discuss the current state of civil rights in our nation, and to offer to you our assistance as you seek equal justice for all Americans."

There is no evidence that Reagan ever knew of the letter. In the staff secretary's office, Diana Lozano, noting that Flemming gave no particular agenda for the meeting and thinking, incorrectly, that the president was about to announce a new staff director and deputy staff director, suggested deferring the meeting until "the new team is in place." Someone circled her recommendation to say "this doesn't make sense," but left the correspondence in the pending file. Gregory Newell, special assistant to the president, wrote Flemming to acknowledge the request for a meeting, which he understood, "as has been done traditionally at the commencement of the incoming administration." They would "contact him again as soon as it is possible."

The commission had heard nothing further from the White House by the July meeting, when the commissioners discussed Louis Nunez's July 8 resignation as staff director. They agreed by unanimous vote that his deputy, John Hope III, would become acting staff director. Nunez left after nine years at the commission, writing the president: "I have had the honor and privilege of serving under four presidents." He expressed a "sincere desire for the success" of the administration.

3. Party efforts to develop a cadre of black conservative Republicans to push their redirection of civil rights were about to bear fruit.

Leading white Republicans convened the Fairmont Hotel conference in San Francisco in December 1980, one month after Reagan's election. Ed Meese, counsel to the president-elect, was there to promise the blacks in attendance that they would gain participation in the administration at higher levels than ever before. Pendleton and others who became Reagan appointees were there, including Clarence Thomas, who was appointed chairman of the Equal Employment Opportunity Commission, and Samuel Pierce, who became secretary of Housing and Urban Development. Pendleton told me that the police report called Meese's attention to the commission.

4. Black Media, Inc., reporter Alfreda Madison. As Ethel Payne, the dean of black newspaper reporters, described Madison: "I think she enjoys it, but it really isn't a hardcore thing with her, like it was with me. But Alfreda is known as a hell-raiser. [Laughter.] She has some real tiny, tiny papers, but she is quick to register offense if she thinks she's

being ignored. I can understand, because I came from the same thing, too." Madison, from Richmond, Virginia, became a reporter after she retired from teaching. She was a feisty personality who had White House credentials, wrote stories for a number of small newspapers, and insisted on being treated respectfully. Washington Press Club Foundation, Ethel Payne, Interview #5 (pp. 85–112), September 24, 1987, in Washington, D.C., Kathleen Currie, Interviewer. James Reston, Jr., *Rolling Stone*, March 1986.

5. Herrington to Berry, October 24, 1983; to Ramirez, to Saltzman; attached memo from Reagan to Herrington, same day: "I have decided to terminate effective today, the appointments of the following members of the Commission on Civil Rights." He directed Herrington to "notify these individuals and Chairman Pendleton of my decision as soon as possible." Attached press release: The reauthorization before Judiciary would require him to keep the incumbents "thwarting the President's ability to exercise his power of appointment." He therefore decided to vindicate the president's "power of appointment" by firing us "holdovers." After all, each "Certificate of Appointment" stated that we served "at the pleasure of the President"; Alfreda Madison's conversation with me, October 1983.

6. George Lardner, Jr., "3 on Rights Commission Terminated," *Washington Post*, October 26, 1983; Robert Pear, "Reagan Ousts 3 from Civil Rights Panel," October 26, 1983; Robert Pear, "Agency Looks for Congressional Resuscitation," *New York Times*, October 30, 1983.

7. Robert Pear, "Two Members of Rights Commission Sue to Bar Dismissal by President," *New York Times*, October 27, 1983; George Lardner, Jr., "Two Rights Commission Democrats Sue to Block Ouster by Reagan," *Washington Post*, October 27, 1983.

8. George Lardner, Jr., "Ex-members of Civil Rights CCR Attest to Its Independence," *Washington Post*, November 8, 1983; Helen Dewar, "Two Victories Reprieve Rights Unit: Judge Bars Firing of Three Members, Senate Passes Bill," *Washington Post*, November 15, 1983.

9. CCR Minutes, July 14–15, 1981.

10. Ibid. After he left the commission, Flemming pursued an active career as a leading advocate for services to the elderly and preserving Social Security until his death at age 91, September 7, 1996. Horn remained president of California State–Long Beach until 1988. Elected to Congress in 1993, he served until 2003.

11. Robert J. Thompson, "The Commission on Civil Rights," in Tinsley Yarborough, ed., *The Reagan Administration and Human Rights* (New York: Praeger, 1985), pp. 187–188; Maurice Dawkins, director of government relations for OIC, in writing to the White House in support of the nomination, expressed just the view that most concerned advocates. He saw the purpose of bringing an appositional view and reforming the law and made no mention of the other major purpose, which was to watchdog and help to recommend implementation of the laws already around. Dawkins to Reagan, March 17, 1982; Robert Detlefsen, *Civil Rights Under Reagan* (San Francisco: Institute of Contemporary Studies, 1991).

12. David E. Rosenbaum, "Files Highlight Legal Stances of Nominee," *New York Times*, July 27, 2005, p. A1; Jeffrey Smith, Jo Becker, and Amy Goldstein, "Documents Show Roberts Influence in Reagan Era," *Washington Post*, July 27, 2005, p. A1, from Justice Department Files National Archives, RG 94. As special assistant to the attorney general, John Roberts drafted a response for Smith to Flemming's request to discuss "the purported need for race-conscious remedies such as busing and affirmative action."

13. Manning Marable, *Race Reform and Rebellion: The Second Reconstruction in Black America, 1945–1982* (Jackson: University Press of Mississippi, 1984), pp. 205–206 (1991 ed.); *Report of the Attorney General of the United States, 1981–8*.

14. *Time*, August 18, 1980; Lou Cannon, *Ronald Reagan: The Role of a Lifetime* (New York: Simon & Schuster, 1991), pp. 269, 303.

15. Thompson, "The Commission on Civil Rights," pp. 186–188 and notes there cited; order designating Pendleton and Smith, March 19, 1982; correspondence on Pendleton's role as only Urban League executive to support Reagan.

16. Thompson, "The Commission on Civil Rights," pp. 189–190.

17. Yzaguirre to President, February 19, 1982; Judith Lichtman, Executive Director, Women's Legal Defense Fund, to President, February 16, 1982; Antonia Hernandez, MALDEf Associate Counsel, to President, February 17, 1982; Karhy Wilson, National Chair, National Women's Political Caucus, to President, February 12, 1982; Mary Purcell, President, American Association of University Women, to President, February 13, 1982; Mary Louise Uhlig, President, Federally Employed Women, to President, February 19, 1982; Ted Weiss and 24 others to President, February 23, 1982; Norman Dicks to President, February 25, 1982; Leonard Denardis to President, February 19, 1982; Phillip Burton to President, February 16, 1982; Albert Lee Smith to President, February 15, 1982; Gordon Jones to President, February 11, 1982.

18. Thompson, "Commission on Civil Rights," p. 190; "President Selects Black Evangelist for Rights Unit," *Washington Post*, February 10, 1982, p. A16; Steven Weisman, "President Defends His Nominee to Civil Rights Agency," *New York Times*, February 19, 1982, p. 18.

19. Steven Weisman, "Reagan Rescinds Rights Nominee in Wake of Outcry," *New York Times*, February 13, 1982, p. 1, Lee Lescaze, "Anti-Gay, ERA, Busing, Rights Nominee Speaks Out," *Washington Post*, February 11, 1982, p. A1.

20. Thompson, "Commission on Civil Rights," pp. 190–191; Bill Peterson, "Hart Owes Back Taxes of $4,400 in Pa. Town," *Washington Post*, February 24, 1982.

21. Pam Turner to Duberstein, February 25, 1982; Duberstein to Baker, Meese, and Deaver, February 26, 1985; Hart to Reagan, White House Central Files, FG 93. Congressional liaison Ken Duberstein reported to Baker, Meese, and Deaver that the meeting to discuss Hart with the senators "essentially went well." However, Specter had "reservations" and Heinz was "less enthusiastic" and remained "negative"; Bill Peterson, "Hart Asks the President to Drop Nomination," *Washington Post*, February 27, 1982.

22. Destro, a native of Akron, Ohio, was educated at Miami University of Ohio and Boalt Hall Law School at the University of California at Berkeley. Destro, Sensenbrenner pointed out, "is in the unique position of being a Democrat who worked in my district for your election, as well as mine." Destro was deeply interested in issues of religious liberty and had "a record of able representation of conservative issues, most recently and significantly the right to life cause." Congressman Clement Zablocki chimed in to point out that Republican congressman Henry Hyde of Illinois and other anti-abortion officials supported Destro. All received the same reply thanking them for their recommendation, which Pendleton James, White House personnel director, would consider carefully. Congressman Mickey Leland recommended Leonard Spearman, president of Texas Southern University in his district and a former education official. Leland to President, October 8, 1981; Sensenbrenner to President, October 13, 1981; Zablocki to President, October 27, 1981.

23. Thompson, "Commission on Civil Rights," pp. 191–192; Robert Pear, "Advocates Fear for Autonomy of Civil Rights Commission," *New York Times* October 2, 1982, p. 1; Felicity Barringer, "New Defiant Tone; Civil Rights Commission Gets Tough," *Washington Post*, December 6, 1982.

24. The CCR had called attention to the existence, in May 1978, of at least seven segregated schools in Mississippi that still had tax-exempt status; Tinsley Yarbrough,

"Tax Exemptions and Private Discriminatory Schools," in Tinsley Yarbrough, ed., *The Reagan Administration and Human Rights* (New York: Praeger, 1985), pp. 110–111. The Carter administration issued standards on August 21, 1978, to establish eligibility, which required a school seeking an exemption to have at least 20 percent of the minority school population in the community or meet other criteria of non-discrimination, with rare exceptions. This was called a quota by opponents. In February 1979, when the administration issued revised guidelines, Senator Jesse Helms (R-N.C.) charged that they were interfering with taxpayers without any congressional direction.

25. Stuart Taylor, "Justice Department Says Dissidents Are Welcome to Leave," *New York Times*, February 4, 1982, p. 12B; and "When Goals of Boss and His Staff Lawyers Clash," *New York Times*, June 22, 1984, p. 14A.

26. The Court agreed with Coleman's arguments and noted that eleven different bills to reverse the IRS policy since 1970 never emerged from the Congress; ibid., pp. 114–128; CCR Minutes, January 18, 1982. In *Bob Jones University v. United States*, 461 U.S. 574 (1983), the Court left open whether religion, without race or other characteristics in our pluralistic society that may go against public policy, could be used to deny an exemption, in a Burger opinion with Rehnquist dissenting,

27. In the Supreme Court, the administration argued in *Grove City College v. Bell*, 465 U.S. 555 (1984), the view that it had expressed internally, that Title IX outlawed sex discrimination only in a specific program that received federal funds in an institution, such as the admissions office or student financial aid office, and not in the entire institution. They argued the validity of this principle, even though the student aid funded the entire institutions. Discrimination, in their view, could occur without federal intervention, everywhere except that specific office.

We also, in January 1983 by a 5–1 vote, criticized the Reagan administration for its opposition to broad-based affirmative action in two major civil rights cases. We cited the New Orleans Police Department case, in which a court had ordered one-for-one promotions, to remedy the non-promotion of African Americans. We also noted the Boston police and firefighters case, in which a lower court ordered that seniority must not make recently hired blacks and Hispanics the first fired. Pendleton dissented from the criticism, saying he agreed with the administration and supported the white employees. Robert Pear, "Rights Panel Criticizes President on Two Affirmative Action Stands," *New York Times*, January 12, 1983.

28. At the press conference on the black farming report that detailed the history of black land loss, he indicated his support of the findings even though it was officially passed and published in February, a month before he was confirmed; CCR Report, *The Decline of Black Farming in America*," February 1982. Bill Prochnau, "Rights Panel Finds Persistent Bias in Hiring," *Washington Post*, November 24, 1982.

29. CCR Report, *Intimidation and Violence: Racial and Religious Bigotry in America*, January 1983.

30. Ibid.

31. CCR Minutes, January 18, 1982; March 8–9, 1982; April 12, 1982; May 3, 1982; July 12, 1982. At Ruckelshaus's suggestion, we added language asking for an end to limitations on the entry into the United States of Amerasian children. We also encouraged the Defense Department to resist pressure from some of our allies to reduce or limit the assignment of African Americans to NATO. At a subsequent meeting, we discussed the issue again in connection with the unexplained "shooting deaths of two African American soldiers at Nuremberg." We also approved a letter asking the president what his position was on the enforcement of Title IX and other civil rights statutes since the Grove City Supreme Court cases narrowly redefined possible coverage; CCR Minutes, December 6, 1982.

32. We had commission briefings in this period on the Simpson-Mazzoli bill reforming immigration as it was debated in Congress. It was pushed by the Leadership Conference, under the leadership of the Latino groups in the coalition. The bill, which included employer sanctions but not ID cards, increased the opportunity for the undocumented to become citizens. It did not become law until November 7, 1986.

33. CCR, *Confronting Racial Isolation in Miami*, January 1982, pp. 317–328.

34. Judy Johnston in OPD told African American special assistant Mel Bradley, who was summarizing the report for the president, that there should be a coordinated effort to address some of the problems involving key local officials. This would be consistent with the administration's "commitment to increasing the participation of the private sector"; Penny to President, June 4, 1982; Johnson to Bradley, June 9, 1982; Bradley memo, June 16.

35. Rhodes to Deaver, Baker, Williamson, May 25, 1982, including handwritten notes of reactions to his idea.

36. The meeting was scheduled from 2:45 to 3:00 p.m.; Bradley to Harper, June 24, 1982; Penny to President, June 28, 1982.

37. Pendleton to Harper, August 11, 1982.

38. Horowitz to Pendleton, August 27, 1982; Pendleton to Horowitz, August 10, 1982, John Hope III to Pendleton on Horowitz comments, August 10, 1982. Pendleton met with Horowitz after a June 25, 1982, letter he wrote to him commenting on the May report on the budget for fiscal 1983; Horowitz to Pendleton, June 25, 1982; Horowitz to Peter Roussel, September 13, 1982; Rhodes to Deaver, Baker, Williamson, May 25, 1982, including handwritten notes of reactions to his idea. Robert Pear, "Reagan Is Rebuked by 33 State Heads of Rights Panels," September 12, 1982, *New York Times*, p. 1.

39. Harper asked Pendleton, "How can I help achieve the vision you put forward?" Harper sent the speech to EEOC chair Clarence Thomas, Reagan Democrat and Vanderbilt professor, Chester "Checker" Finn, Harvard Law School professor Solicitor General Charles Fried, their selection for a Justice Department post and others, telling them: "This is an interesting and important speech."

Speeches given in a variety of settings, including the 35th Annual Conference of the National Association of Human Rights Workers in Kansas City on October 16, 1982, and to the Federal Executive Board of Metropolitan New Jersey Equal Opportunity Luncheon; Harper to Pendleton, October 26, 1982; Harper to Brad Reynolds, Bob Collyer (deputy undersecretary, Employment Standards), Clarence Thomas, Charles Fried same day.

40. CCR Minutes, July 12, 1982; October 12, 1982; December 6, 1982.

41. Chester "Checker" Finn to Harper, November 4, 1982.

42. Pendleton to Fuller, April, 11, 1983; Fuller to Pendleton, April 8, 1983, with attachments; Rusthoven to Fielding, March 21, 1983; Horowitz to Joe Wright, Craig Fuller, Ken Cribb, March 21, 1983; Robert Pear, "Rights Unit Will Subpoena Papers from Two Agencies," *New York Times*, April 12, 1983; Felicity Barringer, "Justice Official Again Hit on Rights," *Washington Post*, May 19, 1983; House Judiciary Subcommittee chairman, Don Edwards, suggested he might subpoena the documents requested by the CCR if the administration continued to stonewall.

43. Meese told Pendleton he had asked the cabinet departments to deliver the policy information the Civil Rights Commission had requested, according to a listing prepared by the CCR staff, which Pendleton had given him. He hoped this would end the controversy. Pendleton to President, January 10, 1983; tracking note indicates on the 15th "The Pres. Briefed by E. Meese," Pendleton to President, March 14, 1983. The data, which included judges, marshals, and attorneys, showed full-time pres-

idential appointees requiring Senate confirmation (PAS): 860 male and 79 female, 37 black and 34 Hispanic, 3 Asian, and no Indians; presidential appointees not requiring Senate confirmation (PA): 132 male, 24 female, 8 black, 2 Hispanic, 0 Asian, 0 Indian; part-time: PAS 231 male, 68 female, 8 black, 11 Hispanic, 1 Asian, 0 Indian; PA 1,097 male, 217 female, 53 black, 25 Hispanic, 13 Asian, 8 Indian.

44. Bradley to Harper, February 7, 1983; Ullman to Harper, February 7, 1983; Connie Bowers, VA Branch/Maurice White, LRD, to Ken Clarkson OMB, December 14, 1982; Horowitz to Clarkson, December 20, 1982; John Hope III, acting staff director, to David Stockman, OMB, January 4, 1983; the previous reauthorization added age and disability to the CCR's jurisdiction.

45. At the April 6, 1983, 8 a.m. staff meeting Baker, Meese, Von Damm, and Harper asked Uhlmann why they had no information on reauthorization until the day before the hearing. Uhlmann and Harper knew about the issue but no one else did. They asked, "Did OPD drop the ball?" When they were briefed, they wondered why an extension of twenty years should be opposed. Baker told Uhlmann to prepare the administration's position to go to the Hill that day and to issue a press release the next day Action "Urgent" to Uhlmann from a.m. senior staff meeting. Horowitz to Dennis Patrick, November 5, 1982; Horowitz to Harper, December 29, 1982; January 10, 1983.

46. Patrick to Harper, March 11, 1983, and E. H. handwritten note. Another nominee, Carolyn Reid-Wallace, had been assistant director of education programs at the National Endowment for the Humanities, had served as a director of the organization of Black Colleges and Universities, the National Association for Equal Opportunity in Higher Education, and was chief academic officer at Bowie State College. She was dropped for Destro. The complication arose when Destro's supporters, led by Sensenbrenner, insisted on the resubmission of his nomination. A few inquiries had already come to the White House about Destro's views and actions that put his renomination in doubt. Barry Goldwater asked for a response for one of his constituents, a woman who had read that Destro recommended the abolition of the CCR, "claiming that it does not investigate discrimination against white minority groups or religious groups." She also objected to Destro's view that the NAACP and NOW can adequately represent the interest of minority groups and women. "If they had succeeded in eliminating discrimination against their constituencies, there would be no need for a CCR."

But, she thought, Destro did not seem to understand that these groups had no legal authority to monitor "anti-discrimination activity." She thought him "not well informed on how the process of government works." David Gergen sent a copy of a news article describing these views of Destro's to senior staff. Ed Harper assigned Mel Bradley to "stay on top of this if it looks like a problem." Destro's supporters who appreciated his anti-abortion views and focus on religious discrimination outweighed any "problem." Patrick to Senator Barry Goldwater, November 5, 1982; Duberstein to Goldwater, August 5, 1982; Goldwater to Duberstein, July 27, 1982, enclosure; Melody Tucker, Phoenix, Arizona, to President, July 14, 1982; Gergen to Baker, Meese, Deaver, Von Damm, Dole, Duberstein, Harper, July 7, 1982; Harper to Bradley, handwritten note, July 8, 1982; Mike Shanahan, "Reagan Nominates One-Time Opponent to Civil Rights Board," *Philadelphia Inquirer,* July 7, 1982.

47. Robert Pear, "Reagan Reported Planning to Name 4 to Rights Panel," *New York Times,* May 21, 1983; Steven Weisman, "Mrs. Ruckelshaus Said to Retain Job," *New York Times,* May 24, 1984; David Hoffman and Juan Williams, "Reagan to Replace 3 Members of Panel on US Civil Rights," *Washington Post,* May 24, 1983. "It's an inescapable paradox, isn't it?" Ruckelshaus said. She had heard, two or three weeks before, that Rea-

gan intended to replace her. "It has nothing to do with Billy's appointment," she said. "It has to do with my performance on the CCR."

Ruckelshaus, a moderate Republican, had voted with the commission majority in support of strong measures to protect the rights of African Americans, women, and Hispanic Americans. Two days later the White House said they had decided not to replace her. I reacted by saying, "If the President goes through with these appointments, the Civil Rights Commission will become just another mouthpiece of the Administration. There would be no need for a Commission on Civil Rights because it would not be independent."

48. Horowitz to Harper, Ken Cribb, Mike Baroody, Mike Uhlmann, May 24, 1983. They should claim that their "distinguished nominees" would improve the CCR's work. Finally they should say they are "not opposed to affirmative action" so long as it is only "outreach, counseling, and training." The CCR staff had on only one occasion made one contract each with NOW and with ADL to write reports where they had expertise. ERA, ADL wrote the report Hate Crimes, and NOW the Equal Rights Amendment statement in 1982. When I was appointed, I explained to commissioners that even though the staff reviewed whatever contractors submitted for accuracy, I thought it was bad practice which invited criticism. We agreed not to contract again with any advocacy group or think tank with obvious biases. After the Reagan take-over the Reaganites made numerous consulting agreements with biased "experts."

49. Von Damm to Ronald Geisler, May 13, 1983, with handwritten note on attached press release; Francis X. Clines, "Reagan Chooses 3 for Rights Panel," *New York Times*, May 26, 1983; Juan Williams, "New Nominees Oppose Quotas, Three Fired from Civil Rights Panel," *Washington Post*, May 26, 1983.

50. Bentsen and Tower to Reagan, May 25, 1983; Pennsylvania Republican senator Arlen Specter to Reagan, May 24, 1983; Carl Holman, President, National Urban Coalition, to Reagan, June 1, 1983; Patrick replies; Duberstein to congressional correspondents; Ralph Neas explained to the press that "the President's attempted wholesale replacement of the United States Civil Rights Commission seriously jeopardizes the independence, the integrity and the effectiveness of the Commission." Some objections concerned specific individuals. New Jersey Democratic congressman Frank Guarini asked for a response to a letter he had received from Dr. Sergio Finzi of the Lupus Foundation of America explaining that he worked with me on that board and regarded me as "one of the most hard-working, competent and intelligent people in any Federal agency." Democratic House of Delegates member Paula Hollinger of Maryland wrote objecting to the replacement of Murray Saltzman.

51. Counsel office staffer Peter Rusthoven, in finalizing the letter, said that even though Jackson made no mention of quotas in his letter, he usually put anti-quota language in letters but decided "the safer and more prudent course is not to do so here." He did not "want to give Jackson anything on which he might seize in any publicity efforts following his receipt of the response." They essentially ignored Jackson's point that an independent CCR can be expected to differ sometimes with a president, and his request for a meeting. Jackson to Reagan, May 23, 1983; White House staffing memo response to Reverend Jesse Jackson re Civil Rights CCR, due by Monday, June 13; Rusthoven to Fielding, June 15, 1983; Fielding to Jackson, June 16, 1983.

52. Office of the White House Press Secretary, May 25, 1983. Pendleton, quoted in Thompson, "Civil Rights Commission," p. 195; Juan Williams, "Beyond the Lunch-Counter Victories; With Basic Rights Guaranteed, Reagan Wants Federal Role Limited," *Washington Post*, June 1, 1983, A3.

53. Williams, "Beyond the Lunch-Counter Victories," *Washington Post*, June 1, 1983, p. A3.

54. Ibid.

55. Ibid.; Thomas Pugh to Pendleton, June 13, 1983, Mattie Crossley, chair of Tennessee SCA, to Pendleton, July 8, 1983; Walter E. Washington, DC SAC, to Pendleton, July 7, 1983; Joseph Russell, Indiana SAC, to Pendleton, July 7, 1983. CCR procedures required the SACs to write to the chair and the staff, who transmitted the letters to the White House.

56. I commented, "I would prefer that the Senate did not approve the new nominees. But if it appears that the Senate will confirm them, I would consider filing a lawsuit to preserve the CCR's independence"; Robert Pear, "Reagan's Power to Change Rights Panel Challenged," *New York Times,* June 1, 1983.

57. Theodore Olson, Office of Legal Counsel to Hauser, Deputy Counsel to the President; memo to Fred P. Fielding, Counsel to the President, June 21, 1983; Rusthoven to Hauser, June 27, 1983.

58. Horowitz to Gergen, Patrick, and Uhlmann, June 22, 1983, and July 5, 1983; Baroody memo, July 12, 1983; Gergen to Senior Staff, materials for hearings on nominees, sent to more than twenty columnists, done by Baroody, Uhlmann, Horowitz, Patrick, and Kennedy from Legislative Affairs. On July 12, 1983, Mike Baroody gave guidance to Darman, Gergen, and Fuller to use when speaking publicly about the nominations.

59. Douglas Brinkley, ed., *Reagan Diaries* (New York: HarperCollins, 2007), p. 166.

60. One hundred fifty-seven members wrote to Reagan, including Robert Garcia of the Bronx, chairman of the Congressional Hispanic Caucus; Democrat Patricia Schroeder of Colorado and Republican Olympia J. Snowe of Maine, co-chairs of the Congressional Caucus on Women's Issues; and Julian C. Dixon of Illinois, chairman of the Congressional Black Caucus. The Republicans were Bill Clinger, Hal Sawyer, Joel Pritchard, Nancy Johnson, John McKernan, Larry Coughi, Clay Shaw, Frank Horton, Ham Fish, Jr., Lynn Martin, Jim Jeffords, Jim Leach, Stewart McKinney, Doug Bereuter, Tom Ridge, Olympia Snowe, Bill Frenzel, and Sid Morrison; Thompson, "Civil Rights Commission," p. 198.

61. Robert Pear, "3 Reagan Rights Nominees Set Off Heated Clash in Senate," *New York Times,* July 14, 1983; George Lardner, Jr., and Helen Dewar, "Congress Heads for Home with Work Undone; House Approves Measure to Thwart the President," *Washington Post,* August 5, 1983. Apparently the administration had decided that if they could smear me they could win. At the July 26 hearing one witness spent more time trying to prove that I was un-American than supporting the president's nominees. He complained about a speech I had made in 1979 at the University of Chicago after a trip to China on an education mission, using it to to to prove I either loved communism or did not understand the dangers of the Communist system. He also lambasted scholarly books I had written with the same point in mind. I not only defended my scholarly work and the misrepresentation of my speech but pointed out I had just returned from a trip to the Soviet Union, where the KGB assaulted one of my delegation members and tried to intimidate me in a rather scary encounter, right before I went to China, and no one had to tell me about the brutal nature of communism. I knew firsthand. I also gratefully received the tip from a reporter at Gannett News Service that Linda Chavez Gersten's special assistant called him to say he should read my books to confirm my un-American tendencies and in fact messengered him a copy of one of my books. The reporter had taped the assistant because he was in Virginia where it was legal, thinking it would be a story he might write. The whole discussion did not propel Reagan's nominations forward. Horowitz to Gergen, Patrick, and Uhlmann, June 22, 1983, and July 5, 1983.

62. Thompson, "Civil Rights Commission," p. 198.

63. On Chavez, Gersten, Robert Mackichan to Becky Dunlap, Legal Memo, August 2, 1983; Mathias to Reagan, September 13, 1983.

64. Robert Pear, "New US Rights Aide Backs Whites for Jobs in Memphis," *New York Times*, September 11, 1983.

65. AP, "Compromise on Civil Rights Panel Reported," *New York Times*, September 30, 1983; George Lardner, Jr., "Civil Rights Commission Expires During Dispute Over Ouster of 3," *Washington Post*, October 1, 1983.

66. Thompson, "Civil Rights Commission," pp. 198–199 and notes there cited; Biden and Mathias to Reagan, November 4, 1983; Martin Tolchin, "Senate Approves Rights Panel Bill," *New York Times*, November 15, 1983.

67. They were following the idea of using signing statements to make constitutional arguments, suggested by Justice Samuel Alito and discussed in his confirmation hearings in 2005 and a subject of extended public discussion thereafter.

68. Gergen to Darman, November 29, 1983; Horowitz to Darman, November 30, 1983; Administration of Ronald Reagan, November 30, 1983, *Messages and Papers of the Presidents*, p. 1626; Robert Pear, "Reagan Signs Bill for Rights Panel," *New York Times*, December 1, 1983.

69. Stockman to President, November 25, 1983.

70. Buckley says she knew nothing about the commission and the controversy into which she was inserted until after her appointment. The White House general counsel staff interviewed her, asking questions about affirmative action and other issues. She had to tell them that in a community that was 99 percent Hispanic, discrimination issues were not a concern. Interview with Buckley, April 23, 2006.

71. Brinkley, *Reagan Diaries*, November 15, 1983, p. 197.

72. Reviewing the text of the Civil Rights Commission proposal on November 14, Michael Uhlmann wrote, "I assume there is no reason to consider reappointing Jill Ruckelshaus and Mary Louise Smith (Smith and Ruckelhaus can be counted upon to oppose Pendleton and Chavez for reappointment)." They needed to have conversations with the Republican leadership on the Hill about their appointees right away to accomplish the "President's goals"; Uhlmann to John Svahn, October 14, 1982, and December 2, 1983; Thompson, "Civil Rights Commission," pp. 199–201 and notes there cited. Juan Williams, "Michel Designates Democrat for Civil Rights Commission," *Washington Post*, December 8, 1983.

73. Robert Pear, "Rift Grows Wider Over Rights Panel," *New York Times*, December 9, 1983.

74. Mary Louise Smith had regarded George Bush as a close friend and almost a relative. They had been co-chairs of the RNC together before he stepped down, and her granddaughter had worked for Barbara Bush. Two hundred of the 585 Democratic women legislators showed up and 150 of the 400 Republican legislators. They paid their own way to the conference. Lee Verstandig to James Baker III, December 5, 1983; Grassley to Reagan, December 6, 1983; Evans to Reagan, December 6, 1983; Lee Verstandig, assistant to the president for intergovernmental affairs, reported that Vice President Bush's appearance became "the highlight of the Conference and he defused what had become a very volatile situation." The women leaders they had worked with before the conference could not "keep unity within the Republican ranks, due to the intensity of feeling and pent-up frustrations" among the Republican women present. She thought on women's issues in general they had a lot of "general uneasiness" about Reagan's record and they had "a lot of work to do" to "increase the visibility of our record."

75. Rusthoven to Fielding, December 19, 1983; Fielding to Darman, December 19, 1983; Fielding to Darman, draft attached, December 22, 1983. Verstandig and Fielding

sparred over how to respond. She wanted to say, "It is important that the President . . . have the privilege to nominate his own choice as Chairman of the CCR, and that the Presidential nominees could support the Chairman with whom they would serve." Fielding thought they should avoid Verstandig's explanation, since her honest draft made it appear "that the decision . . . was simply part of a political calculus involving how many votes the President would have on ratification of his designation of a chairman." In January 2005 Ruckelshaus told Brian Lamb on C-SPAN in a joint interview with her husband, "I disagreed with some of the social policies during the Reagan administration. I didn't think there was enough emphasis on civil rights issues, black and white disparities. And the Civil Rights Commission had historically always been aimed in that direction, and during the time I served, the majority party, then the Republicans, the presidential party, was the majority in the Civil Rights Commission, and we weren't doing what I thought we ought to be doing, which was addressing those issues." They removed Jill Ruckelshaus just a few weeks after he appointed her husband, William D. Ruckelshaus, as administrator of the Environmental Protection Agency. Ruckelshaus did "land on her feet"; she has served on a variety of corporate and nonprofit boards and remained committed to public service since her time on the commission.

76. Herrington to Reagan, with attachment of appointment letters from Congress and materials designating terms, December 19, 1983; Pendleton to Reagan, December 28, 1983; Pendleton to Meese, January 9, 1984; Margaret Shapiro, "Final Vacancy Filled on U.S. Rights Panel, Baker Names Moderate Black," *Washington Post*, December 13, 1983.

77. Robert Pear, "Commission Intends to Reassess Rights," *New York Times*, January 8, 1984. Not understanding, or ignoring, the history of the agency, Reagan supporters asserted that when Reagan began his change in policy direction the CCR issued reports "excoriating administration policies," sent letters to administration officials objecting to decisions affecting civil rights, and voted to subpoena records and officials. According to Reagan supporters, advocates raised the independence issue because they had no other argument; Robert Detlefsen, *Civil Rights Under Reagan* (San Francisco: Institute of Contemporary Studies, 1991).

Chapter VIII

1. Unless otherwise indicated manuscript collections cited in this chapter are in White House subject files, FG93, Ronald Reagan Presidential Library. CCR Minutes, January 16–17, 1984; Robert Pear, "Civil Rights Commission Abandons Backing of Racial Quotas," *New York Times*, January 18, 1984; Michael Wright and Caroline Rand Herron, "Rights Panel Echoes Reagan Point of View," *New York Times*, January 22, 1984; Nancy Dunne, "Reagan Axe Prompts Dissent Over Racial Dividing Line," *Financial Times of London*, April 19, 1984.

2. What appeared to be exceptions like the Baby Doe hearings in 1986 occurred because Robert Destro, one of the Reagan appointees, had a particular interest in right-to-life issues supported by the administration, such as insisting that fetuses were persons who had rights. He wanted the withdrawal of sustenance by the parents and physicians from a Baby Doe to become a disability rights issue. Interview with Destro, February 8, 2006. The Indian civil rights hearings that began in 1988 after Pendleton's death were, it became apparent, part of Allen's attack on the Indian tribal courts that stood in the way of the non-Indian spurious adoptions of Native American children, which he favored but which were opposed by the tribes.

3. CCR Minutes, January 16–17, 1984; Pear, "Civil Rights Commission Abandons

Backing of Racial Quotas"; Wright and Herron, "Rights Panel Echoes Reagan Point of View"; Dunne, "Reagan Axe Prompts Dissent Over Racial Dividing Line."

4. James Reston, Jr., *Rolling Stone*, 1986. To relieve my frustrations and make some contribution to human rights work, in November 1984 I used the notoriety gained from fighting Reagan to support the civil rights movement on human rights issues that the CCR refused to consider. These issues included American complicity with the apartheid regime in South Africa and the Haitian refugee cause, which the CCR had long endorsed. As an individual, I joined in the leadership of a successful direct-action and legislative campaign to help with bringing an end to apartheid in South Africa. My colleagues on the CCR indicated no interest in these activities. After two years of protest, in what became a nationwide movement, we succeeded in encouraging the passage of a vote to sanction U.S. trade with South Africa. As sanctions began to bite, they contributed, along with protest activities in South Africa and opposition to the regime in the world, to the release of Nelson Mandela in 1990 and the crumbling of apartheid.

5. CCR Minutes, March 1984. I successfully moved support of the Senate bill, pressed by civil rights advocates, responding to Japanese internment, including a pardon and liberal review of applicants for restitution.

6. General Accounting Office Report, *The Operations of the United States Civil Rights Commission*, March 25, 1986. The GAO found widespread mismanagement, including the hiring of a large number of political appointees, consultants, and temporary employees instead of career federal workers. The GAO also found that Pendleton had charged the commission $67,344 for 240 days in a year in what was supposed to be a part-time post.

7. CCR Minutes, January 16–17, 1984; Chavez to Baker, February 13, 1984; Rusthoven to Fielding, March 24, 1984, Ronald Reagan Presidential Library. Unless otherwise indicated, manuscripts cited in this chapter are in the Reagan Library. An article in the January 13, 1984 *Washington Post*, "Official Investigates Charges; U.S. Intervenes in Nebraska Religion Controversy," quoted an unnamed White House official saying, "Now that we have the Civil Rights Commission on our side, we can make use of them to run some interference for us." Fielding and Rusthoven decided the president should not respond; Pear, "Civil Rights Commission Abandons Backing of Racial Quotas."

8. The meeting was on August 16, 1984, at 4:15 p.m. for twenty minutes; Ryan to Svahn, August 14, 1984; Gibson to Fuller, July 13, 1984.

9. CCR Minutes, January 16–17, 1984.

10. Francis Guess voted with the majority.

11. Mary Frances Berry and Blandina Cardenas Ramirez, "Civil Rights Commission Majority Versus National Consensus," *New York Times*, February 26, 1984.

12. Nunez to Ken Kramer, January 31, 1984; M. B. Oglesby, Assistant to the President, to Ken Kramer, February 28, 1984.

13. Abrams to Reagan; draft letter circulated April 18, 1984, for White House staff comment; Roberts to Fielding, April 18, 1984; Fielding to Darman, April 18, 1984; Roberts noted that Don Clarey, who handled the correspondence for Staff Secretary Craig Fuller, said the White House "did not direct Education to alter its positions in response to Abram's letter, but simply obtained more accurate information from Secretary Bell." He had no "objection to the President sending a letter correcting Abram's mis-impression about Education's positions." He did suggest revisions. The letter conveys the impression that Reagan discussed this with Bell, and he did not. So the wording should be changed. Roberts also thought "no longer objects" should be taken out because it sounds like Abram's letter caused a change.

14. Bradley to Svahn, April 19, 1984; Svahn to Darman, April 23, 1984; Darman okayed April 7, 1984, file package, new draft from Svahn for his signature being prepared.

15. CCR Minutes, May 1, 1984; Jim Cicconi to Baker et al., April 27, 1984; Kathy Sawyer, "Reagan Repudiates Klan in Letter to Rights Panel," *Washington Post*, April 2, 1984.

16. CCR Minutes, May 1, 1984. At the next meeting of the CCR, in June 1984, I asked that the minutes be modified to reflect my concern about Abram sharing my memo with the White House. CCR procedures did not envision sharing a memo intended for an agenda item with the White House for a response. I had only wanted the CCR to discuss the issue and decide whether action was warranted. I also pointed out that the whole Farrakhan, Jackson, Mondale discussion occurred informally and not as part of the meeting and should not have occasioned any action. CCR Minutes, June 6, 1984, and transcript pp. 14–16, 20–22. I moved that we abandon discussion of the issue and proceed with our work. Bunzel and Abram abstained.

17. CCR Minutes, July 11, 1984; the motion failed when Cardenas Ramirez approved and Buckley and Guess abstained,

18. George Curry, "Attack in New York Stirs U.S. Study of Racial Violence," *Chicago Tribune*, January 14, 1987.

19. George Curry, "Federal Rights Agency Hopes to Find Its Lost Credibility in Violence Study," *Chicago Tribune*, January 18, 1987; George Curry, "Is Race Violence Rising? Bias Panel Can't Find Out," *Chicago Tribune*, March 4, 1987.

20. 467 U.S. 561 (1984).

21. CCR Minutes, February 13, April 16, May 15, June 11, and July 13, 1987. AP Wire, "Agency Rejects Slam at High Court," May 16, 1987. The media reported on the draft Devins had prepared before our vote at the May 1987 meeting. Allen had arrived as Bunzel's replacement. Destro and Buckley voted with us to reject the draft, while the others voted to support it. That meant a statement could be issued, but when *Toward an Understanding of Johnson* was published, they joined in a statement with Allen and Friedman, the three of us wrote separately, and Pendleton issued his own statement approving the memo prepared by Devins; 480 U.S. 616 (1987).

22. CCR Minutes, November 8, 1984, and April 11, 1985.

23. Only one-fifth as many women state chairmen and two-fifths as many nonwhites remained.

24. CCR Minutes, January 17–18, 1984.

25. Terry Hart Lee to Reagan, January 17, 1984; Chavez to Sally Kelly, February 13, 1984; Susan Prado to Cicconi, June 22, 1984. CCR Minutes, April 11, 1985. Peter Perl, "Rights Chief Derides Comparable Worth Studies Released on Controversial Pay Equity Issue for Women," *Washington Post*, November 17, 1984.

26. CCR Minutes, May 10, June 12, and July 11, 1985; Stuart Taylor, "Civil Rights Chief Questions Commission's Future," *New York Times*, July 26, 1985; AP Wire, "U.S. Court Upsets Pay Equity for Women," *New York Times*, September 5, 1985.

27. CCR Minutes, April 11, 1985.

28. CCR Minutes, March 5, 1984; they agreed to Bunzel's revised outline for the Eastern and Southern European report, which would "include an analysis of the adverse consequences of affirmative action programs encouraged by the federal government upon the equal opportunity rights of Americans of Eastern and Southern European descent." When David Richardson, chairman of the Urban Affairs Committee of the Pennsylvania legislature, wrote Reagan to say he was "hard-pressed to understand the importance of the Commission's intended study on the impact of affirmative action on

Americans whose ancestors are from southern and eastern Europe, when there are so many pressing issues facing this nation," Lee Verstandig replied that his letter would be given to the Office of Policy Development "for their benefit"; Richardson to Reagan, April 12, 1984; Verstandig to Richardson, May 21, 1984.

29. CCR Minutes, March 27–28, 1984; Robert Pear, "Trying to Tie Strings to Federal Aid," *New York Times*, March 11, 1984; Juan Williams, "U.S. Rights Panel Urges Limiting Race Bias Laws," *Washington Post*, March 29, 1984.

30. CCR Minutes, July 11, 1984, and November 8, 1984. I also asked for access to the inspector general at the Agriculture Department's report on black farmers and civil rights matters in the department.

31. CCR Minutes, January 1, 1985. We also heard from a panel opposed to minority contracts. Vernie Lindstrom, the president of the Associated General Contractors, expressed glee at the takeover of the CCR. Having the new appointees and discussions leading to an elimination of the contracts guaranteed "civil rights in its truest sense."

32. Wheeler to Reagan, May 24, 1985.

33. Carson to Reagan, November 27, 1984; tracking worksheet, December 11, 1984.

34. CCR Minutes, March 5, 1985; Lindstrom to Don Regan, March 14, 1985; reply from Don Regan, March 27, 1985; Williams to Reagan, March 13, 1985; Reagan to Williams, March 25, 1985.

35. CCR Minutes, January 10, February 11, March 5, and June 12, 1985; 467 U.S. 561 (1984).

36. Bush II withdrew her nomination as secretary of labor in 2001 because she was found to be employing an undocumented immigrant as live-in household help.

37. At the October 1985 meeting, the CCR discussed the desire of some commissioners to meet directly with staff to discuss work in progress. Destro and I expressed an interest in meetings for this purpose. The issue turned on the control of the staff director over the staff and whether commissioners might try to influence a report to reflect their personal views. After debate in executive session, we unanimously passed a motion reaffirming traditional practice: "The commission has the legal authority to obtain from staff information relating to commission projects. Commissioners will exercise this authority through the Staff Director. The Staff Director will arrange meetings and telephone conference between commissioners and staff"; Lawrence Glick, Solicitor to Chairman Pendleton, Vice Chairman Abram and Commissioners, "Motion Passed at Commission Executive Session of October 15, 1985," October 30, 1985.

38. CCR Minutes, November 12, 1985; "Max Green Named Special Assistant," *New York Times*, September 13, 1985.

39. Hatch to Edwards, March 20, 1986. He complained that Rosalyn Kleeman, the GAO project manager, participated in a panel on comparable worth and affirmative action at the invitation of the CCR while evaluating the CCR's comparable worth report. She made comments at the proceeding about the study. Therefore, she and the GAO report suffered from bias. The GAO disagreed absent evidence that the findings were wrong.

40. The rechartered committee membership had increased to 59 percent white versus 49 percent previously and almost 65 percent male versus 29 percent. Chairs were 72 percent white versus 29 percent previously, and 92 percent were male compared to 61 percent previously. "Some records were missing, some were incomplete, and still others were conflicting." Some "documents critical to our ability to determine whether the CCR had followed merit principles in personnel actions were not in the files."

41. Testimony of William J. Anderson, Director, General Government Division, GAO, before the Subcommittee on Civil and Constitutional Rights, House of Representatives, March 25, 1986.

42. Morris Abram testimony, Clarence Pendleton testimony, April 22, 1986. House Judiciary Subcommittee on the Constitution.

43. Wilkins to Abram, April 30, 1986.

44. Abram to Wilkins, May 5, 1986; Wilkins to Abram, April 13, 1986.

45. Testimony of Al Latham, April 22, 1986, House Judiciary Subcommittee on the Constitution.

46. In early April 1986, Kathie Russo, associate director of personnel, told the counsel that a "recent letter by Commissioner John H. Bunzel has suggested the Chairman should resign and presidential personnel would like to be prepared for 'future developments.' " J. Michael Shepherd researched the issue and advised Peter J. Wallison that no one had authority to remove Chairman Pendleton except the president. Shepherd to Wallison, April 11, 1986; Wallison counsel to President to Russo, April 8, 1986.

47. Robert Pear, "Rights Panel Under Fire in House," *New York Times,* June 27, 1986; Max Green to Patrick Buchanan, July 14, 1986; Will Ball to Don Regan, August 14, 1986.

48. Kingdon, Svahn, Tuttle, Request for scheduling, recommendation from Frederick J. Ryan, Jr., August 1, 1986; Pendleton to Reagan, July 30, 1986; Edita to Ellen, October 14, 1986: "Would you happen to know if the Pres. Met w/ the Chairman of the US CCR on Civil Rights, Clarence Pendleton, Jr. Or anyone from that organization?" Handwritten answer: "not anytime recently."

49. Resignation of Abram to Reagan, June 4, 1986; Reagan to Abram, July 8, 1986.

50. Abram to Reagan, July 22, 1986; Robert McFadden, "U.S. Official Quits Civil Rights Post to Lead a Jewish Group," *New York Times,* June 8, 1986.

51. Tuttle to the President, September 10, 1986, and attachments. CCR Minutes, April 11, May 9, June 12, July 11, and September 11, 1986; Pat Buchanan to Tuttle, June 10, 1986; Tuttle replied that as "we discussed over the phone" Linda would be excellent but his concerns were political and he was "waiting for Daniel's discussion with her campaign managers."

52. CCR Minutes, September 26, 1986, and October 24, 1986; Robert Pear, "Black Men Show Gains in Earnings," *New York Times,* September 4, 1986. When he called the question and they refused to vote, we left the meeting. After we left, they voted 5–0 to delay a decision. Pendleton proposed no meeting in December, but everyone disagreed. I asked that we ask the staff for a new reorganization plan instead of a reduction in force. I lost by a vote of 3–2.

53. Latham to Reagan, October 30, 1986; Reagan to Latham, November 25, 1986; Lena Williams, "Rights Panel Expecting Big Cut Is Gearing Down," *New York Times,* September 26, 1986.

54. Latham to Reagan, October 30, 1986; Reagan to Latham, November 25, 1986.

55. Bunzel to Reagan, November 24, 1986; Reagan to Bunzel, December 23, 1986; Robert Pear, "Civil Rights Commission Loses Reagan Man," *New York Times,* November 30, 1986.

56. CCR Minutes, September 27, 1986.

57. CCR Minutes, February 13, April, May 15, June 11, and July 13, 1987. Lena Williams, "Desegregation Plans Aid to Improve Race Balance in Schools," *New York Times,* May 20, 1987. We did not vote against the report because it at least concluded, in a change made after Gary Orfield resigned from the advisory panel in disgust, that white flight and school desegregation do not always go hand in hand.

58. Bradley to Carl A. Anderson, August 7, 1987.

59. CCR Minutes, October 24, November 16, and December 11, 1987. Edwards to Reagan, December 3, 1987; Pendleton to Edwards, January 19, 1988.

60. We heard from CORE's Roy Innis, Alfred Rotondura of the Italian American Foundation, Martin Gerry from the Spina Bifida Association of America, Clint Bolick from the Hudson Institute, advocates from the Arab American Institute, and K. L. Wang, founder of the Organization of Chinese Americans. All wanted reauthorization because the CCR was still needed.

61. CCR Minutes, January 15, February 12, and April 22, 1988.

62. Friedman, Letter to Editor, *New York Times*, April 9, 1988.

63. In December 1987 we heard from an invited panel, which with Abram, Chavez, and Bunzel gone included civil rights advocates, on employer sanctions under the proposed immigration law. GAO, EEOC, Office of Special Counsel, and LILAC and MALDEF testified. "Washington Talk: Briefing AIDS and Civil Rights," *New York Times*, July 21, 1987.

64. Lena Williams, "Washington Talk: Civil Rights Commission: On AIDS Panel Battles Some It Wants to Help."

65. Jack Sirica, "Protestors at AIDS Hearing," *Newsday*, April 13, 1988.

66. CCR Minutes, May 18, 1988, and July 15, 1988. Hatch to Reagan, July 21, 1988; Malcolm Wallop, Kim McClure, Pete Wilson, Gordon Humphrey, Chic Hecht, Jake Garn, Steve Symms to Reagan, July 23, 1988; Tuttle to Reagan, August 11, 1988, including letters to Friedman and response indicating a majority of commissioners concurred. Ramirez and I did not concur.

67. Robert Tuttle to President, September 2, 1988, memo on certificate of appointment, enclosures; Deukmejian to Reagan, July 21, 1988; Matsunaga to Reagan, March 31, 1987; other letters in same file.

68. Hooks to Reagan, February 15, 1983; Reagan to Hooks, February 15, 1983.

69. He cited the attack and reopening of school desegregation cases, efforts to undo employment discrimination remedies in the Boston police and fire department cases, compromising lawsuits in higher education by abandoning previous government agreements on goals and timetables and student admissions, and the equal allocation of resources. He also noted the refusal to file housing discrimination cases, issuing regulations that undermined the contracting process, the EEOC decision to terminate class-action suits, his decimation of the Legal Services Corporation, reductions in job training, higher education grants and loans, and the reduction in federal support for housing for low- and moderate-income families. Hooks to Reagan, February 15, 1983.

70. Thomas Griscom, Assistant to the President for Communications and Planning, to Senior Officers, July 29, 1988; "President Reagan: Seven Years of Accomplishment; The Reagan Record on Minority Opportunity/Civil Rights," April 8, 1988.

Chapter IX

1. Testimony before Select Committee on Indian Affairs, United States Senate, May 15, 1989; CCR Minutes, March 17, 1989.

2. Eleanor Randolph, "Rights Panel Should Quit, Chairman Suggests," *Washington Post*, March 19, 1989; Don Irwin, "Rights Panel Head Agrees to Apologize," *Los Angeles Times*, March 19, 1989.

3. Testimony before Select Committee on Indian Affairs, United States Senate, May 15, 1989; CCR Minutes, March 17, 1989.

4. Johann Neuman, "Rights Agency Caught in Crisis: Conflicts, Infighting Take Toll, *USA Today*, April 27, 1989.

5. Maureen Dowd and Julie Johnson, "Washington Talk: Briefing; One Man's Suspenders," *New York Times*, February 20, 1989.

6. Julie Johnson, "Civil Rights Panel Rebukes Its Chairman," October 6, 1989, *New York Times*, p. A6.

7. Richard Benedetton, "Bush Has Pick for Rights Post, But Incumbent Isn't Budging," *USA Today*, March 23, 1989, p. 4A; Julie Johnson, "Rights Chief Offers to Quit; White House Has Yet to Act," *New York Times*, October 12, 1989, p. B10; Allen to Bush.

8. Bush to Allen, White House Central Files, George Herbert Walker Bush Presidential Library (all manuscript materials cited in this chapter are in the Bush Library in FG 93, unless otherwise indicated). Johnson, "Rights Chief Offers to Quit."

9. Manning Marable, *Race Reform and Rebellion: The Second Reconstruction in Black America, 1945–1990* (Jackson: University Press of Mississippi, 1991), pp. 92–95, 195–197; Gerald Boyd, "President Meets with 20 Blacks," *New York Times*, January 16, 1985, p. A1; "Black America Under the Reagan Administration: A Symposium of Black Conservatives," *Heritage Foundation Policy Review*, Fall 1985, p. 27.

10. *1989 Annual Report of the Attorney General of the United States*, p. 15; *1990 Annual Report of the Attorney General*, p. 14 Marable, *Race Reform and Rebellion*, pp. 205–206; Hearings on Police Brutality Before the House Subcommittee on Civil and Constitutional Rights, 102d Cong., 1st sess., March 20 and April 17, 1991, p. 320.

11. Department of Justice Community Relations Service, *Annual Report*, 1989, pp. 6–9.

12. Friedman to Lee Liberman, October 24, 1989.

13. CCR Minutes, April 28 and October 28, 1989.

14. CCR Minutes, November 17, 1989; Simon to Hatch, June 7, 1989; Hatch to Simon, June 21, 1989

15. Sununu to Hatch, Edwards, Sensenbrenner, and Simon, November 7, 1989. Roger Porter, who drafted the letters, told Sununu he had been trading phone calls with Sensenbrenner but had not reached him; Lucero to Gwaltney, November 7, 1989; Gonzalez to Darman, September 3, 1991; Budget estimate FY 1993, Roger Porter to President, November 16, 1989; Simon to Hatch, June 7, 1989; Hatch to Simon, June 1, 1989.

16. Michelle O'Donnell, "Arthur H. Fletcher Civil Rights Advocate and Affirmative Action Pioneer Dies at 80," *New York Times*, July 14, 2005; conversations with Art Fletcher.

17. Résumé Management Files, Arthur Fletcher, January, 14, 1989; letters to Bush—James Munn, Attorney, Seattle, Washington, December 16, 1988; Fletcher to Bush, December 19, 1988; Malcolm Corrin to Bush, co-chairman with him on Interracial Council for Business Opportunity, December 16, 1988; all letters received the same response from Chase Untermeyer: "The President has decided to appoint another individual." But their comments would be taken into account if another position is available where "this individual's background and expertise can be fully utilized." A letter of support solicited by Fletcher came to the White House from Maurice Dawkins of Leon Sullivan's Opportunities Industrialization Centers, a self-help job-training program focused on the urban poor.

18. Fletcher to Bush, February 10, 1989 (Résumé Management); Bush to Fletcher, March 22, 1989; the staff held the letter until they figured out that he was not violating "legal constraints on committing to a job that's not open"; Untermeyer to Boyden Gray, March 8, 1989.

19. Untermeyer to Bush, March 2, 1990; "Chairman designation with attachments stamped the President has seen"; Maureen Dowd, "Bush Picks a Chief to 'Re-Invigorate' Civil Rights Panel," *New York Times*, February 24, 1990.

20. Dowd, "Bush Picks a Chief."

21. Among the persons considered for the slot, which had to be filled by a Democrat, on March 5, 1990, Andrew Card suggested to Untermeyer, "F.Y.I. A good Democrat for a slot on the Civil Rights CCR. Colby King (of Gwen King Fame)." Untermeyer to Bush, March 2, 1990; "Chairman designation with attachments stamped the President has seen"; Melvin Jenkins, Staff Director to Chase Untermeyer, March 1, 1990, reporting confirmation vote; Press Briefing by Marlin Fitzwater, February 23, 1990, 9:30 a.m., p. 7; Wang to Bush, May 23, 1990; Bush to Wang, June 7, 1990; Dowd, "Bush Picks a Chief." When Wang wrote to thank him, Bush sent him a note saying, "You'll be a valuable member of the Commission on Civil Rights."

22. David Bates to President, February 27, 1990; "Announcement," Cabinet Secretary files; Untermeyer to Bush and attachments, February 27, 1990; "New Rights Chairman Has Heart Surgery," AP Online, March 7, 1990.

23. Michel to Bush, February 9, 1990; Dole to Bush, February 9, 1990; Legislative Affairs, Civil Rights Commission Rose Garden, East Wing files, May 5 and 17, 1990; Dole asked for a swearing-in ceremony for Redenbaugh along with Fletcher, whom he knew from Kansas. Fletcher thought the White House ceremony should take place on May 17, the anniversary of *Brown*, but if not then, April would be acceptable. The White House scheduled a Rose Garden ceremony for the Civil Rights Commission on May 17, 1990, with Fish, Goodling, Dole, Thurmond, Hatch, and Garn at 10 a.m., arranged by the Legislative Affairs Office.

24. *Griggs v. Duke Power Co.*, 401 U.S. 424 (1971); *Wards Cove Packing Co. v. Atonio*, 490 U.S. 642 (1989); *Price Waterhouse v. Hopkins*, 490 U.S. 228 (1989); *Martin v. Wilks*, 490 U.S. 755 (1989).

25. Capital Line, *USA Today*, May 14, 1990.

26. Maureen Dowd, "Trying to Head Off His Own Veto; Bush Holds Meeting on Rights Bill," *New York Times*, May 15, 1990; AP Wire May 15, 1990, "Bush, Black Leaders Seek Compromise on Job Bias Measure."

27. Paul Craig Roberts, "Maneuvering Us Toward Quotas," *Washington Times*, May 21, 1990; Roberts quoted Laurence H. Silberman, undersecretary of labor from 1970 to 1973, as stating on August 11, 1977, that the Philadelphia Plan made "fundamentally unsound policy," because it "introduced a group-rights concept antithetical to traditional American notions of individual merit and responsibility." The "distinction between goals and quotas, perhaps more metaphysical than real, was never truly understandable. It led to the eventual direction of orders and plans toward proportionate minority representation in a given labor market." Employers would avoid governmental scrutiny by earmarking "jobs for minorities without regard to qualifications . . . Some universities abandoned all pretense and adopted outright quotas for minority applicants."

28. CCR Report, *The Civil Rights Act of 1990*, pp. 1–13.

29. Ibid., pp. 81–90.

30. Anderson to John Schmitz, June 21, 1990; Anderson to Commissioners, June 20, 1990; Abram to Bush, June 7, 1990.

31. CCR Report, *The Civil Rights Act of 1990*, p. 97.

32. Michael K. Frisby, "Civil Rights Bill Gets Final OK; Bush Vows Veto," *Boston Globe*, October 18, 1990; Derrick Z. Jackson, "Focus Chamber Speaks, Bush Listens," *Boston Globe*, October 28, 1990.

33. Alexis Moore, "Sign Major Civil Rights Bill, Marchers in D.C. Urge Bush," *Miami Herald*, October 20, 1990, p. A14.

34. Neal Devins, "The Civil Rights Commission Backslides," *Wall Street Journal*, October 19, 1990.

35. Fletcher to Sununu, October 15, 1990 (the Chief of Staff has seen no response).

36. AP Online, November 22, 1990; Terence Hunt, "President Bush Vetoed a Major Civil Rights Bill Monday," *Boston Globe*, October 28, 1990; Derrick Z. Jackson, "Chamber Speaks."

37. Mary Frances Berry, *The Politics of Parenthood: Child Care, Women's Rights, and the Myth of the Good Mother*" (New York: Viking Penguin, 1993), pp. 191–193; Karen DeWitt, "U.S. Plan on Child Care Is Reported to Be Stalled," *New York Times*, January 27, 1991, p. A13.

38. For example, in August 1990 Everett Paup, president of Associated General Contractors, wrote Bush to complain about Fletcher's speech as "simply an attack" on the contractors. Fletcher made the speech shortly before he became chairman. The White House did not respond. Bush to Winkjer and enclosures; Jan Naylor, special assistant and associate director, to associate directors and deputy directors, July 14, 1989; Romey Lucero and Anne Gwaltney list of referrals and dispositions June 1990 to January 29, 1991; Lucero says no résumés were sent prior to her arrival on June 4, 1990; John Eastman to Diane Dracus, Office of Presidential Personnel, April 19, 1989; Linda Walker Sadler, "Civil Rights Agency Chief Brings Fight to Colorado, Arthur Fletcher Will Direct Efforts to Incorporate Civil Rights Policies into Business," *Rocky Mountain News*, September 10, 1991.

39. Michael K. Frisby, "Rights Chief Supports Thomas Nomination," *Boston Globe*, July 27, 1991.

40. Michael Frisby, "Senate Panel Rapped for Handling of Charges Against Thomas," *Boston Globe*, October 8, 1991, p. 12; Myron S. Waldman, "Last-Minute Fury, Senators Defend Thomas, Make No Move to Delay Vote," *Newsday*, October 8, 1991.

41. "Edward's Orthodoxy," Editorial, *Wall Street Journal*, September 23, 1991, p. A14; Edwards letter to *Wall Street Journal*, October 3, 1991, p. A17; "One Report, $14 Million," Editorial, *Washington Post*, October 2, 1991; Steven Holmes, "With Glory of Past Only a Memory, Rights Panel Searches for New Role," *New York Times*, October 10, 1991. "House Extends Civil Rights Panel for Just Two Years," *New York Times*, October 1, 1991, p. A17.

42. Redenbaugh "Rights Staff Deserves Better from Edwards," letter to editor, *Wall Street Journal*, October 21, 1991, p. A19.

43. CCR Minutes, September 13, 1991; Jason De Parle, "Bias Is Found at U.S. Bases in Europe," *New York Times*, August 25, 1991, p. 30.

44. Steven Holmes, "With Glory of Past"; *Congressional Record*, House H7090, September 30, 1991.

45. CCR Minutes, April 28, 1989. The request for fiscal 1992 stood at $10,780.000. The Congress appropriated $7.5 million for fiscal year 1987 and $5.7 in fiscal years 1988 and 1989. The president requested $9.5 million in 1990.

46. Gonzalez to Darman, September 3, 1991, budget estimate fiscal year 1993.

47. Janet Bass, "Government Warns Fiesta Bowl on Civil Rights," UPI Wire, December 4, 1990; Michel Marriott, "Colleges Basing Aid on Race Risk Loss of Federal Funds," December 12, 1990, p. A1.

48. Linda P. Campbell, "Education Chief Quits Amid Rumors of Ouster," *Chicago Tribune*, December 13, 1990; Maureen Dowd, "Cavazos Quits as Education Chief Amid Pressure from White House," *New York Times*, December 13, 1990.

49. Karen De Witt, "U.S. Eases College Stand but Not All the Way," *New York Times*, December 19, 1990, p. A1.

50. Ibid.; Alain Sanders, "Who's in Charge Here: Embarrassed by a Flip-Flop on Minority Scholarships, Bush Chooses a Political Pragmatist as Education Secretary, *Time*, December 31, 1990, p. 16.

51. Karen De Witt, "Ban on Race-Exclusive Scholarships Is Expected," *New York*

Times, December 4, 1991, p. B16; Anthony De Palma, "Theory and Practice at Odds in New Proposal on Minority Scholarships," *New York Times*, December 7, 1991, p. 10.

52. J. Jennings Moss, "Both Parties Claim Victory," *Washington Times*, October 26, 1991, p. 1; Ann Devroy, "President Signs Civil Rights Bill," *Washington Post*, November 22, 1991, p. A1.

53. Moss, "Both Parties Claim Victory," Devroy, "President Signs Civil Rights Bill."

54. Boyden Gray, "We Won, They Capitulated," *Washington Post*, November 14, 1991, p. A23.

55. Devroy, "President Signs Civil Rights Bill."

56. Margaret Wolf Freivogel, "Uncivil Uproar: Signing of Civil Rights Bill Still May Not End Debate," *St Louis Post-Dispatch*, November 24, 1991, p. 18.

57. Fletcher to Bush, November 23, 1991; Card to Gray, November 26, 1991; Gray to Fletcher, December 5, 1991.

58. George Curry, "Rights Panelist Urges Probe in Racial Attacks, *Chicago Tribune*, September 10, 1989, p. 16.

59. CCR Minutes, April 28, 1989.

60. Hearings on Police Brutality Before the House Subcommittee on Civil and Constitutional Rights, 102d Cong., 1st Sess., March 20 and April 17, 1991, p. 320.

61. Ann Devroy, "Bush Reaches Out to Activists for Advice, Presidential Leadership Huge Federal Effort Are Urged," *Washington Post*, May 2, 1992, A1; Ann Devroy, "Bush Links Rioting to 60's Policy," *Washington Post*, May 7, 1992, p. A1; R. W. Apple, "Bush Says Largess Won't Help Cities," *New York Times*, May 7, 1992, p. A22.

62. CCR Minutes, January 31, 1992. I also noted the proposed rule making by Secretary Alexander on minority scholarships and suggested we respond before the March 7 deadline. I also asked that Commissioner Ramirez give us a briefing on the American Council on Education report on minority students in connection with the minority scholarship issue. Everyone agreed to do both.

63. CCR Minutes, July, October, 1992; Darman to Bush, October 5, 1992. With Vice Chair Wang, Anderson, Buckley, Berry, Ramirez present, Wang congratulated Fletcher on dealing with a protester who orally attacked the commission during the hearings.

64. Emma Monroig, Solicitor, to Gonzalez, November 22, 1992; Gonzalez sent copy to Ann Gwaltney; December 3, 1992; Bush to Horner, December 4, 1992; Constance Horner, assistant to the president and director of presidential personnel, to Bush, November 6, 1992, and December 7, 1992; Hyde to Boyden Gray, December 15, 1992; Fletcher to Bush, December 2, 1992.

65. On January 4, 1993, the White House received George's résumé. George, whose father was the son of a Syrian Christian immigrant father and whose grandmother was Italian, grew up in Morgantown, Virginia. In 2006 he directed the James Madison Institute, a conservative think tank at Princeton, and advised George W. Bush on faith-based activities, www.bradleyfdn.org/PR/TranscriptRG.html.

66. Allen left on December 5, 1992, and Buckley on December 24, 1992, to be replaced by Horner and George. After holding a variety of higher education posts in Texas, Blandina Cardenas Ramirez was named president of the University of Texas Pan American in 2004.

Chapter X

1. Alabama State Advisory Committee to the United States Commission on Civil Rights, Burning of African American Churches in Alabama and Perceptions of Race

Relations, transcript, July 1996. The commission published SAC reports and transcripts from each state in which forums were held. Debbie Howlett, "Alabama Forum Targets Church Fires; Civil Rights Panel Returns to Site of Tumultuous '60s," *USA Today*, July 3, 1996, p. 3A.

2. CCR Minutes, June 14, 1996.

3. Alabama SAC, Burning of African American Churches in Alabama and Perceptions of Race Relations, transcript, July 1996.

4. Mary Frances Berry, "Embers of Anger in the South," *New York Times*, July 17, 1997, p. A23.

5. Naftali Bensavid, "Church Arson Probe Rejects Racist Plot: Many Motives Found Behind Burnings," *Chicago Tribune*, June 9, 1997, p. 3.

6. Ibid.

7. CCR Minutes, February 1997.

8. Larry Copeland, "Panel Returns to Mississippi Delta: Chairwoman Ties Failure to Desegregate Schools to Today's Racial Tensions," *Philadelphia Inquirer*, published in *Dallas Morning News*, March 16, 1997, p. 38A.

9. I knew Bill Clinton, only slightly, having met him in August 1979 at Camp David, when President Carter had a series of discussions with opinion leaders who were ferried up and back each day to help him develop themes he could use to compete for reelection. Probably because as assistant secretary I had helped to gain successful passage of the Department of Education bill, I was there with White House staff. I thought Clinton was invited because Vernon Jordan, then the head of the National Urban League, put him on the list. Years later, when he was president, Bill Clinton and I would joke about that episode; he hated having me tell people Vernon brought him, insisting he "got there" on his own. During the Reagan years we both appeared at a forum on voting rights for the LCCR and our papers were published in a book on the subject, and he would send me political notes from time to time; *Romer v. Evans*, 517 U.S. 620 (1996); see also Robert P. George, "The Tyrant State," *First Things* 67 (November 1996): 39–42.

10. Holly Morris, "Civil Rights Leaders Back End to Military's Ban, Coretta King, Lowery at Forefront," *Atlanta Journal and Constitution*, July 1, 1993, p. 8.

11. I joined with her colleagues from the NAACP Legal Defense and Education Fund in helping her when Clinton asked her to come to the White House to meet with him. She had done nothing wrong, and sharing with her my experience after Reagan fired me, I told her that if she decided to stand her ground it would give her an even greater platform for stating her views and doing good work. We suggested she ignore any Clinton tears and make him reject her instead of asking him to withdraw her name. When Lani called our little group of assembled defenders after the meeting, she said it went just as we had predicted and that she had stood her ground. Richard Berke, "Democrats Woo Black Lawmakers," *New York Times*, September 19, 1993, p. 35; my own recollections. CCR Minutes, May 21, 1993; Guinier wanted an up-or-down vote because she had done nothing wrong and thought a confirmation hearing would at least give her a chance to state her actual position to the Senate. At the May meeting, the Republicans raised the subject. Commissioner George wanted to review her writings, but I pointed out that the commission had always refused to take positions on nominations. After much debate and discussion, Clinton withdrew her name. She became a heroine to the civil rights community, and a world opened to her far beyond the limited purview of an assistant attorney general.

12. Berke, "Democrats Woo Black Lawmakers"; my own recollection.

13. Dewayne Wickham, "Clinton Shows Some Muscle on Civil Rights," *USA Today*, September 27, 1993, p. 12A.

14. Al Kamen, "In the Loop," *Washington Post*, November 10, 1993.

15. CCR Minutes, February 26, 1993; the CCR voted 4–3–1, with Fletcher abstaining, to direct Doctor to continue as acting staff director. Associate White House counsel Neil Eggleston thought the president would have only a fifty-fifty chance of defending Ishimaru's acting appointment from a court challenge, but the president wanted to keep his promise. There were no valid reasons to object to Ishimaru except ideological and political ones.

16. I told Doctor that Clinton planned to name Ishimaru and that he should return to Atlanta. I also informed the acting general counsel whom he had detailed to that position that he should return to his previous attorney job. I distributed copies of the Office of Legal Counsel's opinion to the commissioners at the January 1994 meeting. The counsel concluded that just as the president could name a presidential appointee requiring Senate confirmation as acting during a recess, he could name a staff director as acting without concurrence.

I asked the CCR solicitor, Emma Monroig, whose responsibilities included interpreting legal rules, for her written advice. She replied that she had consulted "with legal counsel of the Administrative Conference and with the General Accounting Office," and there was nothing illegal or improper about the actions taken involving Doctor and the acting general counsel, since Fletcher as chairman had asked Doctor to take the acting assignment.

17. Berry to Veronica Biggins, Assistant to President and Director of Presidential Personnel, May 27, 1994, letter in my possession.

18. Aside from Alexis Herman and Ben Johnson in the White House, from the Carter administration and the Jackson campaign, I had known Minyon Moore, the deputy political director, since Jackson 1984. Pat Griffin, who was congressional liaison for a time and has since remained an important lobbyist, had worked for me when I was in the Carter administration, before moving on to one powerful job after another. In the second term, in addition, my former student and protégé from Penn, Josh Gottheimer worked in the White House Intergovernmental Affairs Office with Lynn Cutler, and then he went on to become one of Clinton's speech writers and traveled with the president.

Since our work in the Free South Africa movement, Randall Robinson had organized a number of protest marches in support of returning President Aristide of Haiti to power. Democratically elected, Aristide had been removed in a coup and exiled in the United States. One of the last marches our friend and tennis great Arthur Ashe participated in with us was a protest in front of the White House shortly before his death. One day Randall called to ask me to go on a fast with him to gain an American military intervention to restore Aristide. I told Randall that when we did Free South Africa he needed my media visibility but since then he had become a public figure in his own right and he could do it on his own. He went on a fast in April 1994, and the Haitian cause gained widespread media publicity.

After about a month, as he grew weaker, Randall asked me if I would help him to persuade White House officials of his sincerity, which meant he was willing to die. He wanted to live, but he could not give up. I talked to Mort Halperin on the National Security Council staff, whom I had known when he ran the ACLU's Washington office, and Alexis Herman, and shuttled back and forth between Randall and his physician and the White House for days, emphasizing each time the precariousness of his physical condition. I have no way of knowing how much influence the widely publicized fast had, but the policy changed. Clinton appointed Congressman Bill Gray as a special envoy, and he then sent Jimmy Carter to Haiti to try to resolve the crisis. When that failed, he sent in troops and Aristide was restored. That was not the end of the story, as international agencies refused to come to Haiti's aid, and after the troops were withdrawn, Aristide was later deposed again and went into exile in South Africa, while Haiti descended into chaos.

19. In *Adarand Constructors, Inc. v. Pena*, 515 U.S. 200 (1995), the Court ruled 5–4 that the "strict scrutiny" doctrine they had already applied to overturn affirmative action in state minority contracting cases also applied to federal cases. In ruling this way, Justice O'Connor struck down a Hispanic contractor's agreement, and the Court had already decided *Richmond v. Croson* 488 U.S. 469 (1989), applying this doctrine to state cases.

20. George Stephanopoulos, *All Too Human* (Boston: Little, Brown, 1999), pp. 361–365.

21. Jennifer Corbett, "Civil Rights Rules Not Enforced, Study Says," *Los Angeles Times*, June 24, 1995, p. A23.

22. The leaders were JoAnn Peart, cofounder of Floridians for Immigration Control; Rob Ross, executive director of the Florida-187 Committee; and Enos Schera, of Citizens of Dade United.

23. I took guidance from counsel and discussed the matter with Vice Chair Reynoso, but primarily relied upon Chairman Flemming's resolution of a similar problem at a Boston school busing hearing in June 1975. He decided as matter of resources to use administrative discretion and to abandon any effort to obtain testimony from three recalcitrant witnesses who had staged a similar public relations incident. Sergio Bustos, "Immigration Foes Don't Have to Testify," *Fort Lauderdale Sun Sentinel*, September 13, 1995, p. 38.

24. "Rights Panel Goes Too Far," Editorial, *St. Petersburg Times*, October 1, 1995, p. 2D.

25. Sergio Bustos, "Foes of Immigration Face Its Advocates," *Fort Lauderdale Sun Sentinel*, September 16, 1995, p. 3B; we had managed to preserve the commission's subpoena power.

When we opened our hearings on racial and ethnic tension in South Florida on Thursday morning, since the anti-immigration groups did not appear we heard only one side of Florida's escalating immigration debate on the first day. Immigration advocates argued on Thursday that the movement against illegal immigrants in Florida was racially motivated and divisive. On Friday the founder of the Florida Save Our State Committee arrived to tell us that his organization simply wanted authorities to enforce the nation's immigration laws. "By injecting race into this debate, our opponents have done the people of Florida a disservice," Doug Guetzloe said. "It will only result in the escalation of racial tensions in South Florida."

Cruz Reynoso, the CCR's vice chairman and a Democrat, said California activists who helped pass Proposition 187, which bars illegal immigrants from receiving social services, now want to abolish state-sponsored affirmative action programs. He asked whether Guetzloe intended to do the same. Guetzloe, who consulted with California Prop 187 leaders before launching the effort in Florida, said he was approached about organizing a drive against affirmative action but had declined to become involved.

I asked Guetzloe whether he would consider dropping his proposed amendment if it could be proven that illegal immigrants paid more in taxes than they cost in social service benefits. Not enough, said Guetzloe. He said that as long as illegal immigrants were allowed to skirt the law, his organization would continue to push for passage of his measure. Republican CCR member Constance Horner agreed with Guetzloe, saying the "integrity of the law" was at stake. "The movement to contain illegal immigration is a demand by people to restore respect for the law," she said. "It's about a deteriorating

American social environment and part of it involves this disrespect for the law. We have always winked at illegal immigration."

United States Commission on Civil Rights, *Racial and Ethnic Tensions in American Communities: Poverty, Inequality, and Discrimination: The Miami Report*, October 1997; Canady to Commissioners and Staff Director, March 1, 1996; Mary Mathews, "Subpoena Memorandum to Commissioners," 22 pages, December 7, 1996. At the March 1996 meeting we discussed a letter from Canady asking for handwritten notes kept by the civil service of the lawyers when they were identifying and interviewing witnesses. They were, of course, attorneys' work product, which should have had privacy protection, but we had no ability to resist the Congress. We had now complied with every demand made by the subcommittee.

26. White House announcements of nominations.

27. At the inevitable hearing, Congressman Asa Hutchinson of Arkansas made political mileage out of the fact that our general counsel had taught my usual course at the University of Pennsylvania while I was on leave. He ominously warned that he would pursue the matter. He asked GAO to conduct a further investigation, in which they found nothing wrong at all. When the committee much later published the hearing record as their version of the commission's legislative history, they managed to leave out the GAO letter to the subcommittee, saying that after a full investigation, they determined that I had described the matter truthfully; copy of letter in my possession.

28. Naftali Bendavid, "Affirmative Action Debate: Rights Panel Accused of Blocking Reports," *Chicago Tribune*, April 1, 1998, p. 1.

29. Lee, Berry, Reynoso, Higginbotham, and Redenbaugh voted to confirm her. Al Kamen, "It's Nothing Personnel," In the Loop, *Washington Post*, May 9, 1997, p. A23. *Public Papers of the President*, June 20, 1997, 33 Weekly Comp Pres doc, 411.

30. Ruby Moy, "The Civil Rights CCR Look at the Record," *Washington Post*, July 29, 1997, p. A14; Linda Chavez Gersten, "Its Glory Days Are Long Past," *Washington Post*, July 16, 1997, p. A19.

31. PR Newswire, May 18, June 9, and August 17, 1998.

32. PR Newswire, October 2, 1998.

33. Meeks appointment, *Congressional Record*, April 15, 1999. Meeks was appointed April 15, 1999. Because White House staff told me that Clinton still bristled at Edley's public pronouncements that the president would soon publish a book on race, which Edley was writing for him. S3829; Edley's appointment, *Congressional Record*, April 15, 1999, S3820; May 4, 1999, H2563.

34. Berry to Reno, February 1999, copy in my possession.

35. Jim Newton and Abigail Goldman, "Williams, Union Chief Clash Before U.S. Panel," *Los Angeles Times*, September 13, 1996, p. 1. Katherine Mader, the Police Commission's inspector general, and Mark H. Epstein, who helped prepare a landmark report on the progress of reform at the LAPD, agreed with Williams. They also joined him in opposing two state legislative bills that would remove some police complaint records from the reach of LAPD managers. The union had supported these bills. Mayor Richard Riordan testified that he believed the LAPD had made great progress but that more needed to be done, especially in the area of holding supervisors accountable for the actions of their subordinates. He also defended the decision by his budget team and top LAPD leaders to cut back a proposed expansion of Internal Affairs, the unit charged with investigating other officers. Internal Affairs issues surfaced repeatedly as the major impediment in trying to hold police accountable in a way fair to the officers and the community. Ramona Ripston, executive director of the Southern California ACLU, said the efficiency and effectiveness of Internal Affairs was a major problem. She thought the

"introduction of an adequately sized, easily accessible IAD remains a promise of change that is so far unkept."

Steven H. Rosenbaum, special litigation counsel from the Justice Department's Civil Rights Division, testified concerning whether federal officials would sue the police force for a pattern of condoning improper police conduct. His testimony unnerved local officials. He stressed that the Justice Department would "stay engaged as long as we need to stay engaged."

36. In revisiting the *Who Is Guarding the Guardians?* report, we cited the success of community policing programs in Boston and San Diego for reducing crime as well as the number of complaints of police brutality. We found that "it is less risky for police, in the very tough job that they do, to have the confidence of the community rather than feeling like they are some kind of hostile force in the community." I noted, "It is safer and it is better." We reported that Los Angeles and New York had "made great strides in lowering crime rates" but needed to address lingering concerns in the community about police misconduct. Despite the praise of progress by the police forces, Joe Pasco, executive director of the Fraternal Order of Police, thought we timed the report before the election to help Gore; Eric Lichtblau, "Panel Releases Findings on Police Abuse," *Los Angeles Times*, November 4, 2000, p. 26; "Panel Urges Remedies to Abuses by Police," *New York Times*, November 4, 2000, p. 18.

37. Steve Holmes, "New York City to Face Review of Police Role," *New York Times*, March 6, 1999, p. A1; Bob Herbert, "In America: Policing the Police," *New York Times*, March 7, 1999, p. A15. We published the Wall Street Report in December 1999. We also published a report evaluating the perpetual weaknesses of civil rights enforcement in the Department of Health and Human Services. With its ample share of the Federal domestic budget, the department maintained the largest programs, including support for hospitals, Medicare, and Medicaid—*and* the smallest civil rights compliance staff. This led to such failures as, for example, the lack of investigation of numerous complaints about discrimination that kept black elders from highly desired nursing homes.

38. Elisabeth Bumiller, "Giuliani Blames Democrats for U.S. Inquiry into Police," *New York Times*, April 14, 2000, p. B4; Timothy J. Burger and Lisa Colangelo, "Mayor Hits Cop Report by Hillary Backer," *New York Daily News*, April 14, 2000; Steven Holmes, "A Civil Rights Crusader Unafraid to Challenge Anyone," *New York Times*, May 1, 2000, p. A14. In retrospect, I told Steve Holmes of the *New York Times* perhaps I should not have given $250 to Hillary Clinton's campaign, in order to avoid giving Giuliani an issue to try to undermine the public perception of the report.

39. Kevin Flynn, "Rights Panel Scolds Police on Race Issues," *New York Times*, April 27, 2000, p. B1; Redenbaugh and Anderson echoed the complaints of Giuliani, in addition to claiming the report was inaccurate.

40. Julian Barnes, "Mayor Denounces Panel's Report on Police," *New York Times*, April 28, 2000, p. B4; Joyce Purnick, "2 More Voices in Dissonance Over Police," *New York Times*, August 3, 2000, p. B1.

41. Experts discussed the same issues that had not been resolved and had worsened in 2006; see Erik Eckholm, "Plight Deepens for Black Men, Studies Warn," *New York Times*, March 20, 2006, p. A1. Wilson, who was my editor at Knopf, observed the Diallo hearing and was familiar with the issues; like other valuable members in the past, she brought a non-lawyer perspective. We also had no one from New York and no white women on the commission. I passed her name along to the White House staff. Clinton decided to appoint her; White House Press Release, "President Clinton Names Victoria Wilson to United States Commission on Civil Rights," January 14, 2000.

42. Bill Walsh of Deadwood defended me, saying that if the governor had been at

the forum he would have seen the despair and how I left the chair and "went around to comfort Indian people who were crying in front of our committee." Lee Williams, "Rights Report Will Explore Indian Justice," *Argus Leader,* March 21, 2000, p. 18; Lee Williams, "Study: Indians Jailed More"; Lee Williams, "Special Report: Civil Rights Probe," *Argus Leader,* December 6, 1999, p. 1A.

43. "White Clay Needs Help," *Omaha World-Herald,* March 21, 2000; South Dakota State Advisory Committee to the United States Commission on Civil Rights, *Native Americans in South Dakota: An Erosion of Confidence in the Justice System,* 2000.

44. Jodi Wilgoren, "Rights Panel Criticizes Shift in College Admissions Plans," *New York Times,* April 9, 2000, p. A16; Sara Fritz, "Federal Panel Judges Bush's Plan," *St. Petersburg Times,* April 12, 2000, p. 7B; Charles Ornstein, "More Minorities Enrolling at U.T. But in This Fall's Freshman Class, Groups Percentage Down Slightly," *Dallas Morning News,* September 23, 2000, p. 43A. I recall another letter in February 3, 2000, asking him to correct the record, when a regional official seemed to support, voluntarily, the ending of higher education affirmative action in Florida. The administration subsequently affirmed its continued support for affirmative action in Florida. Bush was reviewing his actions with protests and a sit-in in his office at the time; Anderson and Redenbaugh's two-page dissent said the statement is "littered with inaccuracies and half-truths" and raised questions about the research behind the statement as well as its analytical approach. They produced no data.

Chapter XI

1. Robin Givhan, "The Eyelashes Have It," *Washington Post,* November 18, 2000, accurately describes the reaction evoked by Harris's appearance at our hearings; CCR, *Voting Irregularities in Florida,* 2001, transcript, pp. 265, 298–299.

2. CCR, *Voting Irregularities,* executive summary.

3. Ibid., Transcript, *Voting Irregularities in Florida,* January 11, 2001, pp. 98–125.

4. Ibid., p. 308. Commissioner Edley expressed wonderment at the "tone" of everyone being suddenly interested in "a newfound religion because of the glare of the public spotlight and the closeness of the election" to see to it that everyone fairly votes and is counted. He found missing from the testimony "a confession that, yeah, we blew it, we didn't keep the faith with our constituents . . . we're sorry and we will do the right thing." What he heard was "a lot of denial," a lot of "excuses and a lot of finger pointing, but not stepping up to the plate and saying I made a mistake, my colleagues made a mistake and we regret it."

5. 42 U.S. Code, section 1975c(a) (1).

6. *Bush v. Gore,* 531 U.S. 98 (2000), 42 U.S.C. 1973.

7. Thernstrom's appointment, January 6, 2001, *Congressional Record,* H46; Thernstrom and her husband, Harvard historian Stephan Thernstrom, coauthored *America in Black and White: One Nation, Indivisible,* which attacked affirmative action in higher education, and *Whose Votes Count? Affirmative Action and Minority Voting Rights,* which called into question the focus in the jurisprudence on the Voting Rights Act on giving black voters the opportunity to elect black candidates.

8. CCR, *Voting Irregularities,* chapter 3 and notes there cited.

9. Canady's letter to the commission's general counsel, Edward Hailes, on January 3, 2001, that "it is the secretary of state that has been entrusted by the legislature with the comprehensive obligation to maintain uniformity in the application, operation, and interpretation of the election laws."

10. Harris testimony, transcript, pp. 240, 243, 244.

11. Ibid., pp. 265, 298–299; transcript, pp. 1, 178, 282–284. In the wake of the 1997 Miami mayoral election, state law required the Division of Elections to contract with a private entity to compare information in the central voter file with available information in other computer databases, including those with reliable criminal records and deceased persons. ChoicePoint was given the contract.

12. NPR *Weekend Edition*, February 17, 2001; George Bruder Testimony, Miami Verified Transcript, pp. 220–221; Bruder Unverified Deposition, March 21, 2001, in Miami, Florida; Maya Bell, "Firm Defends Error-Filled List of Voters," *Orlando Sentinel*, February 17, 2001, Madison County Supervisor of Elections Linda Howell, who was not a convicted felon, was purged and received a letter notifying her she had been removed from the rolls. transcript p. 44

13. Sandra Lambert, Director, Division of Driver Licenses, Testimony, Miami Verified Transcript, February 16, 2001, p. 232; CCR, *Voting Irregularities in Florida During the 2000 Presidential Election* (2001).

14. Tucker testimony, Transcript, p. 45.

15. Ibid., pp. 72–73.

16. Hall testimony, Transcript, pp. 112, 118–122, 152–153.

17. Transcript p. 43.

18. Transcript, February 16, 2001, pp. 93–95.

19. Ibid., p. 100.

20. Florida's Inaccessible Polling Places for People with Disabilities, Fred Shotz testimony, Transcript, February 16, 2001, p. 35; Felix Boyle testimony, Transcript, February 16, 2001, pp. 78–79, 90–91.

21. Transcript, February 16, 2001, pp. 69, 97.

22. Ibid., pp. 124–125, 406–407.

23. CCR, *Voting Irregularities*, Statement of Commissioner Wilson.

24. Ibid., pp. 265, 298–299.

25. Mary Ellen Klas, "Harris Assails Rights Report, Calls Leak 'Shameful Violation,'" *Palm Beach Post*, June 8, 2001, p. 2A.

26. CCR, *Voting Irregularities*, Statement of Commissioner Wilson, www.vsccr.gov/pubs/vote2000/report/wilson.htm.

27. Klas, "Harris Assails Rights Report."

28. CCR, *Voting Irregularities*, Voting Systems Controls and Failures, Allan Lichtman testimony, Transcript, January 11, 2001.

29. Robert Pierre, "Rights Panel Criticizes Florida's Bush, Harris," *Washington Post*, June 9, 2001, p. A3; CCR, *Voting Irregularities*, chapter 9, Findings and Recommendations.

30. The White House, Press Briefing by Ari Fleischer, June 27, 2001, www.whitehouse.gov/news/releases/2001/06/20010627-4.html.

31. Transcript, Senate Governmental Affairs Hearing, June 27, 2001; Katharine Seelye, "Senators Hear Bitter Words on Florida Vote," *New York Times*, June 28, 2001, p. A20.

32. Seelye, "Senators Hear Bitter Words."

33. Ibid.

34. General Counsel Edward Hailes to Staff Director Les Jin, July 2001.

35. Ibid.; "Uncivil Fights: The Commissioners Have a Job to Do, but First They Have to Agree to Meet," *Washington Post*, October 30, 2002, p. C1.

36. Richard Morin, "Scholar Invents Fan to Answer His Critics," *Washington Post*, February 1, 2003, p. C1.

37. Jin to Chabot, July 30, 2001, 11-page reply.

38. William Yeomans to Berry, July 19, 2001; Katharine Seelye, "Divided Civil Rights Panel Approves Election Report," *New York Times*, June 9, 2001; Robert Pierre, "Rights Panel Criticizes Florida's Bush, Harris," *Washington Post*, June 9, 2001, p. A3; Katharine Seelye, "Senators Hear Bitter Words on Florida Vote," *New York Times*, June 28, 2001.

39. Jeff Kunerth, Maya Bell, and David Damron, "What a Relief: Election Day Nearly Glitch-Free." *Orlando Sentinel*, November 6, 2000, p. A16.

40. Help America Vote Act of 2002, 116 Stat. 1666 (2002).

41. "Voting Experts Predict Glitches in November," *St. Petersburg Times*, April 10, 2004, p. 7A.

42. Gwyneth Shaw, "Felon Purge Draws Call for Probe," *Orlando Sentinel*, July 16, 2004, p. A1; Ford Fessenden, "Civil Rights Board Wants Inquiry on Florida Voter Purge List," *New York Times*, July 16, 2004, p. 1A. Barbara Arnwine from the Lawyers' Committee for Civil Rights, one of the advocacy groups testifying, said she expects to see lawsuits over the purge list as well as several other issues, including roughly 1,200 people convicted of felonies in other states who were now living in Florida and were being barred from voting. We wanted Justice to investigate to determine whether Florida officials violated the Voting Rights Act, but we knew the Ashcroft Department might continue to ignore us.
Senator Bill Nelson (D-Fla.) came to the hearing to tell us that he wanted the Justice Department to examine the state's electronic-voting machines before the November election. He discussed problems in other elections since 2000 where the machines seemed not to record votes. He wanted an independent review of the machines before the election. In September we discussed voting again, including allegations of abuse in Florida. After Democrat Buddy Dyer's narrow victory in Orlando's mayoral election, opponents charged that a black activist probably illegally filled out absentee ballots for some elderly black voters. Florida Department of Law Enforcement officers interrogated large numbers of voters who cast absentee ballots. Sheldon Bradshaw, principal deputy assistant attorney general with the Justice Department's Civil Rights Division, told us about the investigation after I asked him at our briefing about the complaints. He said, "We are aware, and we have opened an investigation," but he "was not at liberty to discuss details" until they concluded the investigation. The department did not inform us of the results. April Bethea, "Justice Department Probing Claims of Voting Fraud in Florida," Cox News Service, September 17, 2004.

43. PR Newswire, "U.S. Commission on Civil Rights Launches Second Complaint Hotline to Accommodate Great Response; Charges of Vandalism to Personal Property and Harassment by Neighbors, Employers Dominate Calls," September 14, 2001.

44. Bill Douthat, "We Can't Stand It Anymore, Jailed Haitian Woman Says," *Palm Beach Post*, June 22, 2002, p. 1A; Alfonso Chardy, "Civil Rights Commission to Investigate Detained Haitian Refugees," *Miami Herald*, June 22, 2002, p. 1B.

45. Daniel J. Bryant, Assistant Attorney General, to Sensenbrenner, copy to Berry, December 5, 2001.

46. "Embarrassing Berry," Editorial, *Wall Street Journal*, December 10, 2001, p. A10.

47. Gonzales to Berry, December 5, 2001; Conyers and Nadler to Berry, December 6, 2001.

48. Wade Henderson, "The Civil Rights Commission Continues to Have an Important Role in This Nation," *Pittsburgh Post-Gazette*, January 9, 2002, p. A10.

49. Chabot to Berry, November 30, 2001, and December 4, 2001; Katharine Seelye, "Dispute Erupts Over Seat on Civil Rights Panel," *New York Times*, December 6, 2001,

p. 30; Marcia Coyle, "A Small Committee Draws Big Fire in DC Again," *National Law Journal* 24, no. 17 (December 24–31), p. A8; UPI, "House Committee Threatens Berry's Removal," January 9, 2002.

50. *Kirsanow v. United States,* Civil Action No. 01-CV-2541 (GK), intervenors Berry and Reynoso; Neely Tucker, "Judge Rejects Bush Pick for Civil Rights Agency," *Washington Post,* February 5, 2002, p. A1; Neely Tucker and Darryl Fears, "Bush Wins Civil Rights Panel Ruling," *Washington Post,* May 10, 2002, p. A1. The commission had occasionally published reports in draft for public comment before, most notably the 1981 report, *Affirmative Action: Dismantling the Process of Discrimination,* but had not done so routinely.

51. Shawn Windsor, "Groups Call for Ouster of Panelist; Internment Remarks Draw Angry Response," *Detroit Free Press,* July 23, 2002; Lynette Clemetson, "Traces of Terror: Civil Rights Commissioner Under Fire for Comments on Arabs," *New York Times,* July 23, 2002, p. 1A; Anniversary update on commission activities related to September 11, September 2002. In continuing post-9/11 actions we held a briefing in March 2004 at which the American-Arab Anti-Discrimination Committee joined the voices asking, unsuccessfully, for reform of the Patriot Act. The organization's president, former Cleveland congresswoman Mary Rose Oakar, a Christian Lebanese American, documented how the law had contributed to unfair targeting and improper detention of Arabs and Muslims. The American Civil Liberties Union also testified against the law. Supporters told us that the act did not threaten civil liberties and has merely let techniques commonly used in organized-crime investigations be used against suspected terrorists. But they said the law could be fine-tuned. "By and large, I think concerns about the Patriot Act are overblown," said Paul Rosenzweig of the Heritage Foundation, a conservative think tank. Our staff continued to monitor the enforcement of the act.

52. United States Commission on Civil Rights, *Beyond Percentage Plans: The Challenge of Equal Opportunity in Higher Education,* November 2002; Ginsburg dissent in *Gratz v. Bollinger,* joined by Breyer and Souter, 539 U.S. 244 (2003). The staff produced a number of other reports, including one that showed most of the CCR's recommendations for improving civil rights enforcement had been implemented by the enforcement agencies. If they were not, it was because of inadequate resources; *Ten-Year Check-Up: Have Federal Agencies Responded to Civil Rights Recommendations?* They produced the annual funding report and a report with recommendations for the reauthorization of the Individuals with Disabilities Education Act. The funding remained problematic. The act focused on the need for funding to support research, since the gains were still problematic, and the need for monitoring by enforcement agencies that did not have adequate resources to do so. We highlighted the issues of over-placement of minority children as developmentally disabled and the focus of school systems on controlling the behavior of children with disorders instead of addressing their unique needs in order to assure their education. In part these were funding issues and in part discrimination issues. *Funding Federal Civil Rights Enforcement, 2000–2003,* April 2002; *Recommendations for the Reauthorization of the Individuals with Disabilities Education Act,* May 2002.

53. Adam Taylor, "Civil Rights Commission Hears Racial Complaints," *New Journal Wilmington,* September 14, 2002, p. 2B.

54. Lionel Sanchez, "Civil Rights Group Briefed on Border 'Vigilante' Activity," *San Diego Union-Tribune,* November 16, 2002, p. B8.

55. CCR, "Redefining Rights in America: The Civil Rights Record of the George W. Bush Administration, 2001–2004," draft, September 2004.

56. She replaced Yvonne Lee. Braceras was a Puerto Rican lawyer and freelance

writer and the daughter of federal judge Jose Cabranes, who was an appointee of President Carter. Unlike her father, a moderate and supporter of enforcing civil rights laws, Braceras was a member of the Federalist Society and a supporter of the Reagan redirection on civil rights. She had also written articles in right-wing media saying the commission should be abolished.

57. Michael Janofsky, "Study of Bush and Civil Rights Draws Fire," *New York Times*, October 13, 2004, p. 1A. The Republicans knew the report was "coming, they've known for months," I told the *New York Times*. "They should have asked for a change in the timing much earlier." And "to suggest now that the calendar be considered would make it appear that because of political motivations we are violating our own process at the 11th hour." I added I would willingly consider changing the rules again.

58. Their staff director, Kenneth Marcus, came from posts in the Department of Housing and Urban Development and the Department of Education, where he resisted strong enforcement of the civil rights laws.

59. Randall Archbold, "Adviser on Civil Rights Quits, Declining Legal Fight," *New York Times*, December 8, 2004; "Watchdog Muted," Editorial, *New York Times*, December 14, 2004; see also Dina Powell, assistant to the president for presidential personnel, to Chairman Berry, December 1, 2004, copy in my permission.

60. The nonpartisan Government Accountability Office found in June 2007 that the Bush administration, after saying they would not be bound by certain new statutes in signing statements, had not complied with the requirements of the new statutes. Jonathan Weisman, "Signing Statements Study Finds Administration Has Ignored Laws," *Washington Post*, June 19, 2007, p. A4.

61. Commission statements can be found at www.usccr.gov.

Acknowledgments

AFTER PRESIDENT GEORGE W. BUSH essentially "fired" me from the Civil Rights Commission in 2004, I decided against writing a memoir. I had no interest in such a project, but it did seem to me that a history of the commission could prove useful as the nation attempts to conclusively end inequality and injustice caused by prejudice and stereotypes. I knew that listening to ordinary people, conducting investigations, and attempting to persuade presidents and the Congress to take action had been the commission's role for most of its history.

Without the assistance of Walter Hill at the National Archives and the presidential library archivists and their staffs, and staff at a number of other archives and collections, this history would not have been possible. I owe a special debt of gratitude to Deborah Leff, who was the director of the John Fitzgerald Kennedy Library and to archivists Jennifer Sternaman at the Ronald Reagan Library, Jennifer Evans at the Nixon Presidential Materials, Deborah Wheeler at the George Bush Library, Morgan Blue at the Lyndon B. Johnson Library, Kathie Struss at the Eisenhower Library, and Sara Saunders and James A Yancey, Jr., at the Jimmy Carter Presidential Library. I also thank my assistant from the Carter administration, Connie Stewart, who is now a volunteer at the Carter Library and Museum. In addition, staff at the Gerald Ford Presidential Library at the University of Michigan were always helpful.

Staff at the John Hannah Collection, Michigan State University Library, and the Strom Thurmond Collection at Clemson University, Donna Wells at the Moorland-Springarn Collection at Howard University, and Joan Mathys at MJM Film and Picture Research helped to find photographs, including those of the ordinary people who came to plead their cause at the commission. Vanessa Williamson, director of the Civil Rights Commission's Rankin Library, and Lisa Haywood, special assistant to the executive directors at the Leadership Conference on Civil Rights, responded graciously to my inquiries.

Former California Supreme Court Justice Cruz Reynoso, who was vice chair of the commission; Francis Guess, a former commissioner; Kim Alton; Elaine Jones; Bevan Dufty; Paul Cunningham; and Krishna Toolsie helped with my recollections of events during my tenure. Melinda Chateauvert, of the University of Maryland–College Park, shared her deep knowledge of the history of the civil rights movement before and since the 1950s.

Maida Odom aided in the research and made a number of useful suggestions concerning the manuscript. Yael Zekai, V. P. Franklin, T. J. Davis, Barbara Savage, and Genna Rae McNeil made helpful suggestions and asked excellent questions. Discussions on presentations at the Clinton School and Library, the

Woodrow Wilson Presidential Library, and the Association for the Study of African American History helped to refine my understanding of the issues.

My editor, Victoria Wilson, and my agent, Charlotte Sheedy, understood the importance of this work as a history of ordinary people who found a hearing at the commission. Carmen Johnson at Knopf helped to keep us on track. Mindy, as usual, shared her ideas, companionship, and encouragement.

Mary Frances Berry
Washington, D.C.

Index

Meredith, James, 54, 57, 77
Metzenbaum, Howard M., 209
Mexican American Legal Defense and
    Education Fund (MALDEF), 186–7,
    218, 356n
Mexican Americans, 65, 149, 173, 355n,
    356n, 357n
  LBJ's nomination of, 98
  in Los Angeles, 32–3, 98
  Nixon and, 109, 112, 113–15, 124, 127
  in San Antonio, 98–9, 102–4, 103, 104
Miami, Fla., 373n
  hearings in, 197–9, 284–6, 390n–1n
  racial and ethnic conflicts in, 248,
    284–5, 289–90, 390n–1n
  riots in, 179–80, 197, 290
Michel, Robert, 255
Michigan, 6, 32, 34, 94, 95, 324, 329,
    365n
Michigan SAC, 288, 328
Miller, Arnold, 178, 364n
Miller, Charles E., 11
Miller, Loren, 86
Mills, Wilbur, 72
Mineta, Norman, 242
Mink, Patsy Takemoto, 160
Mississippi, 7, 25, 56–60, 67–9, 84, 123,
    272, 344n, 353n, 371n–2n
  civil rights workers murdered in, 73–4,
    74, 76, 78, 79, 190
  hearing in, 69, 70, 76–82, 78, 80, 81,
    88, 101, 351n
  school desegregation in, 54, 57, 77,
    113, 164
Mississippi Southern College, 56
Mississippi State Advisory Committee, 57
Mississippi, University of, 54, 57, 77
Missouri, 165, 174
Mitchell, 109
Mitchell, Clarence, 17–18, 149
Mitchell, James, 343n
Mitchell, Martha "Bunny," 162, 163
Mitchell, Maurice, 97, 133, 139, 354n,
    356n
Mitchell, Parren, 151, 161, 208,
    364n
Mitchell, William, 72–3
Mondale, Walter, 163, 179, 223, 365n,
    380n
Monroig, Emma, 389n

Montgomery, Ala., 49, 353n
  bus boycott in, 10, 11
  hearings in, 10–11, 10, 29
  march to, 82, 83
Moore, Frank, 174, 178
Moore, Minyon, 389n
Morgenthau, Robert M., 296
Morris, Dick, 282
Morrow, E. Frederick, 12, 20, 36, 353n
Morrow, James, 38
mortgages, 48, 146, 193, 349n
Moseley, Rita, 27, 27
Motley, Constance Baker, 350n
Motor Vehicles Department, Florida,
    309–10, 317
Mount Zion Baptist Church, 272, 273
MOVE, 154–5, 156
Moves Camp, Esther, 298
Moy, Ruby G., 289, 320–1
Moynihan, Daniel Patrick, 95, 107–9,
    108, 111, 128, 356n
Mullins, Andrew, Jr., 275
Murray, Charles, 200
Muskie, Edmund, 188
Muskrat, Joe, 136

NAACP, 12, 17, 18, 56, 67, 68, 69, 76, 77,
    140, 149, 224, 236, 262
  affirmative action forum walkout by,
    226
  Destro's views on, 374n
  election of 2000 and, 304, 310
  leadership replacement in, 191–2
  Reagan administration vs., 217, 218
  Youth Council of, 344n
NAACP Legal Defense and Educational
    Fund (NAACP-LDF), 41, 42, 113,
    134, 144, 188, 192, 196, 214, 217,
    388n
  commission firings and, 186–7
  HEW suit of, 142–3
Nadler, Jerrold, 326, 327
Narasaki, Karen, 217, 280
National Academy of Sciences, 226
National Apprenticeship Act, 171
National Asian Pacific American Legal
    Consortium, 217
National Church Arson Task Force, 274
National Coalition Against Domestic
    Violence, 171

Roybal, Edward, 32, 33
Rubin, David, 102
Ruckelshaus, Jill, 187, 212–14, 372*n*,
	374*n*–5*n*, 377*n*
	appointment of, 179
	background of, 179
	C-SPAN interview of, 378*n*
	Hart considered as replacement for,
		193, 196
Ruckelshaus, William D., 179, 375*n*,
	378*n*
Rudman, Warren, 233
Ruiz, Manuel, 113–15, *114*, 149, 357*n*
	resignation of, 179
Rumsfeld, Donald, 142, 143, 149
Runyon v. McCrary, 249
Russell, Richard, 23, 42
Russo, Kathie, 382*n*
Rusthoven, Peter, 375*n*
Rustin, Bayard, 47, 277

Safir, Howard, 295
Saiki, Patricia, 251
St. Louis, 116–19
	hearing in, 117–18, 125
St. Louis Housing Authority, 119
Saltzman, Murray, 142, 149, 195, 196
	Abram as replacement for, 210, 237
	firing of, 184–5, 204, 206, 370*n*, 375*n*
San Antonio hearing, 98–9, 102–5, *103*,
	104, *105*, 107, 111, 355*n*
San Diego, Calif., 213, 330, 377*n*, 392*n*
San Francisco, Calif., 369*n*
	hearings in, 32, 34, 98
Sanchez, Dr., 354*n*
Sanchez, Julian, 320
Scalia, Antonin, 166, 334, 335
Schlesinger, Arthur, 52, 59–60
Schmitz, John, 258
Schneiders, Greg, 365*n*
scholarships, minority, 264–5, 387*n*
Schorr, Daniel, 123
Schroeder, Patricia, 232
Schumer, Charles, 318
Schutt, Jane, 57
Schwartz, George, 155
Schwerner, Michael, 73–4, *74*, 76, 78, 190
Scott, Stanley, 106, 143, 148, 149
Scranton, William, 141
Scully, John, 264

Seamans, Robert, Jr., 118
Seattle, Wash., 6, 290, 336
Securities and Exchange Commission
	(SEC), 146, 147
segregation, 15, 21, 30, 31–2, 34, 42, 44,
	45, 46, 48, 56, 78, 91, 96, 362*n*
	Battle and, 13, 24, 28
	in education, 106, 127, 142–3, 147,
		164, 194, 196, 217, 221–3, 228–9,
		371*n*–2*n*
	of housing, 358*n*
	in Northern schools, 86, 89, 143
	taxes and, 106, 127, 147, 164, 194, 196,
		242, 371*n*–2*n*
	in transportation, 10, 58
Seidman, Eileen, 175
Select Commission on Immigration and
	Refugee Policy, 172
Sellers, Aaron, *10*, 11
Selma, Ala., 82, *83*
Senate, U.S., 7, 12, 19–23, 31, 50, 56, 97,
	111, 149, 176, 188, 203, 277, 321,
	324, 388*n*
	appointments confirmed by, 22–3, 44,
		73, 76, 107, 140, 179, 190, 194, 202,
		210–11, 212, 270, 333, 376*n*,
		389*n*
	civil rights legislation and, 19–21, 22,
		259
	commission compromise and, 187, 210,
		211–12, 214
	commission criticized by, 50, 347*n*
	commission defunding and, 233
	commission independence and, 209,
		211
	commission reauthorization and, 250,
		263
	fair employment office in, 266
	Government Operations Committee
		of, 31–2
	Indian Affairs Committee of, 246
	Judiciary Committee of, 22–3, 25, 44,
		196, 210, 211, 250, 261
	Rules and Administration Committee
		of, 318–19
	Sumner in, 19, 343*n*
	Thomas nomination and, 261
Sensenbrenner, James, 195, 203, 263,
	371*n*, 374*n*, 384*n*
	Bryant's letter to, 325–6

A NOTE ON THE TYPE

THIS BOOK was set in Janson, a typeface long thought to have been made by the Dutchman Anton Janson, who was a practicing typefounder in Leipzig during the years 1668–1687. It has been conclusively demonstrated, however, that these types are actually the work of Nicholas Kis (1650–1702), a Hungarian, who most probably learned his trade from the master Dutch typefounder Dirk Voskens. The type is an excellent example of the influential and sturdy Dutch types that prevailed in England up to the time William Caslon (1692–1766) developed his own incomparable designs from them.

Composed by North Market Street Graphics,
Lancaster, Pennsylvania
Printed and bound by Berryville Graphics,
Berryville, Virginia